British Poetry and the Revolutionary
and Napoleonic Wars

British Poetry and the Revolutionary and Napoleonic Wars

Visions of Conflict

SIMON BAINBRIDGE

OXFORD

UNIVERSITY PRESS

This book has been printed digitally and produced in a standard specification
in order to ensure its continuing availability

OXFORD
UNIVERSITY PRESS

Great Clarendon Street, Oxford OX2 6DP

Oxford University Press is a department of the University of Oxford.
It furthers the University's objective of excellence in research, scholarship,
and education by publishing worldwide in

Oxford New York

Auckland Cape Town Dar es Salaam Hong Kong Karachi
Kuala Lumpur Madrid Melbourne Mexico City Nairobi
New Delhi Shanghai Taipei Toronto
With offices in
Argentina Austria Brazil Chile Czech Republic France Greece
Guatemala Hungary Italy Japan South Korea Poland Portugal
Singapore Switzerland Thailand Turkey Ukraine Vietnam

Oxford is a registered trade mark of Oxford University Press
in the UK and in certain other countries

Published in the United States
by Oxford University Press Inc., New York

ISBN 978-0-19-818758-5

This book is dedicated to my son

CHARLIE

and to the memory of my father

JOHN BAINBRIDGE

Preface

THIS BOOK ARGUES that poetry played a major role in the mediation of the Revolutionary and Napoleonic wars to the British public, and that the wars had a significant impact on poetic practices and theories in what we now think of as the romantic period. Addressing itself to a wide range of readers through a variety of different forms, poetry was part of the cultural contest over the wars, shaping history through narrative and scripting wartime identities and attitudes, often in relation to the nation and gender. The romantic period was an age of war poetry and 'the great national events' that were 'daily taking place', as Wordsworth described them in his 'Preface' to *Lyrical Ballads* (1800), caused poets to re-examine the issues of the poetic role and literary authority.

While this book emphasizes the engagement of poets with the war throughout its twenty-two-year duration, it particularly focuses on two ways in which the conflict can be seen to have shaped poetry. First, it argues that poetry's association with the imagination (or fancy as it was often termed) made it a crucial form for the mediation of the wars to the British public. This book seeks to contribute to the ongoing debate about the relation between the imagination and history in the romantic period by emphasizing the extent to which the imagination was conceived as the faculty that made possible the participation of British readers in the war. For poets of the 1790s such as Samuel Taylor Coleridge, Robert Southey, and Joseph Fawcett, the imagination was essential if their readers were to realize the 'horrors' of the conflict taking place on the continent. For writers like Charlotte Smith and Lord Byron, normally sceptical of 'Fancy', the imagination found a redeeming role in wartime. In his metrical romances, Walter Scott similarly exploited his readers' power to imagine war, but he transformed the process by applying picturesque techniques to the representation of battle, in so doing producing the most influential reimagining of conflict in the nineteenth century. The culmination of this association of the imagination and war can be seen in the writing of Felicia Hemans, for whom warfare became the defining object of imaginative activity.

Secondly, this book argues that the wars were a major factor in the remasculinization of poetry in the romantic period—the attempts by some writers (male and female) to reconceive poetry in a time of crisis as a proper manly pursuit after its feminization in the later stages of the eighteenth century. The wars exerted powerful pressure on those seeking to claim a poetic role, particularly at a time when the nation was demanding manliness embodied in the active figures of the soldier, the sailor, and the volunteer, and femininity in the figures of the mother, lover, or widow. In this context, the adoption, deployment, and negotiation of gendered figures and roles became crucial to poetic authority and self-representation.

I have not attempted a survey of what is a vast subject; indeed, as Betty Bennett has argued, war was perhaps the principal poetic subject of the romantic period (*BWP*, p. ix). Nor have I sought to give comprehensive accounts of how particular poets responded to the wars throughout their twenty-two-year duration. Rather, I have examined moments which combine a sense of historical and poetic crisis, moments when the events of the conflict with France raised most acutely the question of the poetic role in wartime. The size of the subject has made it necessary to be selective, and I have focused on writers who saw the mediation of the war to the public as a crucial part of their role or those who most profoundly shaped their poetic identities in response to the age of war in which they lived. (Space has not permitted the inclusion of William Blake, whose response to the conflict is brilliantly analysed by David V. Erdman in his *Blake, Prophet against Empire: A Poet's Interpretation of the History of his own Times*.) My selection of writers and texts also reflects my argument that the Napoleonic wars witnessed a major transformation in the imagining of conflict, both in poetry and more generally, and that the key figure in this reimagining of war was Walter Scott. Scott is a pivotal figure in this study and in the representation of war in the romantic period.

In the period when I began work on this project, the mid-1990s, Gillian Russell described 'the impact of the Revolutionary and Napoleonic Wars on the work of British Romanticism's "Big Six"' as 'one of the few uncharted territories for canonical Romantic studies'. The excellent book in which she made this claim, *The Theatres of War: Performance, Politics, and Society, 1793–1815*, was one of the first studies to explore what is beginning to be recognized as a crucial area in the culture of the romantic period. Recent years have seen a number of valuable investigations in the field by critics such as Richard Cronin, Mary Favret, Diego Saglia, and Philip Shaw, and 2000 saw the publication of two important volumes on the subject, the collection of essays edited by

Philip Shaw, *Romantic Wars: Studies in Culture and Conflict, 1793–1822*, and Richard Cronin's monograph *The Politics of Romantic Poetry: In Search of the Pure Commonwealth*. As my arguments and footnotes below will reveal, I have learnt much from these stimulating works. Shaw's own monograph, *Waterloo and the Romantic Imagination*, was published as I was in the final stages of completing this book, but I have tried to engage with and respond to the numerous insights of his fascinating study whenever possible. There is one volume that was published prior to this recent upsurge of interest in the cultural dimensions of the wars to which I am especially indebted, Betty T. Bennett's anthology *British War Poetry in the Age of Romanticism 1793–1815*. I have drawn heavily on this tremendous collection of the newspaper and magazine poetry of the period. In this area, I have also found Michael Scrivener's *Poetry and Reform: Periodical Verse from the English Democratic Press, 1792–1824* extremely useful.

I am grateful to Keele University for sabbatical leave and to the AHRB for a Research Leave Award that made possible the completion of this book. The Inter-Library Loan department of Keele Information Services provided an excellent service throughout the period I have been working on this project. I would like to thank my colleagues at Keele University for reading drafts of chapters and for discussing elements of it; I am especially grateful to David Amigoni, Fred Botting, John Bowen, Susan Bruce, Jim McLaverty, David McNaughton, Roger Pooley, Julie Sanders, Helen Stoddart, and Anthea Trodd. Ed Larrissy offered encouragement of the project at its earliest stage, and I am also grateful to Jonathan Bate and Marilyn Butler for their support of it as it was progressing. I have benefited from comments and suggestions made when I have presented earlier versions of this material at conferences and to research seminars, and I would particularly like to thank Christine Battersby, Emma Clery, Philip Cox, Tim Fulford, Vivien Jones, Richard Kirkland, Michael John Kooy, Jacqueline Labbe, Philip Martin, Robert Miles, Sharon Ruston, Nicholas Roe, Philip Shaw, and John Whale. I am also appreciative of the responses offered by three anonymous readers at Oxford University Press which have helped shape the final version of this book. Sophie Goldsworthy at Oxford University Press has been encouraging since I first discussed the proposed book with her and I have also benefited from the expertise of Sarah Hyland and Frances Whistler at the Press. As ever, my greatest debt is to Anne-Julie Crozier who, in addition to reading and valuably commenting on numerous drafts, has been a supportive and stimulating presence throughout the project.

Acknowledgements

Earlier versions of a number of chapters have been published previously and I am grateful to the following for permission to reproduce them here. A version of Chapter 3 appeared in *Romanticism on the Net* (2003). A version of Chapter 4 was first published as an essay in *Romanticism*, 5/2 (1999), 216–31, and appears here by permission of the editors. Parts of Chapter 7 appeared as ' "Of war and taking towns": Byron's siege poems' in *Romantic Wars*, ed. Philip Shaw (Aldershot: Ashgate, 2000), 161–85, and are reproduced by permission of Ashgate Publishers.

Contents

Abbreviations

BLJ   *Byron's Letters and Journals*, ed. Leslie A. Marchand, 12 vols. (London: John Murray, 1973–82).

BWP   Betty T. Bennett (ed.), *British War Poetry in the Age of Romanticism: 1793–1815* (New York and London: Garland, 1976).

EoT   Samuel Taylor Coleridge, *Essays on His Times: in the Morning Post and the Courier*, ed. David V. Erdman, *The Collected Works of Samuel Taylor Coleridge*, Bollingen Series, 75, 3 vols. (London and Princeton: Routledge and Kegan Paul and Princeton University Press, 1978).

GM   *Gentleman's Magazine.*

LWS   John Gibson Lockhart, *The Life of Sir Walter Scott*, 10 vols. (Edinburgh: T. C. and E. C. Jack, 1902).

PR   Michael Scrivener (ed.), *Poetry and Reform: Periodical Verse from the English Democratic Press, 1792–1824* (Detroit: Wayne State University Press, 1992).

RR   Donald H. Reiman (ed.), *The Romantics Reviewed: Contemporary Reviews of British Romantic Writers, Part A: The Lake Poets*, 2 vols. (New York and London: Garland Publishing, 1972).

WD   Frank J. Klingberg and Sigurd B. Hustvedt (eds.), *The Warning Drum: The British Home Front Faces Napoleon: Broadsides of 1803*, Publications of the William Andrews Clark Memorial Library (Berkeley and Los Angeles: University of California Press, 1944).

W & B   H. F. B. Wheeler and A. M. Broadley, *Napoleon and the Invasion of England: The Story of the Great Terror*, 2 vols. (London and New York: John Lane at the Bodley Head, 1898).

CHAPTER ONE

Poetry in the 'Age of War'

IN 1810–11, Captain Adam Ferguson was with Wellington's British army in the Iberian peninsula, fighting the French. The Peninsular War was the latest stage in the conflict which had begun in 1793, initially against the forces of the Revolutionary state and subsequently against Napoleon Bonaparte's imperial army. After nearly twenty years of global fighting seen as unprecedented in nature, scale, and intensity, the war looked no closer to the resolution it would eventually reach at Waterloo in 1815. On one occasion, Ferguson and his men were posted to a position exposed to the enemy's artillery and the soldiers were ordered to lie prostrate on the ground. But that day Ferguson had received a secret weapon, *The Lady of the Lake*, the latest best-selling poem by Walter Scott. As he read aloud to his men the battle scene in canto VI, the effect on morale was instantaneous. As Scott's biographer Lockhart comments, 'the listening soldiers only interrupted him by a joyous huzza, whenever the French shot struck the bank close above them' (*LWS*, III. 286–7).[1] So popular did *The Lady of the Lake* become with 'the rough sons of the fighting Third Division', Ferguson told Scott in a letter from Lisbon of 31 August 1811, that he had 'nightly invitations' to read and illustrate passages of it, and on behalf of his 'messmates of the Black-cuffs' he had written to London for a copy of the music used in a stage adaptation of the poem (the song, 'Hail to the Chief', would become the Presidential anthem for the United States of America). If Scott could help in obtaining the music, Ferguson added, 'I need not say that on every performance a flowing bumper will go round to the Bard' (*LWS*, III. 284).

[1] See also entry for Adam Ferguson in *Dictionary of National Biography . . . from the Earliest Times to 1900*, founded in 1882 by G. Smith, ed. by L. Stephen and S. Lee, 22 vols. (London: Oxford University Press, 1937–8), VI. 1204. References are hereafter cited as *DNB*. I have followed the *DNB* spelling of Ferguson. On stage adaptations of *The Lady of the Lake*, see Philip Cox *Reading Adaptations: Novels and Verse Narratives on the Stage, 1790–1840* (Manchester and New York: Manchester University Press, 2000), 44–76. On 'Hail to the Chief', see *The New Grove Dictionary of American Music*, 4 vols. (London and New York: Macmillan and Grove's Dictionaries of Music, Inc., 1986), III. 485.

These extraordinary scenes of the reading, cheering, singing, and toasting of *The Lady of the Lake* demonstrate poetry's power in mediating, recreating, and imagining war during the conflict with France. Walter Scott, the best-selling and most popular poet of the war years, had a crucial part in this process; his metrical romances, with their spectacular pageants of assembling armies and single combats of knights in armour, transformed the imagining of war, presenting it as heroic, picturesque, and shaped by the conventions of romance at a time when war was seen to have taken on a new form, to have become modern. But Scott's pivotal role comes during a period when, as Betty Bennett has argued, war was 'perhaps the principal poetic subject' and in which the favoured poetic figures of 'the beggar, the orphan, the widow, the sailor and soldier and veteran, the country cottage . . . were largely derived from the war experience' (*BWP*, pp. ix, 47). Poetry played a major role in the ways in which the wars came to be understood, shaping history through narrative and scripting wartime identities and attitudes through deployment of figures such as those listed by Bennett. And while poetry was one of the key forms of cultural practice that mediated the wars to the British public, the wars were influential in shaping poetic theories and practices in the romantic period. Writing in wartime, poets reconceived their poetic identities and literary authority, emphasizing and questioning poetry's power in facilitating the imagining of war. This opening chapter, which will focus primarily on the writing of the 1790s, will begin by illustrating the role that poetry played in the effort to mobilize the country against France, and to resist that mobilization. But if poetry was linked to other cultural forms including song, theatre, and the visual arts in this struggle over the war in the decade that followed the French Revolution, it was also a form for which special claims were made, an area which will be examined in the second section of this chapter. Poetry's links with 'fancy', 'imagination', and 'feeling' were seen to make it crucial for representing the war and poets constantly called on these faculties as vital to their own representational strategies and to their readers' ability to respond to their visions of conflict. As I will argue in the third section, the special claims made for poetry were often presented in gendered terms. While poetry's feminized powers (and powers to feminize) were frequently invoked, the wartime reconceptions and reformulations of poetry were often presented as a need for poetry to become more manly, a major factor in the remasculinization of poetry in the romantic period. Finally, as an introduction to the major poetic transformation in the imagining of war during the conflict, the fourth section will investigate some of the key tropes used to represent the war in the 1790s and the attempts made by several writers to fill the role of national bard prior to Scott.

'The Age of War'

An anonymous poem entitled 'The Spinning Wheel', published in the *Gentleman's Magazine* in April 1794, just over a year after the outbreak of war between Britain and France, forcefully characterizes the world-wide political situation and the role that poetry plays in it:

> In this dread season, when the rage of War
> And din of Anarchy confound the world,
> When madding Nations scorn the scepter'd sway
> Of ancient Rulers, mock the sacred form
> Of Justice, and imbrue their hands in blood;
> Mid this wild uproar, can a single voice
> Be heard, that neither sounds the martial trump,
> Nor swells the frantic mob's tumultuous strife,
> Nor mourns thy fate, poor Louis! but descends
> From Europe's dangers to the Spinning-wheel?[2]

Similar claims for war as the dominant and defining context of the period, and the central theme of the writing produced during it, were made throughout and after the conflict's twenty-two-year duration. For example, in the year of France's declaration of war on Britain, a writer in the *Analytic Review* described it as treated by 'every hireling scribbler' (*BWP*, 6), while of the culminating action of the wars, the battle of Waterloo in 1815, Francis Jeffrey noted that 'All our bards . . . great and small, and of all sexes, ages, and professions, from Scott and Southey down to hundreds without names or additions, have adventured upon this theme.'[3] Betty T. Bennett's estimate that there were over 3,000 short poems on the war published in newspapers, periodicals, and magazines supports such contemporary claims (*BWP*, p. ix). Over 200 individual volumes of poetry with titles referring to the war, battles, or military or naval figures, were reviewed in periodicals between 1798 and 1820, a count which obviously excludes those works not reviewed and does not give any idea of the number of war poems contained in collections of

[2] *GM*, 64 (April 1794), 362.   [3] *Edinburgh Review*, 54 (December 1816), 295.

verse with non-specific titles.[4] Similarly, some brief examples of the popularity of particular writers or forms of writing will help give a sense of the position of war in the poetry of the period. In 1797, the *Anti-Jacobin* declared the key poet figure of these years to be the '*Jacobin* poet' who celebrated Gallic victories while deploring the devastating effect of war on the British poor.[5] During the period of the invasion crisis, from 1797 to 1805, poetry, along with other forms of writing, was seen as almost exclusively devoted to the French threat; as the *Gentleman's Magazine* commented, '[i]n poetry or prose the universal object of patriotic Britons is, to pursue and expose the Invader of the rights of human kind.'[6] The *Gentleman's Magazine*'s own poetry section published well over sixty patriotic invasion poems during the six months from July to December 1803. Nelson's victory and death at Trafalgar in 1805 stimulated a huge outpouring of verses, and the year also witnessed the publication and phenomenal success of *The Lay of the Last Minstrel*, the first metrical romance by Walter Scott, who was described by his son-in-law and biographer John Lockhart as 'the "mighty minstrel" of the Antigallican war' (*LWS*, III. 54). Scott's reign as 'the Monarch of Parnassus', as Byron called him (*BLJ*, III. 219), ran for much of the rest of the war, and the martial and anti-Gallic nature of his metrical romances was matched in shorter pieces by other writers which proved almost as popular. For example, in 1809 John Murray published John Wilson Croker's *The Battles of Talavera*, which went through eight editions in its first year (a number exceeded only by Scott in the period 1809–10), Murray declaring that it had achieved greater success 'than any short poem he knew, exceeding Mr Heber's "Palestine" or "Europe", and even Mr. Canning's "Ulm" and "Trafalgar" '.[7] The Peninsular War, the setting for Croker's poem, was also the subject of important early works by two poets who would continue to write about war after Waterloo and come to rank among the best-selling and most widely read poets of the nineteenth century, Lord Byron and Felicia Hemans.

[4] William S. Ward, *Literary Reviews in British Periodicals, 1798–1820: A Bibliography, with a Supplementary List of General, Non-Review, Articles on Literary Subjects*, 2 vols. (New York: Garland, 1972).

[5] *The Anti-Jacobin*, ed. Graeme Stones, in Graeme Stones and John Strachan (eds.), *Parodies of the Romantic Age*, 5 vols. (London: Pickering and Chatto, 1999), I. 12–14.

[6] *GM*, 75 (February 1805), 145.

[7] Quoted in entry for Croker in *DNB*, V. 125. On the poem's popularity, see A. D. Harvey, *A Muse of Fire: Literature, Art and War* (London and Rio Grande: Hambledon Press, 1998), 27, and A. D. Harvey, *English Poetry in a Changing Society, 1780–1825* (London: Allison and Busby, 1980), 188. Murray's reference is to George Canning, *Ulm and Trafalgar* (London, 1806) and Reginald Heber, *Europe: Lines on the Present War* (London, 1809).

The dominance of war as a poetic subject, and its popularity with both writers and readers, should come as no surprise given the extent to which the war defined Britain during the romantic period. An anonymous lyric entitled 'The Age of War' of 1798, the year of Wordsworth's and Coleridge's *Lyrical Ballads*, powerfully characterizes the martial nature of the epoch:

> This is THE AGE OF WAR the age
> When ev'ry bosom swells with rage,
>   And burns with military fame,
>   When Mamlucks, Pr—sts, and foplings arm,
> Whilst Europe sounds the loud alarm,
>   And pride her children's breasts inflame.   (*BWP*, 215)

Modern historians have concurred with such contemporary characterizations, Clive Emsley writing that 'if there was a common experience shared by all Britons in the last decade of the eighteenth and the early years of the nineteenth centuries, it is to be found less in the changes resulting from the industrial revolution and more in the demands of war.'[8] Britain had experienced a series of wars throughout the eighteenth century but the Revolutionary and Napoleonic wars, conducted on a global stage and engaging most of Europe, were seen as unprecedented; looking back in 1822, the Prime Minister, the Earl of Liverpool, asked 'Who that contemplated the character of the late war could for a moment think of comparing the events of that war, and the state of things growing out of it, with the events and effects of any former war?'[9] The war was described during the period as 'the most extensive and expensive war that ever raged' and as 'unprecedented in the annals of the world'.[10]

The British war effort was indeed huge, '*prima facie* at least as big as France's', according to Geoffrey Best, with the regular army expanding from 40,000 men in 1793 to 250,000 in 1813 and the navy from 45,000 sailors in February 1793 to 145,000 in 1812.[11] These regular armed forces

---

[8] *British Society and the French Wars, 1793–1815* (Basingstoke and London: Macmillan, 1979), 4.
[9] Quoted in A. D. Harvey, *English Literature and the Great War with France: An Anthology and Commentary* (London: Nold Jonson Books, 1981), 1.   [10] Ibid.
[11] Geoffrey Best, *War and Society in Revolutionary Europe, 1770–1870* (Stroud, Gloucestershire: Sutton Publishing, 1998), 125; David Gates, 'The Transformation of the Army, 1783–1815', in David Chandler and Ian Beckett (eds.), *The Oxford Illustrated History of the British Army* (Oxford: Oxford University Press, 1994), 133; Stephen C. Behrendt, ' "A Few Harmless Numbers": British Women Poets and the Climate of War, 1793–1815', in Philip Shaw (ed.), *Romantic Wars: Studies in Culture and Conflict, 1793–1822* (Aldershot: Ashgate, 2000), 16.

were supplemented by volunteer forces which at the height of the invasion crisis of 1803 numbered as many as 400,000 men.[12] It has been estimated that during this period of invasion crisis, from 1797 to 1804, as many as one in six, or even one in five, of all adult males was involved in the armed forces in either a voluntary or an enrolled position.[13] Such a war effort was extremely expensive, in terms of both money and men, and put a huge strain on the society that had to support it. The wars have been estimated to have cost the British about £1,500,000,000, reckoned by Eric Hobsbawm to have been 'between three and four times' what they cost the French.[14] They have also been estimated to have cost 315,000 British lives, which as Best argues by one statistical method can be presented as a higher proportion of servicemen than that lost in the First World War.[15] As David Gates has shown, the casualty rate of the wars was high, with 18,596 dying in 1794 on active service and 40,639 men discharged 'on account of wounds or infirmity' over the next two years. The attrition rate remained high throughout the Napoleonic wars, 16,000–24,000 casualties being incurred each year.[16] Such casualty rates effect more than the unfortunate individuals, of course, and Jordan and Rogers have estimated that as many as one in four families had a direct involvement in the wars;[17] it is striking how many of the women writers of the period, including Charlotte Smith, Jane Austen, and Felicia Hemans, had husbands, brothers, or sons who fought in the wars. Even for those without relatives involved in war, its presence was evident in everyday life in a huge range of forms including returning (and often wounded) soldiers and sailors, the drilling and encampments of militia and volunteer forces, illuminations and celebrations of victories, the building of barracks and Martello towers, invasion scares, sea battles and naval manœuvres, captured French officers, increased taxes, and developments in fashion.[18] As in the poem 'The Age of War', many texts of the period testify to the extent to which British society was militarized

---

[12] Gates, 'Transformation of the Army', 136.

[13] Ian Christie, 'Conservatism and Stability in British Society', in Mark Philp (ed.), *The French Revolution and British Popular Politics* (Cambridge: Cambridge University Press, 1991), 170. See also Emsley, *British Society and the French Wars*, 33, 133. The fullest account of the volunteer movement is J. E. Cookson, *The British Armed Nation, 1793–1815* (Oxford: Clarendon Press, 1997).   [14] Best, *War and Society*, 125.

[15] Ibid.   [16] Gates, 'Transformation of the Army', 137.

[17] Gerald Jordan and Nicholas Rogers, 'Admirals as Heroes: Patriotism and Liberty in Hanoverian England', *Journal of British Studies*, 28 (1989), 217 n. 70.

[18] For a discussion of the presence in British society of some of the elements in this list, see Harvey, *English Literature and the War with France*, 7–11 .

during these years, and especially during periods of invasion crisis.[19] For example, Mary Robinson frequently ridicules the warlike aspirations of the society in which she lives, satirizing 'Schoolboys, smit with Martial spirit' in 'January, 1795' and 'Tradesmen, leaving shops, and seeming | More of *war* than profit dreaming' in 'The Camp' of 1800.[20]

If the Revolutionary and Napoleonic wars were felt to be unprecedented in their scale and intensity, writers on both sides of the channel presented them as a new kind of war altogether. As early as 1791, Brissot described the nascent French republic as undertaking 'a new crusade, a crusade of universal freedom', while an anonymous British pamphlet of 1793 described the war as being fought against 'An Enemy of a new kind ... who fights not merely to subdue States, but to dissolve society—not to extend Empire, but to subvert Government—not to introduce a particular Religion, but to extirpate all Religion'.[21] This sense of the wars as a new kind of conflict, changing in nature from limited to total and fought for ideological rather than territorial reasons, would gain its most powerful and influential expression in Clausewitz's *On War*, published posthumously in 1832–3. Clausewitz described the new military French Republic of 1793, produced by a series of *levées en masse* that created the 'Nation in Arms', as a force that 'beggared all imagination':

Suddenly war again became the business of the people—a people of thirty millions, all of whom considered themselves to be citizens ... The people became a participant in war; instead of governments and armies as heretofore, the full weight of the nation was thrown into the balance. The resources and effects now available for use surpassed all conventional limits: nothing new impeded the vigour with which war could be waged.[22]

The emphasis of Clausewitz and the historians who have followed his argument for a radical change in the nature of war and the advent of the 'Nation in Arms' has been strongly contested by others who have seen the transformation of conflict as anticipated in the wars and invasion threats of the eighteenth century, who have questioned the extent to

---

[19] For examples, see George Cruikshank's portrayal of the impact of volunteering in 1806, quoted in Linda Colley, *Britons: Forging the Nation 1707–1837* (London: Vintage, 1996), 325, and Charles Loftus's reminiscence of himself as a schoolboy in 1808, in Harvey, *English Literature and the War with France*, 12.

[20] Mary Robinson, *Selected Poems*, ed. Judith Pascoe (Peterborough, Ontario: Broadview Press, 2000), 358, 295.

[21] Emsley, *British Society and French Wars*, 3; Clive Emsley, 'Revolution, War and the Nation State: The British and French Experiences, 1789–1801', in Philp (ed.), *The French Revolution and British Popular Politics*, 103.

[22] Quoted in Best, *War and Society*, 63.

which the Revolutionary and Napoleonic wars themselves were 'total', and who have argued that even if such transformations can be detected during the period, they had no lasting effect on British or European society once the wars had finished.[23] However, while there has been disagreement over such issues, there has been a much greater consensus on the increased role of propaganda and of writing that sought to address the newly expanded nation in the years after the revolution and in the importance of public opinion in the conduct of war. As Emsley writes: 'Besides the perceived need, simply because of the Revolution, to address people who were generally outside the political nation, in both Britain and France the new kind of war unleashed by the Revolution, itself required a new kind of mass support. This, in turn, contributed to the propaganda directed towards those previously outside the political nation.'[24]

As the characterization of contemporary verse in 'The Spinning Wheel' quoted earlier both argues and illustrates, poetry was very much part of this address to the newly expanded political nation and played a major role in the 'Revolution Controversy' or pamphlet war of the 1790s.[25] While important claims would be made about poetry's uniqueness and distinctiveness in representing the war, it also needs to be seen as part of the larger cultural contest over the war enacted in a variety of forms including broadsheets, songs, newspapers, magazines, caricatures, and the theatre.[26] Intended for a variety of different readerships (and

---

[23] For an excellent introduction to these issues, see J. E. Cookson, 'War' in Iain McCalman *et al.* (eds.), *An Oxford Companion to the Romantic Age: British Culture, 1776–1832* (Oxford: Oxford University Press, 1999), 26–34. Cookson's arguments are expanded in *The British Armed Nation*. See also Jeremy Black, 'The Military Revolution II: Eighteenth-Century War' and Alan Forrest, 'The Nation in Arms I: The French Wars', in Charles Townshend (ed.), *The Oxford Illustrated History of Modern War* (Oxford: Oxford University Press, 1997), 35–47, 48–63; Best, *War and Society, passim* and esp. 122–49; Emsley, 'Revolution, War and the Nation State' and *British Society and the French Wars*; Michael Duffy, 'War, Revolution and the Crisis of the British Empire' in Philp (ed.), *The French Revolution and British Popular Politics*; Paul W. Schroeder, *The Transformation of European Politics, 1763–1848* (Oxford: Clarendon Press, 1996).

[24] 'Revolution, War and the Nation State', 103.

[25] There is an extensive literature on the pamphlet wars of the 1790s. See Marilyn Butler, *Burke, Paine, Godwin, and the Revolution Controversy* (Cambridge: Cambridge University Press, 1984), and Olivia Smith, *The Politics of Language 1791–1819* (Oxford: Clarendon Press, 1984). On the expansion of reading, see Richard D. Altick, *The English Common Reader: A Social History of the Mass Reading Public, 1800–1900* (Chicago: University of Chicago Press, 1957), and Jon Klancher, *The Making of English Reading Audiences, 1790–1832* (Madison and London: Wisconsin University Press, 1987).

[26] The best discussions of the contexts of production and consumption for poetry published in newspapers and periodicals are provided by Bennett and Scrivener in their introductions to their anthologies, *BWP*, 1–67, and *PR*, 11–34.

audiences), poetry on the war was widely circulated throughout the years of the conflict with France, distributed as broadsides, sung in meetings and taverns, printed in newspapers and magazines, recited in theatres, as well as published in pamphlets and individual volumes. Indeed, in debates over the use of broadsides for ideological purposes in the 1790s, poetry was often seen as a more powerful medium than prose because its metre, rhyme, and frequent association with popular and traditional tunes were seen to make it especially memorable for the 'lower class of people'.[27] Writing in 1840, Douglas Jerrold provides a fascinating account of the role of the broadsheet seller and the ballads he sold in the mediation of the war to the public:

During the war it was his peculiar province to vend half-penny historical abridgements to his country's glory; recommending the short poetic chronicle by some familiar household air, that fixed it in the memory of the purchaser. , , , No battle was fought, no vessel taken or sunken, that the triumph was not published, proclaimed in the national gazette of our Ballad-singer . . . It was he who bellowed music into news, which, made to jingle, was thus, even to the weakest understanding, rendered portable. It was his narrow strips of history that adorned the garrets of the poor; it was he who made them yearn towards their country, albeit to them so rough and niggard a mother.[28]

If Jerrold's retrospective account testifies to the role of the broadsides in making the wars comprehensible and memorable to a broad readership, Betty T. Bennett has argued that 'the chief medium of publication of war poetry were the magazines and newspapers, which provided poets concerned with the war a steady outlet for their encomiums, their warnings, their arguments' (*BWP*, 9).[29] Nearly every important literary periodical had a poetry section and it was common practice for newspapers to include poetry on a regular basis. There were frequently overlaps

[27] See Roy Palmer, *The Sound of History: Songs and Social Comment* (London: Pimlico, 1996), 3, 16–19. See also Robert Hole, 'British Counter-Revolutionary Popular Propaganda in the 1790s', in Colin Jones (ed.), *Britain and Revolutionary France: Conflict, Subversion and Propaganda*, Exeter Studies in History, 5 (Exeter: University of Exeter Press, 1983), 53–69. On the importance of broadsheet ballads in constructing the image and self-image of soldiers and sailors, see Palmer, *The Sound of History*, 12, 271–302, and the entry 'Dibdin, Charles' in McCalman et al., *An Oxford Companion to the Romantic Age*, 484.

[28] Quoted in Palmer, *The Sound of History*, 19. As Jerrold suggests, many of these works focus on military and naval triumphs. The Bodleian Library, *allegro* Catalogue of Ballads includes texts on the following battles: Nile (Harding B 11 (188)), Trafalgar (Harding B 17 (18a)), Barossa (Harding B 16 (16a)), Salamanca (Johnson Ballads 1977Ar), Vittoria (Firth c.14 (25)), Pyrenees (Harding B25 (143)), and Waterloo (Firth c.14(31)).

[29] See also *PR*, 23. For a discussion of magazine poetry, see Robert Mayo, 'The Contemporaneity of the *Lyrical Ballads*', *PMLA*, 69 (1954), 486–522.

between texts published in broadsheet form and those printed in newspapers and magazines. For example, the broadsheet ballad 'Millions be Free: A New Song. Tune—"To Anacreon in Heaven" ', part of the Bodleian ballad collection, was also printed in a less radical version as 'An Ode on the Restoration of Freedom to France' in the *Gentleman's and London Magazine* in January 1793.[30] The broadsheet version of this poem, 'Millions be Free', written in the context of the French decree of November 1792 offering 'fraternity and assistance to all peoples who seek to recover their liberty',[31] concludes each stanza by looking forward to the spread of revolutionary ideology with a variant of the couplet— 'While FRANCE rises up, and proclaims the DECREE, | That tears off our Chains, and bids MILLIONS BE FREE'. The 'Ode' ends each stanza with 'That tears off *their* chains, and bids millions be free' (emphasis added), which like its title ('An Ode on the Restoration of Freedom to France') and certain subtle but significant changes in tenses, allows the poem to be read as a celebration of the Revolution in France without the broadsheet's call for the future spread of revolutionary freedom. The 'Ode' version illustrates Michael Scrivener's argument that ambiguity was a necessary feature of much of the radical verse published in newspapers and magazines, enabling a text to satisfy different factions or 'sides' (*PR*, 28–9), whereas the anonymous broadsheet version was able to present a more direct and extreme message. As this suggests, texts could shift in status and meaning as they were adapted for different forms of production and different audiences, in this case existing in both the relatively elevated form of the ode, to be read by an individual magazine reader, and as a new set of lyrics to a traditional tune, achieving its fullest realization in a communal performance at a political meeting in an alehouse or at a demonstration (*PR*, 26). Much war poetry of the period has this dual status; many songs written for a specific occasion were republished in the poetry sections of newspapers and magazines, while new sets of words were published in the hope they would be adopted for such purposes or with the aim that the tune to which they were set would heighten their impact on the reader.[32] Bellicose war poetry particularly calls on this traditional link with song, often concluding by asking the reader to sing British victories, British heroes, 'Rule Britannia' or 'God

---

[30] Bodleian Library, *allegro* Catalogue of Ballads, Harding B 22 (173), *BWP*, 69.

[31] See Best, *War and Society*, 82.

[32] See Scrivener's discussion of one such song, *PR*, 26–9. For examples from *BWP*, see 'Church and King, A Song. Tune,—"Rule Britannia" ', 71–3, 'THE ARMED YEOMAN: a New Song', 151–3, and 'Song. To the Tune of Nancy Dawson', 161–2.

Save the King'.[33] Similarly, radical and anti-war groups, which often had their origins in dissenting circles, made particular use of the form of the hymn, the words of which would be published in sympathetic newspapers or journals.[34] In this context, it is unnecessary and reductive to make too careful a distinction between 'poetry' and 'song', given that the same text could be experienced in these different ways, though it is important to bear in mind how different realizations of the text may have an impact on its mediation of the war.

In its broadside form, 'Millions be Free' also provides an excellent example of the musical dimensions of war poetry and shows how particular tunes were appropriated and reappropriated by different sides in the war debate.[35] Set to the tune of the well-known drinking song 'To Anacreon in Heaven' (now best-known as 'The Star Spangled Banner'), the ballad's radical politics and especially its implied invitation to the French to 'tear off' Britain's 'chains' made it a target for songs that sought to reappropriate its popular tune and parody its sentiments. The punningly titled 'Song. The REPUBLICANS to the DEVIL. Tune, "To Anacreon in Heaven" ', published in the *Gentleman's Magazine* in June 1794, did this by parodying the structure of the original song, presenting 'A few Rebels from Britain' as offering their petition 'To Satan in Hell, where he sat on his Throne ... | That he for his friends would Republicans own, | And proclaim them, his fav'rite sons of sedition' (*BWP*, 113). As the title tells us, the 'Rebels' are destined to go 'to the DEVIL' and the 'Song' ends with a series of rousing toasts, invoking the source's bibulous spirit to confer communal identity through singing and drinking. In another version, 'Song. Tune, "To Anacreon in Heaven" ', published in the *European Magazine* in July 1794, which celebrates Howe's naval victory of the 'Glorious First of June' of 1794, each stanza ends with a pun on the admiral's name—'And Gallia from henceforth will ne'er forget HOW' (*BWP*, 116)—suggesting that even if all assembled didn't know the words, they could still join in with this final exclamation. 'Song. The REPUBLICANS to the DEVIL' stresses the importance of singing the right song or the right version of a particular song— 'Whilst thus we agree | Let our song ever be | May Britons be Loyal,

---

[33] e.g. 'Imitated from Martial', *GM*, 68 (March 1798), 244; 'The British Volunteers', *GM*, 67 (September 1797), 783.

[34] e.g. 'Hymn, Sung at a Meeting of the Friends of Peace and Reform in Sheffield, held on the last Fast Day', in the *Cambridge Intelligencer* in March 1794 (*BWP*, 111–12).

[35] Other tunes that are subject to similar contests are 'God Save the King' and 'Rule Britannia', e.g. 'Church and King' (*BWP*, 71–3), 'A New Song' (*PR*, 26).

United, and Free' (*BWP* 115). So vital was singing to the war effort, that in yet another version the war becomes primarily a battle of songs:

> ... [we] mean to live happy, while frantic you sing
> Your fav'rite *Ca ira*,
> And hymn *Marseillois*,
> For the true Briton's song shall be 'God save the King'.
>
> (*BWP*, 213)[36]

Conflating the defence of the country with participation in the song, the text enables the singers to prove themselves 'true Britons' and to perform the nation's final triumph through the singing 'with one heart and voice' of the conclusion (*BWP*, 214). The association of national and political identity with the act of singing was emphasized in later versions of the song when it became known as 'The Briton's Song' (*BWP*, 213).

As well as its links with the ballad and song tradition, poetry had strong connections to theatrical and visual culture, which also mediated the war to the British public, frequently calling upon a deep-rooted Francophobia which held a strong place in the popular imagination. The theatre provided one arena for the singing of patriotic songs and the performance of bellicose poetry. As Gillian Russell has argued in an excellent study of the interrelation between the theatre and the war, the various elements of 'an evening's entertainment at the theatre consisting of music, song, interlude, occasional addresses, afterpieces, pantomime, pageants, and spectacle ... considered together ... reveal the extent to which the whole enterprise of the theatre at this time was dedicated to the commemoration of the war and the enhancement of patriotic values'.[37] Theatrical performances offered another source for the news-papers' poetry columns, providing a wide range of materials from elevated addresses through prologues and extracts from plays to songs, some of which were also issued as broadsides.[38]

Similarly, poetry and visual culture were frequently mutually rein-forcing in their constructions of the war. The interrelation of the two forms is well illustrated by the republication in the government-controlled newspaper *The Star* in December 1793 of David Garrick's two

---

[36] 'Song. *Tune*, "To Anacreon in Heav'n" ', first published in the *Gentleman's Magazine* in October 1798 and frequently republished (*BWP*, 213).

[37] *The Theatres of War: Performance, Politics, and Society, 1793–1815* (Oxford: Clarendon Press, 1995), 59–60.

[38] e.g. the broadsheet 'French Cobler: A New Song' (Bodleian Library, *allegro* Catalogue of Ballads, Harding B 22 (98)), published as 'A Favourite Song, Founded on Facts' in *The Star* (*BWP*, 94–5), both drawn from one of Astley's spectaculars, *The Carmagnols Routed*.

inscriptions written to accompany William Hogarth's pair of prints, *The Invasion*.[39] These prints had been published in March 1756, shortly after the outbreak of the Seven Years War with France, and Garrick's verses read like a collection of the clichés of French and English national identity:

FRANCE

With lanthern jaws and croaking gut
See how the half-starv'd Frenchmen strut,
    And call us English dogs;
But soon we'll teach these bragging foes,
That beef and beer give heavier blows,
    Than soup and roasted frogs.

The Priests inflam'd with righteous hopes,
Prepare their axes, wheels and ropes,
    To bend the stiff-neck'd sinner;
But should they sink in coming over,
Old Nick may fish 'twixt France and Dover,
    And catch a glorious dinner.

ENGLAND

See John, the soldier, Jack, the tar,
With sword and pistol arm'd for war,
    Should Mounseer dare come here!
The hungry slaves have smelt our food,
They long to taste our flesh and blood,
    Old England's beef and beer!

Britons, to arms, and let 'em come,
Be you but Britons still strike home,
    And lion-like attack 'em,
No power can stand the deadly stroke
That's given from hands and hearts of oak,
    With Liberty to back 'em.   (*BWP*, 97–8)

The republication of these verses illustrates the extent to which at the outbreak of the war in 1793 there already existed a powerful set of ideas about British and French national identities that could be easily invoked

---

[39] For reproductions of the plates and commentary see Michael Duffy (ed.), *The Englishman and the Foreigner*, The English Satirical Print, 1600–1832 (Cambridge: Chadwyck-Healey, 1986), 172–5.

through stock images and phrases. Garrick's lines appeal to what J. E. Cookson has termed a 'Protestant and francophobic nationalism',[40] providing a verbal equivalent to Hogarth's collection of visual stereotypes and fully exploiting the symbolic power of food which during the eighteenth century had 'taken pride of place in symbolic pictorial propaganda against French despotism', according to Michael Duffy.[41] To construct England as warlike, Garrick also draws on the language of the songs and ballads that were becoming popular in the middle of the eighteenth century. The phrases 'Britons, strike home' and 'Britons, to arms' can be found in a number of the broadsides and folk-songs of the eighteenth century and his reference to 'hearts of oak' anticipates his own song 'Hearts of Oak' of 1759, the so-called 'Year of Victories', which would give a crucial statement of bellicose British identity defined against France.[42]

If the nature of the French state had changed significantly since Garrick's and Hogarth's attacks on the French as hungry and emaciated as a result of the 'taxes of a despotic King and the tithes of a parasitical clergy',[43] the construction of England and France as natural enemies was one that was frequently invoked, as one poem put it:

> Listen how France is still the foe
> Of Britain's Constitution!
> Kings, or Republicans, we know
> In this, no Revolution.[44]

The poetry of the 1790s often stresses the continuity of the French threat, even if Hogarth's and Garrick's embodiment of it in the figures of priests with 'their axes, wheels and ropes' are replaced by sansculottes with their guillotine. For example, a widely read poem of 1793, 'A Word to the Wise. A New Ballad on the Times',[45] presents the French 'Mounseers' (echoing the word used by Garrick) as threatening 'Englishmen' in various ways, including stealing their food, teaching them to dance, talking in clubs, murdering women and priests, destroying the institution of marriage, and indulging in wife-swapping and cannibalism. With its

---

[42] The phrase 'Britons strike home' originates in a set of words interpolated in an adaptation of Beaumont's and Fletcher's play *Bonduca*, set to music by Purcell in 1695. Garrick wrote 'Hearts of Oak' for his *Harlequin's Invasion* of 1759. For further detail on these two songs, see *WD*, 229–30, 235.   [43] Duffy, *Englishman and Foreigner*, 35.

[44] William Young's 'THE ARMED YEOMAN: a New Song', *BWP*, 151. For the wider context of France as Britain's natural enemy in war rhetoric, see Cookson, 'War', 27–8.

[45] Published as the frontispiece to the second half of the 1793 volume of the *Gentleman's Magazine*. Text from *BWP*, 78–80.

presentation of dance teachers as a kind of advanced guard, the poem draws on eighteenth-century anxieties about French fashions and interests making England 'a province of France'. The French national stereotypes are again contrasted with the 'beef and plumb-pudding' fed John Bull and the figures of the soldier and the sailor, while national stereotypes are further represented as contrasting national femininities; the 'fish-wives' of France juxtaposed with the women of England:

> But our ladies are virtuous, our ladies are fair,
> Which is more than they tell us your French-women are;[46]

Despite its reference to France's 'new-fangled nonsense', 'A Word to the Wise' calls on traditional ideas and images to represent what is seen as a familiar threat.

Just as anti-Gallican and pro-war writers and editors had a range of sources from which they could draw in their representations of the war, so too did 'the friends of peace', the various groupings who held a variety of anti-war convictions during the period.[47] For example, a feature of the early issues of the *Cambridge Intelligencer*, which was founded in July 1793 and gained a 'national reputation as it promoted anti-war opinions',[48] was its republication of earlier poems of anti-war protest, such as John Scott's 'The Drum', first published in his *Poetical Works* (1782) and widely reprinted (*BWP*, 80). Opening with 'I Hate that drum's discordant sound', the poem is structured by the contrasting responses to the recruiting drum of 'thoughtless youth', lured to sign up 'To fight and fall in foreign lands', and the poet, horrified at war's 'catalogue of woes':

> To me it talks of ravaged plains,
> And burning towns and ruin'd swains,
> And mangled limbs, and dying groans,
> And widow's tears, and orphans moans,
> And all that *Misery's* hand bestows,
> To fill a catalogue of woes.

---

[46] For a comparable visual representation of national femininities, see T. Rowlandson's 'The Contrast' with its juxtaposition of Britannia with the French Revolutionary Medusa in Duffy, *Englishman and Foreigner*, 286–7.

[47] The authoritative studies are J. E. Cookson, *The Friends of Peace: Anti-War Liberalism in England, 1793–1815* (Cambridge: Cambridge University Press, 1982) and Martin Ceadel, *The Origins of War Prevention: The British Peace Movement and International Relations, 1730–1854* (Oxford: Clarendon Press, 1996), 166–221. For a very valuable discussion of anti-war writing in the period, which includes analysis of poetry to which I am indebted, see Penny Mahon, 'Towards a Peaceable Kingdom: Women Writers and Anti-Militarism, 1790–1825', Ph.D. thesis (Reading, 1997). [48] *PR*, 53.

This 'catalogue of woes' provides a list of anti-war tropes that would be deployed time and again in the poetry of the 1790s. The continued power of 'The Drum' during the wars is illustrated by the pro-war, patriotic parody of it beginning 'I love that drum's inspiring sound', published in the *Gentleman's Magazine* in 1804 (*BWP*, 330). Like its republication of 'The Drum', the *Cambridge Intelligencer*'s publication of a sixteen-line extract from a poem by Bielby Porteous, who became Bishop of London in 1787, written when he was a student at Cambridge in 1759, shows how the anti-war sentiment of the opening years of the war drew on the eighteenth-century enlightenment critique of international conflict. Printed under the title 'The Bishop of London's Opinion on War', the lines present a powerful critique of war as the product of kings' 'Ambitions':

> _____ ONE murder makes a Villain,
> MILLIONS a Hero: Princes are privileged
> To kill, and numbers sanctify the crime.
> Ah! Why will kings forget that they are men?   (*BWP*, 84)

Porteus's enlightenment argument that war was the product of monarchs' ambition has parallels with the critiques of war in Paine's *The Rights of Man* and Godwin's *Political Justice*. Such ideas were widely repeated in poetry of the 1790s, often with echoes of Cowper's famous passage from *The Task* describing war as 'a game' played by kings; as one poem puts it, 'Despots delight in war, to them 'tis sport, | A Royal Game—their subjects lives the stake'.[49] But whereas much loyalist poetry sought to emphasize the continuity of the French threat to Britain, even if presenting that threat in an altered form, radical poetry frequently emphasized that this was a new kind of conflict, fought for political reasons rather than between monarchs, and in doing so it frequently adopted a militant tone. Several poems published in the early years of the war present it as a war of 'Liberty' against 'Tyrants' and of patriots against mercenary slaves, while feminized personifications of France, Liberty, and Freedom frequently become giant, martial figures who overwhelm the monarchical forces of oppression.[50] In such poems, war, in the form of the military triumphs of France, becomes the means for world-wide political change.

As these examples from the early years of the war illustrate, poetry

---

[49] *The Poetical Works of William Cowper*, ed. H. S. Milford (London, New York, and Toronto: Oxford University Press, 1950), 204; 'Effects of War', *BWP*, 109.

[50] For examples from *BWP*, see 'The Triumph of Freedom', 128–9; 'To the Tyrants Infesting France', 110; 'The Genius of France', 98–9; 'Ode to Moderation', 165–7.

played a major role in the way in which the war was mediated to the British reading public and was linked with other cultural forms such as music, the theatre, the visual arts, and political prose. If the early 1790s were the decade in which the poetical contest over the war's meaning and its conduct was at its fiercest, poetry continued to play a key part in the decades that followed, as I will show. But while poetry was part of this broader milieu, it was also claimed as a form which had particular powers in representing war, especially through its association with the imagination and sensibility. It is these particular powers that I will examine in the next section of this chapter.

The Poetic Imagining of War

The battle scene from canto VI of Scott's *The Lady of the Lake* that Captain Ferguson read to his soldiers is important not only as an example of the role of poetry in mediating war, but as an illustration of what was seen as poetry's particular power in representing war through its appeal to the 'fancy' or 'imagination'. In this poem, the imprisoned highland chieftain Roderick Dhu asks the minstrel Allan-Bane to sing him an account of the conflict that has already taken place between his own clansmen and the army of James V. Dhu's request emphasizes how the poetic account of the battle that follows will provide the raw materials for his imaginative realization of the battle and operates as both a tribute to Scott's own poetic powers (especially as a poet of battle) and as a set of instructions to the reader on how to imagine war:[51]

> 'Fling me the picture of the fight
> When met my clan the Saxon might.
> I'll listen, till my fancy hears
> The clang of swords, the crash of spears!'   (VI. 14)[52]

The imaginative response to the poet's picture of war will transport the reader to the battlefield itself, as Dhu believes it will transport him from his prison cell:

---

[51] For an excellent analysis of the 'generic self-consciousness' of this scene, see Philip Cox, *Reading Adaptations: Novels and Verse Narratives on the Stage, 1790–1840* (Manchester and New York: Manchester University Press, 2000), 68–71.

[52] *The Poetical Works of Sir Walter Scott*, The Oxford Complete Edition, ed. J. Logie Robertson (London: Henry Frowde, 1904). Scott's poetry is cited by canto and stanza number.

'These grates, these walls, shall vanish then,
For the fair field of fighting men,
And my free spirit burst away,
As if it soar'd from battle fray.'   (VI. 14)

The power of poetry is such that it enables the hearers or readers to experience the soaring excitement of battle as if they themselves were participants in it. The implication of the anecdote about Ferguson and his soldiers is that Scott's poetry enabled them to imagine themselves as involved in one form of 'battle fray' even as they endured the more modern bombardment of the French artillery.

While Scott crucially transformed the way in which conflict was imagined during the Napoleonic period, as I will argue, his emphasis on poetry's power in enabling the reader to imagine battle exemplifies one of the era's key ideas about the representation of war. As a number of critics have observed, for the majority of the population, war, at least in the form of battle, was something that took place outside their immediate experience. Mary A. Favret has put this case most forcefully in her essay 'Coming Home: The Public Spaces of Romantic War', in which she sees print culture as protecting the population from the conflict, arguing that in 'the years between 1793 and 1815, when England was almost constantly at war with France, publicity raised a paper shield—a shield of newspaper reports, pamphlets, songs and poems—against the destructive violence of war'.[53] Denied the empirical contact with war, the population experience it only through the mediating, filtering, and altering forms of intellectual and verbal conventions which 'shield', 'cloak', and even make 'invisible' 'the first major European war in the era of the public sphere' (539). In this book I want to counter Favret's argument by stressing that writers were acutely aware of this sense of distance between the reading public and the war and that they saw the imagination as the means of bridging this gap and of making war visible. For example, when the publication of the Wickham–Barthélemy correspondence in April 1796 brought to an end Coleridge's hopes that negotiations between Britain and France would lead to peace, he responded by publishing in *The Watchman* extracts from *An Accurate and Impartial Narrative of the War* describing the British campaigns of 1794–5, prefacing them with the

---

[53] *Studies in Romanticism*, 33 (1994), 539. Further page references are cited in parentheses within the text. For an excellent discussion of Favret's argument, with a corrective emphasis on the imagination, see Mark Rawlinson, 'Invasion! Coleridge, the Defence of Britain and the Cultivation of the Public's Fear', in Shaw (ed.), *Romantic Wars*, 110–37.

comment: 'The horrors of war must therefore be re-commenced.—Let those who sit by the fire-side, and hear of them at safe distance attentively peruse the following'.[54] Here Coleridge places his faith in an eyewitness account of the treatment of the wounded and of the casualties of war to bridge the gap between the safety of the fireside and the scene of war, but in much of the war writing of the period it was through the 'imagination' or 'fancy' that readers could themselves become eyewitnesses to the conflict. For example, in his *Enquiry Concerning Political Justice*, first published in 1793, William Godwin gave the imagination a crucial role in the process by which his reader could come to a proper assessment of the moral status of war:

We can have no adequate idea of this evil unless we visit, at least in imagination, a field of battle. Here men deliberately destroy each other by thousands, without resentment against, or even knowledge of, each other. The plain is strewed with death in all its forms. Anguish and wounds display the diversified modes in which they can torment the human frame. Towns are burned; ships are blown up in the air, while the mangled limbs descend on every side; the fields are laid desolate; the wives of the inhabitants exposed to brutal insult; and their children driven forth to hunger and nakedness.[55]

Like Godwin, writers aware of the distance between the site of reading and the scene of war frequently responded to it by invoking the 'fancy' or the 'imagination' as a means of realizing conflict and transporting their readers to the battlefield.

While the period was witnessing the gradual emergence of a distinction between 'fancy' and 'imagination',[56] the terms remained interchangeable in most poetic usage well into the opening decades of the nineteenth century (as the example of Scott illustrates), and were used to mean 'the power of forming ideal pictures; the power of representing things absent to one's self or others', as Johnson had defined both terms in his *Dictionary*.[57] The currency of such a definition in the war years is illustrated in a lecture on the imagination of 1796 in which William Jones commented: 'The word we render *imagination*, has the sense of *forming*

[54] *The Watchman*, ed. Lewis Patton, *The Collected Works of Samuel Taylor Coleridge*, Bollingen Series, 75 (London and Princeton: Routledge and Kegan Paul and Princeton University Press, 1970), 238.

[55] *Enquiry Concerning Political Justice and its Influence on Modern Morals and Happiness*, ed. Isaac Kramnick (Harmondsworth, Middlesex: Penguin Classics, 1985), 510.

[56] See James Engell, *The Creative Imagination: Enlightenment to Romanticism* (Cambridge, Mass., and London: Harvard University Press, 1981), 172–83.

[57] Quoted John Spenser Hill (ed.), *Imagination in Coleridge* (Basingstoke and London: Macmillan 1978), 2.

and *figuring*, as a potter forms the clay, or a seal gives the impression; and when applied to the mind, denotes its faculty of receiving and forming images. When it receives them it is passive; when it forms them it is active . . . the use of the imagination is to give us pictures and images of truth.'[58] As here, the workings of fancy or the imagination were most frequently presented as a process of picturing. For example, Coleridge, who outlined the eyewitnessing role of the 'truth-painting Imagination' in envisioning the miseries of slavery that would be confirmed by the 'fleshly eye', referred in his 1795 lecture 'On the Present War' to his power to 'picture to [the audience's] imaginations the loathsome pestilence that has mocked our Victories in the West-Indies'.[59]

It was the power of the imagination or fancy to form images or to picture what was absent that made it such a crucial faculty for those writing about war for readers distant from the scene of battle. The invocation of the imagination was not limited to poetry, as we have seen from Godwin, nor was it restricted to any particular political position. If Godwin and Coleridge called on their readers in the early years of the war to imagine 'scenes of horror' as part of their critiques of war,[60] writing after the war William Napier calls on the reader's imaginative powers of mentally imaging war as a means of appreciating the bravery of the British troops who stormed Badajoz: 'Let any man picture to himself this frightful carnage taking place in a space of less than a hundred yards . . . and he must admit that a British army bears with it an awful power.'[61] While writing at the beginning and end of the wars and with very different perspectives on the wars, these writers shared the conviction that with the aid of detailed descriptions their readers will be able to use their imaginations to picture to themselves the scene of conflict. Yet as these contrasting examples illustrate, much of the writing on war was a contest over how the war could be imagined, a contest in which a number of the

---

[58] William Jones, *The Nature, Uses, Dangers, Sufferings, and Preservatives, of the Human Imagination. A Sermon, Preached in the Cathedral Church of St. Paul, London, on Sunday, Jan. 31, 1796* (London: F. & C. Rivington, G. G. & J. Robinson, and H. Gardner, 1796), 3–6.

[59] *Lectures 1795: On Politics and Religion*, ed. Lewis Patton and Peter Mann, *The Collected Works of Samuel Taylor Coleridge*, Bollingen Series, 75 (London and Princeton: Routledge and Kegan Paul and Princeton University Press, 1971), 248, 59. Hill argues that during the period 1790–1801 Coleridge used Imagination and Fancy 'interchangeably to denote the mental faculty opposed to Reason and characterized by the ability either of recalling past images or of creating illusions of its own' (*Imagination in Coleridge*, 4).

[60] Godwin, *Political Justice*, 510.

[61] W. F. P. Napier, *The History of the War in the Peninsula and in the South of France, From the Year 1807 to the Year 1814*, 6 vols. (London: Thomas and William Boone, 1838), IV. 432.

writers examined in this book were fully engaged and in which poetry was seen as a powerful weapon. Moreover, while these writers used poetry as a means of defining the imagining of war, war itself becomes a subject that shapes and in some cases defines the activity of imagining in the romantic period. These issues will be of particular concern in later discussions of Charlotte Smith, Samuel Taylor Coleridge, Robert Southey, Lord Byron, and Felicia Hemans, but the rest of this section will show how poetry came to be seen as the form that was best suited for the imagining of war.

It could be argued that the imagining of war is a crucial part of British national identity, as constructed by literature and culture.[62] In the opening speech of Shakespeare's *King Henry V* (a play frequently restaged during the wars), the Chorus invokes the audience's 'imaginary forces' and asks them to 'make imaginary puissance' in response to the staged representations of events that take place on '[t]he vasty fields of France'.[63] This speech emphasizes the inadequacy of such staged enactments of war without the addition of the audience's powers of the imagination and during the eighteenth century poetry came increasingly to be seen as the form most suitable for such imaginative work, as James Engell has shown in his outstanding study of the subject, *The Creative Imagination*. Engell gives an important role to Joseph Warton and to his poem 'Ode to Fancy' in the development of this association between poetry and the imagination, arguing that it 'announced that England needed a new poetry and that this poetry should be inspired by and based upon a faith and confidence in the creative imagination'.[64] As J. Walter Nelson has argued, Warton's poem also marked an important development in the poetic treatment of war.[65] While war poetry had taken a number of forms in the eighteenth century, one important development was the use of war as a subject that could be used to stimulate emotion.[66] In his 'Ode

[62] For one such argument, see Lawrence James, *Warrior Race: A History of the British at War from Roman Times to the Present* (London: Abacus, 2002). For an examination of such arguments with reference to the eighteenth century, see Cookson, 'War', and Colley, *Britons, passim*.

[63] *King Henry V*, ed. Andrew Gurr (Cambridge: Cambridge University Press, 1992), Prologue, ll. 18, 25, 12. [64] Engell, *The Creative Imagination*, 37, 48.

[65] 'War and Peace and the British Poets of Sensibility', *Studies in Eighteenth-Century Culture*, 7, ed. Roseann Runte (published for American Society for Eighteenth-Century Studies by University of Wisconsin Press, 1978), 352–3.

[66] On war poetry in the eighteenth-century, see Nelson, 'War and Peace'; Dustin H. Griffin, *Patriotism and Poetry in Eighteenth-Century Britain* (Cambridge: Cambridge University Press, 2002); Christine Gerrard, 'Political Passions', in John E. Sitter (ed.), *The Cambridge Companion to Eighteenth-Century Poetry* (Cambridge: Cambridge University

to Fancy', the first of his *Odes on Various Subjects* (1746), Joseph Warton
had called on 'Fancy', the 'Parent of each lovely Muse' to 'Animate some
chosen swain' whose 'unequall'd song' would 'O'erwhelm our souls with
joy and pain; | With terror shake, with pity move'.[67] Here poetry
becomes a source of the emotions and effects of the sublime and the
sentimental, and one of the crucial locations for what Warton presents
as a new type of poetry was the battlefield:

> Now let us louder strike the lyre,
> For my heart glows with martial fire,
> I feel, I feel, with sudden heat,
> My big tumultuous bosom beat,
> The trumpet's clangours pierce my ear,
> A thousand widows' shrieks I hear,
> Give me another horse, I cry,
> Lo! the base Gallic squadrons fly;
> Whence is this rage?—what spirit, say,
> To battle hurries me away?
> 'Tis Fancy, in her fiery car,
> Transports me to the thickest war,
> There whirls me o'er the hills of slain,
> Where Tumult and Destruction reign;
> Where, mad with pain, the wounded steed
> Tramples the dying and the dead;
> Where giant Terror stalks around,
> With sullen joy surveys the ground,
> And, pointing to th'ensanguin'd field,
> Shakes his dreadful Gorgon-shield!   (85–6)

As for Roderick Dhu in *The Lady of the Lake* more than sixty years later,
Fancy has the power to transport the poet (and by extension the reader)
to the 'horrid scene' of conflict, taking him from the fringes of battle
with the non-combatant widows and fleeing French 'to the thickest
war'.

Warton's poeticization of war proved extremely influential, both in
making conflict a fitting subject for imaginative writing and in creating
a particular representational register, complete with personifications,

---

Press, 2001), 37–63; Bonamy Dobrée, 'The Theme of Patriotism in the Poetry of the Early
Eighteenth Century: Warton Lecture on English Poetry', *Proceedings of the British
Academy*, 35 (1949).

[67] Text from *The Three Wartons: A Choice of their Verse*, ed. Eric Partridge (Freeport,
NY: Books for Libraries Press, 1927; repr. 1970), 83, 87. References are to page numbers and
are hereafter cited within the text.

classical references, and poetic diction, that was frequently invoked in poetic imaginings of war half a century later ('ensanguin'd field' remains one of the most popular terms for the battlefield throughout the war). For example, Mary Julia Young rewrote the poem as her own 'Ode to Fancy', published in the *Gentleman's Magazine* in January 1794, in which she considers suitable subjects for her 'Muse':

> Or shall she mount Bellona's car,
> And drive amidst the din of war,
> Fearless of the whizzing ball,
> Though dying heroes round her fall?[68]

'Fancy' enables the woman poet to place herself in the thick of war, where 'wading through th'ensanguin'd plain' she can 'View the pride of manhood slain'. However, rather than the sublime of Warton's poem, gestured to in the opening description of battle, Young's response to the battlefield is ultimately elegiac, offering to 'sing a requiem to the silent dead', and reveals both the generic constraints placed on her as a woman poet and the role that sensibility had come to play in responses to the sufferings of war. Warton's imaginative poetics of war are part of a national as well as a cultural project; he ends his poem 'O let each Muse's fame increase, | O bid Britannia rival Greece!' (88) and it is noticeable that the one discernible event in his picture of war as chaotic and destructive is the fleeing French forces. Yet Warton's poem provided a poetic imagining of war that was called on for anti-war poetry.[69] For example, in 'To Horror' the youthful radical Robert Southey calls on horror to transport him to various scenes ('some old sepulchre's moss-cankered seat', a 'wide waste hill', Greenland, a shipwreck, the battle-field, a deathbed, Africa). The battlefield is crucial to this imaginative tour:

> Dark HORROR! bear me where the field of fight
>   Scatters contagion on the tainted gale,
>   When to the Moon's faint beam,
> On many a carcase shine the dews of night,
>   And a dead silence stills the vale
> Save when at times is heard the glutted Raven's scream.
>
> Where some wreck'd army from the Conquerors might
>   Speed their disastrous flight,

---

[68] *GM*, 64 (January 1795), 69.
[69] For other examples, see S. W. 'Ode to Terror' (*PR*, 140–3) and 'Ode to Moderation' (*BWP*, 165–7).

> With thee fierce Genius! let me trace their way,
> And hear at times the deep heart-groan
> Of some poor sufferer left to die alone,
>   His sore wounds smarting with the winds of night;
> And we will pause, where, on the wild,
>   The Mother to her frozen breast,
> On the heap'd snows reclining clasps her child,
> And with him sleeps, chill'd to eternal rest![70]

Southey's poetic technique of calling on horror to transport him to the field of fight clearly draws on Warton, but if Warton used it primarily to evoke the uplifting experience of the sublime, Southey uses it for an explicitly political purpose, emphasizing the experience of revulsion of 'horror'.[71] Whereas Warton describes the battle in full flow, displacing the damage of war onto the 'wounded steed', Southey focuses entirely on the aftermath of battle and the suffering of the wounded, also introducing two key figures of anti-war poetry, the mother and child. Southey also locates his imagining of war within a broader political context. He links his anti-war position with a critique of slavery in the poem's final stanza, and whereas Warton moves easily away from the 'thickest war', Southey's next scene of horror after the battlefield is the deathbed of the individual responsible for war: 'Where he whose murderous power afar | Blasts with the myriad plagues of war'. Though probably written in 1791, prior to the outbreak of the war with France,[72] Southey published 'To Horror' in *Poems* (1797), where it becomes an important part of the anti-war strand of that volume (in which it was followed by two of Southey's best known anti-war poems 'The Soldier's Wife' and 'The Widow') and he heightened the poem's attack on war and linked it to the current conflict by attaching to it a lengthy footnote which presented a 'picture of consummate horror' in the form of the eyewitness account of the campaign of the British expeditionary force in Flanders in 1793–5 that Coleridge had quoted in *The Watchman*.[73]

If the imaginative grand tour of the sublime ode provided one means of transporting the poet and reader to the battlefield, another poetic

---

[70] Robert Southey, *Poems* (Bristol and London: Joseph Cottle and G. G. and J. Robinson, 1797), 140–1.

[71] For the literary and aesthetic contexts for such odes and invocations of 'terror' and 'horror' in terms of Gothic writing, see the extracts and discussions in E. J. Clery and Robert Miles (eds.), *Gothic Documents: A Sourcebook, 1700–1820* (Manchester and New York: Manchester University Press, 2000), 136–72.

[72] William Haller, *The Early Life of Robert Southey, 1774–1803* (New York: Columbia University Press, 1917), 46.   [73] See *The Watchman*, 239–41.

means of paying an imaginative visit to the scene of conflict was provided by the sub-genre of 'The Field of Battle' poem, a category which I have named after Thomas Penrose's highly popular mid-eighteenth-century work of that name.[74] Penrose's poem remained popular throughout the romantic period; it was republished in the *Gentleman's and London Magazine* in May 1794 and *The Courier* in January 1800 and included by Thomas Campbell in his *Specimens of the British Poets* (1819), as well as being widely adapted.[75] 'The Field of Battle' tells the story of Maria who, 'By duty led, for every vein, | Was warm'd by Hymen's purest flame', has followed Edgar to war and now searches for him 'o'er the sad scene of dreariest view', the battlefield, which is presented in gothic and gory terms, presided over by the 'war-fiend' and 'with various carnage spread'.[76] Here she learns that he has been killed in the conflict and finds his body 'Half buried with the hostile dead, | And bor'd with many a grisly wound'. The poem concludes by suggesting Maria's madness; unable to bear the sight of Edgar's body, she is left 'to worse than death—and deepest night!' Within a romantic framework, structured by Maria's love for Edgar, the poem uses the woman on the field of battle as a means of presenting the scene of conflict to the reader. Maria is both the idealized romantic female, seeking to comfort and nurse her 'warrior' and providing support on the battlefield (she presses the hands of the wounded and dying), and the focal point for the viewing of the 'carnage' and 'horrors' of the blood-soaked scene, registered through her sight—'On many a corpse she cast her gaze'— and her hearing—'And turn'd her ear to many a groan!' Maria, like the Muse of Mary Julia Young's 'Ode to Fancy' which, 'wading through th'ensanguined plain, | View[s] the pride of manhood slain', becomes a figure for the poetic experiencing of the battlefield and 'terror' inspired by war.

Penrose's 'The Field of Battle' provided a poeticization of battle that was frequently drawn on in the period. For example, it was the model for 'The Wounded Huzzar' by Thomas Campbell, who wrote both a number of popular patriotic poems on the war such as 'Ye Mariners of England' and 'Battle of the Baltic' and other, more sombre pieces such as 'The Soldier's Dream', 'Hohenlinden', and 'The Wounded Huzzar' itself,

---

[74] For the popularity of the poem, see Harvey, *A Muse of Fire*, 9.

[75] See *BWP*, 112–13. The poem has been interestingly discussed by both Mary A. Favret, 'Coming Home', 547, and Philip Shaw, 'Introduction', in Shaw (ed.) *Romantic Wars*, 3–4, though neither notes the earlier origins of the poem.

[76] Text from *BWP*, 112–13.

which while focusing on the destruction of conflict, tend to contain the violence of war within a romantic framework or displace it onto the natural surroundings. Written in 1797 and published in *The Pleasures of Hope* in 1799, 'The Wounded Huzzar' recounts the journey of 'Fair Adelaide' to the banks of the 'dark-rolling Danube' in search of her wounded husband, who dies in her arms (ll. 2, 1).[77] Campbell removes the gory and gothic elements of Penrose's original, employing a far more euphemistic language to describe war's damage ('From his bosom that heaved the last torrent was streaming' (l. 9)), and makes the passion of love and war equally important elements of his hero ('dim was that eye, once expressively beaming | That melted in love and that kindled in war' (ll. 11–12)). While the poem ends with Henry's death—'he sunk in her arms—the poor wounded Huzzar' (l. 24), Campbell lessens the potential rhetorical force of the narrative by not describing Adelaide's reaction to his death.

Yet if 'The Field of Battle' provided Campbell with a form for emphasizing war's pathos without condemning war itself, it was made to serve a different function by anti-war poets. Robert Southey particularly used the imaginative visit to 'The Field of Battle' to give his reader an adequate idea of the evil of war. His debt to the 'field of battle' form is clearly seen in his Common-Place Book plan for a poem which runs simply: 'Poitiers. The field of battle. The distant wife'.[78] This plan would become his poem 'The Victory', published in the *Morning Post* on 5 September 1798.[79] The poem begins with one act of imagination, as the boy Henry speculates on what must have been the feelings of Edward the Black Prince after the battle of Poitiers (a victory constantly alluded to in the patriotic poetry of the period, such as that which was pouring forth on the battle of the Nile when Southey's poem was published). Henry declares: 'I could for such a moment's joy | Be well content to die!' But this act of martial and self-glorifying imagining is answered by a second voice in the poem, which instructs Henry to accompany him on an imaginative tour of the battlefield:

---

[77] *The Complete Poetical Works of Thomas Campbell*, ed. J. Logie Robertson (London, New York, and Toronto: Oxford University Press, 1907), 197.

[78] *Common-Place Book*, ed. John Ward Warter, 4 vols. (London: Reeves and Turner, 1876), IV. 211.

[79] *The Contributions of Robert Southey to the 'Morning Post'*, ed. Kenneth Curry (Tuscaloosa: University of Alabama Press, 1984), 97–8. For another example of Southey's use of this form in this volume, see 'The Battle of Bosworth. An Eclogue', 105–8.

Come with me in thy spirit, boy!
To view the field of fight—
There, Henry, shall thy young heart learn
To form its wishes right.

Henry becomes a figure for the reader's imaginative viewing of the horrors of the battlefield, such as the raven that 'upon his mangled prey, | Stands idle, gorg'd with blood'. These horrors culminate and the poem concludes with a figure familiar from Penrose:

Look, Henry—what is yonder form
Slow moving o'er the plain?
It is the widow'd wife that comes
To search the field of slain.
Long shall the widow live to mourn,
And long her tears shall roll—
And wouldst thou have at thy death-hour
Her curses on thy soul?

Southey adopts 'The Field of Battle' as a way of imagining war that counters the martial imaginings he implies are essentially childish.

As these versions of the 'Ode to Fancy' and 'The Field of Battle' illustrate, throughout the 1790s poetry was adopted as a form through which the imagination could 'paint', 'picture', or 'portray' war. For example, Elizabeth Moody opened her collection of 1798, *Poetic Trifles*, with a poem entitled 'Thoughts on War and Peace' in which she presented her poetry as undertaking just such an imagining of war:

From Nature's gentlest bosoms Fancy strays
O'er the wide havock of contending bands;
Her glowing pencil each sad scene pourtrays,
The murder'd legions and the pillag'd lands.[80]

The picturing of war through the poetic imagination was used by both those who sought to celebrate war and those who wished to condemn it. Depictions of war's horrors were a standard element of pro-war poetry, emphasizing the bravery of those who fought and the ability of leaders to rise above the chaos of battle. For example, in a poem celebrating the battle of the Nile, 'On Rear-Admiral Lord Nelson's Victory', the Revd Dr Edward Dupre calls for a Miltonic 'Seraph voice' to help him 'paint the fury of the fight, | And all horrors of that dreadful night' and includes reference to the consequences of Nelson's orders: 'The Chief . . . | Calmly

---

[80] *Poetic Trifles* (London: T. Cadell, jun., and W. Davies, 1798), 4.

directs the thunder where to pour: | Loud shrieks are heard, and, ting'd with hostile gore, | The sea runs purple on the frighted shore'.[81] But it was anti-war writers who particularly exploited poetry as a form that facilitated the imaginative visit to the battlefield, frequently making the viewing of the scene of conflict the starting point for their critique of war. For example, in 'Reflections on a Field of Battle', published in the *Monthly Mirror* in May 1797, the poet 'Valdarno' begins by presenting an act of viewing a battlefield (presented in the language of Warton's 'Ode to Fancy')—'When the philanthropist, with pensive eye, | Observes the horrors of th'ensanguin'd plain'—which stimulates the poem's anti-war statements: 'How must he comment of this waste of breath, | This sense-less slaughter of the human kind' (*BWP*, 191). The culmination of the poetic imagining of war as a series of scenes or pictures as a means of anti-war protest was Joseph Fawcett's collection of 1801, *War Elegies*.[82] In 1795, Fawcett had published *The Art of War: A Poem*, over a thousand lines of anti-war blank verse in which he had criticized the argument that modern war was 'civilized'.[83] As Fawcett explained in his 'Preface' to *War Elegies*, whereas in *The Art of War* he had attempted the 'delineation of the *aggregate* calamity of War', in this later collection he presented eleven poems which focused on the 'image of *individual* distress' illus-trative of the evils of war (p. iii), the titles of which read like a list of the key tropes, figures, and narratives of the anti-war poetry of the previous decade: 'The Battle', 'The Siege', 'Famine', 'Victory', 'The Mourning Maid', 'The Despairing Mother', 'Winter', 'The Recruit', 'The Impress', 'The Soldier's School', and 'The Penitent'. Fawcett's explanation of his poetic method, and particularly of his change of approach since *The Art of War*, provides a valuable account of the techniques of much anti-war poetry of the period: 'In my former mode of treating [war], it was my aim to argue, as well as paint. In this, I have little more than endeavoured to paint, and to produce somewhat of a dramatic effect. In reading the first, it is necessary to reflect; the reader of this is only required to feel'

---

[81] *GM*, 68 (supplement 1798), 1133.

[82] Joseph Fawcett, *War Elegies* (London: J. Johnson, 1801). As Fawcett explains in his 'Advertisement', he held back distribution of the volume until 1802. References to this volume are cited by page number within the text.

[83] For an introduction to Fawcett and *The Art of War*, as well as a copy of the text, see Arthur Beatty, 'Joseph Fawcett: The Art of War. Its Relation to the Early Development of William Wordsworth', *University of Wisconsin Studies in Language and Literature*, 2 (1918), 224–69. See also M. Ray Adams, *Studies in the Literary Backgrounds of English Radicalism, with Special Reference to the French Revolution* (New York: Greenwood Press, 1968), 191–226.

(p. vii). Throughout the volume, Fawcett emphasizes the importance of his reader's visual capacity, calling on the reader 'to contemplate, with an eye aroused from the torpid tolerance (into which custom lulls its sense) of a practice humanity cannot endure, an eye awake and open upon its object, the undisguised deformity of War' (pp. v–vi). And it is the reader's visual sense which provides access to the heart: 'Let him open his heart to the pictures of individual wretchedness these little pieces place before him' (p. vi). Fawcett's imaginative poetic is emphasized by the poems themselves, which constantly invoke the reader's viewing of the scenes of war. In the volume's opening poem, 'The Battle', poetry initially gives the reader a bird's-eye view of the conflict; 'Borne by the buoyant muse, aloft ascend, | And view the wide combustion from on high!' (5). This view point gradually moves closer to the action:

> With the descending muse, reduce thy post;
> And, hov'ring o'er the field with nearer flight,
> Trace the distincter forms of either host.   (6)

Like Roderick Dhu's instructions to Allan-Bane, Fawcett's poem provides a step-by-step guide for the imagining of war, though unlike Scott's minstrel, Fawcett focuses in on those suffering in the battle, as he instructs the reader to 'Fix on that agonizing form thine eye, | Tossing and twisting with contorting pain!' and to 'See [the] wounded steeds' (7, 8). For the reader following Fawcett's instructions, there is no escape from the horrors of war: 'The troubled scene denies thine eye repose, | In vain it looks e'en to the peaceful dead' (8). Fawcett's appeal to the visual imagination through poetry is also important in that it seeks to counter the official ways in which the war was mediated to the reading public in Britain. At the conclusion to 'The Battle' he writes:

> Official apathy's cold pen relates
> This harrowing scene, and tells what numbers bled:
> And the vast sum of all these tragic facts,
> Serenely as recorded, shall be read.   (10)

The poetic imagining of war provides an alternative means of reading and writing battle. Fawcett reinforces the overall claim of this poem and of the volume as a whole in a note to this stanza in which he provides a prose equivalent to his poetic strategy, arguing that the cold reports of the newspapers disguise the individual histories of war, in which each statistic:

stands for a long pathetic story (which, if told at length, could not fail to bring tears into all eyes) of a dying man, extended on the cold, uncurtained, unpillowed, unattended couch of earth; trampled on, or passed by, with savage neglect, instead of being surrounded with soothing ministers to his final necessities; and encompassed, instead of the silence of the chamber of death, with scenes of tumult and distraction! Who, that contemplated, in the sum of the slain, at the conclusion of a battle, an accumulation of such affecting pictures as this, could read the tragical amount, without a horror that should cause his head to swim, and strike a sickness into his heart? (11)

Fawcett's collection of poetic pictures emphasizes the link between imagination and sensibility that is generally made in much of the writing of the period, seen in Coleridge's comment to fellow poet William Lisle Bowles in 1797 that 'The base of our politics is, I doubt not, the same. We both feel strongly for whomever our imaginations present to us in the attitude of suffering'.[84] In much poetry, the imagining of war is frequently presented as leading to a sympathetic identification with war's victims, as in 'An Hymn for the Fast Day, To Be Sung by The Friends of Mankind', published in *Politics for the People*:

> Methinks we hear the cannons roar,
> And see a sea of human gore,
> We hear our brethren's dying cries,
> We feel the pangs,—and sympathise. (PR, 89)

As this Hymn suggests, representations of suffering on the battlefield were central to anti-war poetics, contrary to influential recent arguments that the British reading public was protected from the horrors of war by print culture. After all, the *Anti-Jacobin* identified the portrayal of the physical damage of war as one of the central features of Jacobin poetry: 'we are presented with nothing but contusions and amputations, plundered peasants, and deserted looms'.[85] To use the terms of the texts themselves, the war poetry of the period is a poetry of piercing and boring,[86] of wounding and bleeding,[87] of mangling, shattering, breaking,

---

[84] *Collected Letters of Samuel Taylor Coleridge, 1785–1834*, ed. Earl Leslie Griggs, 6 vols. (Oxford: Clarendon Press, 1956–71), I. 183.   [85] *Anti-Jacobin*, 14.

[86] 'manly breasts are pierced with many a wound' ('Lines by John Gabriel Stedman', *BWP*, 103); 'bor'd with many a grisly wound' ('The Field of Battle', *BWP*, 113).

[87] 'Wounds and death left behind' ('The Field of Battle', *BWP*, 112); 'Thousands of wounds and sickness left to die' ('The Wounded Soldier' *BWP*, 244); 'No priest with bloody fingers dy'd | Deep in the gasping victim's side' ('On the Consecration of the Colours of the Military Association of—', *BWP*, 234); 'Gallant Soldiers—fighting—bleeding' ('January, 1795', *BWP*, 142); 'While thousands bleed,—while thousands die' ('On the Return of a Festival', *BWP*, 223).

maiming and scarring,[88] of agonizing pain and groaning,[89] and of dying.[90] The 'horrid scene' of 'The Field of Battle', strewn with 'Slaughter'd men and mangled cattle',[91] becomes the crucial site for the representation of war's damage, whether represented in the poetic diction of the eighteenth century as 'th'ensanguin'd plain' and 'the blood-empurpled plain', or in the graphic terms used to describe the scene of conflict in January 1795, 'Belgia's reeking plain' where 'Alternate horrors rise and reign!'[92] Rather than protecting the British public from the destructive violence of conflict, much of the poetry of the period aimed to make the reader feel war's pain and suffering; war poetry was more like a paper bullet than a paper shield.

Martial Maidens and Trembling Muses: War, Poetry, and Gender

If the battle scene of Scott's *The Lady of the Lake* illustrates poetry's mediation of war to the British public and the importance of the imagination in the process, it also raises the issue of the relationship between war and gender. Prior to the battle of Beal' an Duine with James V's Saxon army, Roderick Dhu orders that the non-combatant Highlanders be placed on the island in Loch Katrine both for their own safety and to act as an inspiration to the warriors:

> Within Loch Katrine's gorge we'll fight,
> All in our maids' and matrons' sight,
> Each for his hearth and household fire,
> Father for child, and son for sire,
> Lover for maid beloved!—   (IV. 8)

Dhu motivates his men by constructing the battle as fought on behalf of familial relations and to protect the domestic sphere, and particularly as one fought under the inspirational gaze of women. While the

---

[88] 'mangled limbs' ('The Drum', *BWP*, 80); 'mangled limb' ('Effects of War', *BWP*, 96); 'Slaughter'd men and mangled cattle' ('Reason Uttering a Soliloquy Over a Field of Battle', *BWP*, 192); 'shatter'd remnants' ('Effects of War', *BWP*, 96); 'broken soldier, maimed and scar'd' ('The Widow', *BWP*, 268).

[89] 'agonising smart' ('Ode to War', *BWP*, 124); 'dying groans' ('The Drum', *BWP*, 80); 'many a groan' ('The Field of Battle', *BWP*, 113).

[90] 'Ghastly and pale the wounded heroes bleed' ('An Elegy on War', *BWP*, 183); 'The Dying Soldier; a Fragment' (*BWP*, 224–5).

[91] 'Reason Uttering a Soliloquy Over a Field of Battle' (*BWP*, 192).

[92] 'Reflections on a Field of Battle' (*BWP*, 191); 'Reason Uttering a Soliloquy Over a Field of Battle' (*BWP*, 192); 'Ode On the Present Times, 27th January 1795' (*BWP*, 141).

non-combatants include the very young and very old, wartime roles are broadly constructed along gendered lines. But during the battle, when the Saxon army find themselves unable to reach the Highland force above them on the ridge, they decide to attack this island, vulnerable due to the absence of men; as Moray tells his troops, 'none are left to guard its strand, | But women weak, that wring the hand' (VI. 20). To enable the rest of the Saxon force to reach the island, a soldier swims to it to capture a boat, as Allan-Bane describes:

> he nears the isle, and lo!
> His hand is on a shallop's bow.
> Just then a flash of lightning came,
> It tinged the wave and strand with flame;
> I mark'd Duncraggan's widow'd dame,
> Behind an oak I saw her stand,
> A naked dirk gleam'd in her hand:
> It darken'd; but, amid the moan
> Of waves, I heard a dying groan;
> Another flash!—the spearman floats
> A weltering corse beside the boats,
> And the stern matron o'er him stood,
> Her hand and dagger streaming blood.   (VI. 20)

Read within the poem's historical framework, the 'stern matron's' violent act could be taken as an example of the fierce, uncivilized nature of the Highlanders. But while the melodramatic flashes of lightning produce tableaux of before and after the killing, suggesting the difficulties of presenting a woman's act of violence, Scott's description of 'Duncraggan's widow'd dame' stresses her familial identity as both a widow and a mother, forced in the absence of men to protect her 'brood' and 'den' (VI. 20). In such a context, it is not hard to read the scene as allegorical of the French invasion threat to the British island and of the symbolic need for the whole nation to become warlike. As Scott wrote in a letter of 1808 advocating the sending of more British troops to reinforce those in the Spanish Peninsula, 'Tell Mr Canning that the old women of Scotland will defend the country with their distaffs, rather than that troops enough be not sent to make good so noble a pledge' (LWS, III. 131–2). As in The Lady of the Lake, while women remain defined by their feminine role, the crisis of war paradoxically enables them to participate in the masculine activity of fighting from which constructions of femininity would normally have excluded them.

As much recent theoretical work has shown, war is inextricably linked to the production, reproduction, and circulation in society of ideas about gender and gender roles.[93] It has been argued that, after biological reproduction, war is the activity where the division of labour along gender lines has been the most obvious and where sexual difference has seemed the most absolute and natural. As Scott's description of the battle of Beal' an Duine illustrates, war both polarizes and pressurizes ideas of manliness and femininity. Constructions of martial masculinity, which link virility and aggression and make war the ultimate testing ground for manhood, are complemented by a vision of domestic femininity, associated with peace, the home, and children, which requires protection, inspires men to fight and rewards them for their heroics. The war poetry of the Revolutionary and Napoleonic wars frequently exhorts individuals to enact these gendered roles. For example, Nathaniel Bloomfield in his *An Essay on War, in Blank Verse*, published at the height of the invasion threat in 1803, writes that at this time of crisis:

> The most humane, the most pacific men,
> Must arm for War, or lose all they hold dear:
> The sorrows of the Aged, Infant cries,
> And Female Tears, resistlessly prevail:
> Can gentlest natures be in love with Peace,
> When Love, most tender Love, excites to War?[94]

Yet, as these lines suggest, while women (along with children and the old) are frequently represented as requiring the protection of men, they also become both a justification for, and a stimulation to, fighting. It is this role of 'excit[ing] to war' that women are often called on to play in the poetry of the period, as in 'The British Heroes' published in the *Anti-Gallican* of 1804, which presents the 'British fair' as 'Like Sparta's matrons nobly great'—a popular analogy during the war years—as the

---

[93] See Miriam Cooke and Angela Woollacott (eds.), *Gendering War Talk* (Princeton: Princeton University Press, 1993); Jean Bethke Elshtain, *Women and War* (Chicago: University of Chicago Press, 1995); William S. Goldstein, *War and Gender: How Gender Shapes the War System and Vice Versa* (Cambridge: Cambridge University Press, 2001); Martin L. Van Creveld, *Men, Women and War* (London: Cassell, 2001); Inger Skjelsaek, and D. Smith (eds.), *Gender, Peace and Conflict* (London: Sage, 2001); Susie Jacobs, Ruth Jacobson, and Jennifer Marchbank (eds.), *States of Conflict; Gender, Violence, and Resistance* (London: Zed Books, 2000); Nancy Huston, 'Tales of War and Tears of Women', *Women's Studies International Forum*, 5.3/4 (1982), 271–82; Sharon MacDonald, Pat Holden, and Shirley Ardener (eds.), *Images of Women in Peace and War: Cross-Cultural and Historical Perspectives* (Basingstoke and London: Macmillan Education, 1987).

[94] Nathaniel Bloomfield, *An Essay on War, in Blank Verse* (London: Thomas Hurst and Vernor and Hood, 1803), 8.

nation's 'Wives, mothers, daughters vie | Who most shall heroes animate | To conquer or to die'.[95]

Yet, if in these examples the crisis of the war prompts a reinforcement of gendered roles, its sense of emergency can also produce questionings, negotiations, or transgressions of them. In Shakespeare's play, Henry V urges his men 'unto the breach' by reminding them that when 'the blast of war blows in our ears' it is necessary to 'Disguise fair nature with hard-favoured-rage'(3. 1. 1–34). While Henry was specifically addressing the issue of what is becoming to 'a man', his exhortation raises the broader issue of how war can demand of individuals that they play a role that will disguise their 'fair nature', an argument applicable to women as well as men. Such acts of disguising or stepping beyond what is constructed as the natural role as the result of war are frequently presented in the poetry of the period. While this poetry is full of highly conventional constructions of women's wartime roles, such as the Spartan mother who sends her son to war or the romance heroine who buckles on her lover's armour, it is also heavily populated by martial maidens and women warriors, such as Southey's eponymous heroine Joan of Arc and his Adosinda (*Roderick, the Last of the Goths*), Scott's Edith (*The Lord of the Isles*), Byron's maid of Saragossa (*Childe Harold's Pilgrimage*, I) and Hemans's Ximena (*The Siege of Valencia*), all of whom will be examined below.[96] Much lyric poetry of the period, such as that which treats the recurring figure of the woman on the field of battle, similarly complexifies the normal gendered division of wartime roles. In all these cases the enactment of a specific role demanded by the emergency of war enables women to move beyond what is perceived to be their natural role, a process which can be presented as either only a temporary necessity before the natural role is resumed or a more radical questioning of the construction of such roles.

The broader dimensions of the interrelation between war and issues of gender are illustrated by the opening of the 1804 poem 'The British Heroes':

> The war's begun, the British fair
>   All weakness overcome;
> The harp and lyre beneath their care,
>   Now hail the sprightly drum.   (*BWP*, 335)

---

[95] 'The British Heroes' (*BWP*, 335).

[96] For eighteenth-century anticipations of such figures, see Dianne Dugaw, *Warrior Women and Popular Balladry, 1650–1850* (Cambridge: Cambridge University Press, 1989).

Another example of the crisis of war causing women to transcend their nature, the poem presents this transformation of gender in terms of national identity and poetic forms. As we shall see, the nation is frequently presented through figures such as Britannia or Mother England and the wars frequently prompted poets to redefine such gendered symbols.[97] If there was a call on the nation to be more warlike, this was frequently symbolized in the representation of martial maidens and warrior women, such as those listed above. But for some writers the pressure of war was such that the nation needed to be regendered, to be made manly, if it was to survive the threat from France (as I shall be arguing in my discussion of Wordsworth's sonnets in Chapter 4). War not only plays a crucial role in the forging of Britain and British national identity, as Linda Colley has influentially argued, it also shapes the gendered forms through which the nation and national identity came to be understood. If 'The British Heroes' illustrates what is seen as a necessary redefinition of gender roles at national level, it links this to a wartime reconception of poetry; the martial muse of the 'sprightly drum', at once the call to volunteers and the beat of war poetry, supersedes the lyric strains of the 'harp and lyre', now deemed unworthy of the reconstituted 'British fair'. As these lines suggest, not only did poetry mediate war to its public but poetry itself was mediated by the theatre of war which it addressed. Constructions of literary and poetic authority have been the focus of much excellent work on the romantic period, in recent years particularly emphasizing the role of gender and the sexual politics of authorship, but they have rarely taken the war into account, despite war's powerful pressure on gender roles and its offering of an arena for the acting out and negotiation of these roles.[98] I will be arguing that the war plays a major role in shaping poetic ideas and practices in the romantic period, particularly in terms of what Gary Kelly has described as the 'remasculinisation' of literary culture in the period.[99]

---

[97] For a general discussion of such figures, see Marina Warner, *Monuments and Maidens: The Allegory of the Female Form* (London: Picador, 1987). For an excellent discussion of such figures in terms of the Peninsular War, see Diego Saglia, ' "O My Mother Spain!": The Peninsular War, Family Matters, and the Practice of Romantic Nation-Writing', *ELH*, 65 (1998), 363–93.

[98] See Marlon B. Ross, *The Contours of Masculine Desire: Romanticism and the Rise of Women's Poetry* (New York and Oxford: Oxford University Press, 1989); Sonia Hofkosh, *Sexual Politics and the Romantic Author* (Cambridge: Cambridge University Press, 1998).

[99] Gary Kelly, 'Revolution and Romantic Feminism: Women, Writing and Cultural Revolution', in Keith Hanley and Raman Selden (eds.), *Revolution and English Romanticism: Politics and Rhetoric* (Hemel Hempstead and New York: Harvester Wheatsheaf and St Martin's Press, 1990), 113.

Kelly argues that in 'certain respects Romanticism . . . was a remasculinisation of a literary culture seen as having become, in the last decades of
the eighteenth century, "merely" feminine' and that 'the remasculinisation of literature and especially poetry was pursued vigorously by men
poets, led in the late 1790s and 1800s by Wordsworth and Coleridge, and
then by Byron and Shelley.'[100] The war, I will argue, played a crucial role
in this transformation of conceptions of poetry from a feminine to a
masculine pursuit.[101]

The feminization of poetry in the early stages of the war is evident in
much of the writing of the 1790s about the relation of the two activities.
The feminine figure of the Muse was frequently used to represent poetry,
especially in elevated forms or with any aspiration to literary value, and
to define it as antithetical to war. Through such feminizing representations, poetry was seen to transcend party politics but to be unable to deal
with the manly subject of war, as in Peter L. Courtier's 'Ode to Peace' of
January 1796 in which he asks the reader to 'Forgive the Muse' because
'Peace is her darling theme':

> Willing from Devastation's reign she turns,
>   With trembling nerves and bitterness of soul,
> To scenes for which with ecstasy she burns!   (BWP, 168–9)

Such representations of the trembling Muse are not new to the period,[102]
but the regularity with which they occur does provide one index of the
increasing perception of poetry as feminized. If Courier presents poetry
as turning away from war, other writers presented the conflict as
hampering, threatening, and potentially destroying the Muse. One poet
comments that 'War, horrid War, untunes the trembling strings, | And
loads Imagination's flagging wings', while in The Art of War Joseph
Fawcett presents the Muse as having a 'long time lain | Beneath the
suffocating weight' of war.[103] In Amelia Alderson's 'Ode on the Present
Times, 27th January 1795', 'pale Fancy' dies when envisioning the war-
produced threat of famine to Britain (BWP, 142) and ten years later the

---

[100]   Kelly, 'Revolution and Romantic Feminism', 113, 126.

[101]   On the feminization of poetry and literary culture in the later decades of the eighteenth century, see Ross, The Contours of Masculine Desire, passim, and Judith Page,
Wordsworth and the Cultivation of Women (Berkeley, Los Angeles, and London: University
of California Press, 1994), 29–53.

[102]   In her poem Peru, Helen Maria Williams writes that 'from the scene where raging
Slaughter burns | The timid muse with pallid horror turns' (VI. 13–14), Poems 1786 (Oxford
and New York: Woodstock Books, 1994), 184.

[103]   N.B., 'Letter to a Sister', GM, 64 (July 1794), 654; Fawcett, 'The Art of War', ll. 554–5.

Gentleman's Magazine was still using this construction of poetry as feminized and forced into retreat by international events when characterizing the literary scene: 'The din of war, and the clang of arms, has been so loud and incessant that the Muses have trembled within their bowers, and retired to weep over the actions of Heroes and Statesman!'[104]

Some writers exploited this gendered opposition of war and poetry, as in Ann Yearsley's 'To Mira, on the Care of her Infant' in which she makes the construction of different wartime roles part of a feminized poetic, grounded in the home, childcare, and education, implicitly critical of masculine violence:

> We are not made for Mars; we ne'er could bear
> His ponderous helmet and his burning spear;
> Nor in fierce combat prostrate lay that form
> That breathes affection whilst the heart is warm:
> No: whilst our heroes from our home retire,
> We'll nurse the infant, and lament the fire.[105]

But for other poets war threatened to overwhelm poetry and to render it irrelevant, an anxiety expressed by Elizabeth Moody in the 'Preface' to her collection of poems of 1798, *Poetic Trifles*:

I am well aware that this is no period favourable to the Muse.

> This is no time for calm familiar talk,
> Like man and maidens in an evening walk.
> War is our business.   POPE'S HOMER

At a season, therefore, like the present,—when the monster WAR is sounding his terrific alarms;—when the spirit of discord is in the air, and pervades every Atmosphere,—when it not only stimulates the combatants in the field of *battle*, but in the field of *Literature*,—when the fiend POLITICS is sharpening the pen to make it like a two-edged sword; and the Pamphleteer builds his hopes of Celebrity on the basis of Spleen and Acrimony—How I presume to ask, may the compilation of a few harmless Numbers be expected to engage the public attention? [106]

Here Moody locates poetry within the context of the ongoing pamphlet war of the 1790s, and suggests the tension between the dominating political concerns of the decade and poetry's supposed ability to transcend

[104] *GM*, 76 (January 1806), p. iii.
[105] *Women Romantic Poets, 1785–1832: An Anthology*, ed. Jennifer Breen (London and Rutland, Vt.: J. M. Dent and Charles E. Tuttle, 1992), 96.
[106] *Poetic Trifles*, pp. i–ii.

such historical crises. While displaying the diffidence required of a woman poet in the later years of this decade (especially in a volume beginning with a poem entitled 'Thoughts on War and Peace'), Moody's comments raise a number of the major concerns of this book. How could poetry, 'a few harmless numbers', engage the attention of the reading public in wartime? Was there a role for it when confronted with 'the monster WAR'? If poetry was constructed as feminized, particularly in its elevated forms, in a period when the nation was demanding manliness embodied in the active figures of the soldier, the sailor, the volunteer, and even the nation itself, how could poets—be they men or women— speak on international events with authority? And at a time when *'Literature'* itself was becoming defined by the field of battle, what would be the impact on poetry of more than two decades of conflict between Britain and France?[107]

'Horror' or 'Glory': The Poetic Contest over War in the 1790s

While the battle scene from *The Lady of the Lake* has proved useful in introducing the major claims and areas of enquiry of this book, Scott himself has a crucial role to play in its argument and structure as the writer who transformed the imagining of war through poetry during the Napoleonic wars, a transformation which we might very broadly categorize as a shift in the representation of conflict from horrific to picturesque. In a review of *The Vision of Don Roderick* of 1811, the *Eclectic Review* argued that Scott's poetic attitude to war was very different from the prevailing modes of the time:

Instead of adopting the mild and pacific tone, by which modern poetry as well as philosophy is distinguished, instead of deploring the calamities of war, exciting a sympathy with the sufferings of mankind, and invoking a just indignation against the wanton contentions of governments, he has taken up the ancient function of a bard, to celebrate military prowess, and set off pride, ferocity, and revenge.[108]

The Eclectic's characterization of what distinguishes 'modern poetry' continues the radical critique of the traditional links between verse and war that was a particular feature of debates over the role of poetry in the

---

[107] For one broad account of the impact of war on European writing in the period, see Nancy L. Rosenblum, 'Romantic Militarism', *Journal of the History of Ideas*, 43 (1982), 249–68. [108] *Eclectic Review*, 7 (1811), 673.

1790s. These attacks on the martial construction of poetry were made on several grounds; it profaned the 'pure gift of poesy',[109] it prostituted poetry for 'the support of great, but guilty men',[110] it threw a 'splendid disguise' over 'the most odious and deformed of all the practices by which the annals of what is called civilized society have been disgraced',[111] and it 'raised | The aspiring spirit to hopes of fair renown | By deeds of violence'. [112] While making Scott the target of an updated version of these arguments, the *Eclectic*'s characterization of the dominant tone, techniques and effects, of 'modern poetry' provides a valuable introduction to some of the major modes of poetic writing on the war. Scott's poetic transformation of war will itself be the subject of a later chapter, but in this section I want to use the *Eclectic Review*'s characterization of 'modern poetry' to introduce these poetic modes and also to argue that prior to Scott's phenomenal success there was seen to be a need for just such a 'martial poet' to inspire the nation in the war against France.

If poetry was a form which could transport readers to the scene of war and assist them in imagining battle, it also brought home the 'calamities of war' in a number of ways, especially through the figures of returning soldiers and sailors telling their tales of the conflict, and through its examination of the broader impact of war on the economic and social condition of Britain. As we have seen from the example of John Scott's 'The Drum', anti-war poetry presented a 'catalogue of woes' and registered the 'Effects of War', to use the title of a poem by 'Pacificus' of 1793 published in the radical provincial newspaper the *Cambridge Intelligencer*, in November 1793 (*BWP*, 96–7). This poem employs many of the key tropes used to bring war home and is structured, like 'The Drum', by the 'amazing change' of war in which conflict is presented as initiating a fall from innocence into experience that constitutes not only a change in world-view but in the world itself.[113] Like Scott, Pacificus opens with a portrayal of the eagerness of the army departing for war, presented from the point of view of the non-combatant—'With glittering arms I saw the soldiers march | With hearts elate, and footsteps light as air'—but rather than following the army overseas, the poem examines the war's impact on those left behind:

---

[109] William Crowe, 'Lines' (*BWP*, 174).   [110] 'Independence' (*PR*, 83).
[111] Joseph Fawcett, 'Preface' to *Poems* (1798), quoted in Beatty, 'Joseph Fawcett', 232.
[112] Crowe, 'Lines' (*BWP*, 175).
[113] The phrase is taken from 'An Elegy on War' (*BWP*, 183).

> Post, after post, soon brings a heavy tale,
> Though gloss'd with victory, fatal to the peace
> Of fathers, mothers, children, wives, and friends.
> Dead, is the hand that long with labour fought
> To feed the little offspring hovering round:
> Vanish'd the hope that sooth'd a parent's age;
> Sunder'd the ties of faithful wedded love,
> And the dear long-tried friend forever gone.   (*BWP*, 96)

As mentioned above, it has been estimated that one in four families was directly involved in the wars and like much of the poetry of the 1790s 'Effects of War' emphasizes that while war is fought abroad its effects are felt at home. Much of this poetry focused on widows and orphans, calling on their tears and sighs as the ultimate indictment of war, a technique with biblical and classical precedent.[114] Already an important figure in the literature of sensibility, the widow was used in numerous poems to represent the cost of conflict, as indicated by the title of Elizabeth Moody's 'Anna's Complaint; or, The Miseries of War; written in the Isle of Thanet, 1794' (*BWP*, 149–50). This ballad is one of many that describes the grief of women for their loved ones killed in the war, which frequently culminate in their own deaths, the subject of a fascinating essay by Mary Favret.[115] The widow also became the subject of the writing of some of the most ambitious poets of the decade, including Charlotte Smith, William Wordsworth, and Robert Southey, whose work will be examined in the next two chapters. These writers made particular use of one of the sub-genres of war poetry in the period, the 'ruined cottage' poem which figures war's impact on the domestic sphere through the image of the increasingly dilapidated building, often a symbol for the widow herself.[116] Poets also used the 'ruined cottage' form to represent the more general social and economic crisis caused by conflict, what one such poem presents as 'sickness, want, | Famine, and

---

[114] 'The Wrongs of Poverty' (*PR*, 54), 'Hymn' (*BWP*, 111), 'Ode to Peace' (*BWP*, 168), 'Lines' by Crowe (*BWP*, 175). For biblical precedent, see *PR*, 55. For classical precedent, see epigram from *Aeneid* in 'Effects of War' (*BPW*, 108). For two excellent discussions of the widow figure in the war poetry of the period, see Favret, 'Coming Home', and Behrendt, 'A Few Harmless Numbers'.

[115] e.g. 'The Widow' (*BWP*, 153–4); Favret, 'Coming Home'.

[116] Southey, 'The Ruined Cottage' in *Poems: The Second Volume* (London: T. N. Longman and O. Rees, 1799), 226–32; Wordsworth, 'The Ruined Cottage', in *William Wordsworth: The Oxford Authors*, ed. Stephen Gill (Oxford and New York: Oxford University Press, 1986), 31–44; Charlotte Smith, 'The Forest Boy', in *The Poems of Charlotte Smith* ed. Stuart Curran (New York and Oxford: Oxford University Press, 1993), 111–16. See also Mary Robinson, 'The Widow's Home', in *Selected Poems*, 207–10.

all the complicated woes, | That haunt the desolating steps of war'. This poem uses the 'piteous scene' of 'yon wretched hovel! once the seat | Of industry and health, content and love' to represent war's economic impact: 'commerce sickens, and the toiling hand | Of industry droops lifeless, unemploy'd' (*BWP*, 108–9).

If Pacificus's 'Effects of War' illustrates the way in which much poetry of the 1790s presents the impact of conflict on the domestic sphere, he also includes one of the major poetic figures used to bring the war home to the reader, the returning soldier, describing the return of a 'shatter'd remnant', devastated both numerically and physically, with 'sickly face and mangled limb' (*BWP*, 96). The returning soldier, often wounded or discharged, is a major figure in the war poetry of the period, with a number of precedents in eighteenth-century writing, and is used to figure the damage done by war both to those who participated in it and those they left behind: soldiers frequently return in these poems to find their loved ones destitute or dead.[117] Robert Merry's poem 'The Wounded Soldier', written *circa* 1795 and printed in *The Spirit of the Public Journals* in 1799, illustrates this fusion of war's damage to the soldier and to the home in startling fashion (*BWP*, 242).[118] Merry had been an enthusiastic supporter of the cause of the French Revolution, celebrating it in a tavern Ode read before 1,500 people, and his poem emphasizes the high casualty rate of the war's early years, as the soldier comments 'Our bravest legions moulder'd fast away, | Thousands of wounds and sickness left to die' (*BWP*, 244). Merry's 'wounded soldier' journeys home, the damage of war registered in his body; he 'feebly mov'd along', 'as with strange contortions lab'ring slow', has a 'hollow and dejected eye' and despite his youth displays a 'helpless prematurity of age' (*BWP*, 243). He is psychologically as well as physically scarred, with a 'tortur'd heart' (*BWP*, 243). Gaining 'the summit of his native hill', the soldier contrasts his past happiness with his present condition, and his reminiscences of his recruitment and his time campaigning lead him to curse 'this warfare of the world' (*BWP*, 242–4). Like many such

---

[117] For a discussion of the historical figure of the returning soldier, see Herman Gaston de Watteville, *The British Soldier: His Daily Life from Tudor to Modern Times* (London: Dent, 1954). For further examples, see E. C. G., 'Written After Seeing Opie's Picture of the Tired Soldier in the Late Exhibition' (*BWP*, 240–1); Anne Bannerman, 'The Soldier', in Andrew Ashfield (ed.), *Romantic Women Poets, 1788–1848*, vol. II (Manchester and New York: Manchester University Press, 1998), 82; Mary Robinson's 'Edmund's Wedding', *Selected Poems*, 259–62, and 'The Old Soldier', *Morning Post*, 31 August 1799.

[118] For the dating of the poem, see the entry 'Merry, Robert' in McCalman, *Oxford Companion*, 601.

poetic figures, including those of 'The Drum', the soldier's innocence had made him vulnerable to the rhetoric of the 'gaudy' recruiting sergeant: 'And as his tongue of war and honour spake, | I felt a wish to conquer or to die' (*BWP*, 243). His experience of warfare has been a process of disillusionment as well as suffering, with war producing the 'wreck of reason and the waste of life' and has also seen him gain a sense of political awareness, realizing that the war in which he fought was one in which the 'savage heart' 'sent the *slave* to fight against the *free*' (*BWP*, 244). Reaching his parent's cottage, the soldier is aware that his presence will alter the nature of the home—'must ye too endure | That I should gloom for e'er your homely mirth'—and that as a result of his disfigurement and maiming his and Lucy's 'cherish'd fondest hopes be vain' (*BWP*, 243). The soldier's fears of his effect on the domestic sphere are horribly literalized in the conclusion to the narrative:

> But when he enter'd in such horrid guise,
>   His mother shriek'd, and dropp'd upon the floor:
> His father look'd to heav'n with streaming eyes,
>   And LUCY sunk, alas! To rise no more.   (*BWP*, 245)

When wars are fought not to protect the home but to stifle 'fair Freedom's call', the ultimate cost of conflict is the home itself (*BWP*, 244). The returning soldier brings home the war in a double sense in the poetry of the period; he is both a physical reminder of war's damage and the bearer of its 'mournful tales' to those distanced from the battlefield. In Pacificus's 'Effects of War', for example, the returned soldier has to break the news of his fellow soldiers' deaths to their relatives:

> If aught can damp *his* joy [at returning home], it is the tale,
> The mournful tale, that he is doom'd to tell,
> Of his lost comrades, in the fatal field,
> Blasting the lingering hope, that yet surviv'd,
> And bade the anxious bosom daily watch,
> For *his* return, who was its only joy.
>   (*BWP*, 96)

The soldier 'doom'd to tell' his 'mournful tale' might appear to anticipate Coleridge's Ancient Mariner, 'forced' to tell his tale, and both suggest something of the psychological necessity of tale telling for those traumatized by the sudden deaths of comrades. John Clare's 'The Wounded Soldier' particularly recalls the Ancient Mariner: 'I'll sit me

down and hear his woful tale . . . | He tells his woful tale to all he meets |
And now he'll tell his woful tale to me'.[119] But the soldier's reporting of
the deaths of his fellow men is also presented as a social responsibility
and narratives of 'A broken soldier, maim'd and scar'd' appearing at the
widow's 'cottage gate' and breaking the 'fatal unexpected news' are
common in the period ('The Widow', BWP, 268).

The returning soldier was a troubling figure, socially, psychologically
and politically, especially if, as in James Gillray's print John Bull's
Progress of 3 June 1793, he could be made to figure the state of the nation
in wartime.[120] In this Hogarthian series of drawings, John Bull joins the
army and is reduced from rotund contentment, drinking beer by the
fireside of his home, a hive of industry and activity, to an emaciated crip-
ple with only one eye and one leg who returns to an impoverished and
desolate family. A number of poems seek to reassure the public about
this unsettling figure, such as Burns's 'When wild War's deadly Blast was
blawn' of 1793, which instructs the reader:

> The brave poor sodger ne'er despise,
>   Nor count him as a stranger;
> Remember, he's his country's stay,
>   In day and hour of danger.[121]

Other poems rewrite returning soldier narratives to contain the troubling implications of the figure. One such piece, 'The Soldier's Return',
published in the Scot's Magazine in April 1804, reads like a rewriting of
Merry's 'The Wounded Soldier' as a returning soldier worries that his
sudden reappearance might produce a similarly fatal effect on his loved
ones:

> What could I do?—If in I went,
>   Surprize might chill each tender heart;
> Some story, then, I must invent,
>   And act the poor maim'd soldier's part.   (BWP, 323)

---

[119] The Early Poems of John Clare, 1804–1822, ed. Eric Robinson and David Powell, 2 vols.
(Oxford: Clarendon Press, 1989), I. 91.
[120] Draper Hill (ed.), The Satirical Etchings of James Gillray (New York: Dover
Publications, 1976), plate 31.
[121] The Poems and Songs of Robert Burns, ed. James Kinsley, 3 vols. (Oxford: Clarendon
Press, 1968), II. 687. Behrendt quotes an earlier version of such poetic reassurance from
Catherine Upton's The Siege of Gibraltar (1781) in 'A Few Harmless Numbers', 13. For a
similar cultural reassurance about the figure of the sailor, see Geoff Quilley, 'Duty and
Mutiny; The Aesthetics of Loyalty and the Representation of the British Sailor c.1798–1800',
in Shaw (ed.), Romantic Wars, 80–109.

The soldier disguises himself as a maimed veteran (indeed, his eye-patch and faked amputated leg particularly recall Gillray's soldier in *John Bull's Glorious Return*):

> I drew a bandage o'er my face,
>   And crooked up a lying knee,
> And found that e'en in that blest place
>   Not one dear friend knew ought of me.   (*BWP*, 323)

The soldier tells his 'feign'd story' to his family and sweetheart who believe him dead, pretending to bring news that 'Hall's [*sic*. Hal's?] not far behind' before pulling off his face patch to reveal his true identity (*BPW*, 323). The poem ends with the father declaring, amidst the joyful reunion:

> 'A wedding first I'm sure we'll have:
> 'I warrant we'll live this hundred year—
>   'Nay, may be, lass, escape the grave.'   (*BWP*, 324)

'The Soldier's Return', then, repeatedly invokes the tropes of anti-war poetry only to present them as fictions; the soldier's injuries are lies and his story 'feign'd'. Published in the year after the breakdown of the Peace of Amiens and during the period of invasion crisis, 'The Soldier's Return' reclaims an anti-war figure for patriotic purposes, making the returning soldier a figure in a comic narrative of war that ends in marriage rather than the grave. Yet it is a narrative shadowed by its tragic other; in a poem of illusions, the father's exclamation that he and his wife may 'escape the grave' strikes a note of romantic fantasy that emphasizes that it is the soldier's own escaping of the grave that is the poem's real illusion.

Merry's and Pacificus's poems establish a link between the tales of war told by returning soldiers and poetry's own tale-telling power and remind us that *The Eclectic*'s characterization of modern poetry saw its display of the 'calamities of war' as having a particular affective and rhetorical aim, 'exciting a sympathy with the sufferings of mankind, and invoking a just indignation against the wanton contentions of governments'. This combination of witnessing, feeling, and speaking out against the sufferings caused by war was frequently called on in the anti-war writing of the 1790s; Southey, for example, uses it to construct his poetic identity in 'The Soldier's Funeral' when, after an attack on those who justify the war, he concludes:

O my God!
I thank thee that I am not such as these
I thank thee for the eye that sees, the heart
That feels, the voice that in these evil days
That amid evil tongues, exalts itself
And cries aloud against the iniquity.   (*BWP*, 232)

Similarly, Merry and Pacificus conclude their poems by combining the exciting of sympathy and the invoking of indignation along the lines suggested by *The Eclectic*. Merry ends 'The Wounded Soldier' seeking to elicit particular responses from different readers:

O, may this tale, which agony must close,
    Give due contrition to the self-call'd great,
And show the poor how hard the fate of those
    Who shed their blood for *ministers of state!*   (*BWP*, 245)

Pacificus concludes 'Effects of War' by outlining the effect he hopes to have on those he sees as responsible for the 'mournful tales' of war:

Long should reflection in a Monarch's mind
Dwell on such themes. Then strongly there impress'd,
War in its various horrors would appear:
And if a spark of virtue in him lives,
Nature must shrink from such a thought accurs'd,
As plunging nations in offensive wars!
                                    (*BWP*, 97)

While the writers of such verse may not really expect their poems to be read by 'the self-call'd great' or 'Monarchs', they use such figures as a means of illustrating poetry's potential power on the reader, calling especially on the language and models of sensibility. As one writer puts it, 'The Muse gives language to the victim's sigh', and its appeal is specifically to 'Pity'.[122] Much anti-war poetry of the 1790s draws on the ethics of sensibility to present poetry's role as awakening the heart's ability to feel. In emphasizing poetry's appeal to the 'pity' or sympathy of the reader, poets were invoking what was seen as a specific power of the form, linked also to the imagination, and such appeals frequently exploited what was seen as its feminine and feminizing influence.[123] For example, in 'Lines Written by a Female Citizen!', published in *The Tribune* in 1795, the explicitly 'female' poet, exploring the function of the

[122] John Towill Rutt, 'The Wrongs of Poverty' (*PR*, 54).
[123] See Engell, *The Creative Imagination*, 143.

Muse at a time when 'savage war depopulates each clime' (l. 2),[124] constructs her role in predominantly feminized terms:

> Here as I turn with sympathy oppress'd,
> With indignation rising in my breast,
> My injur'd country's woes demand my care.   (ll. 15–17)

The effect of her poetry will be to have a feminizing effect, as she awakens her Muse to its task:

> Strike every chord! apall [*sic*] the guilty breast!
> Bid titl'd Pomp his gilded crimes detest;
> Bid fell Injustice melt his heart of stone,
> Nor dare to triumph 'midst the general groan,
> Nor seek fresh plunder from a sinking state,
> Where thousands perish for the proud and great.   (ll. 23–8)

Yet the poem ends by questioning its own claims, and especially the function of pity in the context of world-wide war:

> Pity drops the unavailing tear!
> Unable to relieve, she mourns in vain
> Wrongs that the mass of humankind sustain.   (ll. 42–4)

The poem finishes on a pessimistic note, contrasting the 'great and godlike spirit[s]' of the heroes of the seventeenth century with the 'slave[s]' of the current day (ll. 55, 60). Despite its powerful construction of the poetic role, 'Lines Written by a Female Citizen!' raises the question of whether poetry can produce the transformations it promises.

While the *Eclectic Review* presents Scott's adoption of the 'ancient function of a bard' as anomalous within the context of 'modern poetry' that I have been describing, there had been repeated calls for just such a figure since the opening years of the war and numerous poets had put themselves forward to take on the role of the national, martial poet. Perhaps most famously, in the 'Introduction' to the poetry section of the first number of the *Anti-Jacobin*, the periodical established to combat Jacobinism in all its forms, George Canning had identified a crisis in poetry because of the lack of 'one good and true poet, of sound principles and sober practice' who would take on the role of 'the favourite of the Muses' of earlier times, going on to define this figure as 'an enthusiast in the love of his native soil' and 'a warrior, at least in imagination; . . . [who] sung the actions of the heroes of his country, in strains which

---

[124] *PR*, 122.

"made Ambition Virtue" and which overwhelmed the horrors of war in its glory."[125] Published in November 1797, the *Anti-Jacobin*'s lament predates Nelson's much celebrated triumph at the battle of the Nile of 1 August 1798, yet even before this 'glorious victory' there was no lack of poets keen to sing the actions of British heroes, with the naval victories of Howe over the French on the 'Glorious First of June' 1794 and Duncan over the Dutch at Camperdown in 1797 providing popular opportunities. Similarly there did exist a poetic register for overwhelming the 'horrors of war in its glory', seen, for example, in a poem by 'Panormus' published sixteen months before the declaration of war entitled 'The Triumphant Warrior' which celebrates war as a uniting force that provides an opportunity to prove one's bravery and to gain honour and fame:

> War, and arms, and death prevailing,
>   Front to front we firmly stood;
> And with eager force assailing,
>   Greedy drew each other's blood.
> Brave, brave the death and great the wound,
> Which Fame approv'd, and Honour crown'd.
>
> Be nerv'd the arm, be drawn the sword,
> War, war, when glory is the word!
> As lightning swift the hero flies,
> As lightnings, flash his ardent eyes:
> His flaming faulchion, lo, he draws!
> And gladly, in his country's cause,
>   Or crown'd with conquest mounts to Fame,
>   Or crown'd with honour dies.[126]

Few poems of the period pay as little attention to war's 'horrors' as this piece but the idea of glorious death in the 'country's cause' is regularly repeated and frequently applied to individuals as in 'On the Death of Captain Westcott, Of his Majesty's Ship Majestick; who fell gloriously, on the First of August, 1798', which takes as its epigram the *locus classicus* of the idea of honourable death for one's country, Horace's 'Dulce et decorum est pro Patria mori', and begins by repeating the key terms and ideas of 'The Triumphant Warrior' before applying them to the specific individual:

[125] *Anti-Jacobin*, 12–14. For a similar lament of a lack of a poet to fill this role, see 'Imitated from Martial: From a Gentleman Lamenting the Want of Poetic Merit to Celebrate the Late GREAT VICTORIES' (*GM*, 68 (March 1798), 244).
[126] *GM*, 61 (September 1791), 853.

The gen'rous love of Fame—the noble strife—
That grasps at Honour, at the risk of Life,
(To vulgar souls unknown,) inspires the brave
To bid defiance to the yawning grave: (*BWP*, 219)

In poems such as these, poetry is seen to have an elevated function in wartime as elegiac and commemorative—'While Mars prevails o'er earth and main, | Record, O Muse, the valiant Slain'—while the end of war becomes poetry itself, as the dead are rewarded through these commemorations—'fame eternal is their meed'.[127]

One poet who might have hoped that he filled the *Anti-Jacobin*'s role of 'one good and true poet' was Henry James Pye, appointed Poet Laureate in 1790, whose 'duteous Muse' produced two 'Odes' each year, one for the New Year and one for the king's birthday, as well as other occasional pieces to celebrate particular occasions.[128] These odes were set to music by the court musician and sung before the king at the state drawing rooms, after which they were widely published.[129] Pye's laureate poetry draws heavily on the tropes of eighteenth-century patriotic poetry and particularly on poetic construction of the divinely sanctioned imperial nation found in works such as Edward Young's 'Ocean: An Ode' and James Thomson's 'Rule Britannia'. While presenting Albion as peace-loving and fighting only defensive wars, though particularly fierce when provoked into action, Pye makes Britain essentially a warrior nation defined by conflict against France: 'Albion many an ancient scar | Still bears on her indented breast, | In every age by Gallic war | Or Gallic perfidy impress'd'.[130] He frequently invokes a familiar roll-call of British triumphs—Cressy, Agincourt, the Armada—as proof of Albion's warlike genius and as a demand for the nation to reassert its essential identity as a 'warrior race'.[131] Pye's laureate poetry was an important poetic mediation of the war, presenting to the king, the court, and other influential members of the political hierarchy a familiar yet still powerful vision of Britain and its role in war. Indeed, Pye ended one Ode by inserting 'at the desire of the King' lines from a popular bellicose song from an adaptation of Beaumont's and Fletcher's play *Bonduca*, set to music by Purcell in 1695:

---

[127] 'Ode, To the Memory of the British Officers, Seamen, and Soldiers, who have Fallen in the Present War', *Scots Magazine*, August 1794 (*BWP*, 120).

[128] For Pye's 'duteous Muse', see 'ODE for His MAJESTY's Birth-day', *GM*, 63 (June 1793), 556.

[129] Kenyon West, *The Laureates of England: Ben Jonson to William Wordsworth* (London and New York: Frederick H. Stokes, 1895), 143.

[130] 'ODE FOR THE NEW YEAR', *GM*, 65 (January 1795), 60; 'ODE for His MAJESTY's Birth-day', *GM*, 63 (June 1793), 556.   [131] 'ODE FOR THE NEW YEAR', *GM*, 67 (January 1797), 60.

'To arms, your ensigns straight display!
Now set the battle in array!
The oracle for war declares,
Success depends upon our hearts and spears,
Britons, strike home! Revenge your country's wrongs;
Fight, and record yourselves in Druid's songs!'[132]

Normally seen as a form in which the king's praises are sung before the country—a key element in much of Pye's verse in which the 'Patriot King' comes to stand as a 'bulwark' and symbol of Britain—here the laureate Ode becomes a medium through which the king himself contributes to the poetic call to arms to the nation.[133] (Another royal contribution to this poetic call to arms would be provided during the invasion crisis by Princess Elizabeth, who 'designed' a series of sketches of *Cupid Turned Volunteer* that were engraved for a lavish volume and accompanied by 'poetical illustrations' by Thomas Park[134].)

In his non-laureate verse, Pye sought to use poetry to urge the war's continuation and to inspire his readers' participation in it, publishing translations of the elegies of the Spartan poet Tyrtaeus in 1795, for example.[135] Pye's attempts to inspire martial fervour met with a mixed reception, however, and an amusing account included by T. J. Mathias in a note to the 1796 edition of *The Pursuits of Literature* illustrates the varying appeal of his poetry to different sections of society. According to this account, '[s]everal of the *Reviewing* Generals . . . were much impressed with [the] *weight* and importance' of the translations and had them

read aloud at Warley Common and at Barham Downs, by the adjutants, at the head of five different regiments, at each camp, and much was expected. But before they were half finished, all the front ranks, and as many of the others as were within hearing or verse-shot, dropped their arms suddenly, and were *all found fast asleep!*[136]

---

[132] Ibid. and footnote. For an account of *Bonduca*, see *WD*, 229–30.

[133] 'ODE for His MAJESTY's Birth-Day', *GM*, 62 (June 1792), 556; 'ODE for His MAJESTY's Birth-Day', *GM*, 68 (June 1798), 518.

[134] *Cupid Turned Volunteer: in a Series of Prints, Designed by Her Royal Highness, The Princess Elizabeth and Engraved by W. N. Gardiner, BA, with Poetical Illustrations by Thomas Park, FSA* (London: E. Harding, 1804.)

[135] *The War-Elegies of Tyrtæus, Imitated, and Addressed to the People of Great Britain, with some Observations on the Life and Poems of Tyrtæus* (London: T. Cadell jun. and W. Davies, 1795). For an account of the martial aims of the volume, see *GM*, 65 (May 1795), 412–13.

[136] Quoted in Kenneth Hopkins, *The Poets Laureate* (London: Bodley Head, 1954), 115–16.

The laureate's failure to inspire the troops reinforces the *Anti-Jacobin*'s sense of the lack of 'one good and true poet' and suggests the need for a different poetic mode to bolster the war against France, a mode that would be supplied by the metrical romances of Scott, who would become the unofficial laureate and whose poetry was capable of inspiring soldiers even in the arena of conflict.

If Pye was a poet committed to regular poetic celebrations of the nation, more usually patriotic poetry was inspired by certain events, such as Nelson's victory over the French fleet at the battle of the Nile on 1 August 1798 which became 'the theme of every Muse',[137] and prompted a huge outpouring of poetic celebrations of the victory over the French fleet, dominating the poetry columns of the newspapers and magazines,[138] stimulating the production of numerous volumes of poetry published on the battle,[139] and providing the subject for the Cambridge Tripos.[140] In many of these pieces, the poets sought to adopt the highest genres and registers available, with the battle the subject of verses in Latin,[141] of a dramatic poem modelled on Greek tragedy,[142] of at least one poem which claimed epic status,[143] and of other works which claimed biblical or Miltonic authority. For example, in his 'Song of the Battle of the Nile', William Lisle Bowles adopted the language of biblical translation in presenting the battle as a triumph in a war of religion with the British as the chosen people, his opening line 'Shout, for the Lord hath triumphed gloriously!' echoing the song of triumph over the defeated hosts of Egypt of Exodus (and anticipating Wordsworth's 'Anticipation' sonnet).[144] Of this poem, the *Gentleman's*

---

[137] 'Ode. On the Glorious Victory Gained by Rear-Admiral Nelson, August 1, 1798', *GM*. 68 (October 1798), 880.

[138] See 'Nelson' in 'Index to Poetry' in *GM*, 68 (1798), no page numbers. See also Betty Bennett's reference to 'dozens of verses which celebrated Nelson's victory against the French in Egypt' (*BWP*, 222).

[139] e.g. William Lisle Bowles, *The Song of the Battle of the Nile*; William Sotheby, *The Battle of the Nile* (1799); *The Battle of the Nile* by a Gentleman of Earl St. Vincent's Fleet. These three poems were reviewed in *GM*, 69 (April 1799), 320–1, and (October 1799), 879.

[140] *GM*, 69 (February 1799), 148.

[141] e.g. Auctore Clerico Gallicano, *Nilius* (1799), described in the British Library catalogue as 'A poem in Latin Hexameters on the battle of the Nile'.

[142] Anon., *The Battle of the Nile, a Dramatic Poem, on the Model of the Greek Tragedies* (1799).

[143] J. Hildreth's *The Niliad, an Epic Poem . . . on the Glorious Victory of August* (1799).

[144] *The Poetical Works of William Lisle Bowles*, ed. Revd George Gilfillan, 2 vols. (Edinburgh: James Nichols, 1845), I. 88. See Colin Pedley, 'Anticipating Invasion: Some Wordsworthian Contexts', *Wordsworth Circle*, 21 (1990), 64–70, esp. 65 and 69–70 n. 2.

Magazine declared, 'We have not read a poetical composition so truly Miltonic as the present', though other writers also aspired to this role.[145]

While these examples reveal the extent to which poets prior to Scott 'celebrate[d] military prowess', to use *The Eclectic*'s terms, several also aspired to the specific role that it saw him adopting, that of the 'bard'. During the eighteenth century, the bard had become an increasingly important figure for authorizing poetic practice in relation to national identity and destiny; as Jason Whittaker has commented, 'the bard became a focus for poetic aspirations, combining roles of historian and prophet, fighter for liberty and inspired poet in communion with nature and the national memory . . . The apotheosis of these ideals was Ossian and Gray's Bard.'[146] In the 1790s the bard was often invoked as part of an attempt to reconstruct poetry in wartime, as is illustrated by the verses William Boscawen wrote for the anniversary meeting of subscribers to the Literary Fund in 1795. In this poem, in effect a manifesto for poetry in the context of the current war, Boscawen calls upon the 'sacred Bards of elder time' to inspire a shift from what he sees as the feminized poetics of sensibility that currently characterizes the literary scene ('the voice of Pity floats | In soft, melodious, thrilling notes') to a higher mode of divinely-inspired war poetry:

> Oh, mark the glories of that age
> Which lives in Homer's matchless page,
> When kings, when heroes, could admire
> The glowing verse, th'enraptur'd lyre![147]

In what I have already argued are repeated and important tropes in the period's literary contests, the wartime context makes necessary a manly poetry, suitable for kings and heroes, and the poet's task becomes an imaginative recreation of war:

> And when he tower'd on Fancy's wing,
> And when his touch awak'd the string,
> What sympathetic hearts around
> Re-echo'd to the martial sound!

---

[145] *GM*, 69 (April 1799), 320–1; Revd Dr Edward Dupre, 'On Rear-Admiral Lord Nelson's Victory', *GM*, 68 (supplement 1798), 1133.

[146] *William Blake and the Myths of Britain* (Basingstoke and New York: Macmillan and St Martin's Press, 1999), 99.

[147] 'Ode for the Anniversary Meeting of the Subscribers to the Literary Fund, April 21, 1795.' *GM*, 66 (January 1796), 63.

> Again he bade the battle bleed,
> Pour'd vengeance on th'astonish'd foe,
> With mem'ry of each glorious deed,
> Kindled extatic valour's glow.

Boscawen's model of bardic poetry strikingly anticipates Scott's presentation of the role of Fancy in the imaginative recreation of war in *The Lady of the Lake,* but there is also an important difference; whereas Boscawen presents the poet as facilitating the remembering of deeds for those who have been previously involved in them, Scott's model of the poet is one which facilitates the mental recreation of events by hearers or readers who have played no part in them. Boscawen traces his model of poetry through the classical history of Greece and Rome before he recounts the story of the British bard who inspired resistance to Julius Caesar's invading army in a stanza with obvious applications to the contemporary situation:

> What pow'r their gen'rous valour fir'd?
> The Bard, the patriot Bard, inspir'd!

Boscawen's bard becomes an obvious prototype for the patriotic poet of the 1790s, uniting and inspiring all factions against the invading enemy through his martial song.

Boscawen's figure of the prophetic, national bard opposing Caesar's invading army was a popular one in the 1790s, partly because it facilitated an appropriation of Gray's 'The Bard' that was easily applicable to the contemporary situation, making the bard a figure addressing a united Britain rather than speaking from its Celtic fringes.[148] For example, the Bard figure was drawn on by William Tasker in his play *Arviragus, a Tragedy* which the *Gentleman's Magazine* described as a 'bold attempt towards a national drama' and which, as the *Gentleman's Magazine* account makes clear, again had very obvious contemporary reference: 'the British king Arviragus, the principal character, is represented to be a gallant warrior and a patriot-king, reigning over a free and warlike people; and both are represented as uniting their utmost efforts to resist foreign invasion'.[149] The *Gentleman's Magazine* ends its review: 'we are particularly pleased with the songs, or rather little odes, of the Bard; and the war song, which he recites to the military at large, when they are at the point of engaging with the Romans, is every way worthy of the author of the Ode to the Warlike Genius of Great Britain.' The

---

[148] e.g. 'Ode', *GM*, 62 (April 1792), 367.   [149] *GM*, 66 (September 1796), 771.

Gentleman's Magazine quoted this poem, 'The War-Song of Clewillin, The British Bard', in its poetry section for March 1797, a lively exhortation to martial valour, calling on the soldiers to 'Rush on the foe without dismay, | Like roaring lions on their prey'.[150] But what is most striking about the *Gentleman's Magazine* review of *Arviragus* is the way in which it conflates the Bard with Tasker himself, the 'author of the Ode to the Warlike Genius of Great Britain'. Over the next few years the *Gentleman's Magazine* would adopt Tasker as their version of the bard whose work was 'so well calculated to animate loyal Britons against invaders, and to inspire the necessary unanimity and concord' and was 'exceedingly well adapted to the present times; since it breathes a three-fold spirit of Poetry, Loyalty, and Patriotism'.[151] Over a nine-month period from December 1798 to August 1799 it reprinted the 'Ode to the Warlike Genius of Great Britain', originally published in 1778, in which Tasker presents the Bards as divinely inspired figures whose role was to 'Inspire the sons of Mars in dreams, | And fire their souls in warlike themes'.[152] But the fact that the *Gentleman's Magazine* was forced to reproduce at length a poem written two decades previously again emphasizes what was seen to be the failure of anyone convincingly to fill the role of the Bard until the emergence of Walter Scott. It perhaps comes as no surprise that in the year before achieving fame with *The Lay of the Last Minstrel*, Scott wrote a poem entitled 'The Bard's Incantation. Written under the threat of invasion in the autumn of 1804', in which he called on 'Minstrels and bards of other days' to wake because 'Gaul's ravening legions hither come'.[153] In the poem he summoned into being the figure of 'the "mighty minstrel" of the Antigallican war', a bardic role that he would enact for the final decade of the conflict with France.

While this opening chapter has looked at a wide range of examples, subsequent chapters will focus more closely on particular writers and texts produced at key moments of crisis or emergency to show how poetry was conceived and employed as a vital form in representing and imagining war and how the conflict with France shaped the self-conceptions of individual poets as well as broader formulations of the function of poetry itself. The next three chapters will look at the issue of the poetic

[150] *GM*, 67 (March 1797), 236.
[151] *GM*, 68 (May 1798), 414; 69 (November 1799), 970. It provided further extracts from *Arviragus*, 68 (May 1798), 414, and praised the publication of *Extracts from Tasker's Poems on Military and Naval Subjects*, 69 (November 1799), 970–1.
[152] *GM*, 69 (April 1799), 327.   [153] *Poetical Works*, 702–3.

role in wartime in the writing of four of the major poets of the opening decade of the conflict, Charlotte Smith, Samuel Taylor Coleridge, Robert Southey, and William Wordsworth. Chapter 2 argues that Smith and Coleridge responded to wartime moments of crisis (the declaration of war and the invasion threat respectively) by making the imagining of the conflict a crucial function of their poetry and a key element of their identities as writers. Chapter 3 examines how Southey and Wordsworth defined their poetic identities in relation to war, war poetry, and each other during the years 1798–1802, while Chapter 4 argues that in his political sonnets of 1802–3, written during the invasion crisis, Wordsworth reconceived his poetic role, and poetry and the nation more generally, as 'manly'. Chapter 5 focuses on Walter Scott, who transformed the poetic imagining of war during the conflict (and for a century to come), shifting the emphasis from war's horrors to its picturesque excitements in his metrical romances. The influence of this transformation of war is examined in Chapter 6 which examines the way in which the dominant new understanding of the war as romance was deployed and resisted in poems written on the Peninsular War by Felicia Hemans, Lord Byron, and Robert Southey, as well as by Scott himself. The final chapter will look at two poets writing in the decade after Waterloo whose identities were shaped by their sense of themselves as war poets, Byron and Hemans, and argue that looking back on the Revolutionary and Napoleonic wars they find in the siege a figure for the total and dominating conflict that defined the age through which they had lived.

CHAPTER TWO

The Poetic Imagining of War in the 1790s: Charlotte Smith and Samuel Taylor Coleridge

TWO OF THE major poets of the 1790s made the imagining of war one of the crucial functions of poetry and a key element of their identities as writers. Charlotte Smith's reconception of the role of 'fancy' in her blank-verse poem *The Emigrants*, begun during peacetime but completed in April 1793, two months after France's declaration of war on Britain, forcefully illustrates the way in which the outbreak of war led one of the most popular and influential writers of the closing decades of the eighteenth century to transform her ideas of the imagination and to reconceive her poetic role. Smith begins the poem with a model of fancy as a delusive power to which women are especially vulnerable, a continuation of her conception of it in *Elegiac Sonnets*. But the encounter of her poetic persona with the figures of war in book II forces a reassessment of the poetics of sensibility that had characterized the collection of poems which had made her famous. Moving away from a poetics which finds its metaphors for the self in the suffering other, in *The Emigrants* Smith presents the victims of war as beyond the limits of suffering known to either her persona or to the British public, all of whom are 'safe' from the conflict, 'by the rude sea guarded' (II. 210).[1] It is through imagining war in poetry, and insisting on the public's imagining of war, that the poet can bring the war home to the reading public and bring the conflict to an end. In conceiving of the wartime role of the imagination in this way, Smith transforms the function of a faculty that was becoming particularly associated with women

---

[1] *The Poems of Charlotte Smith*, ed. Stuart Curran (New York and Oxford: Oxford University Press, 1993). All subsequent references to *The Emigrants* are to this edition and are cited within the text by book and line number.

and constructs her poetic role as specifically feminine, finding her model for the poet in the figure of the mother.

If at the outbreak of the war Smith calls on the nation to imagine its horrors, writing five years later in 'Fears in Solitude' Samuel Taylor Coleridge addresses what he sees as a national failure to imagine the war. Like Smith in *The Emigrants*, in 'Fears in Solitude' the poet addresses a nation distant from the scene of conflict—'Secure from actual warfare' (l. 88)[2]—and, like her, he ultimately offers his own imagining as a model for the nation. But while Smith represents her imaginative powers through the feminine figure of the mother, the Coleridgean poet is a specifically masculine figure, mature and paternal. If in Smith's text the imagining of conflict will lead to war's extinction, Coleridge's poem is driven by an opposition between the poet's imagining of war and the nation's failure to do so that threatens to bring 'actual warfare' to Britain. While 'Fears in Solitude' emphasizes the challenge of war to the poet and war's role in the development (and remasculinization) of this figure, it also occupies a place as an important document in the evolution of Coleridge's ideas about the imagination. A text which supports Nigel Leask's 'demand of Imagination' that it occupy 'a position of accountability in the practical realm',[3] 'Fears in Solitude' illustrates the political function that Coleridge outlined for the imagination in much of his writing of the 1790s. Yet in creating an opposition between the 'imagined' and the 'actual', Coleridge was establishing the framework for his influential post-Waterloo accounts of the imagination, the poet, and the absolute genius which would detach them from the world of 'realities'. The imagining of war, then, plays a major role in the development of the romantic imagination.

The 'Mother's Efforts': Imagining War in Charlotte Smith's The Emigrants

In a sonnet added to the fifth edition of *Elegiac Sonnets* (1789), Charlotte Smith analyses the link between fancy and her identity as a woman poet:

---

[2] Coleridge's poetry is quoted from *The Poetical Works of Samuel Taylor Coleridge*, ed. Ernest Hartley Coleridge, 2 vols. (Oxford and New York: Oxford University Press, 1912; rpr. 1983). Unless otherwise stated, hereafter references are cited by line number within the text.

[3] *The Politics of Imagination in Coleridge's Critical Thought* (Basingstoke and London: Macmillan, 1988), 1.

TO FANCY

Thee, Queen of Shadows!—shall I still invoke,
  Still love the scenes thy sportive pencil drew,
  When on mine eyes the early radiance broke
  Which shew'd the beauteous rather than the true!
Alas! long since those glowing tints are dead,
  And now 'tis thine in darkest hues to dress
The spot where pale Experience hangs her head
  O'er the sad grave of murder'd Happiness!
Thro' thy false medium, then, no longer view'd,
  May fancied pain and fancied pleasure fly,
  And I, as from me all thy dreams depart,
Be to my wayward destiny subdued:
  Nor seek perfection with a poet's eye,
  Nor suffer anguish with a poet's heart![4]

As in the examples of the imagination discussed in my previous chapter, Smith presents fancy in terms of its ability to draw or paint pictures, but whereas other writers emphasized the 'truth' of such images, for Smith fancy is a 'false medium' whose 'dreams' exaggerate both the youthful hopes and the mature disillusionments of the self. Though E. J. Furlong sees such unreliability as definitive of 'fancy' as opposed to 'imagination' prior to Coleridge's distinction between the terms, in much poetic usage they were interchangeable well into the nineteenth century.[5] During the period of Smith's career anxieties were expressed about the delusive power of imagination as well as fancy. Such concerns are seen in William Jones's 1796 lecture on the imagination, where his linking of it to sensibility makes it particularly relevant to Smith: 'Persons of lively imaginations have irritable nerves; they suffer more from pain and grief of every kind; and pay a severe tax for their boasted sensibility'.[6] If in this sonnet Smith emphasizes the unreliability of the fancy, in The Emigrants she redeems it as a faculty which can apprehend reality (the function which

---

[4] The Poems of Charlotte Smith, 44.

[5] E. J. Furlong, Imagination (London: Allen and Unwin Ltd, 1961), 20. On the interchangeable nature of the terms 'imagination' and 'fancy' in poetic usage until the end of the eighteenth century, see David Fairer's and Christine Gerrard's discussion of Akenside's The Pleasures of Imagination, which they see as a source for Smith's sonnet, in Fairer and Gerrard (eds.), Eighteenth-Century Poetry: An Annotated Anthology (Oxford: Blackwell Publishers, 1999), 307, n. 10 and 515, n. 4. See also John Spenser Hill, Imagination in Coleridge (Basingstoke and London: Macmillan, 1986), 2–4.

[6] Jones, The Nature of the Human Imagination (London: Rivington, Robinson, and Gardner, 1796), 20–1.

Furlong assigns to the imagination in his definition). Yet Smith's sonnet also makes fancy essential to poetic identity. The renunciation of fancy, necessary for the survival of the self, will involve the loss of the 'poet's eye' and 'poet's heart'; the crisis of fancy constitutes a crisis in the poetic role.

Smith develops this concern with fancy in book I of *The Emigrants*, her two-book blank-verse poem which describes the encounter on the south coast of Britain of her poetic persona with various religious and aristocratic exiles from revolutionary France. Smith began the poem in 1792,[7] three years after the publication of her sonnet, and throughout book I emphasizes the delusive nature of fancy which she associates with women, especially a series of mother figures and her own poetic persona. She introduces fancy in the opening lines when the dawn awakes a nation of sleepers from 'Their fancied bliss (the only bliss they taste!)' (I. 11) and it is associated with 'the dreams | That sooth'd their sorrows' (I. 12–13), providing temporary escape through oblivion from daytime sufferings. Smith embodies this model of fancy in her own poetic persona who, confronted early in the poem with both the universal problem of the human condition—that 'Man, | Mars the fair work that he was bid enjoy, ' (I. 32–3)—as well as with the difficulties of her own specific legal situation (I. 36–41), similarly seeks to escape the world of calamities, 'half abjur[ing] Society' (I. 42) and sighing for 'some lone Cottage' where she may hide herself, a desired retreat described in romance terms as 'deep embower'd | In the green woods' and 'strewn with fairy flowers' (I. 43–4, 49).

As a number of excellent accounts of the poem have emphasized, Smith finds in the émigrés of the poem's title figures who represent not only the worrying developments of the French Revolution (of which Smith had been an enthusiastic supporter) but also metaphors for the internal exile of her own poetic persona.[8] It is 'in witness' of the 'mournful truth' of the

---

[7] Loraine Fletcher, *Charlotte Smith: A Critical Biography* (Basingstoke and New York: Macmillan and St Martin's Press, 1998), 191. Fletcher gives no specific date for the commencement of composition.

[8] Stuart Curran, 'The I Altered', in Anne K. Mellor (ed.), *Romanticism and Feminism* (Bloomington and Indianapolis: Indiana University Press, 1988), 200–2; Jacqueline M. Labbe, 'The Exiled Self: Images of War in Charlotte Smith's *The Emigrants*' in Philip Shaw (ed.), *Romantic Wars: Studies in Conflict, 1793–1822* (Aldershot: Ashgate, 2000), 37–56; Kay K. Cook, 'The Aesthetics of Loss: Charlotte Smith's *The Emigrants* and *Beachy Head*', and Sarah M. Zimmerman, 'Charlotte Smith's Lessons', both in Stephen C. Behrendt and Harriet Kramer Linkin (eds.), *Approaches to Teaching British Women Poets of the Romantic Period* (New York: Modern Language Association of America, 1997), 97–100, 121–8.

universal condition of 'Unhappy Mortals' that Smith's persona turns to these representatives of exile and suffering (I. 92–4). Among the figures the poet describes is a 'softer form' (I. 202), the first of the poem's crucial mother figures. In her essay on *The Emigrants*, Jacqueline Labbe has emphasized the importance of the poem's mother figures and argued that Smith's poetic persona rejects identification with this mother because the exile 'lacks maternal care' and is concerned with 'self at the expense of deep mother-love'.[9] While this is the case, it should also be emphasized that these failings are linked to the exiled mother's vulnerability to fancy; as she stands on the beach, 'lost in melancholy thought' (I. 215) and mindless of her children:

> Fancy brings,
> In waking dreams, that native land again!
> Versailles appears—its painted galleries,
> And rooms of regal splendour; rich with gold,
> Where, by long mirrors multiply'd, the crowd
> Paid willing homage—and, united there,
> Beauty gave charms to empire—Ah! too soon
> From the gay visionary pageant rous'd,
> See the sad mourner start!—and, drooping, look
> With tearful eyes and heaving bosom round
> On drear reality ...   (I. 220–30)

In describing the mother's reverie, Smith recapitulates the poem's early models of fancy; Versailles's visionary pageant (its galleries both painted in the imagination and lavishly decorated) offers a temporary escape from 'drear reality', like the poetic persona's envisioned lone cottage and the sleepers' fancied bliss, from which the 'mourner' is recalled 'too soon'. Fancy's dream world becomes a deceptive yet flattering Hall of Mirrors which places the self centre stage. Notably, none of the male emigrants (who vastly outnumber the mother) are subject to such flights of 'fancy', though the 'sons of France' are deluded by the 'visionary shapes' of 'Chivalry' and 'Heraldry' (I. 247–57). The word 'fancy' seems reserved for women, with one of the male figures, it is his 'high indignant *thoughts* [that] go back to France' (I. 127, my italics). And, as in the sonnet 'To Fancy', Smith links delusive imagining to poetry. After a reference to 'The solitary Shepherd [who] shiv'ring tends | His dun discolour'd flock' (I. 299–300), the poetic persona comments:

---

9 Labbe, 'Exiled Self', 43.

> Shepherd, unlike
> Him, whom in song the Poet's fancy crowns
> With garlands, and his crook with vi'lets binds . . .   (I. 300–2)

The 'Poet's fancy', like the visions of the exiled mother and the poetic persona, shows 'the beauteous, rather than the true'.

It is the demands of war on Smith as a poet that leads her to redeem fancy in book II of *The Emigrants* and to reconstruct her poetic identity and role. France declared war on Britain on 1 February 1793 and, by positioning the two books of *The Emigrants* either side of this date, Smith emphasizes how the change in historical moment from book I to book II is crucial to her poetic reconceptions. Whereas book I is set on '*a Morning in November, 1792*' (p. 135), book II is dated '*an afternoon in April, 1793*' (p. 149); and while the events of war that Smith describes in book II are those of the civil war in France of the previous year, 1792—'The Summer past' (II. 213)—as described by the emigrants, it is Britain's entry into the war that leads to the change of emphasis. No longer a poem about exile, in book II *The Emigrants* becomes a poem about war (a shift emphasized by the epigraph from Virgil (p. 149)) and Smith constructs a very different model of the role of fancy in response to this changed context.

Smith's reconception of her poetics and the changes she enacts in the relations of the self to history begin in a passage which is focused on the next 'wretched Mother' in the poem, Marie Antoinette, who 'petrified with grief, | Views [her son Louis] with stony eyes, and cannot weep!' (II. 152–3). As Labbe points out, Marie Antoinette is differentiated from the émigrée mother of book I because 'unlike that careless mother, she is focused on her son',[10] prompting an explicit act of identification between the poetic persona and the 'hapless Queen!' (II. 154):

> —Ah! who knows,
> From sad experience, more than I, to feel
> For thy desponding spirit, as it sinks
> Beneath procrastinated fears for those
> More dear to thee than life!   (II. 169–73)

This looks like an archetypal moment in Smith's version of the poetics of sensibility, familiar from *Elegiac Sonnets*. Confronted with a figure who occupies the 'eminence | Of misery' (II. 173–4), the poetic persona draws on her own 'experience' to sympathize and identify with the

<hr/>

[10] Labbe, 'Exiled Self', 45.

afflicting object, ultimately presenting herself as pre-eminent in suffering. However, this moment of identification is presented as an inadequate response to either the Queen's or the poet's situation because for both it is a moment of despondency and incapacity through grief, and prompts a rejection of the fancied world of Romance that the poetic persona had earlier desired as a means of escaping reality:

> And, as we view the strange vicissitude,
> We ask anew, where happiness is found?—
> Alas! in rural life, where youthful dreams
> See the Arcadia that Romance describes,
> Not even Content resides!—   (II. 175–9)

As in book I, the rejection of this dream vision of rural life is emphasized by a passage depicting the harshness of the rural labourer's lot, but now, writing in wartime, Smith draws a crucial distinction between the sufferings of the British population and those of the emigrants; for though the British landscape is 'too oft deform'd | By figures such as [the emaciated wretch]' (II. 204–5), it is defined by the absence of war and by protection from war's evils:

>   yet Peace is here,
> And o'er our vallies, cloath'd with springing corn,
> No hostile hoof should trample, nor fierce flames
> Wither the wood's young verdure, ere it form
> Gradual the laughing May's luxuriant shade;
> For, by the rude sea guarded, we are safe,
> And feel not evils such as with deep sighs
> The Emigrants deplore, as they recal
> The Summer past, when Nature seem'd to lose
> Her course in wild distemperature, and aid,
> With seasons all revers'd, destructive War.   (II. 205–15)

These are key lines in Smith's definition of her wartime poetic role and signal an important shift in her poetics away from a career constructed 'out of self-pity', as Curran has described it, towards a public and political poetry in which the sufferings of war transcend the sufferings of self.[11] They challenge the dominant readings of *The Emigrants*, which see it as a development of *Elegiac Sonnets*, and take for granted the poet's continued identification with the émigrés that is certainly a feature of book I. For example, Stuart Curran argues that

---

[11] 'The I Altered', 199.

the underlying metaphorical strategy of *The Emigrants* is to connect Charlotte Smith as center of perception to the exiles from France's Terror . . . as the poem increasingly focuses on them as emblems of alienated humanity, the greater becomes their correspondence to the solitary figure observing them. In an uncanny way Charlotte Smith creates her own identity in the poem by absorbing their emptiness.[12]

Curran's argument holds good up to this point in the poem but here, as for the rest of the poem, it describes a model of poetics that is specifically rejected by the poetic persona. Rather than identifying with the emigrants, the poet associates herself with the British people—'we are safe'—who are differentiated from the emigrants precisely because they cannot achieve easy sympathetic identification with them: 'And feel not evils such as with deep sighs | The Emigrants deplore'. No longer figures of exile, the emigrants have been transformed by the outbreak of hostilities between England and France into figures of war, and as victims of war they cannot be absorbed into the poet's identity. War disrupts the normal workings of Smithian sensibility; if the poetic persona's own 'sad experience' made her pre-eminently qualified to 'feel for' Marie Antoinette's desponding spirit, when confronted with the figures of war, she, like the rest of the nation, lacks the experiential base that would make possible a similar act of sympathetic identification. Significantly, after the section on the French Queen, the poet makes no specific identification between herself and other figures.

It is the poet's and the nation's lack of the empirical knowledge of war which make necessary a redeemed role for fancy. If the evils of war cannot be fully felt, they can be imagined through the 'pictures' and 'melancholy tale[s]' offered by the emigrants (II. 216, 239):

> Shuddering, I view the pictures they have drawn
> Of desolated countries, where the ground,
> Stripp'd of its unripe produce, was thick strewn
> With various Death—the war-horse falling there
> By famine, and his rider by the sword.   (II. 216–20)

The link between the picturing of war described here and the power of fancy is made a little later in the poem when Smith describes a mother whose 'affrighted Fancy paints | The lawless soldier's victims' (II. 271–2). And it is in these picturings and paintings of war that we have Smith's transformation and revalidation of fancy. For if in book I and the sonnet,

---

[12] 'The I Altered', 200–1. See also Jacqueline Labbe's account of the relationship between 'self' and 'history' in the poem in 'Exiled Self', 51–3.

fancy is a 'false medium' that exaggerates both the 'pain' and the 'pleasure' of the life of the self, here it becomes essential for realizing war's horrors for those distant from the scene of conflict. Fancy's potential to exaggerate is no longer a problem when confronted by the sufferings of war; war's horrors are such that they match the excesses of the imagination.

In *The Emigrants* Smith puts her faith in the émigrés' first-hand accounts of the war to provide the basis for her own and her readers' imaginings of conflict. Her attachment of detailed prose footnotes to her poetic pictures of the war seeks to further emphasize the accuracy of her text's representations of the events of summer 1792.[13] However, to guarantee the impact of her recounted depictions of war on her readership, Smith frames them through cultural forms that evoke an emotional response enacted by her poetic persona. Her first 'picture' of war, for example, evokes both the terror of the sublime (deploying one of its favourite images, the volcano) and the emotion of 'pity':

> The moping clouds sail'd heavy charg'd with rain,
> And bursting o'er the mountains['] misty brow,
> Deluged, as with an inland sea, the vales;
> Where, thro' the sullen evening's lurid gloom,
> Rising, like columns of volcanic fire,
> The flames of burning villages illum'd
> The waste of water; and the wind, that howl'd
> Along its troubled surface, brought the groans
> Of plunder'd peasants, and the frantic shrieks
> Of mothers for their children; while the brave,
> To pity still alive, listen'd aghast
> To these dire echoes, hopeless to prevent
> The evils they beheld, or check the rage,
> Which ever, as the people of one land
> Meet in contention, fires the human heart
> With savage thirst of kindred blood, and makes
> Man lose his nature; rendering him more fierce
> Than the gaunt monsters of the howling waste. (II. 221–38)

Similarly, Smith's final 'melancholy tale' of the 'feudal Chief', who 'returning home | From distant lands, alone and in disguise' to his 'Gothic' castle discovers the 'bleeding' corpses of his family (II. 292–5, 304), shifts the depiction of events away from the historic specifics of the 'heavy and incessant rains' of the 'last campaign' with which Smith

---

[13] *Poems of Charlotte Smith*, 157.

began to an emblematic and timeless scene that draws on Gothic conventions to represent war's horrors.[14] Smith's depictions of 'savage War' in these pictures and tales culminate in a daring and powerful denunciation of 'the closet murderers, whom we style | Wise Politicians' (II. 320–1) and the polemical nature of her poem is suggested by her use of the phrase 'plunder'd peasants' in her description of the pictures of war (II. 229). When in 1797 the *Anti-Jacobin* outlined the favoured topics of Jacobin poetry, it commented that 'we are presented with nothing but contusions and amputations, plundered peasants, and deserted looms'.[15] While the *Anti-Jacobin* may not have had *The Emigrants* specifically in its sights here (though I have not found the phrase elsewhere), its use of the phrase does locate Smith's text within a political poetics that the periodical sought to counter and which it strikingly sees as characterized by its emphasis on the physical damage of war.

What distinguishes the uses of fancy in the two books of *The Emigrants* is its shift from a focus on the self to a focus on others. War forces Smith to reconceive not only the imagination but also her sense of the self and its relations to history. In book II, Smith embodies this reconceived and redeeming role for fancy in the now familiar forms of a mother and the poetic persona, setting up a contrast with their equivalents in book I. Smith presents the maternal and poetic responsibility of imagining the fate of others in wartime in the final portrayal of a mother in the poem. One of the 'melancholy tale[s]' of war told by the emigrants (II. 239), the narrative of this 'wretched Woman' tells of her escape with her child to a 'wild mountain' where, 'half repentant now':

> she wishes she had staid
> To die with those affrighted Fancy paints
> The lawless soldier's victims[.]
>   (II. 258, 254, 269–72)

If the escapist, nostalgic fancy of the exiled mother was linked to the neglect of her children, this mother's fancy envisions the horrors of war even as they are enacted on her own family. And her imagining of the fate of others is linked to the fact that, unlike the poem's previous mothers, she remains 'True to maternal tenderness' even as she sinks in death and 'tries | To save the unconscious infant from the storm | In which she perishes' (II. 282–4). While her attempt fails—'alas! | The Mother and the Infant perish both!' (II. 290–1)—this mother nevertheless exemplifies Smith's

---

[14] *Poems of Charlotte Smith*, 157.   [15] *The Anti-Jacobin*, 14.

own wartime maternal poetics. As the mother's fancy paints war's horrors to herself like the pictures the emigrants have drawn for the poet, so she figures the poet's insistence that the reader imagine war and remain true to maternal tenderness. And in a striking passage of self representation near the poem's close, it is in terms of such a maternal poetics that Smith hopes her friends will find a vindication of her writer's career:

> But, if the little praise, that may await
> The Mother's efforts, should provoke the spleen
> Of Priest or Levite; and they then arraign
> The dust that cannot hear them; be its yours
> To vindicate my humble fame; to say,
> That, not in selfish sufferings absorb'd,
> 'I gave to misery all I had, my tears.'   (II. 380–6)

While Smith's quotation from Gray's 'Elegy' emphasizes both her poetic identity and the role of sensibility in her work, she here insists on sensibility being directed away from 'selfish sufferings'.[16] In *The Emigrants*, Smith finds a public role for such sensibility at both a national level, instructing 'English hearts' to 'ever own the sway' of 'just compassion' (I. 360–1), and at international level, calling on 'Power Omnipotent' (II. 421) to:

> Teach the hard hearts
> Of rulers, that the poorest hind, who dies
> For their unrighteous quarrels, in thy sight
> Is equal to the imperious Lord, that leads
> His disciplin'd destroyers to the field.—   (II. 426–30)

If these directions are followed, Smith argues in the poem's closing lines, they will lead to a redeemed world of Freedom and Justice, free of 'Pride, Oppression, Avarice, and Revenge'(II. 434), in a conclusion of millennial optimism:

> Then shall these ill-starr'd wanderers, whose sad fate
> These desultory lines lament, regain
> Their native country; private vengeance then
> To public virtue yield; and the fierce feuds,
> That long have torn their desolated land,
> May (even as storms, that agitate the air,
> Drive noxious vapours from the blighted earth)
> Serve, all tremendous as they are, to fix
> The reign of Reason, Liberty, and Peace!   (II. 436–44)

---

[16] 'Elegy Written in a Country Churchyard', l. 123, *The Poems of Thomas Gray, William Collins, and Oliver Goldsmith*, ed. Roger Lonsdale (London and Harlow: Longmans, Green and Co., 1969), 140.

Smith's reference to her own 'desultory lines' here reveals the extent of her investment in the transformative powers of poetry and the imagination; it is *The Emigrants* that offers the model of sensibility directed to a social and historical end and which has the potential to transform France and ultimately the world. If such a claim for her own poem seems extravagant, she finds a precedent for it in *The Task* by Cowper, to whom the poem is dedicated, and which she describes at the conclusion of her dedication as 'The exquisite Poem [. . .that] was published some years before the demolition of regal despotism in France, which, in the fifth book, it seems to foretell' (p. 134). By implication, *The Emigrants* has the potential to foretell 'The reign of Reason, Liberty, and Peace!'

In *The Emigrants*, then, Charlotte Smith stressed the importance of the poetic imagining of war in not only bringing about the cessation of the current war but in ushering in a new age. But six months after she had completed *The Emigrants*, the nature of her relation with the war would again change, and with it her sense of the authority of her poetic role. For on 6 September 1793 her seventh son Charles, an ensign in the Bedfordshires, was wounded during the Duke of York's campaign on the borders of France and Holland.[17] Smith movingly described her response in a letter:

My gallant Boy lost his leg on the 6th before Dunkirk, & the retreat, which was immediately and rapidly made, compell'd them to remove the wounded at the utmost risk of their lives. My poor Charles was remov'd only two hours after his leg had been amputated and not only sufferd [sic] extremely in consequence of it but has had the cure much retarded. I received this cruel intelligence on the 11th, and it was a shock almost too severe for me. [. . .] My poor invalid, to whom I have sent his next brother, is at Ostend; he has now left his bed and thinks he shall be at home in about three weeks. Nothing can be more dreadful to my imagination than to figure to myself his appearance; a fine active young Man, twenty years old, thus mutilated for life, must appear an afflicting object to a stranger . . . but to me! I really know not, ardently as I wish to have him at home, how I shall support the sight.[18]

Waiting for Charles to return, Smith again calls on the figurative powers of the imagination to bridge the temporal and experiential gap between the battle and the home. But once Charles had returned home, where he recovered well enough to rejoin his regiment in a non-combatant capacity in

---

[17] For an interesting poetic response to this event and examination of the woman poet and the role of fancy in the context of war, see Mary Robinson, 'Sonnet to Mrs. Charlotte Smith, on Hearing that her Son Was Wounded at the Siege of Dunkirk', *Selected Poems*, ed. Judith Pascoe (Waterloo, Ontario: Broadview Press, 2000), 290.

[18] Quoted in Fletcher, *Charlotte Smith*, 201.

1795, only to die of yellow fever in Barbados in 1801, it was no longer necessary to rely on such imaginings.[19] Instead, Smith based her political and poetic response to war on her experience as one who had 'been so sad a sufferer in this miserable contest', as she described herself in a note to her poem of 1797, 'The Forest Boy', and she used this personal experience to authorize this tale of war's devastating effect on a family: 'Late circumstances have given rise to many mournful histories like this, which may be well said to be founded in truth!'[20] Smith draws on the equation of wounding with the knowledge of this 'truth' of war in the conclusion to 'The Forest Boy', when she chastises 'Ye cold statesman! unknowing a scar' who 'let loose the demons of war' (ll. 132, 135). Yet if Smith's self-representation in relation to war changed with Charles's return, she continued to emphasize that the sufferings of war exceeded all others, exclaiming in 'The Forest Boy' note:

Gracious God! will mankind never be reasonable enough to understand that all the miseries which our condition subjects us to, are light in comparison of what we bring upon ourselves by indulging the folly and wickedness of those who make nations destroy each other for *their* diversion, or to administer to their senseless ambition. (111)

And, maintaining this conviction, Smith remained dedicated to the poetic role that underpins *The Emigrants*—her mother's effort—stating that she would '*endeavour* to associate myself with those who apply what powers they have to deprecate the horrors of war' (ibid.). For Smith, who aligns herself in this note with two of the most notorious anti-war poets of the decade, William Crowe and Robert Southey, it was writing, and especially poetry, that best enabled the deprecation of the horrors of war.[21]

Attaching (and Detaching) the Forms and Feelings of War: Coleridge and the Imagining of Conflict

'Written in April 1798, During the Alarm of an Invasion', as its subtitle announces, 'Fears in Solitude' has long been regarded as one of the

---

[19] Ibid. 210, 319.
[20] *Poems of Charlotte Smith*, 111. Further page references to this note are included in parentheses within the text.
[21] For a discussion of Smith's continued writing on the war from 1798 until her death in 1806, see Matthew Bray, 'Removing the Anglo-Saxon Yoke: The Francocentric Vision of Charlotte Smith's Later Works', *Wordsworth Circle*, 24 (1993), 155–8.

crucial accounts of Coleridge's shifting response to the war with France, with the strident anti-war poet, lecturer, and journalist of the mid-1790s seeking to realign his political position as a result of international developments, especially the French occupation of Switzerland in early 1798, itself the subject of Coleridge's 'The Recantation: An Ode', published in the same quarto pamphlet by Joseph Johnson.[22] Yet while a poem of political crisis on both international and personal levels, 'Fears in Solitude' is also a poem which presents the threat of invasion as at least in part the product of a poetic crisis, and specifically a national failure of imagination and feeling. Like Charlotte Smith, Coleridge identifies the separation of the British public from the scene of war as crucial to their response to it:

> Thankless too for peace,
> (Peace long preserved by fleets and perilous seas)
> Secure from actual warfare, we have loved
> To swell the war-whoop, passionate for war!
> Alas! for ages ignorant of all
> Its ghastlier workings, (famine or blue plague,
> Battle, or siege, or flight through wintry snows,)
> We, this whole people, have been clamorous
> For war and bloodshed; animating sports,
> The which we pay for as a thing to talk of,
> Spectators and not combatants!   (ll. 86–96)

Whereas for Smith the British public's safety from war made necessary the imagining of its horrors, for Coleridge the nation's security and its

---

[22] For readings of the poem in these contexts, see Carl R. Woodring, *Politics in the Poetry of Coleridge* (Madison: Wisconsin University Press, 1961), 189–93; David V. Erdman, 'Editor's Introduction', *EoT*, I. lxxxii; Kelvin Everest, *Coleridge's Secret Ministry: The Context of the Conversation Poems, 1795–1798* (Hassocks, Sussex, and New York: Harvester Press and Barnes and Noble, 1979), 270–80; Nicholas Roe, 'Coleridge, Wordsworth, and the French Invasion Scare', *Wordsworth Circle*, 17 (1986), 142–8, and *Wordsworth and Coleridge: The Radical Years* (Oxford: Clarendon Press, 1988), 262–8; Paul Magnuson, 'The Politics of "Frost at Midnight"', *Wordsworth Circle*, 22 (1991), 3–11; Tim Fulford, *Landscape, Liberty and Authority: Poetry, Criticism and Politics from Thomson to Wordsworth* (Cambridge: Cambridge University Press, 1996), 234–6; Morton D. Paley, *Apocalypse and Millennium in English Romantic Poetry* (Oxford: Clarendon Press, 1999), 136–9; Richard Cronin, *The Politics of Romantic Poetry: In Search of the Pure Commonwealth* (Basingstoke and London, and New York: Macmillan and St Martin's Press, 2000), 72–3; Jerome Christensen, *Romanticism at the End of History* (Baltimore and London: Johns Hopkins University Press, 2000), 84–95; Mark Rawlinson, 'Invasion! Coleridge, the Defence of Britain and the Cultivation of the Public's Fear', in Shaw (ed.), *Romantic Wars*, 110–37; Philip Shaw, *Waterloo and the Romantic Imagination* (Basingstoke and New York: Palgrave Macmillan, 2002), 123–4, 126.

ignorance of the 'ghastlier workings' of 'actual warfare' have resulted in its bellicosity. As argued in the previous chapter, during the mid-1790s Coleridge had shown faith in the power of written descriptions of the conflict to bridge the gap between the site of the war and the scene of reading, quoting eyewitness accounts and drawing on them in his own poetry, and the foundations of his political thinking were the faculties of feeling and imagination; as he wrote to fellow poet William Lisle Bowles in March 1797, 'The base of our politics is, I doubt not, the same. We both feel strongly for whomever our imaginations present to us in the attitude of suffering.'[23] As for Smith, the ultimate aim for Coleridge of the exercise of these faculties was the termination of the war itself, as he commented at the close of 'On the Present War': 'And shall we carry on this wild and priestly War against reason, against freedom, against human nature? If there be one among you, who departs from me without feeling it his immediate duty to petition or remonstrate against the continuance of it, I envy that man neither his head or his heart!'[24]

In 'Fears in Solitude', however, Coleridge confronts what he now sees as the national failure to exercise the faculties of feeling and imagination in response to the war. While the conflict remains a topic that 'all read of', the versions consumed are no longer a means of its termination:

> Boys and girls,
> And women, that would groan to see a child
> Pull off an insect's leg, all read of war,
> The best amusement for our morning meal!   (ll. 104–7)

As Coleridge argued in a piece entitled 'Insensibility of the Public Temper' in the *Morning Post* in February 1798, the familiarity of European events to the reading public meant that their impact on the imagination had lessened: 'What is familiar to the imagination ceases to be terrible; and what ceases to be terrible we no longer feel a strong inducement to resist' (*EoT*, I. 22). While Coleridge is writing specifically about 'Revolutions' here, his account of the resulting crisis in reading provides a valuable context for 'Fears in Solitude', as he argues that 'We

---

[23] *Collected Letters of Samuel Taylor Coleridge, 1785–1834*, ed. by Earl Leslie Griggs, 6 vols. (Oxford: Clarendon Press, 1956), I. 183.

[24] *Lectures 1795: On Politics and Religion*, ed. Lewis Patton and Peter Mann (London: Routledge and Kegan Paul and Princeton University Press), 74. On 'benevolence' and 'sensibility' in Coleridge, see Woodring, *Politics in the Poetry of Coleridge*, 45–61, Everest, *Coleridge's Secret Ministry*, 231–6, and Coleridge's poem to Charles Lloyd, 'Addressed to a Young Man of Fortune who Abandoned Himself to an Indolent and Causeless Melancholy', *Poetical Works*, 157–8.

now read with listless unconcern of events which, but a very few years ago, would have filled all Europe with astonishment' and 'We read without emotion that the armies of France have entered the city of Rome'(*EoT*, I. 20, 21). It is a similar national failure to respond imaginatively or emotionally to the language of war that Coleridge identifies at the heart of the current crisis in 'Fears in Solitude':

> The poor wretch, who has learnt his only prayers
> From curses, who knows scarcely words enough
> To ask a blessing from his Heavenly Father,
> Becomes a fluent phraseman, absolute
> And technical in victories and defeats,
> And all our dainty terms for fratricide;
> Terms which we trundle smoothly o'er our tongues
> Like mere abstractions, empty sounds to which
> We join no feeling and attach no form!
> As if the soldier died without a wound;
> As if the fibres of this godlike frame
> Were gored without a pang; as if the wretch
> Who fell in battle, doing bloody deeds,
> Passed off to Heaven, translated and not killed;
> As though he had no wife to pine for him,
> No God to judge him!   (ll. 108–23)

The euphemistic language of war has become detached from what Coleridge elsewhere terms 'realities', realities registered here through the physical damage to the soldier's body, the emotional response of the widow (a variation of a figure previously used in 'On the Present War' and 'Religious Musings')[25] and through divine judgement. Yet it is not the language of war which is itself to blame, after all its 'terms' are only '*Like* mere abstractions' (italics added, ll. 113–15). Rather its sounds have become 'empty' because of the national failure to respond to them specifically with feeling and imagination, 'to which | We join no feeling and attach no form!' (ll. 115–16). This line, and indeed Coleridge's account of language's relation to the abstract and the real, can be glossed through his essay on William Pitt, published in the *Morning Post* on 19 March 1800. In this portrait, Coleridge presents the Prime Minister as like the 'fluent phraseman' of his poem, his element is 'general and abstract phrases' which he learnt to produce at an early age at the cost of the deadening of his 'genuine feelings': 'he acquired a premature and

---

[25] *Lectures 1795*, 59; *Poetical Works*, 120.

unnatural dexterity in the combination of words, which must of necessity have diverted his attention from present objects, obscured his impressions, and deadened his genuine feelings. Not the *thing* on which he was speaking, but the praises to be gained by the speech, were present to his intuition' (*EoT*, I. 223, 219–20). If Pitt fails to join feeling to his words, his 'hothouse' education has resulted in his lack of imagination: 'Imaginary situations in an imaginary state of things rise up in minds that possess a power and facility in combining images.—Mr. Pitt's ambition was conversant with old situations in the old state of things, which furnish nothing to the imagination, though much to the wishes' (*EoT*, I. 220). Coleridge brings together his attack on Pitt's lack of feeling and imagination through an analysis of the prime minister's facility with language that echoes the arguments of 'Fears in Solitude'. Pitt is 'the man of words, and abstractions' and 'GENERAL PHRASES' which are 'unenforced by one *single image*, one *single fact* of real national amelioration' (*EoT*, I. 223–4). It is in such images and facts that reality lies: 'These are *things*, these are realities; and these Mr. Pitt has neither the imagination to body forth, or the sensibility to feel for' (*EoT*, I. 224). As in the use of his word 'form' in 'Fears in Solitude', Coleridge draws on Theseus's description of the imagination as that which '*bodies forth* | The *forms* of things unknown' (italics added) in *A Midsummer Night's Dream*, a source Coleridge also drew on when describing George Washington as among those possessing 'imaginations capable of bodying forth lofty undertakings' (*EoT*, I. 131*)*.[26] Pitt's inability to feel for things and realities or to body them forth through the imagination parallels the nation's failure to exercise its feeling or imagination in response to the language of war.

In 'Fears in Solitude', the national failure is emphasized by contrast with the embodiment of a properly feeling and imaginative response to war in the poet-like figure of the 'humble man' (l. 14), described in the text's opening movement:

> My God! it is a melancholy thing
> For such a man, who would full fain preserve
> His soul in calmness, yet perforce must feel
> For all his human brethren—O my God!
> It weighs upon the heart, that he must think
> What uproar and what strife may now be stirring
> This way or that way o'er these silent hills—

[26] *A Midsummer Night's Dream*, ed. R. A. Foakes (Cambridge: Cambridge University Press, 1984), 5. 1. 14–15.

> Invasion, and the thunder and the shout,
> And all the crash of onset; fear and rage,
> And undetermined conflict—even now,
> Even now, perchance, and in his native isle:
> Carnage and groans beneath this blessed sun!   (ll. 29–40)

As Mark Rawlinson has commented, these lines display 'the poet's capacity to perceive military conflict imaginatively, peopling the region which is perceptively out of range with injurors and injured'.[27] Coleridge's emphasis on the burden of responsibility for this surrogate-poet figure, who 'perforce must feel | For all his human brethren' and imagine 'conflict' 'in his native isle', marks a significant development in his conception of the poetic role. In 'Reflections on having Left a Place of Retirement', a poem written two years earlier but with a number of similarities to 'Fears in Solitude', Coleridge had demanded of the poet that he give up poetry and commit himself to the 'honourable toil' of an active role.[28] In 'Fears in Solitude' the poet's burden of responsibility—the weight upon the heart— becomes the exercising of the poetic faculties of feeling and imagination.[29]

In 'Fears in Solitude', then, Coleridge argues that if the nation had responded properly to the language of war, feeling strongly for whomever its imaginations presented to it in the attitude of suffering, its sense of the conflict as terrible would have been a strong inducement to resist the continuation of the war. But its failure to do so has instead contributed to the war's potential escalation:

> Therefore, evil days
> Are coming on us, O my countrymen!
> And what if all-avenging Providence,
> Strong and retributive, should make us know
> The meaning of our words, force us to feel
> The desolation and the agony
> Of our fierce doings?   (ll. 123–9)

Here violence threatens Britain's shores as a return of meaning,[30] and Coleridge emphasizes the contrast between the bellicose nation and the

---

[27] Rawlinson, 'Invasion!', 119. If we follow John Spenser Hill's account of the development of Coleridge's imagination in the mid-1790s, it is also possible to read Coleridge's 'think' specifically in terms of the imaginative faculty. *Imagination in Coleridge*, 12–13.

[28] Everest, *Coleridge's Secret Ministry*, 270; *Poetical Works*, 108.

[29] One important element in this shift may have been the Wedgwood family's offer to Coleridge of an annuity of £150 in January 1798. See Richard Holmes, *Coleridge: Early Visions* (Harmondsworth: Penguin Books, 1990), 179–81.

[30] See Christensen, 'Romanticism at the End of History', 88.

'humble man' through verbal echo: whereas the 'humble man' *'perforce must feel* | For all his human brethren', the nation's failure may result in Providence's threat to *'force us to feel* | The desolation and the agony | Of our fierce doings' (italics added). Like Smith, Coleridge argues that imagined war can help terminate 'actual warfare', but writing five years later than Smith, he finds himself in a different historical moment which forces a reconsideration of the poet's wartime role. For if Smith could emphasize the safety of the British public—'By the rude sea guarded, we are safe'—Coleridge was writing 'during the alarm of an invasion' that potentially rendered the imagining of war unnecessary. Coleridge's initial reaction to the possibility of an imminent confrontation with death, as it frequently was when faced with deadlines, is to ask for more time:

> Spare us yet awhile,
> Father and God! O! spare us yet awhile!
> Oh! let not English women drag their flight
> Fainting beneath the burthen of their babes,
> Of the sweet infants, that but yesterday
> Laughed at the breast! (ll. 129–34)

Like Smith, Coleridge imagines war through the figure of the fleeing widow and baby, but whereas for Smith such a scene was unimaginable in Britain in 1793, except as an imagining, for Coleridge the feared invasion threatens to turn a literary trope into a reality in his native isle. He responds, as Wordsworth would do five years later when confronted with another invasion threat, by addressing the 'Men of England':

> Sons, brothers, husbands, all
> Who ever gazed with fondness on the forms
> Which grew up with you round the same fire-side,
> And all who ever heard the sabbath-bells
> Without the infidel's scorn, make yourselves pure!
> Stand forth! be men! repel an impious foe,
> Impious and false, a light yet cruel race,
> Who laugh away all virtue, mingling mirth
> With deeds of murder; and still promising
> Freedom, themselves too sensual to be free,
> Poison life's amities, and cheat the heart
> Of faith and quiet hope, and all that soothes,
> And all that lifts the spirit! (ll. 134–46)

Here, Coleridge calls for the remasculinization of the nation, anticipating Wordsworth's sonnets of 1802–3. The nation earlier described as 'A selfish, lewd, effeminated race' must become manly if it is to withstand the threat of France, itself represented as dangerously effeminate.[31] But it is important to differentiate Coleridge's programme for national remasculinization from that demanded by much of the anti-invasion rhetoric of these years which emphasized a more straightforward equation of the martial and the manly enacted in the anticipated triumph over the French. In much of his earlier anti-war writing, Coleridge had similarly appealed to the manliness of his readers or audience, as in his use of St Paul in the conclusion to his 'Introductory Address' of February 1795, a passage which offers the most direct precedent and source for the inspirations and exclamations of this section of 'Fears in Solitude': 'Watch ye! Stand fast in the principles of which ye have been convinced! Quit yourselves like Men! Be strong! Yet let all things be done in the spirit of Love.'[32] As this example illustrates, Coleridge's appeals to manliness do not necessarily link them to the performance of violence, and in 'Fears in Solitude' he minimizes the role of violence in the repelling of the French, speedily defusing the threat they present by consigning them to a limbo reminiscent of the Ancient Mariner's vessel 'As idle as a painted ship | Upon a painted ocean' (ll. 117–18):

> Stand we forth;
> Render them back upon the insulted ocean,
> And let them toss as idly on its waves
> As the vile sea-weed, which some mountain-blast
> Swept from our shores! (ll. 146–50)

While the Miltonic image of the mountain-blast certainly sublimates the violence necessary to repulse the French, it also plays down the necessity for heroic action. Moreover, unlike the majority of invasion poetry (including Wordsworth's of the following decade), the defeat of the French does not resolve the crisis motivating the poem, for the poet's 'fears in solitude' will become the continuing emotional condition of the nation:

> And oh! may we return
> Not with a drunken triumph, but with fear,
> Repenting of the wrongs with which we stung
> So fierce a foe to frenzy! (ll. 150–3)

---

[31] These lines are quoted as variants for the early versions of the poem in *Poetical Works*, 258.   [32] *Lectures 1795*, 49.

The confrontation with the other through war does not solve the poem's crisis of national identity: it merely buys it more time so that it can continue the process of self-scrutiny advocated by the poet and illustrated in the lines that follow with their analysis of the riven state of national politics.[33]

While a reformation of masculinity may be necessary for the tempo- rary survival of the nation threatened by France, the nation's future iden- tity needs to be seen in the context of the poem's models of gendered identity, the 'humble man' presented in its opening and the poet of its close. As I have argued, the nation's failure to imagine the war in which it participates is emphasized through opposition with the 'humble man', a figure 'who, in his youthful years, | Knew just so much of folly, as had made | His early manhood more securely wise!' (ll. 14–16). This personal history of youthful indiscretion anticipates the critique of the nation's 'own folly' (l. 170) which Everest has identified as 'the real problem of society' in the poem,[34] and it locates the lapse within a narrative of growth to 'an early manhood' that is all the 'more securely wise' as a result of these earlier errors. If the nation's sense of being 'Secure from actual warfare' has led to its imaginative failure, the 'humble man's' security of wisdom produces no such isolation from others but rather the responsi- bility to 'feel | For all his human brethren', compelling him to think beyond the solitude in which 'In a half sleep, he dreams of better worlds' (l. 26). This reformed figure, then, offers one model for national refor- mation, attainable through growth to a manhood defined in terms of its acceptance of the responsibilities of feeling and imagining.

Coleridge develops this model of reformed manliness and considers the relation between the individual and the nation in the examination of the poetic persona in the final section of the poem. Defending this persona against the charge that he has been one of the 'enemies' of his country (l. 174), Coleridge traces his persona's growth through his rela- tionship with Britain:

> But, O dear Britain! O my Mother Isle!
> Needs must thou prove a name most dear and holy
> To me, a son, a brother, and a friend,
> A husband, and a father! who revere
> All bonds of natural love, and find them all
> Within the limits of thy rocky shores.   (ll. 176–81)

---

[33] For an interesting reading of the poem which sees the invasion as 'a curious object of desire', see Shaw, *Waterloo in the Romantic Imagination*, 123.

[34] *Coleridge's Secret Ministry*, 277.

As with the 'humble man', Coleridge defines his persona's gendered identity through a narrative of growth to manhood, from 'a son' to 'A husband, and a father', and expands upon the nation's role in shaping his development in the following lines:

> O native Britain! O my Mother Isle!
> How shouldst thou prove aught else but dear and holy
> To me, who from thy lakes and mountain-hills,
> Thy clouds, thy quiet dales, thy rocks and seas,
> Have drunk in all my intellectual life,
> All sweet sensations, all ennobling thoughts,
> All adoration of the God in nature,
> All lovely and all honourable things
> Whatever makes this mortal spirit feel
> The joy and greatness of its future being?
> There lives nor form nor feeling in my soul
> Unborrowed from my country!   (ll. 182–93)

Coleridge's account of his persona's development culminates with his debt to his 'Mother Isle' for the 'form[s]' and 'feeling[s]' that live 'in his soul', setting up an obvious contrast with the failure of the reading public to join feelings and attach forms to the language of war. And it is his persona's possession of these faculties which qualifies him for the role of national poet:

>   O divine
> And beauteous island! thou hast been my sole
> And most magnificent temple, in the which
> I walk with awe, and sing my stately songs,
> Loving the God that made me!—   (ll. 193–7)

The self-conferring of this poetic role on the persona marks the resolution of the poem's crisis, signalled in the wishing away of the invasion threat: 'May my fears, | My filial fears, be vain!' (ll. 197–8).

The final verse paragraph of 'Fears in Solitude' is usually seen as a retreat to the private after the public strains of the poem's middle section, as Coleridge returns to 'beloved Stowey' (l. 221). Yet, as I have been arguing, Coleridge makes his own poetic persona a model for the nation in war and his emphasis on his powers of feeling and imagination produces the positive statement of belief that critics have seen as lacking in the poem.[35] Coleridge's return to Stowey, where he can see the trees

---

[35] See e.g. Roe, *Wordsworth and Coleridge*, 265–7.

that mark 'the mansion of my friend' and imagine 'my own lowly cottage, where my babe | And my babe's mother dwell in peace!' enact his earlier account of himself in a national context as 'a friend | A husband, and a father!' (ll. 223, 225–6, 179). Like Charlotte Smith, who finds authority for her wartime role as poet in the mother figure, Coleridge authorizes his own poetic practice by presenting himself through a parental figure, in his case the father. Such a self-construction is not necessarily a limiting of sympathies to the domestic sphere or, in Burkean fashion, to his native isle; as Coleridge commented in his 'Introductory Address' of 1795: 'The paternal and filial duties discipline the Heart and prepare it for the love of all Mankind. The intensity of private attachments encourages, not prevents, universal Benevolence.'[36] In 'Fears in Solitude', while grounding his identity within its familial roles, Coleridge emphasizes that this is not a turn away from society or the world beyond Stowey; rather Stowey becomes the location for the poem's culminating acts of feeling and imagination:

> With light
> And quickened footsteps thitherward I tend,
> Remembering thee, O green and silent dell!
> And grateful, that by nature's quietness
> And solitary musings, all my heart
> Is softened, and made worthy to indulge
> Love, and the thoughts that yearn for human kind.   (ll. 226–32)

If the poem began by embodying in the 'humble man' the need for feeling and imagination in response to the possibility of war, that figure becomes the model for the poet himself, and in turn for the nation, in a conclusion of 'Universal Benevolence'.[37]

Writing in the 1790s, Charlotte Smith and Samuel Taylor Coleridge both offer the imaginative poet as a model for the nation's response to war, and their detailed poetic examinations of the functions and effects of the imagination reveal the extent to which they saw this faculty as having an essentially political function, contrary to influential accounts of the imagination which see it as transcending, compensating for, or displacing, the political.[38] Yet paradoxically 'Fears in Solitude' can also

---

[36] *Lectures 1795*, 46.

[37] In his 'Remonstrance to the French Legislators' in *The Watchman*, Coleridge presents himself as one who 'speaks in the name of HUMAN KIND', 269.

[38] The two most influential accounts of romanticism in these terms, though very different in their arguments and methodologies, are M. H. Abrams, *Natural Supernaturalism: Tradition and Revolution in Romantic Literature* (New York and London: W. W. Norton

be seen as a text which begins the detaching of the imaginative from the political on which such later accounts are built. For while Coleridge could appeal to the nation's 'truth-painting Imagination' in his 1795 slave-trade lecture, 'Fears in Solitude' distinguishes between the poet's imagining of the war and the nation's failure to do so. The poem differentiates the poet from the rest of the nation and establishes an imaginary world created by him and peopled by the creatures of his imagination. If this imagined world was inherently political in 1798, and remained so for a number of years afterwards, over the next two decades Coleridge would increasingly separate the imaginative from the political in texts such as *Lectures on Literature*, *Biographia Literaria*, and the *Statesman's Manual*.[39] Writing in the context of the ongoing events of the war and the career of Napoleon, in these texts Coleridge elevated the imaginative over the political, and the artist or poet over the politician or soldier, culminating in the post-Waterloo account of the poetic imagining of war in the 'Apologetic Preface to "Fire, Famine and Slaughter"', published with *Sibylline Leaves* in 1817. John Barrell's excellent recent discussion of this text in the context of the treason trials of 1794 and the imagining of the king's death makes unnecessary an extended analysis of this piece.[40] Barrell argues of the 'Apologetic Preface' that it 'is an attempt to take the politics out of the imagination by voiding the imagination of all connection with intention or desire, and so by making poetry, even poetry on political subjects, something which inhabits a quite other universe of discourse from politics itself'.[41] While Barrell finds the context for Coleridge's 'Preface' in the quarrels about imagining the king's death, it is worth emphasizing the extent to which Coleridge rewrites (and so seeks to disclaim) his 1790s manifesto for the poetic imagining of war. In accounting for the war eclogue 'Fire, Famine and Slaughter' he had written more than twenty years before, Coleridge continues to present the poetic role in terms of 'feeling' and 'fancy' (now a lesser form of the imagination), but he now detaches them from 'realities':

and Co., 1971) and Jerome J. McGann, *The Romantic Ideology: A Critical Investigation* (Chicago and London: University of Chicago Press, 1983).

[39] I have discussed these texts, particularly in relation to the career of Napoleon and Coleridge's development of the distinction between 'Commanding Genius' and 'Absolute Genius' in *Napoleon and English Romanticism* (Cambridge: Cambridge University Press, 1995), 26–7. See also Shaw, *Waterloo in the Romantic Imagination*, 126–33.

[40] John Barrell, *Imagining the King's Death: Figurative Treason, Fantasies of Regicide, 1793–1796* (Oxford: Oxford University Press, 2000), 643–56.   [41] Ibid. 651.

Were I now to have read by myself for the first time the poem in question, my conclusion, I fully believe, would be, that the writer must have been some man of warm feelings and active fancy; that he had painted to himself the circumstances that accompany war in so many vivid and yet fantastic forms, as proved that neither the images nor the feelings were the result of observation, or in any way derived from realities. I should judge that they were the product of his own seething imagination, and therefore impregnated with that pleasurable exultation which is experienced in all energetic exertion of intellectual power;[42]

Coleridge's definition of the faculties of the poet remain much the same as in the 1790s, but if in that decade feeling and imagination were the base of his politics, twenty years later they have become entirely separate from it. While the poet's imagination (or 'fancy', as it is now) continues to paint, it is no longer 'truth-painting' and its images would no longer be confirmed by the fleshly eye; indeed the very power of the poetry is proof of the lack of observation of war. Rather than the poem having its origin in 'realities', it is the poet and his 'seething imagination' who becomes its source, in an anticipation of Abrams's expressive model of romantic poetry.[43] In this 'Preface', Coleridge completes one of the major transformations of the imagination in the romantic period, but even while seeking to discredit and disclaim his earlier construction of his poetic identity, his account emphasizes the extent to which his highly influential ideas about poetry and imagination were formulated in relation to the era of war in which he lived.

[42] *Poetical Works*, 598–9.
[43] See *The Mirror and the Lamp: Romantic Theory and the Critical Tradition* (Oxford and New York: Oxford University Press, 1953).

CHAPTER THREE

'Was it for This . . .?': War and Poetic Identity in the Writings of Southey and Wordsworth, 1793–1802

IN ROBERT SOUTHEY'S blank-verse poem 'History', written between mid-1798 and early 1799, the poet asks himself the repeated question 'Was it for this . . .?'[1] Examining the development of his 'young mind' and 'swelling heart' and his aspirations to 'love | his fellow kind', the troubled writer finds himself confronted by the 'crimes' of history and calls on 'gentle Poesy' to receive him from scenes such as 'the fields of war' so that he may 'nurse | My nature's better feelings, for my soul | Sickens at man's misdeeds' (ll. 1–8). This familiar narrative of an overwhelming sense of personal and political crisis producing a turn away from 'History', often figured as here as a retreat to a bower, has been a major feature of accounts of canonical romanticism, and still holds considerable sway. For example, in *The Hidden Wordsworth*, Kenneth R. Johnston writes that Thelwall's 'Lines written at Bridgwater' in July 1797 show that ' "a peaceful retreat" was all that he wanted . . . Like Coleridge's conversation poems and like "Tintern Abbey", Thelwall's "Lines" record the final turn by which the revolutionary hopes and actions of the 1790s turned inward to the form of culture we call Romanticism.'[2] But Southey's account of his poetic development fits Johnston's romantic retreat model only until the second verse paragraph when 'History' answers back. Like Wordsworth's *The Prelude*, also begun in 1798 with the repeated question 'Was it for this . . .?',[3] 'History' is a poem of poetic

---

[1] Robert Southey, 'History', *Morning Post*, 16 January 1799, ll. 16–17.
[2] *The Hidden Wordsworth* (London: Pimlico, 2000), 389.
[3] William Wordsworth, *The Prelude 1799, 1805, 1850*, ed. Jonathan Wordsworth, M. H. Abrams, and Stephen Gill (New York and London: W. W. Norton & Co., 1979), I. 1.

dedication at a time of historical crisis, but while history emerges only at the end of the two-book *Prelude* with the closing references to 'these times of fear' and 'this time | Of dereliction and dismay' (II. 478, 486–7), in Southey's poem it is 'History' itself which offers the solution to the crisis. The poet's initial renunciation of 'History' as a 'chronicle of crimes' prompts the appearance of 'CLIO, the strong-ey'd Muse' of History (l. 10) who, angry and majestic, pours scorn on the poet's longing for retreat and its consequences for his poetry and reminds him of the spirit that formed this particular favoured being:

> Go, young man! she cried;
> Sigh among myrtle bow'rs, and let thy soul
> Effuse itself in strains so sorrowful sweet
> That love-sick maids may weep upon thy page,
> In most delicious sorrow! Oh shame! shame!
> Was it for this I waken'd thy young mind?
> Was it for this I made thy swelling heart
> Throb at the deeds of Greece, and thy boy's eye
> So kindle when that glorious Spartan died?
> Boy! boy! deceive me not! . . .   (ll. 10–20)

Through Clio's severe intervention, Southey presents himself, like Wordsworth in *The Prelude*, as a 'Chosen son', educated for a special task; he has risen 'With nobler feelings, with a deeper love | For Freedom' (ll. 25–6). But whereas Wordsworth presents himself and his poetic identity as formed by Nature, Southey's grand preceptor and inspiring power is History:

> . . . let that spirit fill
> Thy song, and it shall teach thee, boy! to raise
> Strains such as CATO had not scorn'd to hear,
> As SIDNEY in his hall of fame may love.   (ll. 28–31)

At a moment of historical and vocational crisis, History sustains Southey, so that he may in turn sustain History.

It seems likely that Southey and Wordsworth drew on the same sources in Ariosto, Milton, Thomson, and Pope for the phrase 'Was it for this . . .?', but less certain is whether either knew of the other's use of it in their contemporaneous explorations of poetic identity.[4]

References to *The Prelude* are to this edition and are to the two-part *Prelude* of 1799 by book and line number, unless otherwise stated.

[4] For the sources of this phrase, see *The Prelude*, I. 2, n. 2.

Wordsworth was probably the first to use the formula, beginning his first draft of *The Prelude* with the phrase in October 1798 in Goslar.[5] Southey's poem was published in January 1799 and the evidence of his Common-Place Book suggests it was written shortly before this, though in later editions he dated it to Westbury 1798, which would mean it could have been written any time after June 1798.[6] At 31 lines to *The Prelude*'s eventual 8,000, 'History' may seem more like a *reductio ad absurdum* of Wordsworth's epic than a genuine answer to it, but it does offer a manifesto for a different poetic mode to the one normally defined as romantic, one that is politically committed and speaks with what Southey terms in another poem of 1798 'the calm, collected public voice'.[7] Marilyn Butler has presented the political, public Southey as an alternative exemplary romantic figure to the Wordsworth that she sees constructed by the quietist, intellectual agendas of the academy. Southey's assertion of his identity as a historical, politically orientated poet represents an important intervention in contemporary debates about poetry's role in which it was being increasingly elevated and detached from political subject matter.[8] If Southey's poem opens by establishing an opposition between two kinds of writing, History's 'Chronicle' and the strains of 'poesy', only to collapse that distinction in his own historically inspired song, this opening opposition invokes and parodies the way poetry was often feminized in the writing of the 1790s as a trembling or timid Muse who turns away from the subject of 'war, horrid war', seeking like the poet of 'History' the shelter of the bower, removed from 'the court's polluted scenes, . . . dungeon horrors, . . . [and] . . . the fields of war' (ll. 4–5). This chapter will examine the way in which Southey and Wordsworth responded to the war in their poetry and show how the war played a major role in the shaping of their poetic identities.

---

[5] 'The Texts: History and Presentation', *The Prelude*, 512.

[6] *Poems of Robert Southey*, ed. by Maurice H. Fitzgerald (London and New York: Oxford University Press, 1909), 396.

[7] 'Inscription: For a Column in Smithfield where Wat Tyler was Killed!', *The Contributions of Robert Southey to the 'Morning Post'*, ed. Kenneth Curry (Tuscaloosa: University of Alabama Press, 1984), 32.

[8] Marilyn Butler, 'Repossessing the Past: The Case for an Open Literary History', in Marjorie Levinson *et al.*, *Rethinking Historicism: Critical Readings in Romantic History* (Oxford: Basil Blackwell, 1989), 64–84.

Robert Southey and 'War's Varied Horrors'

By the time of his poetic rededication to 'History' in 1798, Southey could make a strong claim for himself as the major anti-war poet of the decade, the author of poems such as 'To Horror' and 'The Victory' discussed in Chapter 1.[9] He had identified 'War's varied horrors' as the subject of his epic *Joan of Arc*, which he had begun in 1793 and which had established his reputation when published in 1796,[10] and he had followed this ambitious work with a series of shorter pieces including the 'Botany-Bay Eclogues' which gave a voice to the victims of war, the poems on the sufferers of the conflict such as 'The Soldier's Wife' that were attacked and parodied in the *Anti-Jacobin*, and several anti-war pieces in the *Morning Post*.[11] The poetic threat that Southey posed to conservative writers like T. J. Mathias, Anna Seward, and the contributors to the *Anti-Jacobin* came not only from '*his principles*' but also from the fact that he was a poet of 'great promise', to use Mathias's terms,[12] capable of adopting the highest literary forms for his political purpose, as he had shown in *Joan of Arc*, echoing Virgil's *Aeneid* in the invocation of a work epic in structure and ambition but seeking to invert the traditional values of the form:[13]

> War's varied horrors, and the train of ills,
> That follow on Ambition's blood-stain'd path
> And fill the world with woe; of France preserv'd
> By maiden hand, what time her chiefs subdued,
> Or slept in death, or lingered life in chains,
> I sing: nor wilt thou FREEDOM scorn the song.   (I. 1–6)

[9] For general accounts of Southey's poetical development in the context of his politics, see Geoffrey Carnall, *Robert Southey and his Age: The Development of a Conservative Mind* (Oxford: Clarendon Press, 1960), and Jean Raimond, 'Southey's Early Writing and the Revolution', *Yearbook of English Studies*, 19 (1989), 181–96.

[10] Robert Southey, *Joan of Arc: An Epic Poem* (Bristol and London: Joseph Cottle, Cadell and Davies, and G. G. and J. Robinson, 1796), 5. Hereafter cited by book and line number within the text.

[11] For a discussion of Southey's widow figures in the context of the war and protest poetry, see C. J. P. Smith, 'Lamb and the Politics of Literary Fashion in Southey's Female Wanderers', *Charles Lamb Bulletin*, 89 (1995) 2 8.

[12] *The Pursuits of Literature. A Satirical Poem in Four Dialogues. With Notes.* (London: T. Becket, 1798), 298.

[13] For a very useful discussion of *Joan of Arc* in the context of the *Anti-Jacobin*'s critique of the Jacobin poet, see Richard Cronin, *The Politics of Romantic Poetry: In Search of the Pure Commonwealth* (Basingstoke, London, and New York: Macmillan and St Martin's Press), 66–9. For discussion of the poem's relations with epic, Stuart Curran, *Poetic Form and British Romanticism* (Oxford and New York: Oxford University Press, 1989), 167–8, and Brian Wilkie, *Romantic Poets and Epic Tradition* (Madison and Milwaukee: University of Wisconsin Press, 1965), 30–58. For a valuable general discussion of the epic genre in the period, see A. D. Harvey, 'The English Epic in the Romantic Period', *Philological Quarterly*, 55 (1976), 241–59.

While a number of reviews praised the poetic powers displayed in this precocious work, they also noted the contemporary nature of its 'liberal' and 'enlightened' sentiments, its anti-war agenda ('War, and the lust of conquest, are every where painted in the strongest colours of abhorrence') and its narrative of a French heroine and people triumphing over an invading English army.[14] Southey presents the conflict in Godwinian fashion not as a national war between England and France but as a political war of guilty 'Mighty Ones' against innocent people, its effects felt most severely by 'the poor man' (II. 717–25; II. 590–1). In her role as God's minister, Joan sees herself not as a representative of France, but of all mankind (VIII. 642–4) and she declares the soldiers of the English invading force to be just as much the 'victims of the mighty' as the French (VIII. 526). Southey's descriptions of the victories of the French people over the invading army in book X particularly allude to the success of the citizen army of the French 'Nation in Arms' in the early years of the war, while also prophesying its further victories:

> And by the Mission'd Maiden's rumour'd deeds
> Inspirited, the Citizens of Rheims
> Feel their own strength; against the English troops
> With patriot valour, irresistible,
> They rise, they conquer, and to their liege Lord
> Present the city keys.   (X. 652–7)

Here Joan becomes an embodiment of the radical vision of Freedom in the early 1790s, a martial female figure inspiring the nation to victory over the oppressive forces of despotism.[15]

Southey reinforces his questioning of the epic and its links with martial culture through his inversion of generic and gender values, as Cronin has argued.[16] If *Joan of Arc* is a poem in which 'the epic is subordinate to the pastoral', it is also one in which the masculine martial urge is subordinated to the feminized powers of feeling, as Coleridge noted when describing the poem as 'frequently reach[ing] the *sentimental*' and Southey as a poet of '*feeling*'.[17] This sentimental emphasis is most evident in the passages describing the victims of war, both combatants and non-combatants;

[14] Lionel Madden (ed.), *Robert Southey: The Critical Heritage* (London and Boston: Routledge and Kegan Paul, 1972), 40–50; quotation is from John Aikin in the *Monthly Review*, 42.

[15] For examples of such constructions of the war in poetry, see 'To the Tyrants Infesting France' (*BWP*, 110), 'A New Song' (*BWP*, 125–8), 'The Triumph of Freedom' (*BWP*, 128), 'Ode to Moderation' (*BWP*, 165).   [16] *The Politics of Romantic Poetry*, 68.

[17] Quoted in *Robert Southey: The Critical Heritage*, 49.

Charles Lamb's comment that the 'very many passages of simple pathos abounding throughout the poem' might have been written by 'the author of "Crazy Kate" ' reveals the extent to which Southey called on the poetics of sensibility in his critique of war.[18] But Southey goes beyond simply juxtaposing the manly epic poetry of war with the feminized anti-war verse of sensibility. Rather he destabilizes the traditional link between war and masculinity. As Cronin argues, one of the 'Jacobin' elements of *Joan of Arc* is its 'dismantling of gender differences . . . [Joan] is a woman who dedicates herself to "active duties" (9, 167), rejecting alike a life of cloistered contemplation, and a life of married love', while Theodore takes on the roles traditionally associated with women, returning to look after his aged mother and disguising himself to follow Joan.[19] Joan's identity as a 'martial maid' assumes a wider significance because it undermines the gender difference which provides the foundation for the sense of power of the English military leaders, for whom defeat by 'a frenzied girl' leads to a loss of manly identity (VII. 511–13; X. 265–76). Southey also uses Joan to figure the poem's feminization of 'just war', which can only be motivated by feelings of 'compassion' and 'pity'. This idea is embodied by the warrior of feeling, Conrade, who presents a justification of his readiness to fight grounded in the ethics of sensibility: 'my heart is fleshly: I do feel | For what my brethren suffer' (I. 372–3). Conrade represents a redefined manliness that is contrasted with the hard-hearted English (VI. 231, 249), especially the 'cold-hearted Foeman' Henry V (II. 617), remembered as 'that merciless man' for his pitiless treatment of women and children at the siege of Rouen (II. 667–70). Conrade's grounding of his war ethic in his 'heart' is a lesson which has to be learnt by Joan, who prior to meeting Conrade 'never dreamt of what the wretched feel' (I. 347) and she in turn teaches it to the French King Charles VII. Whereas the English leaders are constantly represented as fighting for 'glory' (VIII. 276; X. 316, 350, 456–63, 497, 542), it is not only Joan whom 'no lust of glory leads to arms' (IV. 146); the whole French nation is driven to 'holy warfare' by the power of sensibility: 'Thus rous'd to rage | By every milder feeling, they rush'd forth, | They fought, they conquer'd' (X. 98, 104–6).

Southey's combination of the high and manly form of epic and an insistence on the necessity of feminized feeling within a polemical poem made *Joan of Arc* a focus for debates about the compatibility of an elevated conception of poetry with historical subject matter and political purpose. For Coleridge, who in 1796 shared Southey's anti-war agenda,

---

[18] Ibid. 46.　　[19] *The Politics of Romantic Poetry*, 68.

it was 'a poem which exhibits fresh proof that great poetical talents and high sentiments of liberty do reciprocally produce and assist each other'.[20] But for another major poet of the decade, Anna Seward, the poem's explicit politics were irreconcilable with its high aesthetic value. In her 'Lines Written ... after Reading Southey's "Joan of Arc" ', published in the *European Magazine* in August 1797, she begins:

> Base is the purpose of this Epic Song,
> Baneful its powers; but, oh, the Poesy
> ('What can it less when Sun-born GENIUS sings?')
> Wraps in reluctant ecstasy the soul
> Where Poesy is felt.   (*BWP*, 198)

Joan of Arc is problematic for Seward because it is at once politically poisonous, with an explicit 'purpose', yet unmistakably the elevated poetry produced by genius and appreciated only by certain select readers. Seward suggests that it is Southey's youth and lack of manliness that are responsible for his political beliefs, addressing him as 'Oh, unnat'ral Boy; | Oh, beardless Paricide' (*BWP*, 199). She presents his Muse as a monstrous version of the true Muse of poetry, a 'treach'rous Muse | In Comet splendour, in MEDUSA's beauty | Balefully deck'd' (*BPW*, 199). Southey's poem, like Joan of Arc herself, is a debasement of the naturally feminine. It is also dangerous, threatening with its dazzling but deceiving beauty to transform its astonished readers into Jacobins. Seward's use of an evaluative language of gender in her attack on *Joan of Arc* can be compared with the *Anti-Jacobin*'s attack on the '*Jacobin* poet', a figure partly based on Southey. This attack presents the 'coy Muse of *Jacobinism*' as deceptively alluring but falling short of the ideal standard of a 'pure' Muse of poetry to the extent of calling into question its own gendered identity.[21] Despite her many disguises, Jacobin poetry is essentially characterized by the manly features of a 'drunken swagger and ruffian tone', analogous to the cross-dressed figure of Sir John Brute of Vanbrugh's *The Provoked Wife*. Both Seward and the *Anti-Jacobin* recognize that much of the power of Southey's epic derives from its emphasis on the feminized qualities of 'piety and tenderness', to quote the *Anti-Jacobin*, and both seek to present this emphasis as a deception which disguises a manly political purpose. Their arguments illustrate the politics of this evaluative language of gender in suggesting that true poetry is feminine and transcends the factional.

Southey's 'History' can be seen as a retort to these attacks and to these

---

[20] *The Watchman*, 44.   [21] *The Anti-Jacobin*, 14.

constructions of poetry, offering 'Clio, the strong-eyed Muse' as a response to the representations of his verse as the 'treach'rous Muse' and 'coy Muse of Jacobinism' and providing a powerful figuring of his poetry as both elevated and historical. Yet, written in 1798, Southey's rededication can also be seen as a critique of those poets who it seemed to him had indeed deceived the Muse of History and retreated to the 'myrtle bowers' of 'gentle Poesy', supporting Marilyn Butler's suggestion that the most famous collection of that year, Lyrical Ballads, should be seen as a non-political collection, particularly in comparison with the sustained radicalism of Southey's collections of Poems of 1797 and 1799.[22] To Southey, Butler argues, Lyrical Ballads looked like a failure to stand firm against the Anti-Jacobin's attacks. Clio's calm anger, we might say, was Southey's, and the boy who threatened to deceive him, was Wordsworth. It was not Wordsworth alone, perhaps, who asked of his poetic position in 1798, 'Was it for this . . .?'

Wordsworth and the Poetic Figures of War

Southey's accusation that Wordsworth had turned away from history in 1798 was a charge that has since been repeated by a number of important critical assessments of Wordsworth's career. These accounts see the poet's development as characterized by a shift from a polemical humanitarian concern with suffering individuals to an interest in states of mind and being, seen for example in the revision of Salisbury Plain, which Mary Jacobus has described as the 'most impressive protest poem of its time',[23] into the version now known as Adventures on Salisbury Plain. As Stephen Gill has argued, Adventures on Salisbury Plain 'continues the social and political interests of the poem, and even extends them . . . [through] a fully dramatized presentation of human calamities consequent upon war, but Wordsworth's interest was rapidly shifting from social and political phenomena to the more complex phenomena of human motives and behaviour'.[24] For Gill, the later version signals Wordsworth's discovery of his true significance as a

---

[22] Marilyn Butler made this suggestion in her plenary lecture, 'The Bristol Model and the Formation of British Romanticism' at the Bristol: Romantic City conference, 18–22 September 1998, University of Bristol.

[23] Mary Jacobus, Tradition and Experiment in Lyrical Ballads 1798 (Oxford: Oxford University Press, 1976), 148.

[24] The Salisbury Plain Poems of William Wordsworth, ed. Stephen Gill (Ithaca, NY, and Hassocks, Sussex: Cornell University Press and Harvester Press, 1975), 12.

poet and his realization that 'his theme was indeed the mind of man and that his was a major, original genius'.[25]

These developments in Wordsworth's writing, particularly as they affected the relationship between his poetic role and his response to the figures of war, can be examined through a discussion of one of his encounters with history in 'The Discharged Soldier', a blank-verse fragment describing an incident that probably took place in 1788 and that Wordsworth would later include in book IV of *The Prelude*.[26] Written in 1798, the year Southey's encounter with history in the form of Clio prompted his poetic rededication, Wordsworth's encounter also produced a moment of poetic dedication, but one in which 'History' remains an other that troubles the poet's sense of vocation. Wordsworth represents the experience of war through encounter and tale-telling, as his wandering poetic persona, on turning a corner, finds 'Presented to my view an uncouth shape', who he later sees is 'clad in military garb' (ll. 38, 54).[27] Like the figures of war in Wordsworth's earlier poetry and like the many returning soldiers of the newspaper and magazine poetry discussed in the opening chapter, the soldier tells his tale:

> when erelong
> I asked his history, he in reply
> Was neither slow nor eager, but unmoved,
> And with a quiet uncomplaining voice,
> A stately air of mild indifference,
> He told a simple fact: that he had been
> A Soldier, to the tropic isles had gone,
> Whence he had landed now some ten days past;
> That on his landing he had been dismissed,
> And with the little strength he yet had left
> Was travelling to regain his native home.   (ll. 94–104)

---

[25] On Wordsworth's relation to protest poetry, see two articles by Stephen C. Gill, 'Wordsworth's Breeches Pocket: Attitudes to the Didactic Poet', *Essays in Criticism*, 19 (1969), 385–401; ' "Adventures on Salisbury Plain" and Wordsworth's Poetry of Protest 1795–97', *Studies in Romanticism*, 11 (1972), 48–65. For comparable arguments, see Nicholas Roe, *Wordsworth and Coleridge: The Radical Years* (Oxford: Clarendon Press, 1988), *passim* and esp. 137, and Mary Jacobus, *Tradition and Experiment*, 159.

[26] For details of the poem's composition and publication, see Gill's note in *William Wordsworth: The Oxford Authors*, ed. Stephen Gill (Oxford and New York: Oxford University Press, 1986), 687, and Beth Darlington, 'Two Early Texts: "A Night-Piece" and "The Discharged Soldier" ', in Jonathan Wordsworth with Beth Darlington (eds.), *Bicentenary Wordsworth Studies in Memory of John Alban Finch* (Ithaca, NY: Cornell University Press, 1970), 425–48.

[27] Unless otherwise stated, Wordsworth poetry is quoted from Gill, *William Wordsworth*, and referenced by line number within the text.

The soldier's history is a familiar one, and Toby R. Benis has given a powerfully contextualized reading of the poem as one that 'criticizes Britain's leaders', seeing the soldier as a figure 'whose sickly condition and wanderings are direct products of government policy and military service'.[28] Yet in the context of the newspaper and magazine verse on wounded and returning soldiers, what is striking in Wordsworth's presentation of the soldier's telling of his tale is its lack of political and polemical force and its failure to produce the conventional poetic responses of sympathy or indignation on the part of the poet. In its attack on the Jacobin Poet in the second issue of 27 November 1797, the *Anti-Jacobin* had criticized the political use of sensibility 'by many authors ... in sonnets and elegies without end', giving an outline of the standard poetic techniques used by the writers of such verse:

A human being, in the lowest state of penury and distress, is a treasure to a reasoner of this cast. He contemplates, he examines, he turns him in every possible light, with a view of extracting from the variety of his wretchedness new topics of invective against the pride of property. He indeed (if he is a true Jacobin), refrains from *relieving* the object of his compassionate contemplation; as well knowing, that every diminution from the general mass of human misery, must proportionally diminish the force of his argument.[29]

In his treatment of the discharged soldier, it is as if the Wordsworthian narrator is responding to this attack, recommending that he accompany the soldier to the dwelling of a labourer who 'will give you food if food you need, | And lodging for the night' (ll. 114–15). And reinforcing the soldier's failure to fulfil the polemical and emotive role that would be allotted to him in political poetry, the poet again questions him about his 'history', this time providing him with a veritable checklist of the radical agenda of anti-war poetry:

> While thus we travelled on I did not fail
> To question him of what he had endured
> From war and battle and the pestilence.   (ll. 137–9)

But again the soldier's answer fails to produce the 'topics of invective' we have seen in other treatments of the figure:

---

[28] Toby R. Benis, *Romanticism on the Road: the Marginal Gains of Wordsworth's Homeless* (Basingstoke and New York: Macmillan and St Martin's Press, 2000), 198.

[29] *The Anti-Jacobin*, 19–20.

> He all the while was in demeanor calm,
> Concise in answer: solemn and sublime
> He might have seemed, but that in all he said
> There was a strange half-absence and a tone
> Of weakness and indifference, as of one
> Remembering the importance of his theme,
> But feeling it no longer.   (ll. 140–6)

The soldier's delivery of his tale, like the fact that 'He appeared | To travel without pain' (ll. 122–3), undermines the poet's expectation that he would encounter one of the physically damaged victims of war, akin to Robert Merry's 'The Wounded Soldier', discussed in Chapter 1. The normal 'feeling' response to tales of war is blocked by the poet's sense that the soldier himself no longer 'feels' the importance of his theme, and rather than producing expressions of just indignation against contending governments the encounter leads only to silence (ll. 149).

If Wordsworth's treatment of the returning soldier seems to discharge the figure's subversive potential (which Wordsworth himself had drawn on in his earlier poetry), the poem continues to trouble as a result of its supernatural suggestions. The skeletal soldier is described as 'ghastly' and 'ghostly', maintaining even at the poem's close 'the same ghastly mildness in his look' (ll. 51, 125, 163). The soldier's supernatural presence is most explicitly described in a moment of startling identification with the poet:

>   I beheld
> With ill-suppressed astonishment his tall
> And ghostly figure moving at my side.   (ll. 122–4)

The soldier's ghostly figure here becomes the poet's *doppelgänger*, suggesting one reason for his troubling presence in the poem. While a number of critics have seen the soldier in such terms as 'a projection of Wordsworth himself, a sort of alter-ego', as the embodiment of 'a previously hidden or repressed aspect of Wordsworth psyche', as 'a curious version of himself', and as 'Wordsworth's double', what has not been stressed is the martial identity of this double.[30] To paraphrase Jonathan Wordsworth, the poet comes across a curious version of himself as a soldier. Despite the anti-war

---

[30] Warren Stephenson, 'Wordsworth's Satanism', *Wordsworth Circle*, 13 (1982), 176–7; Matthew C. Brennan, 'The "Ghastly Figure Moving at my Side": The Discharged Soldier as Wordsworth's Shadow', *Wordsworth Circle*, 18 (1987), 19; Jonathan Wordsworth, *The Borders of Vision* (Oxford: Clarendon Press, 1982), 12; Paul Magnuson, *Coleridge and Wordsworth: A Lyrical Dialogue* (Princeton: Princeton University Press, 1988), 91.

emphasis of his early poetry, Wordsworth was a poet with a strong sense of martial identity.[31] As Eric C. Walker has commented, in both *The Prelude* and the larger body of the *Recluse* texts, 'warrior and poet ... are twin selves',[32] and in 'Home at Grasmere' Wordsworth guiltily describes his imaginative self-projection to the scene of war:

> I cannot at this moment read a tale
> Of two brave Vessels matched in deadly fight
> And fighting to the death, but I am pleased
> More than a wise Man ought to be; I wish,
> I burn, I struggle, and in soul am there.   (ll. 929–33)

In 'Home at Grasmere', Wordsworth contains and represses his martial identity within a text of poetic dedication which narrates the achievement of his vocation. 'The Discharged Soldier', begun two years earlier, works towards a similar resolution, but with Wordsworth's ill-suppressed 'warrior self' confronting and troubling his 'poetic self'.[33] Wordsworth's ultimate placing of his encounter with the soldier at the conclusion to book IV of *The Prelude* similarly works to contain the haunting presence of this figure of war, locating the encounter after the famous dawn scene of poetic commitment, when 'vows | Were then made' for him and he became 'A dedicated spirit' (1805, IV, 341–4).[34] Wordsworth's poetic vocation is achieved at the cost of his martial identity.

'The Sailor's Mother': Southey's and Wordsworth's Warring Dialogues

Southey's and Wordsworth's poetic encounters with 'History' in 1798, in the forms of Clio and the discharged soldier, exemplify the developments

---

[31] Simon Bainbridge, *Napoleon and English Romanticism*, (Cambridge: Cambridge University Press, 1999), 84–5.

[32] 'Wordsworth, Warriors and Naming', *Studies in Romanticism*, 29 (1990), 224–40. See also Willard Spiegelman, *Wordsworth's Heroes* (Berkeley, Los Angeles, and London: California University Press, 1985), 13, and Mary Moorman, *William Wordsworth: A Biography; The Early Years; 1770–1803* (Oxford: Oxford University Press, 1968), 152.

[33] For a reading of 'The Discharged Soldier' in terms of Wordsworth's commitment to the role of poet, see John Williams, *William Wordsworth: A Literary Life* (Basingstoke and London: Macmillan, 1996), 2–7.

[34] As Brennan and McGavran have shown, Wordsworth's revisions to the passage for the 1805 *Prelude* remove many of the more troubling elements of the portrayal of the soldier. Brennan, 'The "ghastly figure"', 20–2; James Holt McGavran, 'Defusing the Discharged Soldier: Wordsworth, Coleridge, and Homosexual Panic', *Papers on Language and Literature*, 32 (1996), 147–65.

of their poetic identities, evolving out of and continuing to inform their treatment of the figures of war. Their different trajectories as poets and their contrasting poetic responses to the war can be traced through their poetic dialogue over the next few years. While Southey reviewed *Lyrical Ballads* for the *Critical Review* in 1798, more revealing of his response to the collection and to Wordsworth's poetry of the late 1790s in general were the many poems he wrote in 1798 and 1799 which directly echo and rewrite Wordsworth's published and unpublished poetry of the period.[35] As Mary Jacobus has argued, these borrowings should not be seen as plagiarism but as 'a deliberate attempt [by Southey] to put right what he had criticized in his review', restoring the Ballads to the context from which they had been taken, replacing what Jacobus terms their new sophistication, oddity, ambitiousness, imagination, universality, and symbolism with topicality, simplicity, and familiarity.[36] Developing Jacobus's argument, I think Southey's rewritings of *Lyrical Ballads* counters what I have been arguing is one of the fundamental manœuvres that characterizes the development of Wordsworthian romanticism, the shift from a polemical humanitarian concern with suffering individuals to a psychological interest in their state of mind. Instead, Southey writes history back into *Lyrical Ballads*.

A good example of Southey's restoration of history to Wordsworth's poetry and his implied criticism of Wordsworth's poetic development is 'The Sailor's Mother', published in *Poems* (1799), which presents an encounter between a traveller and a woman.[37] After an opening exchange in which the traveller seeks to 'cheer up' the weeping woman, the Wordsworthian nature of this meeting is made quickly apparent when the woman says:

> 'Sir I am going
> To see my son at Plymouth, sadly hurt
> In the late action, and in the hospital
> Dying, I fear me, now.'   (207)

This is an obvious allusion to Wordsworth's 'Old Man Travelling, Animal Tranquillity and Decay, A Sketch', published in *Lyrical Ballads*, where the old man responds to the narrator's question with:

---

[35] For a valuable account, see Christopher Smith, 'Robert Southey and the Emergence of *Lyrical Ballads*', *Romanticism on the Net*, 9 (February 1998).

[36] Mary Jacobus, 'Southey's Debt to *Lyrical Ballads* (1798)', *Review of English Studies*, NS 22 (1971), 20–36, 24.

[37] *Poems: The Second Volume* (Bristol: T. N. Longman and O. Rees, 1799), 206–15. References are to page numbers.

'Sir! I am going many miles to take
A last leave of my son, a mariner,
Who from a sea-fight has been brought to Falmouth,
And there is dying in an hospital.'   (ll. 17–20)

Wordsworth's poem famously stops at this point, setting up a discomforting contrast between the narrator's opening vision of the old man and the old man's own words, and prompted Dr Burney to comment in his review of *Lyrical Ballads* for the *Monthly Review* in June 1799 that 'the termination seems pointed against the war'.[38] Wordsworth's omission of the lines after *Lyrical Ballads* (1805) suggests he came to think that he had gone too far in this specific reference;[39] for Southey, he had not gone far enough, as he makes clear in 'The Sailor's Mother'. Southey extends the encounter with the traveller to enable the sailor's mother to give us the full history of her son, recounting his impoverished childhood, his conviction for snaring hares, his choice of 'the prison or the ship', and his blinding by a French 'fire ball' (210–14). As Christopher Smith has commented: 'At the side of *Old Man Travelling*, which draws back from the particularities of horrific detail, Southey's poem reads like an item on the agenda of the Cabinet of War.'[40] Southey does not simply seek to replace the Wordsworthian emphasis on 'state of mind' with a damning critique of what he calls in a note 'our war systems' (208). Rather, he seeks to show how the ideology of 'Old England' and the war systems have shaped the minds of the figures in the poem. For if the traveller espouses a crassly comforting vision of a protective grateful country, the sailor's mother presents a disturbing figure of a woman unable to reconcile a national ideology of glory and sacrifice with the blinding and imminent death of her son, a juxtaposition of the private and public dimensions of war that Southey examined throughout his war poetry. For example, in response to the woman's statement, quoted above, the traveller replies:

Perhaps your fears
Make evil worse. Even if a limb be lost
There may be still enough for comfort left
An arm or leg shot off, there's yet the heart
To keep life warm, and he may live to talk
With pleasure of the glorious fight that maim'd him,
Proud of loss. Old England's gratitude
Makes the maim'd sailor happy.   (207–8)

---

[38] Quoted Roe, *Wordsworth and Coleridge*, 141.
[39] Gill, *William Wordsworth*, 685 n. 29.
[40] 'Robert Southey and *Lyrical Ballads*', 24.

The traveller speaks like the first issue of the *Anti-Jacobin*, intolerant of the Jacobin Poet's emphasis on 'contusions and amputations' and unregarding of the damage of war to a ludicrous extent. Yet the woman's account goes beyond these standard horrors:

> 'Tis not that—
> An arm or leg—I could have borne with that.
> 'Twas not a ball, it was some cursed thing
> That bursts and burns that hurt him.   (208)

This 'cursed thing', identified by a note as 'The stink-pots used on board the French ships', means that 'my poor boy has lost his precious eyes, | Burnt out' (209). While the poem may seem to strike a pro-British note at this point—the woman tells the traveller that the stink pots are not used 'on board our English ships | It is so wicked!' (208)—as Mary Jacobus argues it 'attacks the complacency of a war-mongering society by juxtaposing the natural despair of the sailor's mother with the crass consolations offered her by the traveller'.[41] Such juxtaposition of different responses to war, and especially of a national and public reaction to an individual and private one, was a major technique of Southey's antiwar poetry, seen in the ironies of 'The Battle of Blenheim' and neatly summed up in his notebook sketch for his poem 'The Battle of Bosworth. An Eclogue', where he outlines its design as 'A woman expecting her husband from that fight, and the utter inconsequence to her of that public event'.[42] Indeed, in his poem 'The Victory' Southey adopted one of the formats widely used by anti-war poets in the decade, juxtaposing the celebrations for 'yet another day | Of glory for the ruler of the waves!' with the individual suffering caused by one fatality, figured particularly through the grief of the widow.[43]

'The Sailor's Mother' works not only through this form of juxtaposition, but also through its parody of the figure of the intermediary that constituted one of Wordsworth's major contributions to the poetry of suffering.[44] The *Anti-Jacobin* had, of course, famously parodied Southey's own poetic persona as the 'Friend of Humanity' addressing the 'Needy Knife-grinder'.[45] Southey uses the eclogue form for the same effect,

---

[41] 'Southey's Debt', 29.   [42] *Common Place Book*, IV. 210.

[43] *Poems* (1799), 174. Other examples of this format include Amelia Opie, 'Lines Written at Norwich on the First News of Peace' (*BWP*, 285–8) and 'The Orphan Boy's Tale' (*BWP*, 247–8), Anne Bannerman, 'Verses on an Illumination for a Naval Victory' (Ashfield (ed.), *Romantic Women Poets*, II. 74–7).

[44] See James H. Averill, *Wordsworth and the Poetry of Human Suffering* (Ithaca, NY: Cornell University Press, 1980), *passim*.   [45] *The Anti-Jacobin*, 21–2.

making the traveller, the spokesman for 'Old England', seem just as ludicrous and removed from the realities he encounters as the *Anti-Jacobin* suggested the poet himself was. If Wordsworth develops the figure of the intermediary as part of his shift to a poetry of the mind, Southey frequently uses this figure to dramatize an inadequate response to the suffering he encounters, as in the conclusion of 'The Sailor's Mother' in which the traveller offers the woman easy reassurance:

> Well! Well! take comfort
> He will be taken care of if he lives;
> And should you lose your child, this is a country
> Where the brave sailor never leaves a parent
> To weep for him in want. (214)

But these words of comfort are met by a response that shifts the terms of reference and suggests a gap between the traveller and the sailor's mother as wide as that between the poet and the old man travelling:

> Sir I shall want
> No succour long. In the common course of years
> I soon must be at rest, and 'tis a comfort
> When grief is hard upon me to reflect
> It leads me to that rest the sooner. (214–15)

The poem ends with the mother going to seek not charity or relief but death which, rather than glory or the nation, offers the only comfort that she can find.

Mary Jacobus has acknowledged the polemical force of Southey's rewritten versions of *Lyrical Ballads*, but in arguing that he replaces individuality with the 'acceptable humanitarian commonplaces of the time' I think she fails to register the sustained radicalism of Southey's poetic output in the late 1790s.[46] As the *Anti-Jacobin*'s attacks illustrate, Southey's poetry was anything but 'acceptable', unlike *Lyrical Ballads*, which Jane Stabler has argued was received in 1798 as 'a soundly reactionary volume', even by the *Anti-Jacobin*.[47] If other critics have found it easy to dismiss these works by Southey, I think at least one contemporary reader appreciated the power of Southey's critique of Wordsworth, and this was Wordsworth himself. For in March 1802, the month before

---

[46] 'Southey's Debt', 28.

[47] Jane Stabler, 'Guardians and Watchful Powers: Literary Satire and *Lyrical Ballads* in 1798', in Richard Cronin (ed.), *1798: The Year of the Lyrical Ballads* (Basingstoke and New York: Palgrave, 1998), 217.

Wordsworth began the reconstruction of himself as a public poet through the Miltonic sonnet that will be examined in the next chapter, he wrote his own 'The Sailor's Mother', a text which not only recalls 'Old Man Travelling' but also answers Southey's reworking of it. This poem follows the basic structure of 'Old Man Travelling', with the narrator's description of the sailor's mother followed by her response to his questioning. Her account reads like the next episode in a now familiar story:

> 'I had a Son, who many a day
> Sailed on the seas; but he is dead;
> In Denmark he was cast away;
> And I have been as far as Hull, to see
> What clothes he might have left, or other property.'   (ll. 20–4)

Whereas Southey had maintained the use of the female war victim characteristic of so much anti-war poetry of earlier in the decade, Wordsworth's version reads less like the late *Lyrical Ballad* it is often taken to be[48] and more like an anticipation of the political sonnets he would start writing in the following month. He describes the sailor's mother in the symbolic language that he would shortly use for English republican heroes, for Westminster Bridge and for England herself:

> A Woman in the road I met,
> Not old, though something past her prime:
> Majestic in her person, tall and straight;
> And like a Roman matron's was her mien and gait.
>
> The ancient Spirit is not dead;
> Old times, thought I, are breathing there;
> Proud was I that my country bred
> Such strength, a dignity so fair: (ll. 3–10)

Here the sailor's mother fulfils exactly the function that the 'good old cause' of English republicanism will serve in the sonnets, as is illustrated by Philip Martin's description of her: 'The sailor's mother steps out of the past, and is used by the narrator as an anachronism, a means by which past glories are evoked and present decadence or degeneration is implied.'[49] Unlike 'Old Man Travelling', here the narrator's impression of the sailor's mother is reinforced by her own account, her possession of her son's song bird reading like an act of memorialization that maintains

---

[48] Johnston, *The Hidden Wordsworth*, 556.
[49] Philip Martin, *Mad Women in Romantic Writing* (Brighton and New York: Harvester Press and St Martin's Press, 1987), 76.

his spirit and even suggests itself as a symbol for the transmutation of war's casualties into song. Refiguring the sailor's mother for the period of the invasion threat, Wordsworth rededicates himself (not uncritically) to his country and to his sense of historical vision, both of which underpin his developing poetic identity. And he does so by reappropriating and rewriting the text by Southey that had attacked his shift away from this poetic model. Moreover, only a few months after he had again been working on *The Prelude*, 'The Sailor's Mother' reads like his version of Southey's 'Was it for this . . .?' poem—in place of the majestic figure of Clio, he offers the sailor's mother, 'majestic in her person', who reawakens his sense of the 'ancient Spirit' and embodies the 'old times' of History.

If the retreat from History figured in the opening of Southey's poem has normally been seen as the major narrative of the formation of canonical romanticism, I have tried to show how Southey offers an important alternative model and to suggest how the rest of the poem's structure with its reassertion of History is played out in Wordsworth's poetic career. But 'History' and *The Prelude* also illustrate another crucial element of these writers' response to historical and vocational crisis during the war, the redefinition of poetry as a manly pursuit after its increasing feminization in the closing decades of the eighteenth century. The phrase 'Was it for this . . .?' reveals both poems to be driven by a vocational crisis that is also a crisis of masculinity. As correspondence on *The Prelude* in the *TLS* initiated by Jonathan Wordsworth has established, the rhetorical device, though with classical precedents, was available from Milton's *Samson Agonistes* where, on beholding his son at the climax of his troubles, Manoa exclaims.

> For this did the angel twice descend? For this
> Ordained thy nurture holy, as of a plant.[50]

These lines, possibly filtered through Thomson, Shenstone, and Pope, could be drawn on by the two poets, Samson's failure to fulfil his divine mission being rewritten in terms of the crises of their own poetic missions. Moreover, as Howard Erskine-Hill has shown, one source for the phrase is Ariosto's *Orlando Furioso*, a favourite of both Southey and Wordsworth, in which the good sorceress Melissa rebukes Ruggiero for having become an unmanly figure like the beautiful youth Adonis or the self-castrated Atys, rather than a heroic conqueror like Alexander, Caesar, or Scipio. In John Harrington's rendering of 1591, the passage begins as follows:

---

[50] John Woolford, '*The Prelude* and its echoes' *TLS*, 6 June 1975, 627.

> Was it for this, that I in youth thee fed,
> With marrow of the beares and lyons fell?
> That I through caves and deserts have thee led . . . [51]

As Erskine-Hill points out, the prominent place given to heroic story in *The Prelude*'s extended preamble suggests that Wordsworth had this passage in mind. Similarly, Southey's Muse Clio particularly resembles the sorceress Melissa. In their use of the phrase 'Was it for this . . .?' in 'History' and *The Prelude*, the two poets draw a parallel between themselves and Ruggiero confronted with a choice between these representative roles. And both poets respond to the suggestions of their failures to fulfil their ordained mission and the highest masculine role by presenting their poetic identities as heroic and manly, defined through a choice of worthy subject matter, a narrative of growth into manhood, and a fitting audience. Wordsworth seeks to be spurred on 'to honourable toil' (I. 452–3), while Southey defines his historical verse against the poesy produced in the feminized space of the myrtle bower. Like Wordsworth, who presents himself as 'in manhood now mature' (I. 452), Southey's growth from boyhood to manhood will be completed with the assumption of the role for which he has been chosen. And if Wordsworth changes his ideal reader from Dorothy in his early verse to Coleridge in *The Prelude* (II. 1), Southey in 'History' resists the temptation to write feminized poesy for a female audience—'strains so sorrowful sweet | That love-sick maids may weep upon thy page' (ll. 18–19)—aiming instead to produce poetry worthy of a readership of the great men of 'History':

> . . . let that spirit fill
> Thy song, and it shall teach thee, boy! to raise
> Strains such as CATO had not scorn'd to hear,
> As SIDNEY in his hall of fame may love. (ll. 28–31)

If Southey's 'History' questions major elements of what we now think of as canonical or high romanticism, nevertheless it contributes to one of the most sustained cultural constructions of the period, that of the Poet as 'a man speaking to men', a construction that I will examine in the context of the war in the next chapter.[52]

---

[51] Howard Erskine-Hill, '*The Prelude* and its echoes', *TLS*, 26 September, 1975, 1094. Curry, *Robert Southey*, 6; Moorman, *William Wordsworth: The Early Years*, 100.

[52] Gill, *William Wordsworth*, 603.

CHAPTER FOUR

'Men are We': Poetry, War, and Gender in Wordsworth's Political Sonnets, 1802–1803

Beating 'the Sprightly Drum': Poetry and the Invasion Crisis

IN AN OTHERWISE critical assessment of Wordsworth's *Poems, in Two Volumes* (1807), the anonymous reviewer of the *Annual Review* made an exception of the poet's efforts in a particular genre: 'The Sonnets, a portion of which are dedicated to liberty, are formed on the model of Milton's and have a certain stiffness—but they hold a severe and manly tone which cannot be in times like these too much listened to—they bear strong traces of feeling and of thought, and convince us that on worthy subjects this man can write worthily.'[1] The reviewer's comment emphasizes the interrelation of the three issues that I will be examining in this chapter: poetry, war, and gender. Wordsworth's political sonnets of 1802–3, on which I will be focusing, were part of the huge outpouring of verse produced to unite, inspire, and animate the nation during the invasion scares of 1797–8 and 1802–5, the period that has been named 'the Great Terror' when 'invasion was the all absorbing and all pervading topic of correspondence and conversation' (W & B, I. p. xii).[2] This vast body of verse, some of which has been collected in the two valuable anthologies *The Warning Drum* and *Napoleon and the Invasion of England*, played an important role in the wartime forging of the British

---

[1] *RR*, I. 19.

[2] For an excellent overall account of the patriotic propaganda of the invasion crisis, see Stella Cottrell, 'The Devil on Two Sticks: Franco-Phobia in 1803', in Raphael Samuel (ed.), *Patriotism: The Making and Unmaking of British National Identity, vol. I: History and Politics*, History Workshop Journal (London and New York: Routledge, 1989), 259–74. See also *WD* and W & B. For a general account of the invasion crisis, see Norman Longmate, *Island Fortress: The Defence of Great Britain 1603–1945* (London: Hutchinson, 1991).

nation, both mediating the war to the British public and providing a means of patriotic expression, a textual equivalent to the volunteering that has been described as 'simply the greatest popular movement of the Hanoverian age'.[3] The volunteer movement saw the formation of up to 2,000 volunteer corps with 400,000 members training to repel the French forces of as many as 140,000 men encamped along the north coast of France.[4] In these years, poetry called the nation to arms and shaped the understanding of the war through the standard tropes of patriotic verse,[5] promising glory and immortality in return for fighting and dying for the country,[6] celebrating national characteristics (landscape, riches, culture, political system, history, women),[7] embodying Britain's natural blessings in its island geography,[8] stressing Britain's destiny and its divinely sanctioned global role,[9] recalling the triumphs of the past and the debt to those who created and defended the country and passed it on to the present generation,[10] emphasizing that the nation is held in trust for future generations,[11] and defining the nation and national identity through opposition to the demonized, dehumanized, and vilified 'Other', France.[12]

---

[3] J. E. Cookson, *The British Armed Nation, 1793–1815* (Oxford: Clarendon Press, 1997), 66.

[4] For accounts of the volunteer movement, see Cookson, *The British Armed Nation*, *passim*, and Linda Colley, *Britons: Forging the Nation 1707–1837* (London: Vintage, 1996), 251–337.

[5] For a valuable overall account of patriotic poetry, which I have drawn on here, see Margaret Canovan, ' "Breathes there the Man, with Soul so Dead . . .": Reflections on Patriotic Poetry and Liberal Principles', in John Horton and Andrea T. Baumeister (eds.), *Literature and the Political Imagination* (London and New York: Routledge, 1996), 170–97. For an idea of the extent to which these poems are calls to arms, see *GM*, 73 (October 1803) 952–55, in which five poems use the phrase 'To arms' or variants of it ('Liberty and Loyalty', 'Unite and Conquer', 'The Spirit of Albion', 'Address of Britannia to her Sons', 'Song. The Volunteer').

[6] e.g. 'Song. The Volunteer': 'Oh! 'tis a gallant thing to die | Preserving all we value here' (*GM*, 73 (October 1803), 954).

[7] e.g. 'The Challenge, A New Song': 'Britannia, though a small land, | Possesses wond'rous wealth' (*GM*, 73 (November 1803), 1058).

[8] e.g. 'Liberty and Loyalty': 'Long, in Freedom's garb array'd, | Has Britain flourish'd great and free' (*GM*, 73 (October 1803), 952).

[9] e.g. George Colman's 'Epilogue' to *The Maid of Bristol*: ''Tis theirs, at length, to fight the world's great cause, | Defend their own, and rescue others' laws' (W & B, II. 261).

[10] e.g. 'Britons' Defiance of France': 'Oh! call to mind the gallant deeds | Your noble Sires have done, | And may the Spirit of the Sires | Descend upon the Son!' (*WD*, 66).

[11] e.g. Thomas Campbell, 'Stanzas on the Threatened Invasion, 1803': ' 'Tis the home we hold sacred is laid to our trust', *Complete Poetical Works*, ed. J. Logie Robertson (London, New York, and Toronto: Oxford University Press, 1907), 200.

[12] e.g. 'Britons Defiance of France': 'A bastard Briton he must be, | His heart contain no oak, | Whose base-born mind could tamely bend | To bear the Gallic yoke' (*WD*, 66).

As the *Annual Review*'s comments on Wordsworth suggest, if poetry shaped understandings of the war in these years, the war in turn shaped poetry, limiting the kinds of writing that could be produced in such an atmosphere of national crisis. One correspondent to the *Gentleman's Magazine* in December 1803 noted that 'the poetical department of your last is almost filled with loyal and patriotic poetry', while a poem of 1805 entitled '*War! War! A Poetical Address to the British Nation*' argued that '[i]n poetry or prose the universal object of patriotic Britons is, to pursue and expose the Invader of the rights of human kind.'[13] The recruitment of poetry to the war against France called into question its wider uses and was frequently accompanied by calls for its reconfiguration, especially along more manly lines, as in the replacement of the 'harp and lyre' by 'the sprightly drum' in 'The British Heroes' (*BWP*, 335). Such calls for more manly poetry echoed the wider cultural invocations of manliness in the writings of the invasion crisis, which instructed readers to 'Awake, . . . be roused, *and shew yourselves* MEN' (*WD*, 181) and to manifest 'a firm Appearance of the same manly Vigour in Defence of every Thing dear to ENGLISHMEN, which purchased with so much Blood, your envied LIBERTY and glorious CONSTITUTION, and which can emanate only from the Spirit of BRITONS!' (*WD*, 114).[14] The war with France not only hardened this construction of British masculinity, but facilitated the claiming of the manly role even by those whose manliness was normally in question, as in 'A New Song, On the Renewed Threat of Invasion' in which 'ev'n' the very *Tailor* | Fight like a *man* for GEORGE' (*BWP*, 326). Here the often effeminized figure of the tailor is able to redefine his gendered identity through fighting. In reverse fashion, to fail to fight Napoleon would be to lose this national manly identity and to become effeminate, as seen in another broadside which argued that a successful French invasion would be proof 'that the | BRITISH LION | is become as docile as a LADY'S LAP-DOG' (*WD*, 175). Manly duty was normally presented in terms of protecting women and the home, as one MP commented: 'The beauty—the goodness—the very helplessness of the sex are so many claims on our support, are so many sacred calls on the assistance of every manly and courageous arm.'[15] But there was also considerable anxiety in the period that domestic ties would lead to the weakening of the nation's manly identity, leaving it vulnerable to French attack. One broadsheet, 'Old

---

[13] *GM*, 73 (December 1803), 1161; *GM*, 75 (February 1805), 145.
[14] For a broader discussion of the construction of British manliness, particularly in relation to French effeminacy, see Colley, *Britons*, 265.
[15] Ibid. 280.

England to Her Daughters. Address to the Females of Great Britain', warns women against the danger that their fears may 'unman' the men of the nation, advising 'Now behave better! or if you will fear, fear to perplex the Men with silly Questions, and an ill-timed Softness!' (WD, 77). At such a moment of national crisis, feminine softness becomes inappropriate for women as well as for men.[16] Hannah More's call to women in Strictures on the Modern System of Female Education of 1799 'to come forward with a patriotism at once firm and feminine for the general good' shows an attempt to balance the conventional constructions of women's roles with the necessary wartime identity in a period when, as Colley has argued, while women were 'being urged to look, feel and behave in ways that were unambiguously womanly, many female Britons were in practice becoming more involved in the public sphere than ever before, not least in terms of patriotic activism'.[17] As Colley describes, women's influence was often felt in what Windham in 1804 termed 'promoting the military spirit', undertaking activities such as providing clothing for soldiers, organizing collections of money and garments, making flags and banners to be presented publicly to volunteer corps, and instigating subscriptions (all of which were celebrated in poetry), but according to one correspondent women also engaged in target practice in readiness for a French invasion.[18] Lord Auckland saw the militarization of the nation as involving not only all classes of men but also women, commenting in 1803 that 'You never saw so military a country, nothing but fighting is talked of. From the highest to the lowest the zeal is wonderful, and I am convinced that, should an invasion be tried, you would see all the ladies letting their nails grow that they might scratch at the invader.'[19] While Auckland defines women's entrance into the violent world of war through an extension of one of their natural features, their nails, rather than through the taking up of arms, his comment emphasizes that the need to fight the French not only changes the character of the nation but leads to a reconception of gender roles.

In this chapter I want to look in detail at one example of the poetic construction of the manly nation and its links to the remasculinization of poetry, Wordsworth's political sonnets. In doing so, I will investigate

[16] For a general discussion of women's activities during the invasion crisis, see ibid. 263–76.

[17] Selected Writings of Hannah More, ed. Robert Hole (London: William Pickering, 1996), 126; Colley, Britons, 267–8.   [18] Colley, Britons, 267–8.

[19] Quoted in Arthur Bryant, Years of Victory, 1802–1812 (London: Collins, 1975), 64.

Wordsworth's fashioning of a virile poetic role for himself and argue that he creates a manly reading position open to women as well as men as he seeks to unite the poetic nation in the war against France and Napoleon. As the comments of the *Annual Review* with which I began illustrate, Wordsworth's sonnets provide a valuable focus for examining the interrelation between poetry, the war, and gender in the period of the invasion crisis. Its response to his *Poems, in Two Volumes* was typical; many reviewers thought the sonnets dedicated to liberty, sometimes linked with the 'Lines on the Character of the Happy Warrior', the only redeeming feature in a collection marred by a choice of low subject matter, a lack of taste, and an increasing egotism. Their ambivalent evaluations of the volume were often expressed in gendered terms, defining the 'manly' sonnets against the 'immature', 'feminine', and 'effeminate' verse of the rest of the collection.[20] The *Annual* reviewer's comments suggest a number of reasons for the widespread praise of the sonnets, linking what is identified as a manly mode of writing, characterized by its stiffness, severity, and strength and authorized by association with Milton, with a choice of 'worthy subject' matter at a time of national crisis—the ongoing war with France. Recognizing with approval Wordsworth's remasculinization of the sonnet form and his reclamation of poetry as a manly, even heroic, pursuit in the sequence, the review articulates through its phallocentric language the pressures poetic and national identities are subjected to during periods of national emergency.[21] The poet and reader themselves become worthy through their ability to produce and prove receptive to 'a severe and manly tone'.

---

[20] For the volume as 'immature', see references to it as 'childish' (*RR*, I. 40, 42, 262; II. 429, 438), 'puerile' (*RR*, I, 41, 42, 136, 261; II. 662), 'babyish' (*RR*, II. 432), the work of an 'unpractised schoolboy', and as unfit for 'any reader or auditor out of the nursery' (*RR*, II. 662). For descriptions of the volume as 'feminine' see references to it as 'pretty' (*RR*, I. 18; II. 432), 'gossip' and 'gossiping' (*RR*, I. 20; II. 846). *Le Beau Monde* combined the accusations of femininity and childishness by placing the collection in the context of *Lyrical Ballads* in which 'Mr. Wordsworth . . . gave considerable testimony of strong feeling and poetic powers, although like a histerical schoolgirl he had a knack of feeling about subjects with which feeling had no proper concern' (*RR*, I. 40). For the volume as 'effeminate', see descriptions of it as 'namby-pamby' (*RR*, I. 136; II. 432, 662).

[21] In his review for *Monthly Literary Recreations*, Byron wrote that many of the poems were 'totally devoid of the tinsel embellishments and abstract hyperboles of several cotemporary [sic] sonneteers' and hoped that the sentiments of 'November, 1806' were 'common to every Briton at the present crisis' (*RR*, II. 661).

Wordsworth and the 'Manly' Sonnet

Any argument for Wordsworth's regendering of poetry as manly may seem to be immediately undermined by the critical response to the 1807 volume. As Judith W. Page has commented, in his review of the collection for the *Edinburgh Review* 'Francis Jeffrey implies that Wordsworth has feminized poetry'.[22] But, like the reviewers, Wordsworth had a varied and hierarchical conception of his own poetic output. In the suppressed 'Advertisement' to the 1807 volume, he describes the majority of the poems as 'chiefly composed to refresh my mind during the progress of a work of length and labour . . . and to furnish me with employment when I had not resolution to apply myself to that work'.[23] If these works were private, occasional, and subsidiary to *The Recluse*, the political sonnets were public verse, published in the *Morning Post* and addressed to the country during the increasingly uneasy Peace of Amiens of 1802–3 and the invasion threat of late 1803. In his epistolary defence of the 1807 volume to Lady Beaumont, Wordsworth made the grand claim that 'these Sonnets, while they each fix the attention upon some important sentiment separately considered, do at the same time collectively make up a Poem on the subject of civil Liberty and national independence, which, either for simplicity of style or grandeur of moral sentiment is, alas! likely to have few parallels in the Poetry of the present day'.[24] Similarly, when the *Morning Post* published several of the sonnets on 29 January 1803, an editorial paragraph by Daniel Stuart accorded them a generic standing beyond their formal status as sonnets. It ran: 'We have been favoured with a dozen Sonnets of a Political nature, which are not only written by one of the first Poets of the age, but are among his best productions. Each forms a little Political Essay, on some recent proceedings.'[25]

While Wordsworth's and Stuart's comments reveal that the political sonnets stood out from the rest of the 1807 volume because they represent Wordsworth's claiming of a particular role at a particular time, they also

---

[22] Judith W. Page, *Wordsworth and the Cultivation of Women* (Berkeley, Los Angeles, and London: University of California Press, 1994), 38.

[23] *Wordsworth's Poems of 1807*, ed. Alun R. Jones (Basingstoke and London: Macmillan, 1987), 145.

[24] *The Letters of William and Dorothy Wordsworth: The Middle Years, 1806–11*, ed. by Ernest de Selincourt, 2nd edn., revised Mary Moorman (Oxford: Clarendon Press, 1969), 147.

[25] Quoted in Mary Moorman, *William Wordsworth: A Biography; The Early Years; 1770–1803* (Oxford: Oxford University Press, 1957; repr. 1968), 571.

suggest that the choice of subject matter leads the sonnets to exceed the expectations associated with the genre to which they belong. Indeed, the language of Wordsworth's claim illustrates his transformation of genre. Charlotte Smith, the most famous figure in the sonnet revival of the later decades of the eighteenth century, defined the form in the 'Preface' to her collection *Elegiac Sonnets*, as 'no improper vehicle for a single Sentiment'.[26] Wordsworth suggests that his sonnets conform to this model, fixing 'the attention upon some important sentiment separately considered', but that they also transcend it, making up 'a Poem on the subject of civil Liberty and national independence'. This phrase not only suggests a work of epic scale and subject but recalls his listing of potential grand subjects in the opening of his own autobiographical epic *The Prelude*, which includes the spirit 'Of independence and stern liberty' (1805, I. 219). In his letter to Lady Beaumont, then, Wordsworth places his sonnets in the context of his more ambitious, epic, and public projects rather than in that of his personal, occasional, and private poetry.

These issues of genre, subject matter, and audience were central to Wordsworth's turn to the sonnet in May 1802 and his subsequent transformation of it. At this period Wordsworth was experiencing a sense of crisis over his poetic vocation and the status of poetry in general, heightened by his sense of increasing responsibility arising from his impending marriage. In 1798 he had committed himself to the role of 'Poet' and in the following year had hoped that the reproachful self-probings of the early drafts of *The Prelude* would 'spur [him] on, in manhood now mature, | To honourable toil' (1799, I. 452–3). Yet, by 1802, having still failed to produce the honourable self-justifying philosophical work he had promised both Coleridge and himself, Wordsworth's desired manly poetic identity was threatened by intersecting developments in the gendered constructions of poetry. The closing decades of the eighteenth century had witnessed the increasing feminization of poetry as it became characterized as a pursuit most suitable for women, heightening one popular construction of the male writer as effeminate.[27] The war had led

---

[26] *The Poems of Charlotte Smith*, ed. Stuart Curran (New York and Oxford: Oxford University Press, 1993), 3.

[27] On the feminization of poetry, culture, and the reading public, see Marlon B. Ross, *The Contours of Masculine Desire: Romanticism and the Rise of Women's Poetry* (New York: Oxford University Press, 1989), *passim* and Judith W. Page, *Wordsworth and the Cultivation of Women*, (Berkeley, Los Angeles, and London: University of California Press, 1994), 29–53. On the male poet as 'effeminate', see G. J. Barker-Benfield, *The Culture of Sensibility: Sex and Society in Eighteenth-Century Britain* (Chicago and London: University of Chicago Press, 1992), 104–5.

to the increasing remasculinization of both English national identity, defined in opposition to the feminine or effeminate French,[28] and poetry, which had been recruited to, but also increasingly limited by, the fight against France. The sense of national emergency caused by fear of invasion also further threatened to undermine and emasculate poetry, giving a new urgency to the 'arms versus letters' debates of the seventeenth and eighteenth centuries.[29] If poetry needed to be allied to volunteering, as one correspondent to the *Gentleman's Magazine* suggested,[30] what claims could be made for its status or that of the poet in wartime? Writing within this context, in his political sonnets Wordsworth seeks to legitimize poetry at a time of war and to validate it as a pursuit worthy of a reconstructed masculinity—a 'manhood now mature'—for both reader and writer.

Contemporary and modern critics have seen Wordsworth's adoption of the model of Milton as central to his reconstruction of his poetic identity in his sonnets[31]—an argument strongly supported by reference to Wordsworth's own writings and that of his sister Dorothy. Dorothy, in her journal for 21 May 1802, reports that 'William wrote two sonnets on Buonaparte after I had read Milton's sonnets to him'.[32] Writing in 1843, over four decades after the event, William gave a fuller if rather different account:

In the cottage of Town End, one afternoon in 1801 [May 1802], my sister read to me the Sonnets of Milton. I had long been well acquainted with them, but I was particularly struck on that occasion by the dignified simplicity and majestic harmony that runs through most of them,—in character so totally different from the Italian, and still more so from Shakespeare's fine Sonnets. I took fire, if I may be allowed to say so, and produced three Sonnets the same afternoon, the first I ever wrote except an irregular one at school. Of these three, the only one I distinctly remember is 'I grieved for Buonaparté'.[33]

---

[28] See Colley, *Britons*, 251–337, and Michèle Cohen, *Fashioning Masculinity: National Identity and Language in the Eighteenth Century* (London and New York: Routledge, 1996), *passim*.

[29] Barker-Benfield, *The Culture of Sensibility*, 114.

[30] On the links between volunteering and writing poetry as forms of patriotic expression, see *GM*, 73 (December 1803), 1161 where W. B. prefaces his poem addressed to the 'Men of Kent' with the comment 'I am ... desirous, through the medium of your respectable publication, to evince my principles and sentiment; which I have already done in the place of my residence by entering a troop of cavalry.'

[31] e.g. Stuart Curran, *Poetic Form and British Romanticism* (Oxford and New York: Oxford University Press, 1989), 41.

[32] *The Journals of Dorothy Wordsworth*, ed. Mary Moorman, 2nd edn (New York and Oxford: Oxford University Press, 1976), 127.

[33] Fenwick note, in *The Poetical Works of William Wordsworth*, ed. E. de Selincourt and Helen Darbishire, 5 vols. (Oxford: Clarendon Press, 1940–9), III. 417.

Noticeably distinguishing the work of his model from that of the sonnet writers of the romantic tradition, William's recollections give Milton the position of an inspiring force, his 'dignified simplicity and majestic harmony' causing William to take 'fire'. Importantly, looking back over forty years, Wordsworth is keen to mark this out as his first real attempt at the sonnet form; his slightly embarrassed dismissal of his composition of 'an irregular one at school' glosses over the fact that he had in fact written several sonnets before his day of Miltonic inspiration—a suppression that I will return to.

The implication of Wordsworth's adoption of the model of Milton's sonnets seems clear: to write like Milton is to write like a man. As the reviews of the 1807 volume reveal, the Miltonic sonnet on worthy public subjects was gendered masculine; a manliness all the more necessary at a time of national emergency. Wordsworth participated in this gendering of the form, describing Milton's sonnets as 'manly and dignified compositions' in a letter of November 1802.[34] Yet Wordsworth's achievement of the manly Miltonic role, if indeed it is ever realized, is neither as instantaneous nor as straightforward as his account suggests. Wordsworth has to construct his poetic manliness and he does so by negotiating between different models of sonnet and their associations; defining himself, poetry, and the nation against the feminine, the childish, and the effeminate.

Wordsworth, Gray's Sonnet, and Effeminacy

Despite Wordsworth's later claim that the three sonnets he produced on the afternoon of 21 May 1802 were 'the first I ever wrote except an irregular one at school', his first published poem had in fact been a Shakespearian sonnet printed in March 1787 in the *European Magazine*. Entitled 'Sonnet, on seeing Miss Helen Maria Williams weep at a Tale of Distress', the poem is, as Janet Todd has argued, typical of the magazine verse of the 1780s and 1790s and of the feminized sonnet of sensibility, emphasizing the poet's capacity to feel and weep in response to Williams's imagined tears.[35] Wordsworth's later suppression of this sonnet and of several like it indicates his increasing concern over the

---

[34] *The Letters of William and Dorothy Wordsworth: The Early Years 1787–1805*, ed. E. de Selincourt; 2nd edn revised Chester L. Shaver (Oxford: Clarendon Press, 1967), 379.

[35] Janet Todd, *Sensibility: An Introduction* (London and New York: Methuen, 1986), 62–3.

feminization of poetry. His 1843 account, while offering a powerful emblematic scene of inspiration and composition as the trumpet of the Miltonic sonnet is handed down from poetic father to poetic son, glosses over his own early engagement with other versions of the form and fails to acknowledge the numerous sonnet writers of the closing decades of the eighteenth century when the form became particularly associated with women writers such as Charlotte Smith and Helen Maria Williams, whose works were well known to Wordsworth.[36] Wordsworth had himself subscribed to the fifth edition of Smith's *Elegiac Sonnets* of 1789[37] and ironically, given his failure to acknowledge her influence over his own sonnets in the account of 1843, he described Smith in 1835 as 'a lady to whom English verse is under greater obligations than are likely to be either acknowledged or remembered'.[38]

A number of critics have argued that Wordsworth can be seen to react to the rise of women writers and the feminization of poetry by reasserting his own masculine self-conception. For example, Roger Lonsdale has argued that Wordsworth's formulations of the poet in the 'Preface' to *Lyrical Ballads* as one who writes in a 'manly' style, who uses the 'real language of men', and who is a 'man speaking to men' can be seen as an attempt to recover poetry from the woman writer and woman reader who, it appeared, had come to dominate it.[39] His argument offers one way of reading Wordsworth's adoption of the Miltonic sonnet; as an assertion of the 'manly' and a suppression of the feminine in poetry, a reading offered by a number of critics and supported by Wordsworth's later comments.[40] But such a reading establishes too rigid a set of binary

[36] For the sonnet as 'a genre which could be seen as directly related to the productions of women poets and also implicitly feminised as regards its salient generic features', see Philip Cox, *Gender, Genre and the Romantic Poets* (Manchester and New York: Manchester University Press, 1996), 42–50. See also Daniel Robinson, 'Reviving the Sonnet: Women Romantic Poets and the Sonnet Claim', *European Romantic Review*, 6 (1995), 98–127; Page, *Wordsworth and the Cultivation of Women*, 55; and Andrew Ashfield (ed.), *Romantic Women Poets, 1770–1838* (Manchester: Manchester University Press, 1995), p. xiv. For an excellent discussion of Wordsworth and the feminized sonnet, to which I am indebted, see Ramona Marie Ralston, 'Wordsworth and the Feminized Sonnet: A Suppression of Eighteenth-Century Poetic Influences', Ph.D. thesis (University of Southern California, 1987), 108–95.   [37] Cox, *Gender, Genre*, 46.

[38] De Selincourt and Darbishire (eds.), *Poetical Works*, IV. 403.

[39] *Eighteenth-Century Women Poets: An Oxford Anthology* (Oxford and New York: Oxford University Press, 1990), pp. xl–xli.

[40] See Cox, *Gender, Genre*, 50; Page, *Wordsworth and the Cultivation of Women*, 7 and 40; Jennifer Ann Wagner, *A Moment's Monument: Revisionary Poetics and the Nineteenth-Century English Sonnet* (Madison, Teaneck, and London: Fairleigh Dickinson University Press and Associated University Presses, 1996), 13, 17, 27, 43.

oppositions between sonnet traditions and gender categories and fails to acknowledge Wordsworth's more complex engagement with different versions of the form, an engagement that both calls into question and redefines the manly while also reasserting it as an authorizing category. It also simplifies the ways in which manliness is constructed both in the discourse of gender in the period and in the sonnets themselves. Significantly, the sonnet that Wordsworth uses to illustrate his argument in the 'Preface' is Thomas Gray's 'Sonnet on the Death of Richard West' rather than one by a woman writer.[41] The basis of Wordsworth's attack has proved something of a puzzle for critics; as Peter Manning has commented, '[g]enerations of readers have sensed that the issue of poetic diction to which Wordsworth confines the discussion does not adequately explain the handling of the poem.'[42] He argues that Wordsworth's 'cryptic' discussion of Gray's poem suggests 'a shift in the poetic decorum of bereavement'[43] and I will be developing this to argue that, for Wordsworth, Gray's sonnet comes to represent a particular kind of sensibility, an expression of isolated and static grief that becomes invalid at a time of national crisis. Yet, as Manning has also pointed out, drawing on Roger Lonsdale's analysis of the sonnet's use of the conventions of Italian Renaissance love poetry in which the lover mourns the loss of the beloved, the 'adaptation of heterosexual conventions for a lament over a friend is striking'.[44] Extending this reading of the poem, Linda Zionkowski has analysed the 'homoerotic resonances' of Gray's poem within the context of the poet's contemporary reputation for 'effeminacy', noting that the sonnet's private nature meant Gray never published it during his own lifetime.[45]

Zionkowski's work on the contemporary construction of Gray as effeminate suggests that Wordsworth may have chosen his sonnet as an example of 'unmanly' poetry against which he could define his own. Indeed, Manning's argument for a 'shift in the poetic decorum of bereavement' from Gray to Wordsworth can be developed in terms of contemporary constructions of gender. His argument that Wordsworth attacked Gray's sonnet because its mourning is 'fruitless' and static, lacking 'the

---

[41] *The Prose Works of William Wordsworth*, ed. W. J. B. Owen and Jane Worthington Smyser, 3 vols. (Oxford: Clarendon Press, 1974), I. 133–5. Hereafter references are cited within the text.

[42] Peter J. Manning, 'Wordsworth and Gray's Sonnet on the Death of West', *SEL*, 22 (1982), 506.   [43] Ibid. 507.   [44] Ibid. 515.

[45] Linda Zionkowski, 'Gray, the Marketplace, and the Masculine Poet', *Criticism*, 35 (fall 1993), 589–608.

strength to begin life anew', can be linked to Hazlitt's definition of effeminacy in his essay 'On Effeminacy of Character' of 1821.[46] Hazlitt opens this essay by arguing that 'Effeminacy of character arises from a prevalence of the sensibility over the will: or it consists in a want of fortitude to bear pain or to undergo fatigue, however urgent the occasion'.[47] In similar terms, Manning argues that Wordsworth criticizes the speaker of Gray's poem for being the victim of an overly refined sensibility: 'Gray's grief feeds on itself and perpetuates its own condition.'[48] By contrast, Wordsworth's poetry looks to move forward from grief, as the conclusion of his famous 'Ode' ('There was a time . . .') declares: 'We will grieve not, rather find | Strength in what remains behind,' (ll. 182–3). As Hazlitt's essay illustrates, effeminacy in the period was conceived as a matter of style as well as subject; he echoes the language of Wordsworth's 'Preface' when he describes 'effeminacy of style' as 'one that is all florid, all fine; that cloys by its sweetness, and tires by its sameness'.[49] As an example of 'effeminacy of style' he cites the Della Cruscan school, the grouping of poets who have often been taken to be Wordsworth's target in his attack on 'the gaudiness and inane phraseology of many modern writers'.[50] Though Wordsworth's attack on Gray in the 1800 'Preface' as 'more than any other man curiously elaborate in the structure of his own poetic diction' (132) does not explicitly formulate his argument in gendered terms, one of the additions of 1802 does develop the argument in this way. The 1802 additions, written the year Wordsworth begins the sonnets, emphasize the manliness of the poet, especially in the 'What is a Poet?' section, which introduces the formula 'He is a man speaking to men' (138) and makes the link between the poet and the 'Man of science' (140), emphasizing the vocational nature of the poetic role. In one passage of this section, Wordsworth develops the argument of 1800 on language which he had initially illustrated with Gray's sonnet. Positioning himself against those who see the poet as a 'translator who does not scruple to substitute excellencies of another kind [language] for those which are unattainable by him [passion]', he argues that such a process will 'encourage idleness and unmanly despair' (139). This rather

[46] Manning, 'Wordsworth and Gray's Sonnet', 509.
[47] *The Complete Works of William Hazlitt*, ed. P. P. Howe, 21 vols. (London and Toronto: J. M. Dent and Sons, 1930–4), VIII. 248.
[48] Manning, 'Wordsworth and Gray's Sonnet', 508.
[49] Hazlitt, *Complete Works*, VIII. 254.
[50] e.g. *Wordsworth and Coleridge, Lyrical Ballads 1805*, ed. Derek Roper (Plymouth: MacDonald and Evans, 1968; 2nd edn., 1982), 272, 280.

obscure phrase becomes clearer if it is read in the context of Wordsworth's and others' critiques of Gray. In attacking 'idleness', Wordsworth reproduces Johnson's criticisms of Gray for his failure to produce poetry, one element of the emphasis in his 'Life' on the poet's effeminacy and lack of maturity and manliness.[51] Wordsworth's phrase 'unmanly despair' recalls the Gray sonnet and links a critique of its content, static grieving, with one of its style, the failure to fit language to passion. The 'unmanly' figure of Gray again functions to exemplify the weakness of modern poetry.

If Wordsworth's critique of poetic diction in the 'Preface' can be read as an attack on the effeminacy of modern poetry, a fuller examination of effeminacy and of Wordsworth's construction of Gray (itself an act of 'self-definition')[52] will help develop our understanding of Wordsworth's wartime construction of his own gendered role as poet. 'Effeminacy' is a complex and elusive term, much discussed by recent scholars of the eighteenth century who have linked it variously with homosexuality, sodomy, and femininity.[53] In a very useful analysis of the term in *Fashioning Masculinity: National Identity and Language in the Eighteenth Century*, Michèle Cohen argues that part of its meaning in the eighteenth century was the 'admission of the qualities of a woman, softness, unmanly delicacy' as well as implying the effect that women or the feminine could have on men.[54] A word with national as well as personal resonances, 'effeminacy' is perhaps most usefully seen as a word which could be used to call into question the 'manliness' of society or the individual, as in Kathleen Wilson's definition of it as denoting 'a degenerate moral, political and social state that opposed and subverted the vaunted "manly" characteristics—courage, aggression, martial valor, discipline and strength—that constituted patriotic virtue'.[55] Drawing on the work of Peter Fletcher, Cohen argues that effeminacy, rather than femininity or homosexuality, was the defining otherness for manliness in the eighteenth century.[56] This delineation, she argues, was interwoven with ideas about language; the manly English language was defined not only against the French of both sexes but against the English spoken by women and effeminate men. Cohen's work provides a useful context for thinking

[51] Zionkowski, 'Gray, the Marketplace, and the Masculine Poet', 606 n. 15.
[52] Manning, 'Wordsworth and Gray's Sonnet', 505.
[53] Cohen, *Fashioning Masculinity*, 4–6.   [54] Ibid. 7.
[55] *The Sense of the People: Politics, Culture and Imperialism in England, 1715–1785* (Cambridge: Cambridge University Press, 1995), 186–7.
[56] Cohen, *Fashioning Masculinity*, 9.

about Wordsworth's gendered constructions of the poetic roles of Milton and Gray in his critical writing (and, ultimately, for thinking about his gendered construction of the nation). In the 'Preface', Wordsworth's critique of Gray is immediately preceded by praise for Milton's poetry, as if Wordsworth is drawing an implicit distinction between the 'manly' Milton and the 'unmanly' Gray (132). Similarly, in his discussion of Milton's 'manly' sonnets in his letter of 1802, Wordsworth praises them as 'distinguished by simplicity and unity of object and aim, and undisfigured by false or vicious ornaments'.[57] The latter part of this sentence has usually been associated with the work of women poets but it can also be read in terms of Wordsworth's critique of Gray's poetic language as 'ornament' rather than as 'incarnation of thought'.[58] In this context, Wordsworth's juxtaposition of Milton and Gray in the 'Preface' and his attack on Gray's sonnet suggests that Wordsworth's assertion of the manly may be an attempt to recover poetry not only from women but from the effeminate or unmanly man.

Wordsworth's critique of Gray can be read in the broader terms of the eighteenth-century anxiety over effeminacy and used to provide a context for a reading of his own 'manly' Miltonic sonnets. In *The Culture of Sensibility*, J. G. Barker-Benfield has examined the concern over the effeminizing effects of sensibility on men in the eighteenth century, arguing that the tempering powers of reason were deemed necessary to hold in check the 'softening' that was part of the reformation of male manners.[59] This is a pattern which can be traced in the one sonnet that we know Wordsworth wrote on 21 May 1802 and which, rather than simply adopting the 'manly' Miltonic mode, engages with the conventions of previous generations of the sonnet, reworks gender categories and prefigures some of the major strategies of the rest of the sonnet sequence:

> I grieved for Buonaparte, with a vain
> And an unthinking grief! the vital blood
> Of that Man's mind what can it be? What food
> Fed his first hopes? What knowledge could *He* gain?
> 'Tis not in battles that from youth we train
> The Governor who must be wise and good,
> And temper with the sternness of the brain
> Thoughts motherly, and meek as womanhood.

---

[57] De Selincourt, *Letters: Early Years*, 379.

[58] Cox, *Gender, Genre*, 50 and 57 n. 25. For an examination of this issue, see James E. Swearingen, 'Wordsworth on Gray', *SEL*, 14 (1974), 489–509, esp. 503.

[59] Barker-Benfield, *The Culture of Sensibility*, 104–53.

Wisdom doth live with children round her knees:
Books, leisure, perfect freedom, and the talk
Man holds with week-day man in the hourly walk
Of the mind's business: these are the degrees
By which true Sway doth mount; this is the stalk
True Power doth grow on; and her rights are these.[60]

For many critics, such as Lee M. Johnson, this sonnet on a public figure exemplifies Wordsworth working in the Miltonic mode.[61] Yet to read the sonnet purely in terms of the Miltonic tradition is to overlook its engagement with other traditions of sonnet writing and with the cult of sensibility, as Ralston has argued.[62] Perhaps most striking here is the poem's opening which, with its stress on 'grieved', invokes both the tradition of the feminized sonnet, particularly Charlotte Smith's *Elegiac Sonnets*, and Gray's elegiac 'Sonnet on the Death of Richard West'. Like Wordsworth's sonnet on Williams, 'I grieved' initially appears to find value in sensibility, both in the emotion of grief that the speaker feels for Bonaparte and the sensibility that Bonaparte has been denied as a result of his upbringing. In addition, the sonnet undermines the traditionally 'manly', juxtaposing Bonaparte's masculine upbringing in the public field of war with the private, domesticated upbringing of the 'Governor who must be wise and good' presided over by the maternal figure of Wisdom from whom he imbibes 'Thoughts motherly, and meek as womanhood' (ll. 6–9). 'True Power' (l. 14), gendered feminine, is defined against the false power wielded by Bonaparte. As Alan Richardson has written, Wordsworth 'makes clear that femininity is no less central to politics than to poetics ... The good patriarch must himself grow matriarchal; a ruthless figure like Napoleon must have been early deprived, Wordsworth implies, of the milk of human kindness.'[63] For Richardson, the sonnet exemplifies what he terms the 'colonization of the Feminine' in which the male romantic poet incorporates the feminine qualities developed by sensibility.

If the poem in this reading reconstructs masculine authority, it nevertheless reimposes more conventional gender hierarchies. It is clear that

---

[60] The texts for the sonnets are taken from *William Wordsworth: The Oxford Authors*, ed. Stephen Gill. Gill prints the first published versions of the poems.

[61] *Wordsworth and the Sonnet*, Anglistica, 19 (Copenhagen: Rosenkilde and Bagger, 1973), 45.

[62] Ralston argues that the sonnet contains echoes of one of Wordsworth's early personal sonnets, 'Sonnet. Written at Evening', 'Wordsworth and the Feminized Sonnet', 179.

[63] 'Romanticism and the Colonization of the Feminine' in *Romanticism and Feminism*, ed. Anne K. Mellor (Bloomington and Indianapolis: Indiana University Press, 1988), 16–17.

the role of governor, despite its feminization, is open only to men. It is a man who will hold weekday talk with other men, the phrase 'the mind's business' (l. 12) equating what could be seen as desultory intellectual pursuits with the professionalized activities of the public sphere. Similarly, children round the governor's knees would interfere with the pursuits of books, leisure, and perfect freedom that complement and develop the upbringing provided by Wisdom, reminding us perhaps of the way in which Wordsworth's cultivation of the role of poet was dependent upon the support of a domestic economy run by women: an issue which has been the subject of a number of recent studies.[64] If the feminine is appropriated in the sonnet, the female is confined to the domestic and maternal role. Exemplifying Barker-Benfield's argument, characteristics of mind traditionally constructed as masculine are presented as necessary to hold in check others that are specifically associated with the feminine: the Governor must 'temper with the sternness of the brain | Thoughts motherly, and meek as womanhood' (ll. 7–8). If we follow Barker-Benfield's and Cohen's arguments here, this tempering is necessary to guard against effeminacy. Likewise, within the sonnet, the poet is constructed against the effeminate through allusion to the 'unmanly despair' of Gray. The poem begins with an expression of feminized grief but immediately dismisses this spontaneous overflow of powerful emotions as 'vain' and 'unthinking' (ll. 1–2), invoking the opening of Gray's sonnet:

> In *vain* to me the smiling mornings shine,
> And reddening Phoebus lifts his golden fire:
> The birds in *vain* their amorous descant join,
> (ll. 1–3, emphasis added)[65]

As Lonsdale has suggested, the repetition of 'in vain' to describe the poet's own grief at the close suggests the 'fruitless circling' of his sorrow:[66]

> I fruitless mourn to him who cannot hear,
> And weep the more because I weep *in vain*.
> (ll. 13–14, emphasis added)

In the opening of 'I grieved', the poet signals that his sonnet will not stop at fruitless mourning but progress to show how the qualities of sensibility

---

[64] e.g. Page, *Wordsworth and the Cultivation of Women*, 3.

[65] *The Poems of Thomas Gray, William Collins, and Oliver Goldsmith*, ed. Roger Lonsdale (London and Harlow: Longmans, Green and Co., 1969), 67–8.

[66] Ibid. 67.

characterizing both Gray's sonnet and those of the following generation of women writers will become an integral yet subordinate part of his masculinist programme for the education of the governor, an education strikingly similar to that described in the epic autobiography *The Prelude*.

Wordsworth and the Gendering of the Nation

If 'I grieved for Buonaparte' constructs manly roles for the Governor and the poet, Wordsworth's sonnet 'On the Extinction of the Venetian Republic' creates a nation of manly readers. The sonnet's subject is the destruction of the Republic of Venice by Napoleon in 1797 through the Treaty of Campo Formio and serves as a lesson to England as both a nation threatened by Napoleonic France and a developing trading power prone to the dangers of luxury and decline:

> Once did She hold the gorgeous East in fee;
> And was the safeguard of the West: the worth
> Of Venice did not fall below her birth,
> Venice, the eldest Child of Liberty.
> She was a Maiden City, bright and free;
> No guile seduced, no force could violate;
> And when She took unto herself a Mate
> She must espouse the everlasting Sea.
> And what if she had seen those glories fade,
> Those titles vanish, and that strength decay,
> Yet shall some tribute of regret be paid
> When her long life hath reached its final day:
> Men are we, and must grieve when even the Shade
> Of that which once was great is passed away.

Like 'I grieved', this sonnet initially appears to offer an image of female power but turns on the contrast between the octet's celebration of Venice's former power and the sestet's representation of her in decline, recalling the figure of forlorn and ultimately defeated womanhood central to Smith's *Elegiac Sonnets*. Again making grief the central emotion of the poem, the poet argues not only that sensibility is something available to men, but that it is something essential to his own manliness and that of his readers—'Men are we, and must grieve'. This reclaiming of the masculinity of emotion, as Marlon B. Ross has termed it,[67] is familiar from much late eighteenth- and early nineteenth-century poetry, but importantly here grief becomes a public emotion, displayed for a great political cause, and it unites the speaker of the poem with his fellow men, unlike the private griefs of Smith's sonnets or, more particularly, the speaker of Gray's sonnet who is divided from 'happier men' (l. 10) as a result of his isolating, unarticulated mourning. Like 'I grieved', the sonnet can be read as an implicit critique of the vain grief—the 'unmanly despair'—of Gray's sonnet; at a time of national crisis grief is validated if expressed for what the *Annual* reviewer termed 'a worthy subject'. Manly grieving creates national unity and the sonnet constructs a gendered reading position which must be adopted if this unity is to be achieved. To adopt a formula from one of the 1802 additions to the 'Preface', in this sonnet the poet becomes a man speaking to men (138).

In the context of the sonnet sequence, Wordsworth's Venetian sonnet is exceptional in its initial representation of the female republic as powerful, albeit if only for the poet and his readers to regain the position of mastery through the expression of grief. More characteristic is Wordsworth's representation of England as a passive female figure entirely dependent on the actions of men, particularly the poet and his readers who are placed in the 'virile role of the chivalric saviour', as Marlon B. Ross has termed it.[68] Wordsworth represents female England in terms of a familiar duality, as fallen and in need of redemption by the poet, as in 'London, 1802' in which 'she is a fen | Of stagnant waters' (ll. 2–3), or as idealized and in need of protection, as in the nuptial 'Composed by the Sea-side, near Calais, August 1802' in which the poet fears for his 'dear Country' (ll. 13–14). It could be argued that the Venice sonnet also draws on this duality, contrasting the Republic's past status as a 'Maiden City, bright and free' (l. 1) with its present fallen status. However, it is noticeable that while the octet introduces and stresses the language of sexual conquest, suggesting the Republic's subsequent violation by Bonaparte, the sestet presents the fall of the Republic as a process of ageing. Yet in many of the sonnets, particularly the increasingly bellicose ones of 1803 written during the heightened fear of French invasion, female figures are notably absent, despite the part women played in the war effort during the invasion scare, the development of the figure of Britannia and the range of roles that are normally scripted for women

---

[67] 'Romantic Quest and Conquest: Troping Masculine Power in the Crisis of Poetic Identity', in Mellor (ed.), *Romanticism and Feminism*, 34.   [68] Ibid. 32.

during wartime.[69] Like the *Annual Review*, with its reference to 'times like these', several sonnets stress that this is a moment of particular crisis—using phrases such as 'at this hour' ('London, 1802', l. 1), 'the time is come' ('England! the time is come when thou shouldst wean', l. 1), and 'Now is the time' ('To the Men of Kent, October, 1803', l. 4)—and they link this moment of crisis with a need to reformulate individual and national gender identities. The defence of the country is represented as an exclusively 'manly' role, undertaken by 'the *men* of Kent', but in which the entire readership participates—'We are with you now from Shore to Shore' ('To the Men of Kent, October 1803', ll. 1, 13). The female figures of 'Wives' and 'Grandame', like 'Old Men' and 'little Children', only enter the invasion sonnets when 'Victory', and so peace, is 'Anticipated' ('Anticipation; October, 1803').

Yet the threat to the nation is also represented as an internal crisis of masculinity for a nation which has fallen away from the heroic manly past of the Republic evoked in sonnets such as 'Great Men have been among us' with its roll call of 'The later Sydney, Marvel, Harrington, | Young Vane, and others who called Milton Friend' (ll. 3–4). These figures, like that of 'the Governor', represent a reformed masculinity, characterized by 'magnanimous meekness' (l. 9), a quality associated with 'womanhood' in 'I grieved'. However, at the present time the nation is presented as being in danger of becoming corrupt, decadent, and effeminate in a new commercialized present when 'Men change Swords for Ledgers, and desert | The Student's bower for gold' ('When I have borne in memory what has tamed', ll. 3–4). In one of the sonnets quoted with approval by the *Annual Review* and anticipating its phallocentric language, the poet fears 'that noble Feelings, manly Powers, | Instead of gathering strength must droop and pine' ('There is a bondage which is worse to bear', ll. 11–12). In another, the twenty-first of the sequence, he begins: 'England! the time is come when thou shouldst wean | Thy heart from its emasculating food'. This reads like a refutation of Wordsworth's first political sonnet, 'I grieved for Buonaparte'. Whereas that sonnet advocated the absorption of the feminine, albeit tempered by masculine qualities, this sonnet emphatically rejects the feminine and the maternal through the use of the verb 'wean'; the influence of the maternal breast, central to Richardson's argument about the

---

[69] See Colley, *Britons*, 263–76; Marina Warner, *Monuments and Maidens: The Allegory of the Female Form* (London: Picador, 1987), 45–9; Nancy Huston, 'Tales of War and Tears of Women', *Women's Studies International Forum*, 5.3/4 (1982), 274–5; Jean Bethke Elshtain, *Women and War* (Chicago: University of Chicago Press, 1995), *passim*.

self-feminizing of the romantic poet, is now seen as a threat to the nation's masculine identity. The model of individual development that Marlon Ross has traced in Wordsworth's poetry in which the maternal figure is a primary force in constructing identity and fostering the passage into manhood but is then superseded by the assertion of masculine maturity, independent of the maternal or feminine influence, is here applicable to the nation. The narrative of the sequence itself follows a similar pattern, placing an increasingly bellicose emphasis on virility in the later sonnets, particularly those written in October 1803, the month Wordsworth joined the Grasmere Volunteers,[70] such as 'To the Men of Kent, October 1803', with its instruction 'Now is the time to prove your hardiment!' (l. 4) and its assertion of transhistoric and essential masculinity, defined primarily in the martial terms and imagery which had been rejected in 'I grieved'.

Indeed, 'To the Men of Kent' could be used to represent the regendering of the form that made the sonnets stand out for the reviewers who otherwise found the 1807 collection 'namby-pamby'. Identifying his readership with the defenders of his country and equating the reading of poetry with the traditionally masculine realm of the martial, Wordsworth strives to make the writing and reading of poetry a pursuit that is heroic, akin to the defence of the country, and, above all, worthy—worthy of the time and worthy of men. For at least one reader he was successful. Anticipating the mixed responses of the reviewers, Robert Southey wrote to his friend C. W. Williams Wynn in 1807 about Wordsworth's new collection:

Have you . . . seen Wordsworth's new poems? Some are very childish, some very obscure, though not so to me, who understand his opinions; others of first rate excellence—nothing comparable to them is to be found anywhere except in Shakespeare and Milton. Of this character are most of the sonnets which relate to the times. I never saw poetry at once so philosophical and heroic.[71]

Southey's assessment of the political sonnets as uniquely combining the 'philosophical' and the 'heroic' emphasizes Wordsworth's regendering of the form and grants them a martial as well as intellectual value. If his comments recall those of the Annual Review, it is worth returning to that piece to provide a conclusion to this chapter and to the issue of the role played by women in the 'manly' nation. For the reviewer who approved

<hr>

[70] Moorman, William Wordsworth: The Early Years, 602–3.
[71] Letter of 11 June 1807, Selections from the Letters of Robert Southey, ed. J. W. Warter, 4 vols. (London: 1856), II. 15.

of the sonnets with their 'severe and manly tone' and denounced the 'mere gossip' of much of the rest of the volume was Lucy Aikin, a poet and historian (*RR*, I. 13). We might put Aikin's response down to conservatism, propriety, or a sense of poetic decorum and argue that she is conspiring with Wordsworth's exclusion of the feminine from the discourse of poetry, despite her own professional and creative investment in it. Alternatively, we might argue that under the guise of anonymity she is creating her own self-authorizing manly voice. But Aikin's praise of the political sonnets brings us back to the issue of what happens to constructions of gender at a time of national emergency and illustrates that the manly reading position which Wordsworth constructs is open to women. Aikin offers one example of a woman reader who, rather than feeling excluded by Wordsworth's 'severe and manly tone', felt that it could not 'be in times like these too much listened to'.

CHAPTER FIVE

Walter Scott's Picturesque Romance of War, 1805–1814

Metrical Romance, the History of war, and the Picturesque

Walter Scott was by far the best selling and most popular poet of the Napoleonic wars and his metrical romances played a crucial role in mediating conflict to a nation at war. In a period when warfare was seen to have taken on a new form, to have become 'modern', Scott's phenomenally successful tales of 'Border chivalry' transformed the imagining of war, presenting it as heroic, shaped by the codes of romance, and framed by the conventions of the picturesque.[1] Having made his name with his ballad collection *Minstrelsy of the Scottish Border* in 1802–3, Scott published the first of his metrical romances, *The Lay of the Last Minstrel*, in 1805, at the climax of the invasion crisis. This tale of border rivalry between two Scottish clans and of the hostilities between England and Scotland, set in the middle of the sixteenth century and full of knights in armour, massing armies, and single combats, was immediately successful, selling 12,500 copies in the first two years.[2] As Lockhart comments, 'In the history of British Poetry nothing had ever equalled the demand

---

[1] On Scott and romance, see Alice Chandler, *A Dream of Order: The Medieval Ideal in Nineteenth-Century English Literature* (London: Routledge and Kegan Paul, 1971); Jerome Mitchell, *Scott, Chaucer and Medieval Romance: A Study in Sir Walter Scott's Indebtedness to the Literature of the Middle Ages* (Lexington: University Press of Kentucky, 1987); Mark Girouard, *The Return to Camelot: Chivalry and the English Gentleman* (New Haven and London: Yale University Press, 1981), 29–38; David Duff, *Romance and Revolution: Shelley and the Politics of a Genre* (Cambridge: Cambridge University Press, 1994), 120–3; Marlon B. Ross, 'Scott's Chivalric Pose: The Function of Metrical Romance in the Romantic Period', *Genre*, 18 (1986), 267–97; Anne-Julie Crozier, 'The Influence and Concept of Romance in Scott's Early Narrative Poetry', MA dissertation (University of York, 1989).

[2] The details of the sales of Scott's poetry are taken from Peter T. Murphy, *Poetry as an Occupation and an Art in Britain, 1760–1830* (Cambridge: Cambridge University Press, 1993), 138–9.

for the Lay of the last Minstrel' (*LWS*, II. 195). These phenomenal sales reflect not only the expanded market but also Scott's ability to appeal to a wide range of readers; as the *Monthly Review* commented, 'Mr Scott's Lay of the Last Minstrel kindled a sort of enthusiasm among all classes of readers.'[3] Scott's next two poems were even more successful, consolidating his status as 'the Monarch of Parnassus', as Byron termed him (*BLJ*, III. 219). *Marmion*, his tale of the English victory over the Scots at Flodden Field, was published in 1808, and sold 25,000 copies in four years. *The Lady of the Lake*, which presents the conflict between the army of James V and the Highland Clan-Alpine, was published in 1810 and was Scott's best-selling poem of all; as Lockhart describes, 'in the space of a few months, the extraordinary number of 20,000 copies were disposed of'.[4] As Peter Murphy has argued, one of the best ways to gauge Scott's popularity is to amalgamate the sales for the years 1809–11, when he had four books of verse on the market, during which two-year period he sold 'a breathtaking 50,500 copies'.[5]

The Lay of the Last Minstrel was reviewed for the *Annual Review* by Anna Barbauld who, as an anti-militarist writer of some distinction, was acutely aware of the relationship between the representation of war and propagation or termination of conflict.[6] In her review, Barbauld identified Scott's treatment of war as one reason for its power over contemporary readers' imaginations. Contrasting the forms of warfare in the periods of the poem's setting and its publication, Barbauld argues that in the 'half-civilized times' of the middle of the sixteenth century 'the bands of government were so loosely twisted, that every man depended for safety more on his own arm, or the prowess of his chief, than on civil power' but in modern, civil society fighting is undertaken by the professional soldier (601). Barbauld emphasizes the difference in imaginative appeal of these two forms of warfare:

---

[3] Quoted in *The Poetical Works of Sir Walter Scott, Bart., Author's Edition*, ed. J. G. Lockhart (Edinburgh: Adam and Charles Black, 1869), 7.   [4] Ibid. 174.

[5] Murphy, *Poetry as an Occupation*, 139.

[6] 'Art. XXXIV. *The Lay of the last Minstrel; a Poem*', *Annual Review and History of Literature for 1804*, 3 (1805), 600–4. Hereafter page references are cited in parenthesis within the text. Anonymous review identified as by Mrs Barbauld in J. H. Alexander, *Two Studies In Romantic Reviewing: Edinburgh Reviewers and the English Tradition, Vol. 2: The Reviewing of Walter Scott's Poetry: 1805–1817*, Romantic Reassessment, 49, ed. Dr James Hogg, Salzburg Studies in English Literature (Salzburg: Institut für Englische Sprache und Literatur, Universität Salzburg, 1976), 301. For a discussion of Barbauld's anti-militarist writing, see Penny Mahon, 'Towards a Peaceable Kingdom: Women Writers and Anti-Militarism, 1790–1825', Ph.D. thesis (Reading, 1997), 150–68.

War is always most picturesque where it is least formed into a science: it has most variety and interest where the prowess and activity of individuals has most play; and the nocturnal expedition of Diomed and Ulysses to seize the chariot and horses of Rhesus, or a *raid* of the Scots, or the Kerrs to drive cattle, will make a better figure in verse than all the battles of the great king of Prussia. The *sleuth-dog*, the *beacon-fires*, the *Jedwood-axes*, the *moss-troopers*, the yell of the *slogan*, and all the irregular warfare of predatory expeditions, or feuds of hereditary vengeance, are far more captivating to the imagination than a park of artillery and battalions of drilled soldiers. (601)

Barbauld's assessment of *The Lay of the Last Minstrel* is particularly useful because it locates Scott's poem within two of the period's major sets of ideas, one historical, the changing nature of war as a result of social progress, the other aesthetic, the cult of the picturesque. Scott shared Barbauld's belief in the changing nature of warfare within an enlightenment narrative of social progress, being familiar with ideas derived from the works of Scottish philosophical historians such as Adam Smith's *The Wealth of Nations* and Adam Ferguson's *Essay on the History of Civil Society*.[7] Scott gave his fullest account of the history of war in relation to the development of civil society in his *Life of Napoleon* of 1827. Like Barbauld, in this work Scott traces the development of nations from their 'savage state' in which they are 'constantly engaged in war' to their civilized state when 'the character of the soldier begins to be less familiarly united with that of the citizen'.[8] And, like her, he sees war in its modern form as becoming a 'science', characterized by the organization of forces and by the evolution of tactics that reached their culmination in Napoleon. He writes that:

as war becomes a profession, and a subject of deep study—it is gradually discovered, that the principles of tactics depend upon mathematical and arithmetical science; and that the commander will be victorious who can assemble the greatest number of forces upon the same point at the same moment, notwithstanding an inferiority of numbers to the enemy when the general force is computed on both sides. No man ever possessed in a greater degree than Buonaparte, the power of calculation and combination necessary for directing such decisive manoeuvres.[9]

---

[7] See Peter. D. Garside, 'A *Legend of Montrose* and the History of War', *Yearbook of English Studies*, 4 (1974), 159–71. On the philosophical context for Scott's arguments, see Duncan Forbes, 'The Rationalism of Sir Walter Scott', *Cambridge Journal*, 7 (1953), 20–35, and Peter D. Garside, 'Scott and the "Philosophical" Historians', *Journal of the History of Ideas*, 36 (1975), 497–512.

[8] *The Miscellaneous Works of Sir Walter Scott, Bart.*, 28 vols. (Edinburgh: Adam and Charles Black, 1880–1), X. 4.   [9] Ibid., X. 5.

Scott had developed these ideas about the history of war throughout the Anglo-French conflicts, particularly emphasizing the scientific character of its modern form. In 1811, for example, he argued in a letter that the Peninsular campaigns 'will teach us what we have long needed to know, that success depends not on the nice drilling of regiments, but upon the grand movements and combinations of an army. We have hitherto been polishing hinges, when we should have studied the mechanical union of a huge machine' (*LWS*, III. 274). Here we have a strikingly early example of the 'war machine' image that would frequently be used in the later nineteenth and twentieth centuries.[10] In Scott's account, the individual soldier becomes absorbed into the huge machine of war: as the Marquis of Montrose says of Dugald Dalgetty, the professional soldier and representative of modern war in Scott's novel *A Legend of Montrose*, there is 'something convenient in commanding a soldier, upon whose motives and springs of action you can calculate to a mathematical certainty'.[11]

However, the ambiguity of the war machine image illustrates the changing conceptions of war in the period in which Scott was writing. If, on the one hand, the image represents the enlightenment vision of the refinement of war under man's control, on the other, it suggests the post-enlightenment anxiety of the machine running out of control, of the 'unstoppable engine of war'. Scott's sense of how war had become 'modern' as part of the progress of society was called into question by the unprecedented scale and intensity of the Revolutionary and Napoleonic wars. As we have seen, since Clausewitz these wars have frequently been pointed to as the first examples of 'modern' or 'total' warfare, the birth of the 'Nation in Arms' transforming war from the smaller-scale encounters of professional armies that characterized eighteenth-century conflict. This change in the nature of warfare can be seen to have called into doubt Scott's narrative of war's development. As Clausewitz argued, far from being the specialized province of professional soldiers, 'war again became the business of the people'.[12] In his later prose accounts, Scott negotiated this problem by presenting the Britain of the invasion crisis as a nation of professional soldiers, the product of the discipline and drilling of the volunteer movement. As he wrote in the *Life of Napoleon*: 'On a sudden, the land seemed converted to an immense

---

[10] See Daniel Pick, *War Machine: The Rationalization of Slaughter in the Modern Age* (New Haven: Yale University Press, 1993).

[11] Quoted in Garside, '*A Legend of Montrose*', 162.

[12] Quoted in Geoffrey Best, *War and Society in Revolutionary Europe* (Stroud Gloucestershire: Sutton Publishing, 1998), 63.

camp, [and] the whole nation into soldiers'.[13] But during the war itself, Scott's belief that the soldier had been divided from the citizen created a crisis for a nation faced with the threat of invasion and forced to rely on its civilian population for its defence. As Adam Smith had argued in *The Wealth of Nations*, one of the dangers of the professionalization of war was that the rest of civil society lost the 'martial spirit' that characterized earlier stages in the nation's history.[14] It was through his poetry that Scott sought to transform the 'whole of the nation into soldiers' and through his turn to the pre-modern world of the sixteenth century that he aimed to restore the 'martial spirit' of the earlier warlike period to his modern readership.

As Barbauld commented in her review of *The Lay of the Last Minstrel*, 'War is always most picturesque where it is least formed into a science' and if as a philosophical historian Scott viewed modern war as a science, as a poet and volunteer he responded to it in aesthetic terms. In 1803 he wrote to Anna Seward:

For myself, I must own that to one who has, like myself, *la tête un peu exaltée*, the 'pomp and circumstance of war' gives, for a time, a very poignant and pleasing sensation. The imposing appearance of cavalry, in particular, and the rush which marks their onset, appear to me to partake highly of the sublime. (*LWS*, II. 119)

Here Scott presents the 'pleasing sensation' produced by war in terms of the sublime, which Edmund Burke had defined in his *Philosophical Enquiry* of 1757 as produced by the experience of 'terror'.[15] In 1811, writing to the playwright Joanna Baillie, Scott identified another aesthetic category as best suited to convey the nature of war, better even than accounts of soldiers who had experienced conflict, commenting: 'I don't know why it is I never found a soldier could give me an idea of a battle. I believe their mind is too much upon the *tactique* to regard the picturesque ... The technical phrases of the military art, too, are unfavourable to convey a description of the concomitant terror and desolation that attends an engagement' (*LWS*, III. 256). The category of the picturesque, then, not only gives the 'idea of a battle' but also contains the 'terror' normally associated with the sublime.[16] The suggestion of the potential of the

---

[13] *The Miscellaneous Works of Scott*, XI. 296.

[14] See Garside, 'A *Legend of Montrose*', 161.

[15] Edmund Burke, *A Philosophical Enquiry into the Origin of our Ideas of the Sublime and Beautiful*, ed. Adam Phillips (Oxford: Oxford University Press, 1990), 36.

[16] Like Scott here, critical responses to his poetry do not always clearly differentiate between the sublime and the picturesque. While nearly all critics see his work in terms of the picturesque, there is more of a debate about whether he achieves the sublime. Other critics see his work in terms of the 'picturesque sublime'. See Alexander, *Reviewing of Scott's Poetry*, 339–44, 341.

picturesque as a means of making war aesthetically pleasing is confirmed by the rest of this letter to Baillie. Scott tells her that had he been able to visit 'Lord Wellington and his merry men in Portugal', as he had hoped to do, he would have been 'able to communicate some personal anec-dotes on the subject' of 'Fear', which he considers 'of all passions . . . the most universally interesting' (*LWS*, III. 254). However, one of his friends had travelled to the Peninsula and had 'witnessed the Battle of Busaco, of which he describes the carnage as being terrible' (*LWS*, III. 255). While battle produces fear and terrible carnage, Scott goes on to praise the form of his friend's account of his experience: 'The narrative was very simply told, and conveyed, better than any I have seen, the impressions which such scenes are likely to make when they have the effect (I had almost said the charm) of novelty' (*LWS*, III. 255–6). It is this unsoldierly account of a battle which prompts Scott to invoke the picturesque, suggesting that its distancing and framing effect, while enabling the reader to gain an 'idea of a battle', may also transform war into a source of visual pleasure.

The term picturesque helps us to understand the aesthetic nature of Scott's response to war and the imaginative power of his construction of it for his readers.[17] The eighteenth-century aesthetic theory of the picturesque sought to explain why certain phenomena pleased the eye and was primarily concerned with the placement of objects in a field of vision. As the term suggests, for a scene to be picturesque, whether painted or written, it had to be 'worthy of a picture', such as those by the seventeenth-century Italian history and landscape painter Salvator Rosa, with their wild landscapes, often peopled by shepherds, soldiers, and bandits.[18] According to William Gilpin, one of the main eighteenth-century theorists of the picturesque, what particularly distinguished such paintings and land-scapes was the quality of 'roughness', which defined them against the regu-larity, smoothness, and neatness of non-picturesque beauty. For Gilpin,

---

[17] For valuable general discussions of Scott and the picturesque, see Peter D. Garside, 'Picturesque Figure and Landscape: Meg Merrilies and the Gypsies', in Stephen Copley and Peter D. Garside (eds.), *Politics of the Picturesque: Literature, Landscape and Aesthetics since 1770* (Cambridge: Cambridge University Press, 1994), 145–74; Alexander M. Ross, *The Imprint of the Picturesque on Nineteenth-Century British Fiction* (Waterloo, Ontario: Wilfrid Laurier University Press, 1986), 1–72; Marcia Allentuck, 'Scott and the Picturesque: Afforestation and History', in Alan Bell (ed.), *Scott Bicentenary Essays: Selected Papers Read at the Sir Walter Scott Bicentenary Conference* (Edinburgh: Scottish Academic Press, 1973), 188–98; Catherine Gordon, 'The Illustration of Sir Walter Scott: Nineteenth-Century Enthusiasm and Adaptation', *Journal of the Warburg and Courtauld Institute*, 34 (1971), 297–317.

[18] William Vaughan, *Romantic Art* (London: Thames and Hudson, 1978), 36.

roughness produces the key qualities of the picturesque which include irregularity, ruggedness, variety, and contrast, particularly of light and shade.[19] It was in such picturesque terms that Barbauld assessed Scott's presentation of war in *The Lay*, emphasizing 'variety', 'interest', and 'irregularity'.

In describing battle as 'picturesque', then, Scott responded to it aesthetically and he saw war as the most suitable subject for his own picturesque efforts. In the Ashestiel Memoir of 1808 he drew a 'distinction between a sense of the picturesque in action and in scenery' and to illustrate that his own ability was in the former offered the following reminiscence: 'shew me an old castle or a field of battle and I was at home at once, filled it with combatants in their proper costume and overwhelmed my hearers by the enthusiasm of my description'.[20] In his poetry, Scott structured war through the picturesque and he wanted this to be recognized, as is seen in his reactions to two responses to the success of *The Lay*. The first of these came in reply to a suggestion from the statesman Warren Hastings, whose wife could repeat parts of the poem by heart. Hastings and his wife both felt 'inspired' with the wish that Scott would 'compose a poem of the nature of the old Minstrellsy, and make our gallant Nelson the Subject of it'.[21] Scott's polite refusal of this suggestion from 'a quarter of such high authority' was made on aesthetic grounds, and specifically the 'insurmountable object' of the impossibility of producing a picturesque poem on the current conflict:

In order to produce a picturesque effect in poetry, a very intimate knowledge of the subject described is an essential requisite. I do not mean that this knowledge should be pedantically or technically brought forward, but it seems to me indispensably necessary that the poet should have enough of seafaring matters to select circumstances which, though individual and so trivial as to escape general observation, are precisely those which in poetry give life, spirit, and, above all truth to the description. (XII. 383)

Scott goes on to argue that his lack of such knowledge, as well as the speed with which his errors would be spotted by sailors—'some hundred critics in blue and white'—make it impossible for him to produce such a picturesque effect in a poem on Nelson, while there

---

[19] For a discussion, see Ross, *The Imprint of the Picturesque*, 4.

[20] Walter Scott, *Scott on Himself*, ed. David Hewitt (Edinburgh: Scottish Academic Press, 1981), 37. For a discussion of the idea of 'picturesque in action', see Ross, *Imprint of the Picturesque*, 41, and Peter Garside, 'Picturesque Figure and Landscape', 148.

[21] Quoted in *The Letters of Walter Scott*, ed. Herbert J. C. Grierson, 12 vols. (London: Constable, 1932–7), XII. 382. Further references are included within parentheses in my text.

were no such difficulties in the poetic treatment of 'my ancient *preux chevaliers* and border moss troopers' (XII. 383), the picturesque figures singled out by Barbauld in her review. Similarly, it was suggested to Scott that *The Lay* should be illustrated by John Flaxman, a painter and sculptor who was seen as the epitome of British classicism and who had gained an international reputation as a result of his illustrations of Homer's epics. While Scott's reply emphasized the link between the imagination and the process of picturing by adopting the phraseology of Theseus in *A Midsummer Night's Dream*, he rejected the suggestion because: 'I should fear Flaxman's genius is too classic to stoop to body forth my Gothic Borderers. Would there not be some risk of their resembling the antique of Homer's heroes, rather than the iron race of Salvator's engravings?'[22] Rather than the classical elegance of Flaxman's outline drawings with their linearity and clarity, Scott wanted his warriors to look like the wild and fierce soldiers of Rosa's 'Figurine series' of 1656–7, one of the standard sources of the picturesque.[23]

If the scientific and technical character of modern warfare made it resistant to artistic representation, it was by turning to the 'half-civilized' times of the sixteenth century that Scott was best able to capture war's picturesque essence and the imaginations of his readers. As Francis Jeffrey commented in his review of *Marmion* for the *Edinburgh Review* in 1808, 'the times of chivalry, it may be said, were more picturesque than the present times. They are better adapted to poetry; and every thing that is associated with them has a certain hold on the imagination, and partakes of the interest of the period.'[24] Like Barbauld, Jeffrey sees the 'charm' of this picturesque period of history, 'the days of knightly adventure', as arising from its martial character: 'the interest which we take in the contemplation of the chivalrous era, arises from the dangers and virtues by which it was distinguished,—from the constant hazards in which its warriors passed their days, and the mild and generous valour with which they met those hazards.'[25] Yet what made this period of

[22] Quoted Allentuck, 'Scott and the Picturesque', 190. For Scott and illustrations, see Catherine Gordon, 'The Illustration of Sir Walter Scott', *passim*.

[23] On Rosa's figurine series as a source of the picturesque, see Garside, 'Picturesque Figure and Landscape', 146, 148; and Allentuck, 'Scott and the Picturesque', 190.

[24] Quoted in John O. Hayden (ed.), *Scott: The Critical Heritage* (London: Routledge and Kegan Paul, 1970), 46.

[25] Ibid. See also, *La Belle Assemblée*: 'He passes with a bold retrospective genius into these times of turbulence and arms, in which are found those materials of the picturesque and savage sublime, which have so often astonished and charmed us in extraordinary ballads and obsolete romances'—Alexander, *Reviewing of Scott's Poetry*, 341.

history particularly picturesque was its transitional nature, an idea that Scott articulated most fully and famously in his 'Introduction' (1831) to *The Fortunes of Nigel*:

The most picturesque period of history is that when the ancient rough and wild manners of a barbarous age are just becoming innovated upon, and contrasted by, the illumination of increased or revived learning, and the instructions of renewed or reformed religion. The strong contrast produced by the opposition of ancient manners to those which are generally subduing them, affords the lights and shadows necessary to give effect to a fictitious narrative.[26]

While we may need to beware of applying a later account of history's picturesqueness to the poetry, Scott's metrical romances do focus on such periods of transition in a way that anticipates the historical novels. J. H. Alexander, for example, has examined *Marmion* as a poem that presents late chivalric society in a period of decline, and Scott's friend George Ellis pointed to the combination of savage and civilized elements in Scott's poems written up to 1813: 'That mixture of ferocity and courtesy, of religion and barbarity, of rudeness and hospitality, of enthusiastic love, inflexible honour and extravagant enterprize, which distinguished the manners of the middle ages, opens the happiest and most fertile sources of poetic invention.'[27]

As Barbauld argued in her review, Scott's choice of the 'half-civilized' period of the middle of the sixteenth century and his picturesque approach to war determined the forms in which he could represent conflict. Rather than the parks of artillery, the drilled soldiers, or the vast machine of the modern army, Scott focused on forms of warfare in which 'the prowess and activity of individuals has most play'. Again, this was a matter of aesthetics as well as history. Like Barbauld, Scott believed that narrative poetry was best suited to portraying individual endeavour, commenting in 1815 of what he felt was his failure to do justice to the great modern battle in *The Field of Waterloo*, 'it is not always the grandest actions which are best adapted for the arts of poetry and painting' (*LWS*, V. 87–8). In his 'Preface' to *The Bridal of Triermain* of 1813, he illustrated this general principle about the appeal of modern poetry with a military example:

Modern poets may therefore be pardoned in seeking simpler subjects of verse, more interesting in proportion to their simplicity. Two or three figures, well

---

[26] Quoted in Allentuck, 'Scott and the Picturesque', 190.

[27] J. H. Alexander: '*Marmion*': *Studies in Interpretation and Composition*, Salzburg Studies in English Literature, 30, ed. James Hogg (Salzburg: Insitut für Anglistik und Amerikanistik, 1981); Alexander, *Reviewing of Scott's Poetry*, 301.

grouped, suit the artist better than a crowd, for whatever purpose assembled. For the same reason, a scene immediately presented to the imagination, and directly brought home to the feelings, though involving the fate of but one or two persons, is more favourable for poetry than the political struggle and convulsions which influence the fate of kingdoms. . . . We would, for example, be more interested in the fate of an individual soldier in combat, than in the grand event of a general action . . .[28]

While Scott did not shy away from the poetic representations of general actions, as we shall see, his depiction of war in his verse romances certainly emphasized heroic individual action. This is seen particularly in the importance of single combat which provides the key narrative action in the first three metrical romances. In *The Lay of the Last Minstrel* the disputes between the two clans, the Scotts and the Kerrs, and between the Scots and the English, are resolved not through massed battle, but through single combat of national champions fought according to the rules of chivalry. The assembled armies, who have now joined each other in 'social cheer', act as spectators to the duel.[29] In *The Lady of the Lake*, the battle between King James V's army and the Highland Clan-Alpine is halted when news reaches the combatants that James has already defeated the highland Chieftain, Roderick Dhu, in single combat. Even in *Marmion*, which culminates in a famous description of the battle of Flodden, the motif of single combat constructs violence as a moral force through which justice operates. While the poem's villain Marmion dies at Flodden in fulfilment of a prophecy that sees death in battle as a punishment for his crimes, this punishment is symbolically anticipated earlier in the poem when he is defeated but spared in single combat by the poem's hero, De Wilton. While these acts of single combat work at a narrative level to prove the valour of the poem's heroes and to validate a ritualized form of violence, they can also be read in the context of the Napoleonic war. Writing during a war which witnessed a huge escalation in the size of armies and the scale of conflict, Scott presents national disputes as resolvable through a ritual contest which costs only one life.

However, there is a doubleness in the picturesque, and especially its treatment of war, that can be seen to influence Scott's portrayal of conflict. As we have seen, one model for Scott's picturesque warriors was

[28] *Poetical Works*, 586.
[29] For an interesting discussion of this scene in terms of Anglo-Scots relations, see Cronin, *The Politics of Romantic Poetry: In Search of the Pure Commonwealth* (Basingstoke, London and New York: Macmillan and St Martin's Press, 2000), 104–5.

the 'Figurine series' in which Rosa presented single soldiers or small groupings of them, recalling Scott's preference for 'Two or three figures, well grouped'. Like Scott's single combats, Rosa's 'book of figures' emphasized the martial prowess of these exotically dressed and heavily armed individuals. Yet Rosa was equally well known for his picturesque landscape paintings, in which figures occupied a much less significant place. In such paintings, war and its representatives are seen from a distance, framed by the natural landscape and potentially absorbed into nature itself. Scott's poetic depiction of battles, for which he employed the techniques of picturesque description, can be seen to distance the reader from the devastation of war, absorbing the individual combatant into a pleasing aesthetic spectacle. Scott was a poet frequently described in terms of painting,[30] the vividness of whose descriptions carried the reader 'back in imagination to the time of action',[31] and he was seen to be particularly skilled as a picturesque writer; as Coleridge commented: 'the powers of presenting the most numerous figures, and figures with the most complex movement, and under rapid succession, in *true picturesque unity*, attests true and peculiar genius.'[32] For his readers, Scott excelled in his application of his picturesque genius to armies and conflicts; the *British Critic*, for example, assessed his portrayal of Flodden in *Marmion* as 'at least the most picturesque of all the fields of battle that were ever exhibited in poetry'.[33] Scott's picturesque structuring of battle is well illustrated by the battle scene from canto VI of *The Lady of the Lake* that Adam Ferguson read to his soldiers in Portugal and that I discussed in my opening chapter. What is most striking about this exemplary scene is the emphasis it places on the picturesque as the means by which such an imagining of war can take place. Roderick Dhu's request immediately establishes the form of the battle narrative to follow as picturesque: 'Fling me *the picture* of the fight | When met my clan the Saxon might' (VI. 14, my italics). And Roderick Dhu's account of how he will imagine the battle—'I'll listen, till my fancy hears | The clang of swords, the crash of spears' (VI. 14)—can be read in terms of Gilpin's account of the picturesque, which as Alexander M. Ross comments, emphasized 'the importance of imagination in the creative process—

[30] The *Quarterly Review* commented in a review of *The Lady of the Lake*: 'Never, we think, has the analogy between poetry and painting been more strikingly exemplified than in the writings of Mr Scott. He sees everything with a painter's eye.' Quoted in *Scott's Poetical Works: Author's Edition*, 176.   [31] Ibid. 7.

[32] Quoted in Allentuck, 'Scott and the Picturesque', 192.

[33] Quoted in Alexander, *Reviewing of Scott's Poetry*, 367.

especially in representing "scenes of fancy" '.[34] In line with Gilpin's
argument, Scott calls on the imaginative powers of the reader to
respond to the poet's description, working on its raw materials with his
or her 'fancy' to create a satisfying realization of the battle that will
transport the reader to the battlefield itself, as Dhu believes it will
mentally liberate him from his prison cell. However, while the imaginative response to the poet's picture of war enables the hearers to experience the soaring excitement of battle as if they themselves were
participants in it—as Dhu comments his 'free spirit [will] burst away, |
As if it soar'd from battle fray' (VI. 14)—Allan-Bane does not plunge
Roderick or the reader into the thick of the fight. Rather his account of
the battle is based on his own distant view of what he 'witness'd from
the mountain's height' combined with 'what old Bertram told at night'
(VI. 14).[35] He maintains this crucial element of distance in his description of the battle which begins as an exercise in appreciation of
picturesque landscape:

> 'The Minstrel came once more to view
> The eastern ridge of Benvenue,
> For, ere he parted, he would say
> Farewell to lovely Loch Achray:
> Where shall he find, in foreign land,
> So lone a lake, so sweet a strand!'   (VI. 15)

War enters this landscape in the form of the King's army, though it is
initially indistinguishable from the forms of nature:

> 'Is it the thunder's solemn sound
> That mutters deep and dread,
> Or echoes from the groaning ground
> The warrior's measured tread?
> Is it the lightning's quivering glance
> That on the thicket streams,
> Or do they flash on spear and lance
> The sun's retiring beams?'   (VI. 15)

Here, the aural and visual impact of the army is assimilated to natural
forms and Scott uses Allan-Bane to exemplify the implied reaction of the

---

[34] Alexander, *The Imprint of the Picturesque*, 7.

[35] Similarly, in *Marmion*, the battle of Flodden is viewed from a non-combatant
perspective 'by a Cross of Stone, | That, on a hillock standing lone, | Did all the field
command' (VI. 22, see also VI. 23). This position produces a viewpoint from which the
spectators 'Could plain their distant comrades view' (VI. 25).

ideal reader to this picturesque description, with the visual experience of war surpassing anything that can be felt in peacetime:[36]

> I see the dagger-crest of Mar,
> I see the Moray's silver star
> Wave o'er the cloud of Saxon war,
> That up the lake comes winding far!
>   To hero bound for battle-strife,
>   Or bard of martial lay,
>   'Twere worth ten years of peaceful life,
>   One glance at their array!   (VI. 15)

Allan-Bane's description of the battle draws on the conventions of the picturesque, emphasizing contrast and variety through juxtaposition of light and darkness, silence and noise, and stillness and movement, and his metaphors and similes of ocean and storm assimilate the violence of war into the natural world (VI. 16–17). As a result of the distant viewpoint, the casualties remain indistinguishable: 'None linger now upon the plain, | Save those who ne'er shall fight again' (VI. 18). The battle's function in enabling the reader to experience war's picturesqueness is emphasized by its inconsequential nature: just as the two armies close 'in desperate fight' the battle is halted by the news that the conflict has already been resolved through the single combat of James and Roderick (VI. 21). Scott's picturesque treatment of battle frames, contains, and distances the violence of conflict, transforming war into a source of imaginative pleasure.

Scott's picturesque treatment of battle was frequently remarked on, as we have already seen in the comments of the reviewers of the *Annual Review* on *The Lay of the Last Minstrel* and the *British Critic* on *Marmion*, and was a key element in his popularity and critical reputation, as seen in *Monthly Review*'s comment on *The Lord of the Isles* that 'the battle of Bannockburn will remain for ever as a monument of the fertile poetical powers of a writer, who had before so greatly excelled in this species of description.'[37] Indeed, Scott became regarded as not only the pre-eminent war poet of the period, but of all time. As Francis Jeffrey wrote in his review of *Marmion* in the *Edinburgh Review* in 1808, 'Of all the poetical battles which have been fought, from the days of Homer to those of Mr Southey, there is none, in our opinion, at all

---

[36] For an interesting discussion of the viewing of armies in *Marmion*, see Cronin, *The Politics of Romantic Poetry*, 105.

[37] Quoted in Scott's *Poetical Works: Author's Edition*, 455.

comparable, for interest and animation,—for bredth [*sic*] of drawing and magnificence of effect,—with this of Mr Scott's.'[38] Much of Scott's significance as a poet lay in offering this version of war to the reading public at a particular moment; at a time when war had become modern, it could be experienced imaginatively through the more appealing forms of Scott's romances. And it is the relation between the sixteenth-century wars of Scott's poetry and the Napoleonic wars during which they were best-sellers that will be explored in the next section of this chapter.

Writing and Reading 'to the Sound of the Bugle'

In his *Life of Sir Walter Scott*, first published in 1833, Lockhart commented that Scott 'must ever be considered as the "mighty minstrel" of the Antigallican war'(*LWS*, III. 54) yet such a claim might seem strange about a poet whose most popular poems were set in the early sixteenth century and whose subject matter—the internal tensions within Scotland and national conflicts between Scotland and England—would seem to emphasize division rather than the unity necessary at a time of crisis. Francis Jeffrey praised the opening of the minstrel's tale in *The Lay of the Last Minstrel* for its ability to 'transport us at once into the days of knightly daring and feudal hostility'[39] and the minstrel's account of the vigilance of the knights of Branksome Hall provides a good example of the violent world into which Scott plunged his readers:

> Nine-and-twenty knights of fame
>   Hung their shields in Branksome hall;
> Nine-and-twenty squires of name
>   Brought them their steeds to bower from stall;
>   Nine-and-twenty yeomen tall
>   Waited, duteous, on them all:
>   They were all knights of mettle true,
>   Kinsmen to the bold Buccleuch.
>
> Ten of them were sheath'd in steel,
> With belted sword, and spur on heel:
> They quitted not their harness bright,
> Neither by day, nor yet by night:

---

[38] Ibid. 138.   [39] Ibid. 10.

> They lay down to rest,
> With corslet laced,
> Pillow'd on buckler cold and hard;
> They carv'd at the meal
> With gloves of steel,
> And they drank the red wine through the helmet barr'd.   (I. 3–4)

If the violent world of Branksome Hall seemed strange to readers of 1805, it may also have seemed familiar, for its picture of a community awaiting attack paralleled the context in which Scott was writing, encamped as a member of the Royal Edinburgh Volunteer Light Dragoons awaiting the invasion of Napoleon's army. Scott, who described himself as having a 'strong military bent' (*LWS*, III. 152), had always wanted to be a soldier but had been prevented by the disability he had developed as a result of a childhood bout of polio.[40] During the invasion scare of 1797, Scott and some of his friends had formed the Volunteer Dragoons and his role in them enabled him to experience the excitements of armed service.[41] He drilled each morning at 5 o'clock, attended regular encampments at Portobello beach, and delighted in wearing uniform. One of his contemporaries described Scott's enthusiasm for volunteering as follows:

It was not a duty with him, or a necessity, or a pastime, but an absolute passion, indulgence in which gratified his feudal taste for war, and his jovial sociableness. He drilled, and drank, and made songs, with a hearty conscientious earnestness which inspired or shamed everybody within the attraction. I do not know if it is usual, but his troop used to practise, individually, with the sabre at a turnip, which was stuck on top of a staff, to represent a Frenchman, in front of the line. Every other trooper, when he set forward in his turn, was far less concerned about the success of his aim at the turnip, than about how he was to tumble. But Walter pricked forward gallantly, saying to himself: 'Cut them down, the villains, cut them down!' and made his blow, which from his lameness was often an awkward one, cordially, muttering curses all the while at the detested enemy.[42]

It was within this specific context that *The Lay of the Last Minstrel* was written, as Lockhart describes. In the autumn of 1802, Scott was kicked by a horse while at Portobello on his cavalry exercises, and while recovering began the poem: 'his accidental confinement in the midst of a volunteer camp gave him leisure to meditate his theme to the sound of

---

[40] John Sutherland, *The Life of Walter Scott: A Critical Biography* (Oxford: Blackwell Publishers, 1997), 66.
[41] For a full account of Scott's involvement in the Volunteers, see Major J. R. Marshall, T. D., 'Walter Scott, Quartermaster', *Blackwood's Magazine*, April 1930, 511–32.
[42] Quoted in Sutherland, *Life of Walter Scott*, 67.

the bugle;—and suddenly there flashes on him the idea of extending his simple outline, so as to embrace a vivid panorama of that old Border life of war and tumult' (*LWS*, II. 181). Lockhart's 'flash' of inspiration marks the transformation of the wartime context in which Scott was writing 'to the sound of the bugle' into 'the old Border life of war and tumult'. Read within this context, the armed vigilance of the knights of Branksome Hall could be seen as another form of the kind of military self-projection Scott frequently enacted in his letters, as when writing to Ellis in 1803:

The necessity of the present occasion ... has kept almost every individual, however insignificant, to his post. God has left us entirely to our own means of defence, for we have not above one regiment of the line in all our ancient kingdom. In the mean while, we are doing the best we can to prepare ourselves for a contest, which, perhaps, is not far distant. A beacon light, communicating with that of Edinburgh Castle, is just erecting in front of our quiet cottage. My field equipage is ready, and I want nothing but a pipe and a *schnurbärtchen* [mustachios] to convert me into a complete hussar. (*LWS*, II. 135)

Like the knights of Branksome Hall, Scott spent the years 1802–5 watching to 'see the midnight beacon gleaming' and the 'sound of the bugle' remained a crucial inspiration for Scott's poetry, volunteer activities providing the environment for composition as well as an eager first audience. Another friend, James Skeene, described Scott's writing of the battle of Flodden to Lockhart as follows: 'In the intervals of drilling, . . . Scott used to delight in walking his powerful black steed up and down by himself upon the Portobello sands, within the beating of the surge; and now and then you would see him plunge in his spurs, and go off as if at a charge, with the spray dashing about him. As we rode back to Musselburgh, he often came and placed himself beside me, to repeat the verses that he had been composing during these pauses of our exercise' (*LWS*, III. 7). For Scott, who described himself as someone 'through whose head a regiment of horse has been exercising since he was five years old' (*LWS*, II. 223), the delights of riding, volunteering, and composing poetry were strongly associated, as Philip Shaw has argued.[43] He drew them together, for example, in his description of the standard octosyllabic line of his poetry as 'a light-horseman sort of stanza' (*LWS*, II. 96) and in the 'War Song' he wrote for the Dragoons which began 'To horse! to horse!'.[44] Scott's success as a poet also helped him maintain his

---

[43] Philip Shaw, *Waterloo and the Romantic Imagination* (Basingstoke and New York: Palgrave Macmillan, 2002), 48.

[44] *Poetical Works*, 701. See also Shaw's account of the composition of 'The Bard's Invocation', *Waterloo and the Romantic Imagination*, 47–8.

war effort—when his horse Captain was killed in a riding accident, Scott used some of the profits from *The Lay of the Last Minstrel* to buy a new horse, Lieutenant, for use as his charger in the volunteer cavalry (*LWS*, II. 196).

If Scott's poetry gave expression to his 'feudal taste for war' in general, passages in it specifically invoked the context of the war with France, such as the dramatic descriptions in both *The Lay of the Last Minstrel* and *The Lady of the Lake* of Highland forces gathering to repel invasion, which both John Sutherland and Michael C. Gamer have seen as allegorical celebrations of the rallying of British volunteer forces to resist Napoleon.[45] Scott increasingly referred to the contemporary context as a framework for his historical tales, in his second poem *Marmion* adding the verse epistles that frame the sixteenth-century tales with contemporary history, including the elegiac analysis of the current state of Britain after the deaths of Pitt, Fox, and Nelson and the celebration of his own involvement in the volunteers.[46] In these epistles, Scott transforms the current wars into romance, fought according to the laws of chivalry, so that William Pitt, the former Prime Minister who had died in 1806, becomes a chivalric knight, serving his distressed damsel Albion ('Introduction to Canto First'), and the Duke of Brunswick, the Prussian military leader, is an embodiment of 'valour' pitted unsuccessfully against the 'dragon' Napoleon ('Introduction to Canto Third').[47] The romance register that Scott deploys in the main poem to describe 'Flodden's fatal field, | Where shiver'd was fair Scotland's spear, | And broken was her shield' (VI. 34) is also used to represent contemporary events: 'Scotland hurried to the field, | And snatch'd the spear, but left the shield'. Scott makes the Napoleonic wars equivalent to the 'knightly tale[s] of Albion's elder day' that he presented in his poems ('Introduction to Canto First'). And while Scott focuses on the wars between England and Scotland within the poems, these wars are seen as part of a necessary historical progress towards the construction of a unified Britain.[48] In *Marmion*, while the

[45] Michael C. Gamer, 'Marketing a Masculine Romance: Scott, Antiquarianism, and the Gothic', *Studies in Romanticism*, 32 (1993), 531–2; Sutherland, *Life of Walter Scott*, 87.

[46] These epistles have been the subject of much discussion. See David Hewitt, 'Scott's Art and Politics', in Alan Bold (ed.), *Sir Walter Scott: The Long Forgotten Melody* (London: Vision Press, 1983), and J. D. McClatchy, 'The Ravages of Time: The Function of the *Marmion* Epistles', *Studies in Scottish Literature*, 9 (1972), 256–63.

[47] See Crozier, 'The Influence of Romance in Scott', 34–8, and Duff, *Romance and Revolution*, 122.

[48] For discussions of this issue in the poetry, see Cronin, *The Politics of Romantic Poetry*, 103–9, and Sutherland, *Life of Walter Scott*, 125–6.

main text laments the defeat of the Scots at Flodden, in the epistles Scott addresses himself to 'every British heart' ('Introduction to Canto First').

Even when Scott acknowledges that the forms of war have changed, he sees the emotions it evokes as remaining constant over history, in line with his philosophical belief stated in the first chapter of his novel *Waverley* that certain 'passions common to men in all stages of society ... have alike agitated the human heart, whether it throbbed under the steel corslet of the fifteenth century, the brocaded coat of the eighteenth, or the blue flock and white dimity waistcoat of the present day'.[49] In the apostrophe to war in *The Lord of the Isles*, for example, Scott presents the emotions evoked by war as common to Robert the Bruce, in 1314, and to his own readers 500 years later in 1814:

> Oh, War! thou hast thy fierce delight,
> Thy gleams of joy, intensely bright!
> Such gleams, as from thy polish'd shield
> Fly dazzling o'er the battle-field!
> Such transports wake, severe and high,
> Amid the pealing conquest-cry;
> Scarce less, when, after battle lost,
> Muster the remnants of a host,
> And as each comrade's name they tell,
> Who in the well-fought conflict fell,
> Knitting stern brow o'er flashing eye,
> Vow to avenge them or to die!
> Warriors!—and where are warriors found,
> If not on martial Britain's ground?
> And who, when waked with note of fire,
> Love more than they the British lyre?–
> Know ye not, hearts to honour dear!
> That joy deep, deep-thrilling, stern, severe,
> At which the heartstrings vibrate high,
> And wake the fountains of the eye?
> And blame ye, then, the Bruce, if trace
> Of tear is on his manly face,
> When, scanty relics of the train
> That hail'd at Scone his early reign,
> This patriot band around him hung,
> And to his knees and bosom clung?   (IV. 20)

---

[49] Sir Walter Scott, *Waverley; or 'Tis Sixty Years Since*, ed. Claire Lamont, World's Classics (Oxford: Oxford University Press, 1986), 5.

In this passage, Scott not only presents his readers as familiar with the 'fierce delight' and 'gleams of joy, intensely bright' evoked by war, but addresses them as 'Warriors', constructing Britain as the exemplary 'Warrior' nation: 'where are warriors found | If not on martial Britain's ground?' Writing for a civilized age in which according to his own version of history the soldier had been separated from the citizen, Scott seeks to restore through his poetry the martial spirit necessary during time of war. To respond to Scott's poetry fully here it is necessary to respond as a 'Warrior', even if all that one knows of war's 'fierce delight' has been learnt from Scott's poetry itself.

Scott's transformation of his readers into warriors was identified as the reason for his popularity in the *Eclectic Review*'s account of the poet of 1811 discussed in the opening chapter. Writing of Scott's *The Vision of Don Roderick*, the anonymous reviewer sought to identify what distinguished Scott's poetry from that of his contemporaries and to account for his power over the reader's imagination. Scott, the reviewer argues, 'has taken up the ancient function of a bard, to celebrate military prowess, and set off pride, ferocity, and revenge'.[50] This bellicosity, the reviewer continues 'is the general tendency of his poems. Almost their only moral effect is, to inspire a passion for strife and violence, inducing a contempt for the insipid comforts of peaceful and civilized society, and a secret but decided preference for the times of lawless and sanguinary adventure'(673). As a result, Scott's readers are 'hardened' and 'brutalized' (685), but the reviewer is alert to how Scott achieves this effect through his poetic technique, providing a valuable gloss on the poet's use of the picturesque. He writes that the poems are 'exquisite delineations—of a fierce and licentious age: they captivate the fancy with beautiful scenes, and excite the passions by striking events; but at the same time they reconcile us to the manners they illustrate, and assimilate us to the characters they describe' (685). As readers of Walter Scott, the reviewer is arguing, we become like one of his sixteenth-century warriors. If the *Eclectic* reviewer's comments are helpful in understanding the appeal and effect of Scott's poetry for the readers at the time of the Napoleonic wars, they are also illuminating in emphasizing how successfully Scott filled the role of the pro-war, national poet after more than a decade in which the dominant strain of war poetry had asked readers to imagine war's horrors and to feel for its victims. Scott fulfilled

---

[50] *Eclectic Review*, 'Scott's *Vision*', 673. Further page references are included in parenthesis within the text.

the traditional role of the 'favourite of the Muses' outlined in the *Anti-Jacobin* in 1797.[51] Who better than Walter Scott could be described as 'a warrior, at least in imagination' whose strains 'overwhelmed the horrors of war in its glory'? Scott's commitment to such a response to war is illustrated by a letter he wrote consoling his correspondent over the death of a friend who had been killed in the Peninsular campaign, when he commented, 'I grieve for your loss at Barossa, but what more glorious fall could a man select for himself or friend, than dying with his sword in hand and the cry of victory in his ears?' (*LWS*, III. 275). With Scott's verse, the eighteenth-century emphasis on war's horrors gives way to the nineteenth-century stress on its glory.

Scott and the Remasculinization of Romance

In addressing his readers as 'Warriors' in his last extended verse romance in 1814, Scott completed his remasculinization of the reader and of poetry more generally, contributing, like Wordsworth in his sonnets, to the wartime revalidation of poetry as a manly pursuit for writer and reader alike. In turning to romance with *The Lay of the Last Minstrel* in 1805, Scott had adopted what was seen as a feminized genre,[52] something dramatized in the poem itself in which the minstrel addresses his song to an audience made up entirely of women in the court of the Duchess of Buccleuch. As a number of critics have pointed out, in his metrical romances Scott emphasizes the heroic rather than the amatory elements of the genre,[53] and his position as the author of *The Lay* is paralleled in the figure of the minstrel, torn between his own identity as a war poet— 'full many a tale he knew | Of the old warriors of Buccleuch' ('Introduction')—and the demands of his audience of 'fair dames' who want to hear 'a melting tale, | Of two true lovers in a dale' (II. 29). This tension between the minstrel's identity and the audience for which he sings is illustrated most fully in his account of the single combat between Cranstoun and Musgrave, where an awareness of the sensibilities of his hearers causes him to restrict the natural impulse of his song:

[51] *The Anti-Jacobin*, 12–14.
[52] See Gamer, 'Marketing a Masculine Romance', *passim*, esp. 524. Gamer argues that 'Scott attempts to reclaim gothic romance by resituating it in the masculine realm of antiquarian history', 524.
[53] Gamer, 'Marketing a Masculine Romance', 531, and Crozier, 'The Influence of Romance in Scott', 71.

> Ill would it suit your gentle ear,
> Ye lovely listeners, to hear
> How to the axe the helm did sound,
> And blood pour'd down from many a wound;   (V. 21)

The audience's sensibility prevents the minstrel from the true poetic self-expression that would be facilitated by a change of listener:

> But, were each dame a listening knight,
> I well could tell how warriors fight!
> For I have seen war's lightning flashing,
> Seen the claymore with bayonet clashing,
> Seen through red blood the war-horse dashing,
> And scorn'd, amid the reeling strife,
> To yield a step for death of life.   (V. 21)

In the conclusion to *The Lay of the Last Minstrel*, Scott begins the transformation of the genre and reconceptualization of the reader that the minstrel desires and that Scott would achieve over the next decade. The success of the minstrel's poem is rewarded with 'A simple hut' beneath Newark Castle which provides the location for the minstrel's performances:

> Then would he sing achievements high,
> And circumstance of chivalry,
> Till the rapt traveller would stay,
> Forgetful of the closing day;
> And noble youths, the strain to hear,
> Forsook the hunting of the deer;
> And Yarrow, as he roll'd along,
> Bore burden to the Minstrel's song.
>   (VI. 'Conclusion')

No longer addressing an audience of women who require a tale of love, the minstrel sings of heroic subjects—'achievements high | And circumstance of chivalry'—to 'travellers' and 'noble youth' who listen rather than going hunting. In Scott's verse, hunting is analogous to war—Douglas comments in *The Lady of the Lake* that 'the chase I follow far, | 'Tis mimicry of noble war' (II. 26)—and in this conclusion to his first romance, Scott makes listening to poetry an activity fit for potential warriors.

Scott's concluding vision of the minstrel prefigures the direction of his own poetic career. Following the success of *The Lay of the Last Minstrel*, in his next poem, *Marmion*, Scott himself takes on the role of the minstrel (like him he is located in a 'little garden'[54]) and sings of 'achievements high' for an audience that includes men as well as women—'knights' as well as 'dames'. With the subject of 'Flodden Field'—the original title of the poem—and his famous description of the battle, Scott gives full expression to his minstrel's desire to 'tell how warriors fight'. In the first epistle he presents such martial adventures as the natural subject matter of nineteenth-century minstrels as much as their sixteenth-century counterparts, 'the legendary lay | O'er poet's bosom holds its sway' and

> our hearts at doughty deeds,
> By warriors wrought in steely weeds,
> Still throb for fear and pity's sake;
> ('Introduction to Canto First')

In *Marmion*, such martial subject matter intended for a manly readership coexists with a romantic narrative that will appeal to female readers, as Scott emphasizes in the final stanza of the poem proper:

> I do not rhyme to that dull elf,
> Who cannot image to himself,
> That all through Flodden's dismal night,
> Wilton was foremost in the fight; . . .
> Nor sing I to that simple maid,
> To whom it must in terms be said,
> That King and kinsman did agree,
> To bless fair Clara's constancy;
> Who cannot, unless I relate,
> Paint to her mind the bridal state;   (VI. 38)

If these lines differentiate the imaginative response to romance along gendered lines, in the 'L'Envoy' which follows, Scott presents his poem as being read not only by 'every lovely lady bright' and the 'school boy', the typical representatives of the feminized audience, but also by 'Statesmen grave', the 'hero', the 'faithful lover', 'the studious sage', and 'the head of age'—a catalogue of authentic manly figures including the leaders of the wartime nation ('L'Envoy'). Such a claim about the readership of his poetry comes as the culmination of the arguments presented in the verse epistles that preface each canto, which seek to validate romance as a form worthy of men at time of war, uniting Pitt and Fox as readers of *The Lay* ('Introduction to Canto First'). Like

---

[54] Crozier, 'The Influence of Romance in Scott', 71.

Wordsworth, who in 'Scorn not the sonnet' sought to defend a form by constructing it in terms of the authority of previous literary figures and ultimately by claiming it as a political rather than an amatory form, Scott validates the romance by associating it with the great national poets of the past, Spenser, Milton, and Dryden, 'The mightiest chiefs of British song | [who] Scorn'd not such legends to prolong' ('Introduction to Canto First'). With the authority derived from such readers and predecessors, Scott is able to present himself in heroic terms:

> Warm'd by such names, well may we then,
> Though dwindled sons of little men,
> Essay to break a feeble lance
> In the fair fields of old romance;
> ('Introduction to Canto First')

Here the poet becomes the chivalric knight of his own romances and, even if diminished from its earlier glory, such chivalric jousting is not to be scorned, as Scott emphasizes in his continued adoption of the terms of romance in his address to the romance scholar William Stewart Rose: 'Well has thy fair achievement shown, | A worthy meed may thus be won' ('Introduction to Canto First'). Scott equates the writing of poetry and the more traditionally manly activity of fighting, as he will do in the fourth epistle, which focuses on his role as a volunteer, the memory of which 'inspires my strain':

> And mark, how, like a horseman true,
> Lord Marmion's march I thus renew.
> ('Introduction to Canto Fourth')

Scott's past life in the Volunteer Dragoons here provides both the inspiration and the authority for his narration of 'A knightly tale of Albion's elder day.'

In *The Lady of the Lake*, Scott again constructs his audience through the gendered roles of romance laid out by the characters within his poems; poetry has the power to 'bid a warrior smile' and 'teach a maid to weep' (I, 'Introduction'). But in *The Lord of the Isles*, as has been argued, Scott makes all his readers 'warriors'. This construction of the reader is consistent with the overall emphasis of *The Lord of the Isles*, which was well characterized by the *Port Folio* in 1815: 'The SENTIMENTS are bold, masculine and lofty, rather than tender, delicate and refined— befitting the rough and hardy warrior, rather than the persons of a softer texture. This is as it should be: the poem being chiefly of a heroic cast, they are, therefore, in their nature, the more appropriate.'[55] *The Lord* is the most explicit of Scott's narrative poems in its treatment of violence, and marks the culmination of his poetic development away from the feminized romance form. Instead of the censorship of violence on behalf of polite ears in *The Lay*, Scott offers his most graphic depiction of the damage of war:

> Unsparing was the vengeful sword,
> And limbs were lopp'd and life-blood pour'd,
> The cry of death and conflict roar'd,
> And fearful was the din!   (V. 31)

Indeed, if *The Lord* was the culmination of Scott's wartime transformation of poetry into something manly and heroic, as the *Port Folio* suggests, as his first peacetime poem it also signals the beginning of his retreat from the genre and the start of his critique of the violence of war that he would undertake most fully in the novel. Scott's comment in the 1830 afterword to the poem that the sales of *The Lord* were enough to enable 'the author to retreat from the field with the honours of war' illustrates, as John Sutherland has argued, that he 'saw *The Lord of the Isles* as marking the "close" of his serious poetic career'.[56] But Scott's use of military language also reminds us that he was retreating from the poetic field at the same time as the armies of Europe were withdrawing from battlefields, and *The Lord of the Isles* would prove to be his last extended metrical romance. The poem was written in the autumn and early winter of 1814, finished in December, and published on 8 January 1815 and, as such, was Scott's first post-war poem, written and published after Napoleon's abdication and exile to Elba in spring 1814 and prior to his return during the hundred days (*LWS*, IV. 12–14). If this peacetime context makes it possible for Scott to fulfil his minstrel's desire to 'tell how warriors fight' without having to worry about the effect his depictions of violence may have on the wartime morale of the nation, the graphic nature of some passages suggests a renewed awareness of war's physical damage that would be compounded by his visit to the battlefield of Waterloo. Scott visited this battlefield and was shocked by the evidence of war's physical damage.[57] On his return home he made a significant renunciation when he was thrown three times by his horse, a 'high-spirited and very handsome' charger named, perhaps

---

[55] Alexander, *The Reviewing of Scott's Poetry*, 337.
[56] *Life of Walter Scott*, 179.
[57] Ibid. 186, and Shaw, *Waterloo in the Romantic Imagination*, 35–66.

inappropriately, Daisy (*LWS*, V. 85). Scott commented, 'I was obliged to part with Daisy—and wars and rumours of wars being over, I resolved thenceforth to have done with such dainty blood. I now stick to a good sober cob'(*LWS*, V. 86). John Sutherland, Scott's most recent biographer, has rightly seen this incident as 'Scott's discharge from the military', commenting 'He was a cavalryman no more'.[58] But given Scott's mental association of riding, volunteering, and composing poetry, we can also see it as his resignation of the role of 'the "mighty minstrel" of the Anti-Gallican war'. After Waterloo Scott exchanged the charger of poetry for the sober cob of the novel, the form to which he would devote most of the rest of his literary career and in which he would be much more critical of war's picturesque sensations.[59]

Scott's transformation of the reader into a warrior during the final decade of the Napoleonic war, like Wordsworth's address to the manly English nation discussed in the previous chapter, raises the question of the woman reader and, more generally, of his poetic construction of wartime gender roles. Not only did Scott adopt a form that was seen as feminized but a large proportion of his readers were women, something that he frequently acknowledges in his poetry, as in the 'L'Envoy' in *Marmion*, in which he addresses 'every lovely lady bright'. As this phrase would suggest, Scott constructs his female readers in terms of the conventional female roles of romance, interested in love rather than war and in need of protection from the war's violence, be it acted or represented. Within the poems themselves, women generally play wartime's supporting roles, sanctioning their heroes' engagement in acts of violence, rewarding them when they are triumphant, and nursing the wounded. For playing such roles, the heroines are themselves rewarded with marriage. For example, Clare enacts all these roles in the final canto of *Marmion*. Reunited with De Wilton prior to the battle of Flodden, she initially questions whether he must 'Trust fate of arms once more', offering the pastoral and domestic retreat of a cottage in 'an humble glen' as an alternative to martial engagement (VI. 10). While De Wilton does not reply to this suggestion, from his expression Clare realizes the symbolic importance of participation in the battle:

---

[58] *Life of Walter Scott*, 188.

[59] For discussions of this issue, see Ross, *The Imprint of the Picturesque*, 46–72 and Joseph E. Duncan, 'The Anti-Romantic in *Ivanhoe*', reprinted in D. D. Devlin (ed.), *Walter Scott: Modern Judgements* (London: Macmillan, 1968), 142–7.

'That reddening brow!—too well I know,
Not even thy Clare can peace bestow,
   While falsehood stains thy name:
Go then to fight! Clare bids thee go!'   (VI. 10)

Clare recognizes that the masculine values of honour, secured through violence, outweigh her feminine desire for peace and she symbolically enacts this recognition by buckling on De Wilton's spurs, belting him 'with brand of steel' and sending him 'forth to fame!' (VI. 10). Such moments are frequently re-enacted in Scott's poetry, most powerfully in the fiery cross sequence in *The Lady of the Lake* in which Scott presents a number of emblematic scenes in which individuals receive and answer the call to arms, including a bridegroom who leaves his recently married bride and a widow at her husband's funeral who sends forth her son in place of his father (III. 14–24). If Clare enacts this female role of sanctioning war, Scott also makes her embody another archetypal female role when she nurses the wounded and dying Marmion, prompting his famous apostrophe:

O, Woman! in our hours of ease,
Uncertain, coy, and hard to please,
   And variable as the shade
By the light quivering aspen made;
When pain and anguish wring the brow,
   A ministering angel thou!   (VI. 30)

Clare's reward of marriage to De Wilton anticipates the poet's hopes for his female readers: 'To every lovely lady bright, | What can I wish but faithful knight?' ('L'Envoy').

While women generally play the supporting roles in war in Scott's poetry, there are notable occasions when they participate actively as combatants in battle or as inspirers of armies, though these examples are never straightforward, illustrating the problematic position of women in wartime. In my opening chapter I have already discussed how 'Duncraggan's widow'd dame' in *The Lady of the Lake* can be read as a figure of necessary transformation of the nation in wartime. Similarly, in *The Lord of the Isles*, Scott again emphasizes the role of women in a crisis of national defence when the needs of the nation extend beyond the regular army:

The multitude that watch'd afar,
Rejected from the ranks of war,
Had not unmoved beheld the fight,
When strove the Bruce for Scotland's right;

> Each heart had caught the patriot spark,
> Old man and stripling, priest and clerk,
> Bondsman and serf; even female hand
> Stretch'd to the hatchet or the brand;   (VI. 30)

At this moment of crisis Scotland becomes unified in war, undivided by differences of age, profession, class, or gender. Indeed, the nation in arms is inspired to further heroics by the poem's heroine, 'Fair Edith', though the manner in which she does so again emphasizes the difficulties of assigning a public role to woman in wartime. At this point in the poem Edith is disguised as a page and, so as not to be given away by her voice, is pretending to be mute. But on seeing reinforcements join the English army, she cries out:

> 'O God! the combat they renew,
>   And is no rescue found!
> And ye that look thus tamely on,
> And see your native land o'erthrown,
> O! are your hearts of flesh or stone?'   (VI. 29)

This speech is interpreted as a miracle by the 'multitude' of the Scottish nation who see in it a symbol of the divinely inspired transformations necessary in wartime: 'And he that gives the mute his speech | Can bid the weak be strong' (VI. 30). Inspired by this change, the Scots adopt the language of the British invasion writing of 1797–1805, crying: 'The choice, 'twixt death or freedom, warms | Our breasts as theirs—To arms, to arms!' (VI. 30). In this crisis of national emergency, then, Scott presents a woman who inspires her nation to heroic deeds and whose example makes the weak strong, but her role is assumed by accident, made possible by disguise, and is only temporary. After the battle, Edith is firmly relocated within her traditional female role. As she runs from the battlefield, her 'plume and bonnet drop', revealing her 'lovely brow' and 'dark locks' and she is immediately proposed to by Ronald (VI. 36–7). The poem ends with Bruce looking forward to 'The bridal of the Maid of Lorn' (VI. 37).

If Clare appears less interesting than the cross-dressing figure Edith, as the conventional heroine of romance she provides a useful figure for thinking about the participation of women within Scott's nation of 'Warriors'. For while she enacts the archetypal supporting roles of women in war, she is able to imagine herself a warrior, as she says to De Wilton when sending him off to fight: 'Clare can a warrior's feelings know, | And weep a warrior's shame'(VI. 10). Similarly Ellen, the heroine

of *The Lady of the Lake*, while emphasizing her gendered identity, is able
to imagine herself as a version of her warrior father:

> 'My soul, though feminine and weak,
> Can image his; e'en as the lake,
> Itself disturb'd by slightest stroke,
> Reflects the invulnerable rock.'   (IV. 10)

Ellen's imagery of reflection both consolidates gender difference,
contrasting the yielding vulnerability of the lake with the resisting invul-
nerability of the rock, and dissolves it. As she emphasizes at the close of
her speech, she is able to experience the masculine emotions of her father
even if, as a woman, she is not able to act on them: 'He goes to do—what
I had done, | Had Douglas' daughter been his son!' (IV. 10). As these two
heroines illustrate, Scott makes accessible to women the sentiments of
his poetry that the *Port Folio* described as 'bold, masculine and lofty'.
Though 'feminine and weak', women can become part of Scott's warrior
nation.

CHAPTER SIX

'History in the Land of Romance': Poetry and the Peninsular War, 1808–1814

IN AUGUST 1808, Robert Southey wrote excitedly to his brother Tom describing his reaction to the Spanish risings that followed Napoleon's diplomatic chicanery and the subsequent French invasion:

> Landor is gone to Spain! to fight as a private in the Spanish army, and he has found two Englishmen to go with him. A noble fellow! this is something like the days of old as we poets and romancers represent them,—something like the best part of chivalry,—old honours, old generosity, old heroism are reviving,—and the career of that cursed monkey nation is stopt, I believe and fully trust, now and for ever.[1]

While Walter Savage Landor's volunteering is a notable incident in the war of British poets against Napoleon, what is most striking about Southey's letter is the extent to which the unfolding events in Spain have already been imagined, and written, as romance. Southey was a scholar and translator of Spanish romances and had described Spain as the 'Land of Romance' as early as 1797,[2] but he was not alone in responding to the war in the Peninsula as already shaped by the representations of 'poets and romancers'. Walter Scott wrote in June 1808 that 'It strikes me as very singular to have all the places mentioned in Don Quixote and Gil Blas now the scenes of real and important events. Gazettes dated from Oviedo, and gorges fortified in the Sierra Morena, sounds like history in the land of romance' (*LWS*, III. 82). Similarly, Thomas Campbell commented that 'We shall hear in the language of Cervantes, all the great

---

[1] Quoted in Geoffrey Carnall, *Robert Southey and his Age: The Development of a Conservative Mind* (Oxford: Clarendon Press, 1960), 85.
[2] 'Recollection of a Day's Journey in Spain', *Poems of Robert Southey*, ed. Maurice H. Fitzgerald (London: Oxford University Press, 1909), 393.

principles of British liberty . . . Oh, sweet and romantic Spain!'[3] For both Scott and Campbell, Cervantes's *Don Quixote* becomes the archetypal romance text through which the war will be imagined; as Scott commented of its hero, his 'gallantry was only impeachable from the objects on which he exercised it' (*LWS*, III. 82). But such a generic shaping of the war was not limited to poets, as Diego Saglia has shown with reference to George Ellis's and George Canning's opening article of the first issue of the *Quarterly Review* of 1809, in which they wrote: 'In surveying the transactions recorded or referred to in these papers, we are almost tempted to doubt whether we are reading the events of real history . . . [The situation] presents a spectacle, certainly, not less improbable than the wildest fictions of romance.'[4] This combination of geography and genre in the imaginative shaping of the latest stage of the war was compounded by the fashion for romance produced by the popularity of Scott's poetry. As *Blackwood's* commented retrospectively in 1817:

The 'Lay' converted thousands, and 'Marmion' tens of thousands, and the *whole* world read poetry . . . The whole secret is, that Mr Scott gave to the world a series of brilliant romances, and turned into this new-made channel all who ever in their lives read and relished fictitious compositions. All the poets, good and bad, forthwith wrote metrical romances . . .[5]

While it is obviously overstating the case to say that 'the *whole* world read poetry', the popularity and model of Scott's romances coalesced with the sense of Spain as a land of romance to provide the major poetic framework for the British understanding of the war. In a period when Britain was taking an increasingly active role in the conflict, its army in the Peninsula constituting its largest commitment on land to the war with France, romance and its associated values provided a powerful construction of Britain's role that would influence the way in which the nation saw its global role for the rest of the century.[6] In this chapter, I will examine the poetic use of romance to shape and give meaning to the

---

[3] Quoted in Arthur Bryant, *Years of Victory, 1802–1812* (London: Collins, 1944; repr. 1975), 228.

[4] Quoted in Diego Saglia, 'War Romances, Historical Analogies and Coleridge's *Letters on the Spaniards*', in Philip Shaw (ed.), *Romantic Wars: Studies in Culture and Conflict, 1793–1822* (Aldershot: Ashgate, 2000), 142.

[5] Quoted in Marlon B. Ross, *Contours of Masculine Desire: Romanticism and the Rise of Women's Poetry* (New York: Oxford University Press, 1989), 270.

[6] See Mark Girouard, *The Return to Camelot: Chivalry and the English Gentleman* (New Haven and London: Yale University Press, 1981), *passim*.

war, looking at the representational challenges this presented and at the poetic questioning and subversion of this generically inflected understanding of the conflict.

Felicia Hemans, the Peninsular War, and the 'Songs of Spain'

The central place that war came to occupy in the poetic imagination during the Peninsular War, and the role of romance in shaping poetic representations of conflict subsequent to Scott, are nowhere better illustrated than in the early poetic career of Felicia Hemans, the writer who would go on to become 'the most widely read woman poet in the nineteenth-century English-speaking world'.[7] That Hemans made war the topic on which she most often exercised her poetic 'fancy' owes much to the early power over her imagination of the events of the Peninsular War, seen in her comments to her aunt in December 1808: 'Glorious, glorious Castilians! may victory crown your noble efforts. Excuse me for dwelling so much on this subject; for Spain is the subject of my thoughts and words—"my dream by night, my vision of the day".'[8] Hemans's allusion here is to Thomas Campbell's *The Pleasures of Hope*, and specifically to dreams and visions of 'Thy fairy worlds, Imagination',[9] and through it Hemans gives the war the supreme position in her imagination. There were a number of reasons why the Peninsular War should dominate the imagination of the aspiring teenage poet, most obviously the fact that her two elder brothers were in the 23rd Royal Welch Fusiliers serving in the Peninsula, George with the armies of first Sir John Moore and later the Duke of Wellington, and

---

[7] *Felicia Hemans, Selected Poems, Prose, and Letters*, ed. Gary Kelly (Peterborough, Ontario: Broadview Press, 2002), 15. Valuable considerations of the theme of war in Hemans's poetry include: Tricia Lootens, 'Hemans and Home: Victorianism, Feminine "Internal Enemies," and the Domestication of National Identity', *PMLA*, 109 (1994), 238–53; Susan J. Wolfson, ' "Domestic Affections" and "the Spear of Minerva": Felicia Hemans and the Dilemma of Gender', in Carol Shiner Wilson and Joel Haefner (eds.), *Re-Visioning Romanticism: British Women Writers, 1776–1837* (Philadelphia, Pennsylvania University Press, 1994), 128–66; Diego Saglia, 'Epic or Domestic? Felicia Hemans's Heroic Poetry and the Myth of the Victorian Poetess', *Rivista di Studi Vittoriani*, 2/4 (July 1997), 125–47; Kevin Eubanks, 'Minerva's Veil: Hemans, Critics, and the Construction of Gender', *European Romantic Review*, 8 (1997), 341–59; E. Douka Kabitoglou, 'The Pen and Sword: Felicia Hemans's Records of Man', in Tony Pinkney, Keith Hanley, and Fred Botting (eds.), *Romantic Masculinities: News from Nowhere 2: Theory and Politics of Romanticism* (Keele, Staffs.: Keele University Press, 1997), 101–20.

[8] *Felicia Hemans*, ed. Kelly, 413.   [9] Ibid.

Henry as part of Wellington's headquarters staff.[10] Hemans's early volumes, *Poems* (1808) and *The Domestic Affections* (1812), include a number of poems addressed to these brothers in which she presents the imagination as performing a crucial function in maintaining a link between the physically separated siblings, her fancy enabling her to imagine George's plight in a personalized version of the imagining of war's horrors:

When the heroes of Albion, still valiant and true,
    Were bleeding, were falling, with victory crown'd;
How often would fancy present to my view,
    The horrors that waited thee round![11]

In reciprocal fashion, Hemans's brothers' imaginative powers enable them to make a spiritual return from the scene of war to the home, as in 'To My Eldest Brother, With the British Army in Portugal':

Does fancy oft in busy day-dreams roam,
And paint the greeting that awaits at home?
Does memory's pencil oft, in mellowing hue,
Dear social scenes, departed joys renew; . . .
Yes! wanderer, yes! thy spirit flies to those,
Whose love unalter'd, warm and faithful glows![12]

'Fancy' breaks down the sense of distance between the home and the scene of war, undermining any simple construction of the private and the public space. The home becomes the space for imagining war's horrors while the scene of war becomes the site for the imagining of home.

Hemans's poetry addressed to her brothers is also important in that it authorizes her as a woman to write about what might be perceived as public or political issues. Her own sense of the way in which these familial attachments sanctioned her interest in such matters is well illustrated by her letter to her aunt:

You have, I know, perused the papers (as I have done,) with *anxiety*, though, perhaps, without the *tremors* which I continually experience. The noble Spaniards! surely, surely, they will be crowned with success: I have never given

---

[10] Ibid. 412 n. 1.

[11] 'To My Younger Brother, On his Return from Spain, After the Fatal Retreat Under Sir John Moore, and the Battle of Corunna', in Felicia Dorothea Browne [Hemans], *The Domestic Affections, and Other Poems* (London: T. Cadell and W. Davies, 1812), 51.

[12] *The Domestic Affections*, 146–7.

up the cause, not withstanding the late disastrous intelligence; but I think their prospects begin to wear a brighter appearance, and we may hope that the star of freedom, though long obscured by clouds, will again shine with transcendent radiance. You will smile, my dear aunt, but you know what an *enthusiast* I am in the cause of Castile and liberty: my whole heart and soul are interested for the gallant patriots, and though females are forbidden to interfere in politics, yet as I have a dear, dear brother, at present on the scene of action, I may be allowed to feel some ardour on the occasion.[13]

While Hemans ends with an expression of anxiety for her brother, this comes only after a lengthy account which emphasizes her enthusiasm for the 'noble Spaniards'. Similarly, Hemans's presentation of herself in *Poems* (1808) and *The Domestic Affections* (1812) as one who has 'a dear, dear brother, at present on the scene of action' sanctions a much broader poetic articulation of her enthusiasm for the Peninsular War, and indeed for war in general. Her early works display an interest and a proficiency in patriotic themes and tropes and in celebrating the heroes and triumphs of Britain's past and present.[14] Yet in this poetry Hemans also reveals an impressive range of perspectives on political events, seeing them in cosmic terms through the 'truth-enlighten'd eye' of 'The Angel of the Sun' as well as in national terms in 'The Wreath of Loyalty'.[15] She adopts a wide range of voices in her treatment of the war, from those of the combatants themselves, as in the 'War-Song of the Spanish Patriots', and the abstract persona of Liberty,[16] through the bardic,[17] to the prophetic, as in the ambitious 'War and Peace', the longest poem in *The Domestic Affections*, which, as Nanora Sweet and Julie Melnyk comment, suggests in its title the true concerns of the volume, and in which the Muse sees with 'bright, prophetic eyes'.[18]

Hemans's adoption of a prophetic role to treat the war was not only ambitious, but also risky, as was illustrated by Anna Barbauld's *Eighteen Hundred and Eleven*, published in the same year as *The Domestic*

[13] *Felicia Hemans*, ed. Kelly, 411–12.

[14] See e.g. 'Sacred to the Memory of Lord Nelson' and 'To Patriotism' in Felicia Dorothea Browne [Hemans], *Poems* (London: T. Cadell and W. Davies, 1808), 55–6, 64.

[15] *The Domestic Affections*, 69, 122–35.

[16] Ibid. 39–41; 'The Call of Liberty. May 1809', ibid. 139–44.

[17] 'The Bards, To the Soldiers of Caractacus', ibid. 63–6. On Hemans and the bardic voice, see Kabitoglou, 'The Pen and Sword', *passim*.

[18] *The Domestic Affections*, 116. Nanora Sweet and Julie Melnyk (eds.), *Felicia Hemans: Reimagining Poetry in the Nineteenth Century* (Basingstoke and New York: Palgrave, 2001), 5.

Affections, which was dealt with so harshly by critics that it ended Barbauld's poetic career.[19] Much of the hostility to Barbauld's poem focused on her as a woman poet who had adopted the prophetic mode; reviewing the poem for the *Quarterly*, John Wilson Croker, the Secretary to the Admiralty who had himself played a considerable role in the romancing of the Peninsular War with his poem *The Battles of Talavera* (which I will consider in the next section), wrote that 'We had hoped, indeed, that the empire might have been saved without the intervention of a lady-author'.[20] A number of critical accounts of the reception of *Eighteen Hundred and Eleven* have emphasized the link between gender and genre in these attacks,[21] but as the lack of any such outcry against Hemans's adoption of the prophetic mode suggests, these responses to Barbauld's poem also need to be seen in the context of the poem's anti-war politics.

While there was considerable opposition to the continuation of the war in Parliament during this period, the vast majority of poetic writing was supportive of the war effort (Byron's attacks on the British conduct of the war in *Childe Harold's Pilgrimage* would make him the target for personal criticism, such as Ellis's suggestions of cowardice in the *Quarterly*).[22] At a time when war was dominantly structured as romance, Barbauld invoked the diction and modes of the anti-war poetry of the 1790s only to suggest that even they were not adequate to the war-related desolations of famine, disease, and rapine: 'war's least horror is the ensanguined field' (l. 22).[23] And Barbauld's use of these modes of representation certainly proved provocative, as is seen in Elizabeth Cobbald's reaction, which draws on the imagery of the poem's opening: 'Britain in bending her ear to the Death Drum and feeding the fierce strife appears to me to be accused of voluntarily protracting and exciting the Horrors of War.'[24] In her attacks on the construction of the island nation in patriotic poetry, Barbauld recalls Smith's and Coleridge's concerns over its isolation and insulation from the war, and like Coleridge in 'Fears in Solitude' suggests that the consequence will be a rebounding of the conflict on the nation itself:

[19] William Keach, 'A Regency Prophecy and the End of Anna Barbauld's Career', *Studies in Romanticism*, 33 (1994), 569–77.

[20] *Quarterly Review*, 7 (1812), 309.

[21] See Penny Mahon's account of such arguments, 'Towards a Peaceable Kingdom: Women Writers and Anti-Militarism, 1790–1825', Ph.D. thesis (Reading, 1997), 132–3.

[22] *Quarterly Review*, 7 (1812), 183.

[23] Text from Duncan Wu (ed.), *Romantic Women Poets: An Anthology* (Oxford: Blackwell Publishers, 1997), 10–18.

[24] Quoted in Mahon, 'Towards a Peaceable Kingdom', 133.

> And think'st thou, Britain, still to sit at ease,
> An island queen amidst thy subject seas,
> While the vexed billows, in their distant roar,
> But soothe thy slumbers, and but kiss thy shore?
> To sport in wars, while danger keeps aloof,
> Thy grassy turf unbruised by hostile hoof?[25]
> So sing thy flatterers—but, Britain, know,
> Thou who hast shared the guilt must share the woe. (ll. 39–46)

As part of her prophetic project, Barbauld even reclaims 'Fancy' for what Julie Ellison has described as a 'visionary tour' through time, a development of the techniques of Warton's 'Ode' that looks to a future in which the British empire is in ruins.[26] Barbauld's poem was attacked not just as a result of 'a mismatch of gender and genre', then, but as a result of the vision of conflict that they produced.[27] And as the comparison with Hemans emphasizes, she was attacked not just for being a woman writing in the prophetic mode, but as a particular kind of woman. Hemans sanctioned her political interest not only by drawing attention to her family links to the war, but also by stressing her young age; the subtitle of 'War and Peace' is 'Written at the Age of Fifteen', constructing the poet as one who speaks with the inspired innocence of uncorrupted youth. By contrast, in his attacks on Barbauld, Croker both removes her from a family context and stresses her age by falsely describing her as a 'spinster' when she was a widow. As William Keach has emphasized, such criticisms undermine 'her claim to the kind of proper domestic or familial identity' necessary to gain authority as a woman writer, and they show how important such a domestic and familial identity would be for Hemans as a woman poet writing about war.

While celebrating patriotic topics, Hemans's early poetry also reveals the attraction that war has for her as a poetic theme, and specifically as one that attracts and inspires 'Fancy'. In 'The Ruined Castle' in *Poems* (1808), the gothic scene of 'moss-grown battlements' and 'ivy'd towers' provides the stimulus for a series of exercises of the imagination as the poet oscillates between descriptions of the tower's current ruined condition and its previous wartime function:

---

[25] Barbauld here echoes Smith's *The Emigrants*: 'And o'er our vallies, cloath'd with springing corn, | No hostile hoof shall trample' (II. 205–6).

[26] Julie Ellison, 'The Politics of Fancy in the Age of Sensibility', in Wilson and Haefner (eds.), *Re-Visioning Romanticism*, 238. [27] Ibid. 241.

Here, where I muse in meditation's arms,
Perhaps the battle raged with loud alarms;
Here glory's crimson banner waving spread,
While laurel crowns entwin'd the victor's head;
And here, perhaps, with many a plaintive tear,
The mourner has bedew'd the soldier's bier.
The scene of conquest pensive fancy draws,
Where thousands fell, enthusiasts in their cause . . .
Ah! where is now the warrior's ardent fire?
Where now the tuneful spirit of the lyre?
The warrior sleeps; the minstrel's lay is still;
No songs of triumph echo from the hill.
Ah! yet the weeping muse shall love to sigh,
And trace again thy fallen majesty;
And still shall Fancy linger on the theme,
While forms of heroes animate her dream.   (42–3)

Like Scott, by whom this passage is heavily influenced, Hemans establishes a contrast between a past martial age and a present more civilized and less warlike one. But as for Scott, and in the tradition of Warton's 'Ode to Fancy', war becomes an inspiring subject for the imagination, animating Fancy's dream and stimulating her to 'draw' 'the scene of conquest'. Hemans would give a striking example of such an imaginative recreation of a time of war, as mediated by romance, in the opening of her post-Waterloo poem 'The Abencerrage', from *Tales and Historic Scenes, in Verse* of 1819, in which she juxtaposes the deserted and silent Alhambra of modern day with the atmosphere of an earlier period of history:

Far other tones have swell'd those courts along,
    In days romance yet fondly loves to trace;
The clash of arms, the voice of choral song,
    The revels, combats, of a vanish'd race.

And yet awhile, at Fancy's potent call,
    Shall rise that race, the chivalrous, the bold!
Peopling once more each fair, forsaken hall,
    With stately forms, the knights and chiefs of old.   (I. 21–8)[28]

If war has the power to animate fancy in Hemans's poetry, here Hemans's fancy has the power to reanimate the days of war and romance.

[28] 'The Abencerrage' is quoted from Felicia Hemans, *Selected Poems, Letters, Reception Materials*, ed. Susan J. Wolfson (Princeton and Oxford: Princeton University Press, 2000), 90–134. Further references are given by canto and line number within the texts.

It was in terms of such a reanimation of the romantic past that the events of the Peninsular War appealed to Hemans. As she later commented 'I could almost fancy I passed that period of my life in the days of Chivalry, so high and ardent were the feelings they excited'.[29] It was through the framework of Spanish romances and ballads that Hemans imagined the Peninsular War,[30] as in 'The Abencerrage' in which she brings together the country's legendary associations with the recent events of the war:

> Fair land! of chivalry the old domain,
> Land of the vine and olive, lovely Spain! . . .
> Blest be that soil! Where England's heroes share
> The graves of chiefs, for ages slumbering there;
> Whose names are glorious in romantic lays,
> The wild, sweet chronicles of elder days,
> By goatherd lone, and rude serrano sung,
> Thy cypress dells, and vine-clad rocks among.
> How oft those rocks have echo'd to the tale
> Of knights who fell in Roncesvalles' vale;
> Of him, renown'd in old heroic lore,
> First of the brave, the gallant Campeador;
> Of those, the famed in song, who proudly died,
> When 'Rio Verde' roll'd a crimson tide;
> Of that high name, by Garcilaso's might,
> On the green Vega won in single fight.   (II. 1–28)

Here writing half a decade after its conclusion, Hemans associates the Peninsular War with chivalric history as celebrated by the popular ballads on Roland, who died heroically at Roncesvalles in 778, Rodrigo Díaz de Bivar (the 'Campeador' or 'El Cid'), who fought the Moors in the eleventh century, and Garcilaso de la Vega, who defeated a Moor in single combat.[31] It was in such romantic and chivalric terms as 'champions' who 'defend' Freedom's 'sacred cause' that Hemans presented both the British and the Spanish forces in the poem she published on the Peninsular War in 1808, *England and Spain; or, Valour and Patriotism*. In this poem, Hemans links the contemporary success of the British army with the legendary and mythical ('doubtful') exploits of King Arthur:

---

[29] Quoted in Saglia, 'Epic or Domestic?', 142.
[30] On the British literary interest in things Spanish, see Diego Saglia, *Byron and Spain: Itinerary in the Writing of Place* (Salzburg: Edwin Mellen Press, 1996), 29–56.
[31] See *Selected Poems*, ed. Wolfson, 114.

From doubtful Arthur, hero of romance,
King of the circled board, the spear, the lance;
To those whose recent trophies grace her shield,
The gallant victors of Vimiera's field;
Still have her warriors borne th'unfading crown,
And made the British flag the ensign of renown.   (323)[32]

Similarly, in celebrating the Spanish forces, Hemans associates them with the romantic past of Spain which was inspired by the 'Genius of chivalry!' (329). While the medieval forms of chivalry—'the tilt, the tournament, the long crusade'—are a thing of the past—'Those times are fled'—they continue to inspire the imagination ('Whose faded splendour fancy oft recalls') and live on in 'Iberia's sons' as 'virtues': 'Genius of chivalry! Thy noble train, | Thy firm, exalted virtues yet remain!' (329–30). Hemans explores how these virtues ('truth', 'emulation', 'love', 'ardour', 'courage', 'loyalty', 'untainted faith', 'unshaken fortitude', and 'patriot energy' (330)) have inspired 'Iberia's Sons' from the heroes of 'remotest days' (330) down to the current 'champions of their country's cause' (335) who 'proudly emulate their father's fame' (334).

By plotting the Peninsular War through romance in *England and Spain*, Hemans constructs Britain's role as a crusade fought for noble reasons, sanctioning it on a number of levels: moral ('the injured to defend and save'(337)), political ('The reign of Freedom let your arms restore' (337)), historical ('By Albion's thousand, thousand deeds sublime, | Renown'd from zone to zone, from clime to clime'(337)) and religious ('Look down, oh, Heaven! the righteous cause maintain, | Defend the injured, and avenge the slain!'(335)). These justifications also act as prophecies of victory for the crusading forces over the 'despot' (337), ushering in an era of peace, as in Hemans's long poem 'War and Peace', in which the triumph of Albion will lead to the appearance of the angel-form of sweet Peace. While 'War and Peace' does juxtapose its celebration of British heroes and triumphs (Wolfe, Nelson, Moore) with examinations of those damaged by conflict (including the mother who dies of grief after the death of her own son, the daughter lost to anguish, and 'the thousands doom'd to moan, | Condemned by war, to hopeless grief unknown!'),[33] suggesting the tensions of Hemans's post-Waterloo

---

[32] As neither of the recent authoritative editions of Hemans includes a full text of *England and Spain*, I have taken my text from *The Works of Mrs Hemans, with a Memoir by her Sister*, 7 vols. (Edinburgh and London: William Blackwood and Sons and Thomas Cadell, 1839), I. 319–40, citing references by page number.

[33] *The Domestic Affections*, 105.

writing that I will be examining in my final chapter, it is important to emphasize that during the conflict with Napoleon Hemans saw war as entirely necessary:

> For never, *never*, in holier cause,
> Nor sanction'd e'er by purer, nobler laws;
> Has Albion seiz'd the sabre and the shield,
> Or rush'd impetuous to th'ensanguin'd field![34]

In *England and Spain*, Hemans's plotting of the war also draws on the sexual politics of romance, structuring national identity through gender roles. Thus Britain becomes the chivalric protector of feminized Portugal—'brave defenders of her injured cause' (324)—shielding her from any further outrages that might be attempted by 'insulting France' (325). Britain, France, and Spain are embodied as different forms of masculinity; whereas Briton's 'To brave Castile their potent aid supply' (325), the French are led to war by 'cruel rapine' as well as 'mad ambition' (326). This over-virile form of Gallic masculinity is in turn contrasted with the manliness of the 'brave Castilians', whose martial roles are constructed in familial forms as 'fathers' and protectors of 'the maid adored', fighting for 'love' and 'friendship' as well as the 'country's name' (326).

Hemans's continued poetic representation of the deeds of the Spanish and the British in the Peninsular War as a re-enactment of the romantic and chivalric past of Spain can be seen in her retrospective account of the Peninsular War in the second edition of 'The Restoration of the Works of Art to Italy', a post-Napoleonic poem of the restoration period in which Hemans takes stock not only of art history but the recent history of Europe. Calling on the 'Muses' of Italy, she instructs them to sing of the British army and of Wellington:

> Sing of that Leader . . .
> Who bade once more the wild, heroic lay,
> Record the deeds of Roncesvalles' day; . . .
> And 'midst those scenes renew'd the achievements high,
> Bequeath'd to fame by England's ancestry.[35]

Wellington not only revives England's chivalric past but re-enacts the heroics of the Spanish hero Roland. Hemans's reference to Roncesvalles presents the battle fought between Wellington's British army and Soult's

---

[34] Ibid. 115. See Lootens, 'Hemans and Home', for an excellent reading of the ambiguities of 'War and Peace', 240–1.   [35] *Selected Poems*, ed. Wolfson, 19–20.

French troops in that pass in northern Spain on 25 July 1813, during which General Cole's 4th division succeeded in delaying the French advance despite heavy casualties, as a retelling of the story of Roland and his knights, who in medieval romances such as the *Chanson de Roland* fought an army of 400,000 Muslims to cover the retreat of Charlemagne's army. While Roland's army was defeated, their protection of the retreat led to the return of Charlemagne's army and ultimate triumph over the Muslim Saracens.[36] As this paralleling of modern history and medieval legend suggests, for Hemans the significance of the Peninsular War was not just that it looked like 'history in the land of romance', as it did for Scott, but that modern history had become romance. As she emphasizes in *England and Spain*, much of the imaginative power of England's and Spain's chivalric past lay in its legendary and poetic status, as with 'doubtful Arthur, hero of romance' (323) and Chivalry's Gothic reign in Iberia, of which 'all thy glories, all thy deeds of yore, | Live but in legends wild, and poet's lore' (329). For Hemans, the past survives not through history but through legends and poetry— 'romantic lays', 'artless lays', 'heroic tales', 'fabling numbers'—and these forms have a double function, as she writes of the 'gallant Cid' in *England and Spain*: 'And still his deeds Castilian bards rehearse, | Inspiring theme of patriotic verse!' (331). Patriotic verse is not only inspired by the Cid's heroic deeds but in its turn inspires acts that will themselves become the theme of poetry; as Hemans writes in 'The Wreath of Loyalty', the British troops who died 'Mingling blood with Tajo's tide' will themselves 'inspire, | Many a bard and many a lyre, Songs of Spain'.[37] In the poetry of Felicia Hemans, the British contribution to the Peninsular War becomes itself a 'Song of Spain'.

Scott and the Triumph of Romance

In the autumn of 1809, John Murray published John Wilson Croker's *The Battles of Talavera*, a poem on Wellington's victory over Marshall Jourdan of 27–8th July 1809, which proved remarkably popular, going through eight editions in its first year, a number exceeded only by Scott in the period 1809–10.[38] One possible reason for *The Battles of Talavera*'s

---

[36] Chandler, *Dictionary of the Napoleonic Wars* (London: Greenhill Books, 1993), 384; *Felicia Hemans*, ed. Kelly, 114.   [37] *The Domestic Affections*, 127.

[38] A. D. Harvey, *English Poetry in a Changing Society, 1780–1825* (London: Allison and Busby, 1980), 188.

extraordinary success was offered by the anonymous reviewer of the *Quarterly Review*, who commented in November 1809 that the poem 'is written in that irregular Pindaric measure first applied to serious composition by Mr Walter Scott, and it is doing no injustice to the ingenious author to say, that in many passages, we were, from the similarity of the stanza and of the subject, involuntarily reminded of the battle of Flodden, in the sixth book of *Marmion*'.[39] Croker had adopted the irregular stanza form of Scott's metrical romances and the techniques of battle description of his best-seller of the previous year and applied them to a contemporary British victory, presenting Talavera through the picturesque techniques that proved so successful for his model; the *Quarterly* reviewer pointed to the 'picturesque merit' of the poem's description of battle (295). Walter Scott himself wrote to congratulate Croker on his poem and commented enthusiastically: 'Many a heart has kindled at your Talavera which may be the more patriotic for the impulse as long as it shall beat. I trust we shall soon hear from the Conqueror of that glorious day such news as may procure us "another of the same".'[40] In other words, the main outcome of a further British victory will be another Croker poem and, indeed, the success of Croker's poem prompted a huge number of similar pieces; as Richard Cronin has observed, after the success of Croker's poem 'every allied victory, and especially any victory by Wellington, had prompted a poem'.[41] The writers of such poems frequently used Croker as their model, like the author of *The Battles of the Danube, and Barrosa* (1811), who dedicated his volume to Croker and commented that 'The just celebrity and extensive circulation of "the Battles of Talavera", induced the Author of the following poems to try how far the sanguinary conflicts on the banks of the Danube, upon a similar plan, might prove successful.'[42] The poetic transformation of modern war into romance, achieved through the forms and tropes of Scottian poetics, would seem to be complete. Indeed, a revealing comment on the effect of this transformation of war was provided by the Conqueror of Talavera himself. Wellington, who considered Talavera to be one of the bloodiest battles that he had ever fought,[43] and who was

---

[39] Scott, *Miscellaneous Works* (Edinburgh: Adam and Charles Black, 1880–1), XVII. 293. References to this review are hereafter cited by page number within the text.

[40] *The Letters of Walter Scott*, ed. Herbert J. C. Grierson (London: Constable), XII. 404.

[41] *The Politics of Romantic Poetry: In Search of the Pure Commonwealth* (Basingstoke, London, and New York: Macmillan and St Martin's Press, 2000), 130.

[42] *GM*, 82 (January 1812), 57.

[43] Chandler, *Dictionary of the Napoleonic Wars*, 435. The British had lost 5,365 in all (or one-quarter of their strength), the Spanish 1,200, and the French 7,268.

notoriously matter-of-fact in his own accounts of battles and critical of those he considered to be too fanciful, wrote to Croker from Badajoz saying that he had read the poem with great pleasure, adding 'I did not think a battle could be turned into anything so entertaining'.[44]

It perhaps comes as no surprise that the anonymous reviewer of the *Quarterly* was none other than Scott himself, and his review of Croker's poem can be seen as both a self-justification and self-criticism of his own role as poet. Scott makes writing verse a martial and manly activity, presenting Croker as a 'volunteer' who has 'rushed forward' (293). He begins his final sentence: 'It is *"the heart, the heart"*, that makes the poet as well as the soldier' (300), clinching the association of poetry with fighting and constructing Croker as a kind of surrogate of himself. The rhyming of the poet is as necessary as the drilling of the volunteer when faced with the threat of Bonaparte. Scott uses this martial register particularly when commenting on Croker's use of the irregular Pindaric form, particularly appropriate for his subject because:

in passages of vivid, and especially of tumultuary and hurried description, the force of the poet's thought, and the intenseness of the feeling excited, ought to support his language. He may be then permitted to strip himself as to a combat, and to evince that 'brave neglect' of the forms of versification which express such an imagination too much exalted, and a mind too much occupied by the subject itself, to regard punctiliously the arrangement of rhymes or the measurement of stanzas. (294)

The very irregularity of form, a looseness for which reviewers frequently criticized Scott's own poetry, is ideally suited to a patriotic subject like Talavera because the poet's exalted imagination transcends the petty considerations of regular form: 'In this point of view, few themes present themselves which can better authorize a daring flight, than that which had been selected by the author of Talavera'(294). Yet Scott's emphasis on his manly and martial stanza form itself constitutes a daring, or even scandalous, regendering of poetry and rewriting of literary history akin to Wordsworth's regendering of the sonnet and elision of Charlotte Smith from its own literary history. Contrary to Scott's argument in the review, the irregular form had not been 'first applied to serious composition by Mr Walter Scott' in *The Lay of the Last Minstrel* but by Coleridge in *Christabel*, written in 1797 and 1800 but not published until 1816. Scott would later acknowledge the influence of *Christabel* on his *Lay* in the 1830 'Introduction' to the poem, echoing his review when

[44] *DNB*, V. 125.

commenting that 'it was in Christabel that I first found it used in serious poetry, and it is to Mr. Coleridge that I am bound to make the acknowledgement due from the pupil to his master.'[45] But during the period of his greatest success as a poet, Scott made no such acknowledgement and to many of those who knew Coleridge's unpublished poem, including the Wordsworths and Southey, Scott's Lay seemed at best to borrow many elements from Christabel (the gothic setting, the enchantress figure, and particular phrases, as well as the verse form), and at worst to plagiarize it.[46] Yet, as we have seen, if The Lay of the Last Minstrel did originate in part in the feminized gothic of Coleridge's tale of the supernatural and same-sex relations, Scott turned away from the more feminized elements of romance, emphasizing instead the masculine chivalric elements of war and heroism. In Scott's hands romance becomes manly, and by writing Christabel out of his short history of the irregular stanza form Scott both disqualifies the feminized romance of Christabel from the category of 'serious poetry' and severs his versions of the genre and verse form from its feminized origins.

Scott's account of Croker can be seen to give his own writing a major role in what he presents as a necessary transformation of verse in wartime when too many writers 'amuse themselves with luscious sonnets to Bessies and Jessies', 'roam back to distant and dark ages', and 'wander to remote countries, instead of seeking a theme in the exploits of a Nelson, an Abercromby, or a Wellesley' (292). In my previous chapter, I argued that Scott's own roaming 'back to distant and dark ages' needs to be understood within the wartime context, but the potentially morale-boosting effect of the application of his romance form to the specific events of the war with France had seemed apparent from the very start of his career as a romancer, as we saw in Warren Hastings's wish that Scott 'would compose a poem of the nature of the old Minstrellsy, and make our gallant Nelson the Subject of it'.[47] While Scott turned down this suggestion partly as a result of his lack of expert knowledge of naval matters, Hastings's proposal also raised the more challenging question of the adequacy of poetry for representing contemporary history at all, prompting Scott to comment that 'Trafalgar is almost too grand in its native simplicity to be heightened by poetical imagery' and that, though he has 'repeatedly sat down to the task, it has always

---

[45] Poetical Works, ed. J. Logie Robertson (London: Henry Frowde, 1904), 52.
[46] See Sutherland, The Life of Walter Scott: A Critical Biography (Oxford: Blackwell Publishers, 1997), 100–2, 147–50.   [47] Letters of Walter Scott, XII. 382.

completely overwhelmed me'.[48] It is with precisely this question of poetry's adequacy as a means of responding to the grandeur of contemporary events that Scott begins his first attempt to write an expanded poem on the conflict with France, *The Vision of Don Roderick* (1811). In this poem, Scott uses a visionary machinery to survey the history of Spain from the Moorish invasion of 711 up to the French incursions in the Peninsula, and he opens by considering the relationship between modern war and forms traditionally used for representing conflict:

> Lives there a strain, whose sounds of mounting fire
> May rise distinguish'd o'er the din of war;
> Or died it with yon master of the lyre,
> Who sung beleaguer'd Ilion's evil star? (I. 1)[49]

Scott's motives in writing *Don Roderick* are normally seen as a result of his enthusiasm for British involvement in the Peninsular War, which found an occasion for expression with the formation of the committee to raise money for the Portuguese victims of the conflict to which the profits from the poem were to be presented (*LWS*, III. 276). Assessing the poem within this context, Scott and many of his critics have presented it as a work which should not be taken too seriously, but *Don Roderick* can also be seen as a more ambitious attempt to meet Hastings's challenge and to respond to his own criticism of modern poets and rhymers in his review of *The Battles of Talavera*. This new seriousness is immediately apparent in Scott's shift from the octosyllabic line to the Spenserian stanza, a formal shift which Canning, who had frequently criticized Scott's use of the irregular stanza, wrote to him to praise, describing the newly adopted verse form as 'at once the most artificial and the most magnificent that our language affords' (*LWS*, III. 281). Yet Scott's shift to the Spenserian stanza also indicates the difficulty for him in responding poetically to contemporary events. While the irregular Pindaric measure was good enough for Croker's *The Battles of Talavera*, the 'theme' authorizing Croker's 'daring flight', it does not seem to have been good enough for Scott's own poem on the national theme. And while Wellington's feats provide a theme for an epic strain akin to Homer's, the romance form that Croker had applied to Talavera is here presented as unworthy of representing them:

---

[48] Ibid. 384.

[49] References to *The Vision of Don Roderick* are by part and stanza number.

> But we, weak minstrels of a laggard day,
>   Skill'd but to imitate an elder page,
> Timid and raptureless, can we repay
>   The debt thou claim'st in this exhausted age?   (I. 3)

In the stanzas that follow, an exchange between the poet and the voice of the 'Mountain Spirit' of his native Scotland, the reason that modern poetry is in crisis and written by 'a faint degenerate band' (I. 3) is presented as the lack of a living relationship between poetry and war:

> 'If to such task presumptuous thou aspire,
>   Seek not from us the meed to warrior due:
> Age after age has gather'd son to sire,
>   Since our grey cliffs the din of conflict knew,
> Or, pealing through our vales, victorious bugles blew.
>
> 'Decay'd our old traditionary lore,
>   Save where the lingering fays renew their ring,
> By milk-maid seen beneath the hawthorn hoar,
>   Or round the marge of Minchmore's haunted spring:
> Save where their legends grey-hair'd shepherds sing
>   That now scarce win a listening ear but thine,
> Of feuds obscure, and Border ravaging,
>   And rugged deeds recount in rugged line,
> Of moonlight foray made on Teviot, Tweed, or Tyne.'   (I. 7–8)

No longer a vital force due to the increasing peacefulness of modern Scotland, poetry has degenerated into two different forms of romance, the feminized tales of the supernatural or the archaic and obscure rhymes collected by the antiquarian Scott himself. However, if the minstrelsy of the poet's native land cannot supply the necessary strain, the Mountain Spirit directs him to a source where poetry exists as a vital form:

> 'No! search romantic lands, where the near Sun
>   Gives with unstinted boon ethereal flame,
> Where the rude villager, his labour done,
>   In verse spontaneous chants some favour'd name
> Whether Olalia's charms his tribute claim,
>   Her eye of diamond, and her locks of jet;
> Or whether, kindling at the deeds of Græme,
>   He sing, to wild Morisco measure set,
> Old Albin's red claymore, green Erin's bayonet!   (I. 9)

Unlike the feminized or antiquarian forms of romance of his own land, Scott presents the poetry of 'romantic lands' as spontaneous, living and manly—associated with the noble savage figure of the 'rude villager' who sings both love songs and war songs. If Spain is at an earlier stage of development than peaceful Scotland, its poetry is still inspired by the events of the war taking place on its soil. In turning to Spain for his theme, Scott presents himself not as applying the forms of his minstrelsy to the events of war, but as producing a more genuine and living romance form, which will reanimate poetry, a point emphasized by the 'Mountain Spirit':

> 'And cherish'd still by that unchanging race,
>   Are themes for minstrelsy more high than thine;
> Of strange tradition many a mystic trace,
>   Legend and vision, prophecy and sign;
> Where wonders wild of Arabesque combine
>   With Gothic imagery of darker shade,
> Forming a model meet for minstrel line.
>   Go, seek such theme!' The Mountain Spirit said:
> With filial awe I heard; I heard, and I obey'd.   (I. 12)

While attempting a theme higher than anything he has tried previously, Scott will also establish continuity with the poets previously invoked, becoming the latest in the 'minstrel line' that links him with the epic poets Milton and Homer, solving the poetic crisis outlined in stanza III. Scott aligns this sense of poetic continuity with a continued tradition of Scottish heroism. While the example of the 'rude villager' offers a model for reanimated romance, it is emphasized that he sings not of Spanish heroics but of the exploits of British forces—'the deeds of Græme', 'Old Albin's red claymore, green Erin's bayonet.' Scott includes references to the English and Irish elements of the army, but as Sutherland has observed he particularly praises Scottish heroes in the poem.[50] In a note to this stanza, he described Græme as 'a name sacred for ages to heroic verse' and in the penultimate stanza of the poem, after his visionary machinery has brought him to contemporary events in Spain, he returns to sing the praises of this 'hero of a race renown'd of old, | Whose war-cry oft has waked the battle-swell' (III. 17) in a passage which, as Scott comments in a note, 'alludes to the various achievements of the warlike family of Græme, or Grahame'.[51] In singing 'the deeds of Græme' in his 'Conclusion', then, Scott not only models his revived romance on that of the 'rude villager' from the introduction, a figure for the spontaneity and vitality of the form, but presents its as part of a continuous line of 'heroic verse' that sang this 'name sacred

---

[50] *Life of Walter Scott*, 159.   [51] *Poetical Works*, 611, 618.

for ages'. In embracing the events of the Peninsular War, Scott presents his poetry as transformed from the imitations of an elder page to become the 'living descendant' of the romance form.

However, while Scott presents his turn to Spanish subjects as reviving his romance, he leaves unresolved the relation between the 'strain' he invoked at the poem's opening, and the 'patriot's parting strain' (II. 63), as he characterizes his concluding verses on the Scottish heroes of war— Cadogan, Beresford, and Græme. Despite the epic demands of the theme fit for Homer and Milton, the best that Scott can offer is romance. Indeed, with only five stanzas to go, Scott continues to seek the appropriate verse for the celebration of these heroes with the apostrophe:

> O for a verse of tumult and of flame,
>   Bold as the bursting of their cannon sound,
> To bid the world re-echo to their fame!
>   For never, upon gory battle-ground,
> With conquest's well-bought wreath were braver victors crown'd!
>
> (III. 13)

Scott's apostrophe, like his opening search for 'a strain . . . of mountain fire | [which] May rise distinguish'd o'er the din of war' (I.1), recalls Shakespeare's *Henry V*: 'O for a muse of fire, that would ascend | The brightest heaven of invention' (Prologue, 1–2).[52] If Scott seeks to associate his poem with a play popular at the time and seen as a patriotic celebration of English triumph over the French, he also invokes the representational problems posed by war. For Scott, these challenges are heightened by the need to represent modern battle, symbolized here as throughout his poetry by 'cannon sound'. For Scott, as he would argue in his 'Essay on Chivalry', it was the widespread use of gunpowder which contributed to, and symbolized, the shift from chivalric to modern war, a distinction he had drawn in *Marmion* in which the sounds of the cannon come 'Not in the close successive rattle, | That breathes the voice of modern battle' (VI. 23).[53] In *Don Roderick*, Scott emphasizes this role of gunpowder in the transformation of war during the shift from the first to the second period of Roderick's vision:

> For War a new and dreadful language spoke,
>   Never by ancient warrior heard or known;
> Lightning and smoke her breath, and thunder was her tone. (II. 26)

---

[52] He may also be recalling Croker's *The Battles of Talavera*, which includes the lines 'Oh, for a blaze from heaven to light | The wonders of that gloomy fight'. Quoted *GM*, 82 (1812), 56.   [53] 'Essay on Chivalry', *Miscellaneous Works of Walter Scott*, VI. 107–9.

In seeking 'a verse of tumult and of flame', Scott aspires to a new poetry that will match this new language of war, a strain which 'with all o'er-pouring measure, | Might melodize with each tumultuous sound' (I. 2). Such verse must not only register the dramatic nature of modern battle, but be aesthetically pleasing, creating melody out of the tumultuous sounds of modern war.

In his two extended poems on the war with France, *The Vision of Don Roderick* and *The Field of Waterloo*, Scott offers very different responses to the aesthetic challenge of representing modern war in poetry. In *The Vision of Don Roderick*, Scott's poem builds inexorably through the history of Spain to the battles of the Peninsular War, and the poet prepares his audience for the imagining of British triumphs:

> Now on the scene Vimeira should be shown,
> On Talavera's fight should Roderick gaze,
> And hear Corunna wail her battle won,
> And see Busaco's crest with lightning blaze: (II. 61)

This was the moment Scott's readers had waited for, in Warren Hastings's case since 1805, as the writer celebrated for his description of the battle of Flodden prepared to give his account of the 'Atchievement' of the British army in the style 'of the old Minstrellsy'. Indeed, in the preceding stanzas in which Scott described the arrival of the British forces—'It was a dread, yet spirit-stirring sight' (II. 56)—he already seemed to be writing history in terms of romance, combining the patriotism and form of Spenser ('From mast and stern St. George's symbol flow'd'(II. 55)) with allusions to his own poetry, such as the celebrated description of the arrival by boat of the Clan-Alpine in *The Lady of the Lake* (which John Sutherland has seen as itself a tribute to Highland Regiments).[54] Scott even echoes Croker's *The Battles of Talavera*, including what he had described in his review as the 'beautifully described' passage on the 'approach of the Gallic army' which began 'And is it now a goodly sight, | Or dreadful to behold . . .'.[55] Yet just as in 1805, when Scott found himself 'completely overwhelmed' by Trafalgar, the poet turns away from the task that this time he appeared to have set himself, though for different reasons:

---

[54] *The Life of Walter Scott*, 143.
[55] Quoted in *Miscellaneous Works of Walter Scott*, XVII. 297.

> But shall fond fable mix with heroes' praise?
> Hath fiction's stage for truth's long triumphs room?
> And dare her wild-flowers mingle with the bays,
>   That claim a long eternity to bloom
> Around the warrior's crest, and o'er the warrior's tomb!   (II. 61)

While the structure of Scott's poem seemed to have been chosen to enable the transformation of British deeds in the Peninsula into romance, romance now becomes an inadequate mode for celebration and commemoration of British heroes. Scott's placing of history over poetry in a hierarchical relation to truth anticipates his comment of 1813 that: 'If the want of sieges, and battles, and great military evolutions, in our poetry, is complained of, let us reflect, that the campaigns and heroes of our days are perpetuated in a record that neither requires nor admits of the aid of fiction.'[56] It is history, what in *Don Roderick* Scott describes as 'the glorious past, | The deeds recorded, and the laurels won' (II. 63), that constitutes for Scott the true record of the British role in the war.

If during the course of the Napoleonic wars Scott's reflections on the role of romance in the representation of modern war would appear to constitute a move away from poetry and towards history as the most appropriate form for responding to the contemporary conflict (a shift that anticipates his move from poetry to the novel),[57] the final triumph of Wellington over Napoleon at Waterloo in 1815 provided an opportunity too good to miss for one final poetic charge. And in *The Field of Waterloo* Scott did follow Croker's example in using the stanza form and descriptive style of his metrical romances to represent a British victory. For example, Scott's description of the heroic resistance of the Scottish army at Flodden in *Marmion* is practically interchangeable with his portrayal of the British infantry at Waterloo.[58] Indeed, Scott's portrayal of Waterloo was so reminiscent of his earlier poetic battles that his printer, James Ballantyne, raised objections in the margins to the proof sheets. For example, in a passage describing the charge of the French cavalry, Scott had written:

> Down were the eagle banners sent,
> Down, down the horse and horseman went.

---

[56] 'Introduction', *Bridal of Triermain, Poetical Works*, 586.
[57] See Philip Shaw's excellent discussion, *Waterloo and the Romantic Imagination* (Basingstoke and New York: Palgrave Macmillan, 2002), 35–66.
[58] Compare *Marmion* VI. 34 with *The Field of Waterloo*, 12.

Ballantyne commented that 'This is very spirited and very fine; but it is unquestionably liable to the charge of being very nearly a direct repetition of yourself', and he quoted *The Lord of the Isles*, adding emphasis:

> *Down! down!* in headlong overthrow,
> *Horseman and horse*, the foremost go,[59]

To write *Waterloo*, then, Scott borrowed from his own metrical romances, and his poem on the battle is structured by its conventions. Wellington, for example, is introduced through the chivalric imagery Scott had employed in his previous poems as 'his country's sword and shield' (10), and while he commands rather than fights, his own valour is stressed by his positioning 'in the battle-front . . . | Where danger fiercest swept the field' (10).

In a brilliant and stimulating discussion of *The Field of Waterloo*, Philip Shaw sees the battle as the ultimate triumph of history over romance—'History itself has done away with the need for mythopoeic representation; the force of romance is, as it were, immanent within the field of actuality.'[60] As we have seen, Scott had been aware of the possible redundancy of romance, and poetry more generally, since confronted by the grandeur of Trafalgar in 1805, and he had continued to juxtapose the forms of 'fable' and 'fiction' with those of 'truth' ever since. For Shaw, Waterloo provides the perfect conclusion to this argument: 'The judgement of literary history, that *The Field of Waterloo* cannot "come up" to the event it narrates, suggest that Waterloo itself is the great poem that Scott can never write.'[61] While Scott may well have agreed with this assessment of his own poem, reminding a friend to whom he was sending a copy that 'it is not always the grandest actions which are best adopted for the arts of poetry and painting' (*LWS*, V. 87–8) and making the standard gestures of poetic deference ('Forgive, brave Dead, the imperfect lay' (22)), in the final lines of the main part of his poem he suddenly transforms his evaluation of his narrative and reverses his hierarchy of history and romance. Describing the damage to the 'sad Field', he asks 'Has not such havoc brought a name | Immortal in the rolls of fame?' (23). We might expect these 'rolls of fame' to be the same as the 'record' that rendered redundant 'the aid of fiction' in his comment of 1813. But Scott's answer to his question in 1815 is surprising:

---

[59] Quoted in *LWS*, V. 92. [60] *Waterloo and the Romantic Imagination*, 60.
[61] Ibid.

> Yes, Agincourt may be forgot,
> And Cressy be an unknown spot,
>   And Blenheim's name be new;
> But still in story and in song,
> For many an age remember'd long,
> Shall live the towers of Hougomont,
>   And field of Waterloo.   (23)

Here history becomes redundant in assessing Waterloo, because the modern battle transcends the British victories of the past. Instead, as for Hemans writing about the Peninsular War, it is the fictional and fabular forms of 'story' and 'song' that are necessary for the remembering of Waterloo. At the end of the wars, and the end of his poetic career, Scott finds in Waterloo an event which, rather than making romance redundant, redeems it. And this reclaiming of romance as a mode of historical understanding is signalled in the immediate formal change in the poem, as Scott swaps his octosyllabic line for the Spenserian stanza in which he presents the British triumph over France:

> Now, Island Empress, wave thy crest on high,
> And bid the banner of thy patron flow,
> Gallant Saint George, the flower of Chivalry,
> For thou hast faced, like him, a dragon foe,
> And rescued innocence from overthrow,
> And trampled down, like him, tyrannic might,
> And to the gazing world mayst proudly show
> The chosen emblem of thy sainted Knight,
> Who quell'd devouring pride, and vindicated right.[62]

If Scott's comparable shift of form in *Don Roderick* had been accompanied by questions about the status of romance as a means of representing war, after Waterloo there remains no doubt about the appropriate genre for understanding the events of the last twenty-two years and Britain's role in them. For Scott in *The Field of Waterloo*, the defeat of Napoleon represents the triumph of romance.

The Pilgrim on the Plains of War: Childe Harold in the Spanish Peninsula

While the role of *Childe Harold's Pilgrimage* in making Byron famous in 1812 is one of the best-known literary anecdotes of the romantic period,

---

[62] *Poetical Works*, 627 (no stanza or line number given).

the controversy over Byron's use of genre in the poem is less familiar. Subtitled *A Romaunt*, Byron's poem was published at a moment when the genre and its associated values had become integral to contemporary understandings of the war with France and particularly the Peninsular War.[63] For many of the reviews, such as the *Monthly Review*, Byron's title-page raised 'magnificent expectations' of 'chivalrous antiquity' and 'heroic adventure' that the poem failed to satisfy.[64] The *British Review* wrote that 'When we first heard of the poem of Childe Harold—a Romaunt—what could we expect, but a new assortment of chivalrous tales, of amours and battles, of giants and deliverers, of knights and Saracens, of dwarfs and demons?'[65] Such chivalric tales of valiant deliverance would have a clear relevance to contemporary events, but the poem, and especially its hero, represented a falling away from the genre's noble traditions: 'the Childe Harolde [*sic*] is no child of chivalry. Neither virtue nor enterprize is his.'[66] As the *Anti-Jacobin Review* commented, *Childe Harold* was 'a perfect anomaly in the annals of chivalry, or in the history of romance', and, what was worse, the figure who was expected to embody ideal national character was used for a wholesale attack on war:

He arraigns wars, generally and indiscriminately, confounding the just with the unjust, the defensive with the offensive, the preservative with the destructive, not with the judgment of a sage, but with the settled moroseness of a misanthrope; victories, though gained by courage exerted in the best of causes, excite only the sarcastic sneers of this querulous vagabond; and the profession of a soldier, deemed honourable by wise and good men, is the subject of his ridicule and contempt.[67]

In his anomalous romance, Byron had made the genre a vehicle for anti-war sentiment, and he specifically ridiculed the failure of the British leaders to live up to the chivalric roles that were being scripted for them, as in his stanzas on the Convention of Cintra.[68] Using an allegorical style derived from, and parodying, Spenser, Byron satirizes the 'champions'

---

[63] For valuable general accounts of Byron's treatment of the Peninsular War, see William A. Borst, *Lord Byron's First Pilgrimage* (New Haven: Yale University Press, 1948), 42–9; Saglia, *Byron and Spain*, 67–93; Cronin, *The Politics of Romantic Poetry*, 128–44.

[64] Quoted in Donald H. Reiman (ed.), *The Romantics Reviewed: Contemporary Reviews of British Romantic Writers, Part B: Byron and Regency Society Poets*, 5 vols. (New York and London: Garland Publishing, 1972), IV. 1731.   [65] Ibid., I. 396.

[66] Ibid., I. 397.   [67] Ibid., I. 11.

[68] As David Duff has pointed out in a valuable discussion of romance in the poem, Byron does apply the notion of chivalry 'to the political struggle of the Spaniards themselves', *Romance and Revolution: Shelley and the Politics of a Genre* (Cambridge: Cambridge University Press, 1994), 125, and see 123–7.

with 'names known to chivalry' who have been defeated by a scoffing, impish figure that recalls the Goblin Page of Scott's *Lay of the Last Minstrel*: 'Convention is the dwarfish demon styl'd | That foil'd the knights in Marialva's dome' (I. 24–6).[69]

If *Childe Harold's Pilgrimage* subverts romance and its intrinsic link with martial ideology and national identity, in it Byron particularly attacks poetry as the form that mediates the war to the reading public (unlike his later treatment of the subject in *Don Juan*, he makes no reference to other forms of mediation such as gazettes, bulletins, or newspapers). In this attack, he targets traditional as well as contemporary practice, writing for a readership which he expects to recognize his allusions. For example, in his stanzas on Talavera, Byron describes those killed in the battle as follows:

> There they shall rot—Ambition's honoured fools!
> Yes, Honour decks the turf that wraps their clay!
> Vain Sophistry! (I. 42)

Here Byron compresses two lines from William Collins's celebrated 'Ode, Written in the Beginning of the Year 1746', which begins 'How sleep the brave' and describes the 'sod' where the brave 'sink to rest | By all their country's wishes blest!' (ll. 1–2):

> There Honour comes, a pilgrim grey,
> To bless the turf that wraps their clay (ll. 9–10)[70]

Byron undercuts Collins's euphemistic poetic eulogizing through his own monosyllabic, matter-of-fact emphasis on corporeal decomposition and through direct denunciation. His pilgrim comes to the battlefield not to cover the war dead with laurels but to view the corpses that 'feed the crow in Talavera's plain, | And fertilize the field that each pretends to gain' (I. 41). Byron had been even more explicit in his attack on the mediation and consumption of war as poetry in his manuscript draft:

> There shall they rot—while rhymers tell the fools
> How honour decks the turf that wraps their clay!
> Liars avaunt![71]

---

[69] Unless otherwise stated, references to Byron's poetry are to *Byron: The Oxford Authors*, ed. Jerome J. McGann (Oxford: Oxford University Press, 1986). References to *Childe Harold's Pilgrimage* are given by canto and line number.

[70] *The Poems of Thomas Gray, William Collins, and Oliver Goldsmith*, ed. Roger Lonsdale (London and Harlow: Longmans, Green and Co., 1969), 437.

[71] Quoted in *The Works of Lord Byron*, 13 vols., *Poetry*, ed. Ernest Hartley Coleridge (London and New York: John Murray and Charles Scribner's Sons, 1899), II. 50.

The explicitness of this attack on poets is a feature of the manuscript drafts in which Byron denounces poets as 'poets, prone to lie' and 'fabling poets'.[72]

By the time he came to publish *Childe Harold's Pilgrimage*, Byron was aware that he was entering a market that was already well supplied with poetical works on Spain, as he notes in his 'Preface'.[73] Byron may have composed the majority of *Childe Harold* without knowledge of the success of Croker's *The Battles of Talavera* (published in November after he had left on his tour) or of the many poems written along similar lines that took later battles as their subjects, yet on his return he became quickly aware of such works, in the stanza on 'Albuera! Glorious field of grief' added at Newstead in August 1811 denouncing these poetic celebrations of the battle: 'Thy name shall circle round the gaping throng, | And shine in worthless lays, the theme of transient song' (I. 43).[74] In an excellent discussion of the relation of *Childe Harold's Pilgrimage* to other poems on the Peninsular War, Richard Cronin has argued that Byron had Scott specifically in mind in his attacks on the versification of war, though Cronin goes on to argue that as 'he tours the field, imagining the battle in which so many died, Byron becomes the representative of all those countrymen of his who eagerly scanned their newspapers for the latest bulletin from the Peninsula, who triumphed in the news of each victory and grieved over every fresh defeat'.[75] While following Cronin's suggestion of reading Byron's treatment of the Peninsular War in the context of Scott's poetry, I want to argue that Byron's poem was critical of the 'imaginative consumption of war' rather than representative of it.

The paradoxes of Byron's attack on the Scottian poeticizing of war are particularly apparent in his famous description of the battle of Talavera. Crucial to Byron's poetic authority in *Childe Harold's Pilgrimage* is his presentation of himself as one who had seen the sights he describes,[76] and to validate his stance on the Peninsular War he presents himself as an eyewitness of the battle of Talavera, even though he was in Seville when it was being fought:[77]

[72] Coleridge (ed.), *Poetry*, II. 32.   [73] *Byron: Oxford Authors*, 20.

[74] For details of Byron's additions and revisions, see Jerome J. McGann, *Fiery Dust: Byron's Poetic Development* (Chicago: University of Chicago Press, 1968), 101–2.

[75] *The Politics of Romantic Poetry*, 131, 135. See also Jerome Christensen's argument that 'the imperial character emerges in *Childe Harold* as the blithe consumer of the representations of the bloody delights of others', *Lord Byron's Strength: Romantic Writing and Commercial Society* (Baltimore and London: Johns Hopkins University Press, 1993), 72.

[76] See 'Preface' (*Byron: Oxford Authors*, 19) and I. 60–2.

[77] See Coleridge (ed.), *Poetry*, II. 49 n. 1.

> By Heaven! it is a splendid sight to see
> (For one who hath no friend, no brother there)
> Their rival scarfs of mix'd embroidery,
> Their various arms that glitter in the air!   (I. 40)

Ironically, while emphasizing his own position as an eyewitness to the conflict, Byron relies on techniques of battle poetry that Scott had used in *Marmion* to transform conflict into picturesque romance. Indeed, his picturesque description of it is comparable to similar moments in the battle poetry of Scott—'It was a dread yet spirit-stirring sight' (*Don Roderick*, II. 56)—and Croker:

> And is it now a goodly sight,
>   Or dreadful to behold,
> The pomp of that approaching fight,
> Waving ensigns, pennons light,
> And gleaming blades and bayonets bright.[78]

Indeed, while both these writers call into question the nature of the aesthetic experience of watching battle, Byron allows the aesthetic experience to stand unquestioned at this point, so that his undermining of it in the second half of the stanza becomes more powerful:

> What gallant war-hounds rouse then from their lair,
> And gnash their fangs, loud yelling for the prey!
> All join the chase, but few the triumph share;
> The Grave shall bear the chiefest prize away,
> And Havoc scarce for joy can number their array.   (I. 40)

For a number of critics this stanza exemplifies Byron's unstable attitude to war, oscillating between admiration and denunciation.[79] Yet the passage on Talavera is not marked by alternation so much as a sonnet-like turn in the modes of representation that occurs between the chivalric 'gallant' and the bestial 'war-hounds', Byron's use of the formal possibilities of the Spenserian stanza anticipating the juxtapositions and deflations that would become characteristic of his use of the ottava rima stanza. Contrary to his own implicit claim, Byron's attack on the representation of war works not through a juxtaposition of the poetic and the real, or the fictional and the factual, but through a clash of rival poetic modes. The picturesque techniques of romance made popular by Scott

---

[78] *The Battles of Talavera*, quoted in Scott, *Miscellaneous Works*, XVII. 293.
[79] Cronin, *The Politics of Romantic Poetry*, 135; Saglia, *Byron and Spain*, 76.

are set against the techniques of the sublime or horrific ode on war, familiar from the writings of the 1790s, seen in the personifications of 'Red Battle' and the 'Giant' War in the previous stanzas frequently compared to the sublime figures of Goya's war paintings (I. 38–9).[80] It is the framing and containing of violence through romance and the picturesque that Byron exposes in his stanzas on Talavera and which he later figures in his description of the bullfight in Seville, tracing the degeneration of chivalric spectacle to violent savagery. Like the passage on Talavera, Byron begins his description of the bullfight with an emphasis on the coming conflict as a visually appealing chivalric display:

> Hush'd is the din of tongues—on gallant steeds,
> With milk-white crest, gold spur, and light-pois'd lance,
> Four cavaliers prepare for venturous deeds,
> And lowly bending to the lists advance;
> Rich are their scarfs, their chargers featly prance: (I. 73)

But, as in his account of Talavera, Byron undermines this picturesque mediation of violence to the 'gaping throng', the word 'gallant' again signalling the shift from the chivalric to the horrific:

> One gallant steed is stretch'd a mangled corse;
> Another, hideous sight! unseam'd appears,
> His gory chest unveils life's panting source,   (I. 77)

As at Talavera, which culminates with corpses rotting on the battlefield, so in the bullring we are left with the body of the bull—'sweet sight for vulgar eyes' (I. 79). Byron attacks the romantic and picturesque framing of violence which produces the 'splendid sight' of war or the 'sweet sight' of the bullfight.

Often presented as the most sceptical of the canonical poets of the romantic period in his ideas about the imagination,[81] throughout the first canto of Childe Harold Byron attacks the poetic imagining of war, be it in the forms of the songs and romances of Spain, the eighteenth century elegiac mode of Collins, the romance genre with its endorsements of national crusades, or the picturesqueness of Scott's descriptions

---

[80] On the 'bloody giant' as Byron's 'chief essay in sublime war reportage', and the link with Goya, see Christensen, Lord Byron's Strength, 71.

[81] M. H. Abrams omits Byron from his classic study of the romantic imagination, Natural Supernaturalism: Tradition and Revolution in Romantic Literature (New York and London: W. W. Norton and Co., 1971); see 13.

of battle. But in the additional stanzas Byron wrote in August 1811 once he had returned to England, his continued reflection on the war in Spain led him to reconceive the role of poetry, fancy, and even romance (in a manner that recalls Charlotte Smith's wartime revalidation of 'fancy' in *The Emigrants*). For McGann these additions and revisions radically altered not only the poem but Western culture, changing '*Childe Harold's Pilgrimage I–II* from an interesting, at times brilliant, but always highly derivative personal travelogue (with a truly "pointless" titular hero) to the revolutionary confessional poem which so decisively influenced Romantic and post-Romantic art'.[82] But what I want to emphasize here is the extent to which Byron's new direction in poetry was the result of his sustained reflection on war, the subject of all these additions to canto I. Whereas in the first version of stanza 87, initially a satire on the travel writer Sir John Carr, Byron had directed to 'the Boke of Carr' readers 'who would more of Spain and Spaniards know, | Sights, Saints, Antiques, Arts, Anecdotes and War', war featuring as only one of the elements that constitute Spain, in his revised version war becomes the country's defining condition: 'Ye, who would more of Spain and Spaniards know, | Go, read whate'er is writ of bloodiest strife' (I. 87).[83]

As William A. Borst has argued, Byron's additional stanzas are politically more optimistic than the rest of the poem. Contrasting his exclamation of 1809—'Ah! Spain! how sad will be thy reckoning-day' (I. 52)—with that of 1811—'Nor yet, alas! The dreadful work is done' (I. 89)—Borst comments that the 'added stanzas are less occupied with predicting Spain's certain downfall than they are with lamenting that her day of deliverance is not nearer at hand. The assumption now is that day will eventually come.'[84] And as Borst observes, Byron's imagery for the moment of political redemption—'And Freedom's stranger tree grow native of the soil!' (I. 90)—anticipates the celebrated picture of Freedom in canto IV of *Childe Harold*, in both passages Byron reusing the imagery of the French Revolution to construct this envisioned future.[85] But the most important development in Byron's treatment of the Peninsular War in these stanzas is that in the first of them he locates the conflict within a much grander historical framework, anticipating the prophetic tone of his later poetry:

[82] *Fiery Dust*, 105.
[83] Manuscript version quoted in Coleridge (ed.), *Poetry*, II. 78.
[84] *Lord Byron's First Pilgrimage*, 48.   [85] Ibid. 49.

Flows there a tear of pity for the dead?
Look o'er the ravage of the reeking plain;
Look on the hands with female slaughter red;
Then to the dogs resign the unburied slain,
Then to the vulture let each corse remain;
Albeit unworthy of the prey-bird's maw,
Let their bleach'd bones, and blood's unbleaching stain,
Long mark the battle-field with hideous awe:
Thus only may our sons conceive the scenes we saw!   (I. 88)

While drawing on the techniques of the 'field of battle' poem, his instruction to 'Look' invoking the reader's imagining of the crucial site, Byron presents firsthand experience of the battlefield as the only way in which war can be conceived. He offers his own witnessing of the 'reeking plain' as an alternative to poetic imaginings of the conflict. But the most striking line of this powerful stanza is the final one in which he envisions a future without war; the collective experience of conflict of Byron's generation, 'the scenes we saw', is something that will be unknown to later generations, hence the battlefield's importance for them as a signifier of the truth of this otherwise vanished age of war.[86] Changing tense to the future perfect, Byron shifts the temporal perspective of his poem, and the current war in Spain becomes part of a historical process which will ultimately result in a millennial age of peace when all that remains of war are the bleached bones on the battlefield of Spain.

If Byron's additional stanzas add this optimistic, prophetic note to the poem, they also develop a new role for poetry in wartime. In the second of the two additional elegiac stanzas on his friend John Wingfield, who had died of disease at Coimbra in Portugal in May 1811, while serving in the army, Byron suddenly finds a new role for 'Fancy':

Oh, known the earliest, and esteem'd the most!
Dear to a heart where nought was left so dear!
Though to my hopeless days for ever lost,
In dreams deny me not to see thee here!
And Morn in secret shall renew the tear
Of Consciousness awaking to her woes,
And Fancy hover o'er thy bloodless bier,
Till my frail frame return to whence it rose,
And mourn'd and mourner lie united in repose.   (I. 92)

---

[86] For a fuller deployment of similar techniques and images, in which Byron looks to a future in which the world is free, see *Don Juan*, VIII. 135–7.

For McGann, these additional stanzas play a crucial role in determining the new direction of Byron's poetic achievement in making Byron himself 'assume the place of first importance in the poem'; in the context of his friend's death 'the melancholy political events over which he had lamented earlier are now seen to have had an even greater personal relevance than he had ever realized'.[87] But these two stanzas also constitute a regaining of poetic faith on Byron's part and his finding in poetry a meaningful way of responding to war and its desolations. This is partly in his adoption of the elegiac mode which Tim Webb and Philip Shaw have shown to be crucial to his later poetic response to war, particularly in the Waterloo stanzas of *Childe Harold's Pilgrimage*.[88] In his elegy for Wingfield, Byron reclaims the form from its uses for 'the boasted slain' (I. 91), emphasizing the effect of one individual loss and act of remembrance over the anonymizing tributes of official culture. But, if these stanzas anticipate Byron's later emphasis on elegy as the mode that can give meaning to war, they also reveal an awakening to the role that poetry and the creative powers might play in response to the loss of war. For here Byron turns to the forms and faculties that he would normally associate with the illusory world of poetry, the 'dreams' of night-time and the daytime powers of 'Fancy'. In his *Hours of Idleness* poem 'To Romance', for example, Byron had rejected 'Fancy' as he left the realms of romance, where 'Fancy holds her boundless reign', for those of 'Truth' as part of what he presents as a coming of age, a narrative similar to that presented by Charlotte Smith in her sonnet 'To Fancy'.[89] Vowing that he will 'No more on fancied pinions soar', he embodies the faculty's failings in the 'genial Nymphs', 'Whose bosoms heave with fancied fears, | With fancied flames and phrenzy glow'. But the pressures of war compel Byron, like Smith, to revalidate 'Fancy'. Confronted in *Childe Harold's Pilgrimage* by the 'unavailing woe' which 'Bursts from [his] heart' (I. 91), Byron finds in 'dreams' and 'Fancy' powers that will sustain his image of Wingfield and, indeed, himself. The loss of war stimulates a tentative exploration of the creative power of the imagination, a power that Byron would come to define most famously in the third canto of his romance:

---

[87] *Fiery Dust*, 105, 110.

[88] Timothy Webb, 'Byron and the Heroic Syllables', *Keats–Shelley Review*, 5 (autumn 1990), 53–8; Shaw, *Waterloo and the Romantic Imagination*, 165–91.

[89] Text from Coleridge (ed.), *Poetry*, I. 174–7 (no line numbers given).

'Tis to create, and in creating live
A being more intense, that we endow
With form our fancy, gaining as we give
The life we imagine, even as I do now.   (III. 6)

And Byron's sense of his renewed faith in his poem, and in his larger poetic project, can be seen in one of the stanzas he added to the canto in 1811 where he specifically alludes to the poetic tradition of romance:

Oh, Albuera! glorious field of grief!
As o'er thy plain the Pilgrim prick'd his steed,
Who could foresee thee, in a space so brief,
A scene where mingling foes should boast and bleed!   (I. 43)

If *Childe Harold* had been begun as a parody of Spenser, in the late additions Byron constructs his poem as a serious reconceptualization of the romance form. Rewriting the opening line of the *Faerie Queene*—'A Gentle Knight was pricking on the plaine'[90]—Byron presents his pilgrim as the hero of a new kind of romance, a form in which its imaginative response to Albuera and the other fields of grief of the Peninsular War competes with the 'worthless lays' and 'transient songs' which had so far defined the poetic response to the conflict.

Warrior Women and the Sons of Spain: Southey's Roderick and the Gendering of the Peninsular War

At the symbolic climax of *Roderick: The Last of the Goths*, Robert Southey's version of the legendary story of the Moorish invasion of Spain of 711,[91] the eponymous hero witnesses the acclamation of Pelayo as King of Spain. This event founds the Spanish monarchy and symbolizes the ultimate triumph of the nation after the invasion of the Moors, the immediate cause of which was Roderick's rape of Florinda and the subsequent alliance with the Moors of her father, Count Julian. For Roderick, the acclamation of Pelayo vindicates the role of his imagination, as watching the ceremony he recalls an earlier vision:

---

[90] Edmund Spenser, *The Fairie Queene*, ed. Thomas P. Roche, with the assistance of C. Patrick O'Donnell, Jr. (Harmondsworth: Penguin, 1978), I. 1.

[91] On Scott's, Wordsworth's and Landor's allegorical use of this myth to represent the French invasion of the Peninsula, see Charles Mell Hudson, Jr., 'The Roderick Legend in English Romantic Literature: Scott, Landor and Southey', D.Phil. thesis, (Yale, 1943).

[He] recall'd that thrilling shout
Which he had heard when on Romano's grave
The joy of victory woke him from his dream,
And sent him with prophetic hope to work
Fulfilment of the great events ordain'd,
There in imagination's inner world
Prefigured to his soul.

(XVIII. 185–91)[92]

As for Wordsworth and Coleridge in their writing on the Peninsular War, the 'inner world' of the 'imagination' becomes a vital force in war and the source of ultimate triumph.[93] Southey wrote *Roderick* over a six-year period that ran from the Spanish risings to Napoleon's abdication in 1814, and in it he presents war as a means of national and individual redemption for Spain and Roderick. If it is a poem about apostasy, as Mark Storey had suggested,[94] it is also a poem about how an individual, through penitence, can embrace and inspire the country which he feels he has betrayed, and how he can be restored to that country. Like the *Ancient Mariner* (echoed in book I)[95] or the *Prelude*, it is a tale of a sinner and a penitent, and it represents Roderick as a hero whose misplaced but understandable and ultimately forgivable desire comes close to threatening the destruction of his country through invasion, but from which he eventually saves it. It is the work of a sometime '*Jacobin* poet' who has become Poet Laureate.[96]

If the vindication of Roderick's political imagination figures the triumph of Southey's poetic imagining of the defeat of France, his vision particularly emphasizes the extent to which the Peninsular War was imagined through gendered figures. In a poem in which Southey frequently represents Spain as a woman (IV. 16–18, 45–8) and as a mother (VIII. 127), he uses women characters to figure both the crisis of the nation which has necessitated its punishment and the means of its redemption through war. The vision which Roderick recalls during the

---

[92] The text for *Roderick: The Last of the Goths* is taken from Southey's *Poems*, ed. Maurice H. Fitzgerald (London: Oxford University Press, 1909), and is cited within parentheses by book and line number.

[93] For this idea in Wordsworth and Coleridge, see my discussion in *Napoleon and English Romanticism* (Cambridge: Cambridge University Press, 1995), 95–134.

[94] Mark Storey, *Robert Southey: A Life* (Oxford and New York: Oxford University Press, 1997), 232.   [95] l. 129–30.

[96] For detailed accounts of Southey's political development, see Storey, *Robert Southey*, and Geoffrey Carnall, *Robert Southey and his Age: The Development of a Conservative Mind* (Oxford: Clarendon Press, 1960).

acclamation was first described in book II and is of one such figure, his
mother, Rusilla:

> her form was changed!
> Radiant in arms she stood! a bloody Cross
> Gleam'd on her breast-plate, in her shield display'd
> Erect a lion ramp'd; her helmed head
> Rose like the Berecynthian Goddess crown'd
> With towers, and in her dreadful hand the sword
> Red as a fire-brand blazed. Anon the tramp
> Of horsemen, and the din of multitudes
> Moving to mortal conflict, rang around;
> The battle-song, the clang of sword and shield,
> War-cries and tumult, strife and hate and rage,
> Blasphemous prayers, confusion, agony,
> Rout and pursuit and death; and over all
> The shout of victory . . . Spain and Victory!   (II. 210–23)

The mother from whom the 'sinful child' (II. 172) seeks forgiveness and
blessing becomes a figure for the nation transformed by war and an image
of the means of redemption. For Roderick, who initially 'as the strong
vision master'd him | Rush'd to the fight rejoicing' (II. 224–5), the vision
proves an inspirational force and one which prompts a particularly
masculine devotion to action—'He girt his loins' (II. 249). If Southey uses
Rusilla to figure the means of national redemption, throughout the poem
he represents Spain's fall and the corruption of its leaders through sexu-
alized and adulterous women who fail to perform properly the duties of
wife and mother. Such representations are a major feature of the poetic
romances on the Peninsular War, and are worth examining before
returning to look at Southey's particular use of these figures.

In their poems on the Peninsular War, both Scott and Byron identified
the complex diplomatic and personal triangle of Charles IV (who abdi-
cated in favour of his son Ferdinand VII, in turn replaced by Napoleon's
brother Joseph), his queen Maria Luisa of Parma, and her lover, the Prime
Minster Manuel Godoy, as the cause of the current crisis in Spain, and
they present this situation as one in which conventional gender roles have
become reversed, with the Queen sexually and politically dominant over
her husband and her lover. In *The Vision of Don Roderick*, Scott presents
Charles IV as 'grown impotent of toil' and having 'Let the grave sceptre
slip his lazy hold', his lack of political or sexual potency leaving his 'rule'
'the spoil | Of a loose female and her minion bold' (II. 35). Godoy, while
politically powerful—'bold'—remains subordinate to the sexually

immoral Maria Luisa in the role of minion. In *Childe Harold's Pilgrimage* I, Byron similarly emasculates Charles, describing him as 'The royal wittol' (an acquiescent cuckold), and traces the origin of the war to 'the day | When first Spain's queen beheld the black-ey'd boy, | And gore-fac'd Treason sprung from her adulterate joy' (I. 48). Anticipating his later examinations of powerful and desiring women, such as Gulbeyaz and Catherine the Great in *Don Juan*, Byron presents the Queen as sexually aggressive while making Godoy passive and, as a boy, less than a man— later in the poem Byron will describe the 'black eye' of the Spanish maid (I. 55). For both Scott and Byron, then, Spain's current crisis is a result of a failure of masculinity that has left the country in the hands of a transgressive and immoral woman, complicating the more usual figure of invasion as rape.[97] The invasion of Spain is the natural consequence of such 'loose' or 'adulterous' behaviour, as the writers apply the narrative and ethics of domestic relations to the national situation.

For Scott, the crisis of masculinity in the Spanish court is representative of a national effeminacy that characterizes the country in the period between the conquests and the French invasion. Having allegorized Spain through the figures of Valour and Bigotry, Scott presents them as becoming effeminate in the 'third period' covered by Roderick's vision:

> Valour had relax'd his ardent look,
> And at a lady's feet, like lion tame,
> Lay stretch'd, full loth the weight of arms to brook;
> And soften'd Bigotry, upon his book,
> Patter'd a task of little good or ill: (II. 34)

Sexually and physically weakened, chivalric Spain is unable to defend itself against the French invasion, the result of the Queen's intriguing. But war has a revivifying and remanning effect on Spain, as Scott revives the figure of Valour to represent the national uprisings:

> with a common shriek, the general tongue
> Exclaim'd, 'To arms!' and fast to arms they sprung.
> And Valour woke, that genius of the land!
> Pleasure, and ease, and sloth, aside he flung,
> As burst th'awakening Nazarite his band,
> When 'gainst his treacherous foes he clench'd his dreadful hand.
>   (II. 44)

---

[97] For rape as a figure of the invasion of the Peninsula, see Diego Saglia, ' "O My Mother Spain!" The Peninsular War Family Matters, and the Practice of Romantic Nation-Writing', *ELH*, 65 (1998), *passim*.

Through war the nation not only regains its manly identity, casting off its effeminate indulgences, but achieves a purified version of it, free of the bigotry which had earlier been equally representative of national character. Byron too calls on the 'sons of Spain' to 'Awake' (I. 37), though he was more equivocal than Scott about whether it would do so. While Portugal was the particular target of his accusations of national cowardice,[98] the context for his lines on the Spanish court is a contrast of the 'rustic', aware of the threat of war, and the decadent inhabitants of Seville, who rather than bleeding 'with their country's wounds' indulge in the 'feast, the song, [and] the revel' in a city personified by 'Folly', 'young-eyed Lewdness', and 'Vice' (I. 46–7). Similarly Cadiz is presented as a place of 'riot', inhabited by 'Revel's laughing crew' where 'Devices quaint, and frolicks ever new, | Tread on each other's kibes' (I. 67). As in Scott's poem, Byron presents Spain's chivalric past as having degenerated into indulgence, and his poem leaves open the question of whether the war will lead to the regeneration of the country or its destruction.

Like Scott and Byron in their representations of Napoleon's invasion of Spain, Southey locates the cause of the Moorish invasion not with the invader but with the invaded. The opening lines of the poem present Roderick's rape of Florinda as the last in a series of national sins committed by 'inhuman priests' and 'iron servitude': 'Long had the crimes of Spain cried out to Heaven; | At length the measure of offence was full'(I. 4, 6, 1–2). This opening emphasis on national sin is developed in the analysis offered by Siverian, something of a wise chorus in the poem, who gives a fuller account of the bloody (and complex) recent history of Spain:

> Have we not seen Favila's shameless wife,
> Throned in Witiza's ivory car, parade
> Our towns with regal pageantry, and bid
> The murderous tyrant in her husband's blood
> Dip his adulterous hand? Did we not see
> Pelayo, by that bloody king's pursuit,
> And that unnatural mother, from the land
> With open outcry, like an outlaw'd thief,
> Hunted?   (V. 83–91)

As in Scott's and Byron's accounts of the Charles–Maria Luisa–Godoy triangle, Siverian represents Spain's crimes through the unnamed figure of the adulterous wife of Favila who had become mistress of Witiza, King of the Wisi-Goths. In her failure to perform properly her feminine duties

---

[98] See Borst, *Byron's First Pilgrimage*, 6–22.

and in her intervention in public affairs, she exemplifies the breakdown of the family unit of the nation. Similarly, Roderick's Queen, Egilona, who has become the 'concubine' of Abdalaziz, the Moorish Governor of Spain, is presented as destructive of both the family and the nation (V. 124–236). While Diego Saglia has argued that Southey uses rape as his main trope for national dissolution in *Roderick*, I would argue that Southey figures it primarily through the disruption of hierarchy caused by these sexually aggressive women.[99] The threat of such figures persists in Guisla, the daughter of the wife of Favila, who is seen to have inherited her corruption and whose adultery, like Egilona's with 'the enemy, | The Moor, the Misbeliever' (V. 235), combine sexual, national, and religious treachery. For Pelayo, her brother, Guisla's sexual aggression is a matter of 'domestic shame' (XV. 65) but it is also linked with public affairs, for she betrays the whereabouts of Pelayo's family to the Moors, who plan to use the information to destroy Pelayo and his race. Count Julian's comment when he hears of Guisla's treachery emphasizes the structural and symbolic significance of the poem's female figures:

> 'Tis the old taint!
> Said Julian mournfully; from her mother's womb
> She brought the inbred wickedness which now
> In ripe infection blossoms. Woman, woman,
> Still to the Goths art thou the instrument
> Of overthrow; thy virtue and thy vice
> Fatal alike to them!
>   (XXII. 138–44)

It is 'woman', then, who is presented as the cause of the destruction of Roderick's reign, whether in the virtuous form of Florinda who represents a temptation Roderick cannot withstand or in the vicious figures of the Wife of Favila, Egilona, and Guisla.

If Southey uses women to figure the fall of Spain, he also uses them to represent the means of redemption, Roderick prophesying the rebirth of the nation as a redeemed femininity:

> The nation will arise regenerate;
> Strong in her second youth and beautiful,
> And like a spirit which hath shaken off
> The clog of dull mortality, shall Spain
> Arise in glory.   (IV. 44–8)

---

[99] Saglia, 'O My Mother Spain', 370. I should add that I am indebted to this article, and particularly its penetrating analysis of the link between the family and the nation.

While Roderick's vision of his mother represents the necessary transformation of the wartime nation at a symbolic level, in the narrative of the poem this adoption of martial identity is enacted by Adosinda, a war victim encountered by Roderick in book III whose parents, warrior husband, and child have all been killed by the invading Moors. Adosinda's new-found devotion to a particular role is paralleled with Roderick's— 'like one | Who ... girds himself | For this world's daily business' (III. 264–7)—and the suggestion of the renunciation of her gendered identity is fulfilled in her avowal of revenge when she symbolically entombs her female identity: 'All womanly tenderness, all gentle thoughts, | All female weakness too, I bury here' (III. 294–5). Adosinda here recalls Byron's 'maid' of Saragossa from *Childe Harold's Pilgrimage*, I, who also operates as an example of the transformations of identity caused by war:

> Is it for this the Spanish maid, arous'd,
> Hangs on the willow her unstrung guitar,
> And, all unsex'd, the Anlace hath espous'd,
> Sung the loud song, and dar'd the deeds of war?   (I. 54)

While both women warriors disclaim their female identity, the maid through Lady Macbeth's call on the 'Spirits' to rid her of her femininity and to fill her 'top-full | Of direst cruelty',[100] both are also represented as fighting for domestic motives. Byron presents the involvement of the Spanish maid as a redirection of feminine instincts and roles, 'aroused' not by her lover but by war and 'espoused' not to her husband but to the dagger, while during the siege in which her family die it is Adosinda's maternal qualities, her 'ever anxious love' and 'noble heart', which sustain the city (IV. 155, 147). But the uses which Byron and Southey make of their women warriors are different. Byron emphasizes both the temporary nature of the maid's transformation and her essential femininity. Generalizing out from the maid to the women of Spain, he presents them as motivated by love and defines them against the figures of monstrous female otherness:

> Yet are Spain's maids no race of Amazons,
> But form'd for all the witching arts of love:
> Though thus in arms they emulate her sons,
> And in the horrid phalanx dare to move,
> 'Tis but the tender fierceness of the dove,
> Pecking the hand that hovers o'er her mate.   (I. 57)

[100] William Shakespeare, *Macbeth*, ed. Kenneth Muir (London and New York: Routledge, 1984), 1. 5. 40–3.

Byron's figure of the dove contains the potentially transgressive woman warrior within a construction of femininity that was not only conventional but highly appealing to contemporary readers. The reviewer of the *General Chronicle and Literary Magazine*, for example, thought the passage on the maid one of the poem's most memorable 'beauties' and the image of the dove 'one of the happiest-chosen figures' which helped the poet in 'making us feel that neither nature nor any of her sympathies are out of unison with such an assumption of character: in other words, that the female warrior is still a woman'.[101] Despite being 'foremost in the ranks of war' and 'active in deeds of violence and slaughter', the heroine of Saragossa retained 'all the qualities and all the charms that embellish and endear the sex' (pp. 1057–8). While women may inspire men, either through individual example or as symbols, for Byron it is the 'sons of Spain' who must fight to redeem the country. By the end of the canto women occupy the role of those who must be protected—'So may he guard the sister and the wife'—or of the victims of war—'Look on the hands with female slaughter red' (I. 87, 88). In constructing the warring nation in this way, Byron foreshadows the emphasis of the second canto in which, as Caroline Franklin has observed, he strives 'to reach the authentically male warrior cultures of the Ottoman empire' as part of a 'conscious attempt to masculinize poetry'.[102]

Southey conceives Adosinda in much grander and more symbolic terms than Byron represents the maid of Saragossa, embodying Southey's construction of the Peninsular War as a holy conflict (and paralleling his earlier woman warrior, Joan of Arc). Adosinda's martial identity becomes a model for the nation and through a parallel with the biblical story of Judith and Holofernes she constructs herself as performing a role that is divinely sanctioned, God having given her 'A spirit not mine own and strength from heaven' (III. 382). Southey's representation of Adosinda emphasizes her participation in the bloody business of war:

> A helm
> Presses the clusters of her flaxen hair;
> The shield is on her arm; her breast is mail'd;
> A sword-belt is her girdle, and right well
> It may be seen that sword hath done its work
> To-day, for upward from the wrist her sleeve
> Is stiff with blood.   (XIV. 133–9)

---

[101] Quoted in Reiman, *Romantics Reviewed B*, III. 1058.
[102] Caroline Franklin, *Byron: A Literary Life* (Basingstoke and London: Macmillan, 2000), 57.

Unlike other poetic warrior women, including Byron's maid and Scott's Edith, Adosinda is not restored to the domestic sphere at the poem's conclusion. Nor is she the only woman to participate in fighting. During the attack on the Moorish forces in the vale of Covadonga the women 'aid in the destruction' (XXIII. 184), rolling rocks onto the army below, while Adosinda presides over the scene:

> In the midst there stood
> A female form, one hand upon the Cross,
> The other raised in menacing act; below
> Loose flow'd her raiment, but her breast was arm'd,
> And helmeted her head.
>
> (III. 226–30)

The destruction of the Moorish force takes place under the twin symbols of the cross and the 'female form' of the warring nation.

The transformations of Rusilla and Adosinda into martial forms figure the necessary transformation of the nation if it is to gain salvation. For Roderick, who repeatedly links these two figures (III. 352–80; XIV. 140–61), they combine to offer the model for national and self redemption that he dedicates himself to:

> Even so I swear; my soul hath found at length
> Her rest and refuge; in the invader's blood
> She must efface her stains of mortal sin,
> And in redeeming this lost land, work out
> Redemption for herself. (IV. 14–18)

For the other male characters women offer a more practical example of the necessity for manliness in wartime. For example, when Pelayo's wife sends him a message of support he comments:

> Brave spirits! cried
> Pelayo, worthy to remove all stain
> Of weakness from their sex! I should be less
> Than man, if, drawing strength where others find
> Their hearts most open to assault of fear,
> I quail'd at danger. Never be it said
> Of Spain, that in the hour of her distress
> Her women were as heroes, but her men
> Perform'd the woman's part. (VII. 98–106)

The heroism of women not only redeems them of their 'stain | Of weakness' but provides a model for the men of the nation. This need for manliness is all the greater because, as in Wordsworth's sonnets of 1802–3 and Scott's and Byron's poems on the Peninsular War, the need for national redemption is partly the result of a crisis in masculinity. In *Roderick,* the crimes that have caused the nation's downfall, figured through the sexually aggressive adulteress, are implicitly critiques of the nation's masculinity, men having 'perform'd the woman's part' and failed to exercise proper political or domestic authority. This crisis of masculinity is represented partly as a lack of martial vigour, as in Siverian's comments after the disguised Roderick has killed a Moor—'A manly Gothic heart doth ill accord | With these unhappy times' (V. 221–2)—and partly in terms of the breakdown of the family unit, seen in Siverian's parallel of the domestic and the national in response to a question from Pelayo about the welfare of his family:

> They are as thou couldst wish, the old man replied,
> Wert thou but lord of thine own house again,
> And Spain were Spain once more.   (VII. 60–2)

It is through war that the nation regains its lost masculinity. Roderick presents the conflict as an opportunity offered by 'The Highest' 'To prove and purify the sons of Spain' (XII. 150) and in the final battle scene Southey emphasizes the regained manliness of the Spanish forces: 'manfully | They stood' (XXV. 424–5). It is in this final battle that Roderick gains full redemption, achieving 'victory | Over the world, his sins, and despair' (XXV. 395–6) and becoming an agent of divine punishment, 'the Avenger' (XXV. 449).

Yet while Roderick's martial heroics are crucial to the Spanish victory, as the last representative of his line and of a warlike age he does not represent the form of masculinity on which the new nation of Spain can be constructed. With the extinction of the line of Roderick, the last of the Goths, Spain is refounded around the figure of Pelayo, 'Restoring in Pelayo's native line | The sceptre to the Spaniard' (IV. 276–7).[103] While certainly a good leader and heroic fighter, Pelayo's 'calm and manly spirit' (IV. 249) is constructed in familial and domestic terms, especially when he is compared with Roderick. As Siverian comments, Pelayo is 'Not happier in all dear domestic ties | Than worthy for his virtue of the bliss | Which is that virtue's fruit' (XVII. 122–4). If Spain is the 'Motherland', as Pelayo himself terms it (VIII. 127), then he is 'like a father' to his people (XIV. 74), and his own status as such is emphasized by Roderick

---

[103] Saglia provides an excellent discussion of the dynastic elements of the poem in 'O My Mother Spain', 374.

during the acclamation scene when he 'wed[s]' Pelayo to 'our dear Spain' (XVIII, 247–51). It is in the model of the family that Spain finds its salvation, as Pelayo comments:

> Spain is our common parent: let the sons
> Be to the parent true, and in her strength
> And Heaven, their sure deliverance they will find.   (XVI. 327–9)

Southey figures the need for the nation to become manly but also the construction of this new-found manliness in familial terms in the figure of Alphonso, the son of Count Pedro and future King of Spain by marriage to Pelayo's daughter, Hermesind. Alphonso is initially presented as in transition from boyhood to manhood—'The blossom of all manly virtues made | His boyhood beautiful' (VIII. 80–1)—and dreaming of participating in battle (VIII. 148–54). His induction into war is symbolized by his father's ceremonial presentation to him of the armour he himself had worn in earlier wars, a moment from which, as Pedro instructs him, he will 'as from a birth-day ... date | Thy life in arms' (XII. 69–70). This spiritual rebirth through war parallels those of Roderick ('thou beholdest me | A man new born'(V. 259–60)) and Spain when Pelayo becomes king ('Spain is born again' (XVIII. 279)). Yet if Alphonso's life in arms is associated with the gaining of an identity, he still remains a boy, even as he almost immediately kills a Moor in a skirmish: 'The gallant boy | Gave his good sword that hour its earliest taste | Of Moorish blood' (XIII. 27–9). Rather it is in the final battle that Alphonso is represented as entering into manhood:

> Rejoicing like a bridegroom in the strife,
> Alphonso through the host of infidels
> Bore on his bloody lance dismay and death.   (XXV. 175–7)

Conflating a martial and a sexual coming of age, Southey here presents Alphonso's power on the battlefield in terms of his potency in the bedroom. In battle, Alphonso enacts both his domestic and his political authority as future King of Spain; if Spain is brought down by sexually aggressive adulterous women, its future is secured through the figure of the virile bridegroom. And this secure future has already been guaranteed by a prophetic moment as the poet foresees the future for Alphonso and his bride, 'laid side by side' and projected beyond mortality in 'the everlasting marriage-bed' (XVI. 269–89). The future of Spain is safe in the virile but domestic figure of Alphonso, who will restore order to the family of the nation.

CHAPTER SEVEN

'Of War and Taking Towns': Byron's and Hemans's post-Waterloo Poetry, 1816–1828

WAR REMAINED A dominant poetic subject in the decade after Waterloo, with a vast amount of poetry produced and published on the topic in addition to that which celebrated the battle itself.[1] Percy Shelley, whose *Esdaile Notebook* includes several anti-war poems written during the period of the conflict, continued to examine war's place in the modern world in *The Revolt of Islam* (1817–18), *Prometheus Unbound* (1818–19), and *The Triumph of Life* (1822). John Keats's Miltonic *Hyperion: A Fragment* (1818–19) reflects on dynastic change in the aftermath of war, while his Dantean reworking of the material in *The Fall of Hyperion: A Dream* (1819), with its examination of the poetic role through the narrator's encounter with Moneta, again illustrates the creative dynamic that links the envisioning of conflict and the poetic imagination. Laetitia Landon displayed the impact of war on the family and the home in several poems in *The Improvisatrice* (1824), while in the inserted narratives of *The Troubadour* (1825) she offers tales of war's destructiveness and analyses the role of poetry within martial societies. But in this final chapter I want to examine the work of two of the best-selling and most widely read poets of the period whose obsession with war developed out of their engagement with the Peninsular War and whose poetic identities were profoundly shaped by their continued reflection on conflict, Felicia Hemans and Lord Byron. The chapter will

---

[1] I have discussed some of the poetic responses to Waterloo in *Napoleon and English Romanticism* (Cambridge: Cambridge University Press, 1995), 153–82. See also Philip Shaw, *Waterloo and the Romantic Imagination* (Basingstoke and New York: Palgrave Macmillan, 2002); Richard Cronin, *The Politics of Romantic Poetry: In Search of the Pure Commonwealth* (Basingstoke and New York: Macmillan and St Martin's Press, 2000), 85–91; and Carl Woodring, 'Three Poets on Waterloo', *Wordsworth Circle*, 18/2 (1987) 54–6.

particularly focus on one way in which these two writers represented war, the siege. Writing with a degree of historical distance from the Revolutionary and Napoleonic conflicts, they found in the siege a means of representing to their readership the entirety of modern war, as Byron tells the 'Cockneys of London' and 'Muscadines of Paris', by contemplating 'one annihilated city, | Where thousand loves, and ties, and duties grow' they can 'ponder what a pious pastime war is' (VIII. 124).[2] The siege illustrates war's effects on the whole of society and it conflates within one site—the fortress, the citadel, or the walled city—the two spaces that we have seen poetry so frequently striving to link, the scene of conflict and the home, as Joseph Fawcett had emphasized in his poem 'The Siege', published earlier in the period: 'Domestic scenes no safe recess afford: | The peaceful hearth the missile battle feels'.[3] War is not something that can be contained within the public, professional, or masculine sphere, as Hemans shows in her poetic examinations of women caught up in besieged cities and as Byron emphasizes in *Don Juan* when he comments that the aim of the Russian bombardment is to 'knock down | The public buildings, and the private too, | No matter what poor souls might be undone' (VII. 23). Both writers use the siege to explore the relations between war, gender, and history, exploiting the siege's rich allegorical and symbolic potential, and ultimately find in it a figure for their own poetic identity.

'To Paint' the 'Appalling Sight' of a Siege

The figurative and symbolic elements of Hemans's and Byron's uses of the siege are emphasized when seen in terms of developments in military history during the Revolutionary and Napoleonic wars. Though once the dominant form of warfare in Europe and still a significant feature of the military scene, particularly during the British campaign in the Spanish Peninsula, regular sieges played a considerably less important part in the warfare of the Revolutionary and Napoleonic period than they had in the mid-eighteenth century.[4] Byron had, of course, treated the siege of

---

[2] References to *Don Juan* are to *Byron, The Oxford Authors*, ed. Jerome J. McGann (Oxford: Oxford University Press, 1986), and hereafter are cited by canto and stanza number within the text.

[3] Joseph Fawcett, 'The Siege', *War Elegies* (London: J. Johnson, 1801), 16.

[4] David G. Chandler, *Dictionary of the Napoleonic Wars* (London: Greenhill Books, 1993), 410–12.

Saragossa in *Childe Harold's Pilgrimage*, I, but none of the siege texts I will be examining in this chapter were set during the Revolutionary and Napoleonic wars. Byron wrote his verse narrative *The Siege of Corinth* (1816) during the closing years of the war, from 1812 to 1815, and in it he describes the Turkish attack on the Venetian fortress in 1715 during the war between Venice and the Ottoman empire for control of the Peloponnesus.[5] Similarly, in her first collection of narrative poems, *Tales, and Historic Scenes, in Verse*, published in 1819, Hemans turned to historical sieges to examine the impact of war in a number of poems, perhaps most powerfully 'The Wife of Asdrubal' set during the siege of Carthage in 146 BC. But it was in the early years of the 1820s that these two writers particularly exploited the siege as a dramatic situation through which they could examine the place of war in the modern age. Thus 1823 witnessed the publication of two of the great poetic investigations of war in the romantic period, Byron's *Don Juan*, cantos VII and VIII, and Hemans's *The Siege of Valencia* volume. In the war cantos of *Don Juan*, written in 1822, Byron depicts the Russian assault on the Turkish fortress at Ismail of November to December 1790, part of the Russo-Turkish War of 1787–91. He reworked and developed a number of his themes in *The Deformed Transformed*, written in 1822–3 and published in 1824, which dramatizes the siege of Rome of 1527 by Charles V's army of Spanish, German, and Italian troops under the leadership of Charles, Duc de Bourbon.[6] Hemans's *The Siege of Valencia* volume includes no fewer than three siege texts. The verse drama from which the volume takes its title presents a fictional sixteenth-century siege of the city by the Moors while her collection of lyrics 'The Songs of the Cid' is set during the 1090s when 'The Moor had beleaguer'd Valencia's towers' ('The Cid's Funeral Procession', l. 1).[7] In *The Last Constantine*, initially intended as an entry for the Royal Society of Literature's poetry prize, Hemans focuses on the siege and fall of Constantinople to the Turks in 1453.

To a writer of exciting verse narratives such as Byron, siege warfare may have seemed a particularly attractive topic, offering a series of

---

[5] *Lord Byron, The Complete Poetical Works*, ed. Jerome J. McGann (Oxford: Clarendon Press, 1980–93), III. 479–82. References to *The Siege of Corinth* are to this edition and are hereafter cited by line within the text.

[6] Ibid., VI. 725–38. References to *The Deformed Transformed* are to the McGann edition and are hereafter cited by act, scene, and line within the text.

[7] Unless otherwise stated, references to Hemans's poetry in this chapter are to Felicia Hemans, *Selected Poems, Letters, Reception Materials*, ed. Susan Wolfson (Princeton and Oxford: Princeton University Press, 2000). References are cited by line number within the text.

dramatic set-piece actions (trenching, cannonade, assault) that had become particularly formalized during the seventeenth and eighteenth centuries (following the manuals of the French military architect Vauban) and that contributed to a single, decisive action—the taking of a fortress and the annihilation or total surrender of the enemy. In all three poems, Byron exploits and increasingly scrutinizes the exhilaration of this form of combat, presenting the action of the siege from the attackers' point of view and using the structured events of the siege to structure his own works. By contrast, Hemans shows little interest in the formalities and technicalities of the siege. Rather, writing from the perspective of the besieged confined within the city walls and limited in their sphere of action, she is more concerned to represent the psychological impact of war through a focus on individuals caught up in the conflicts of history.

If sieges played a less important part in the Revolutionary and Napoleonic conflicts than they had in earlier centuries, the action of the siege none the less constituted modern warfare at its most intense and devastating,[8] and both poets emphasize this shocking physical destructiveness of modern war by presenting it as surpassing in horror the military actions of classical poetry. In *The Last Constantine*, Hemans addresses 'Olympus, Ida, [and] Delphi' and informs them that:

> there is yet a more appalling sight
> For earth prepared, than e'er, with tranquil brow,
> Ye gazed on from your world of solitude and snow!   (41)[9]

Similarly Byron informs 'eternal Homer' that he has:

> To paint a siege, wherein more men were slain,
> With deadlier engines and a speedier blow,
> Than in thy Greek gazette of that [Trojan] campaign;   (VII. 80)

However, there is a major difference in the way in which the two poets 'paint' the 'appalling sight' of a siege for their readers in *The Last Constantine* and *Don Juan*. While Hemans describes 'the mangled heap, | In the red moat, the dying and the slain' over which the assailants climb to

---

[8] See e.g. the accounts of the British siege of Badajoz in Michael Glover, *The Napoleonic Wars, 1792–1815: An Illustrated History* (London: Book Club Associates, 1979), 160, and Christopher Duffy, *Fire and Stone: The Science of Fortress Warfare, 1660–1860* (London and Vancouver: David and Charles, 1975), 149.

[9] As *The Last Constantine* is not included in either Kelly's or Wolfson's modern editions, I have taken my text from *The Works of Mrs Hemans, with a Memoir by her Sister* (Edinburgh and London: Thomas Blackwood and Sons and Thomas Cadell, 1839), III. 178–224. References are to stanza numbers.

attack the city (83), the smoke of the cannons and fires obscures the action of the siege from the vision of the poet and her readers, drawing a discreet veil over its horrors: beyond 'the compass of our gaze | . . . fearful things, unknown, untold, are there, | Workings of wrath and death, and anguish, and despair!' (85). By contrast, much of Byron's war poetry is directed to precisely the aim of making known and telling the 'fearful things' of war. In his dedication to Wellington at the start of Canto IX of *Don Juan*, Byron describes war as a 'brain-spattering, windpipe-slitting art, | Unless her cause by Right be sanctified'(IX. 4) and throughout the poem he insists upon the factual nature of his 'true Muse' and 'true portrait of one battle-field' (VIII. 1, 12), emphasizing the shocking physicality and gory nature of martial combat when describing Juan and Johnson 'trampling' over 'dead bodies' and 'wallow[ing] in the bloody mire | Of dead and dying thousands' (VIII. 19–20). Byron uses two particular tropes to represent the devastation of the siege of Ismail. The first is the sea, initially used to figure the unholy destructive potential of mankind—' "Let there be light! said God, and there was light!" | "Let there be blood!" says man, and there's a sea!' (VII. 41)—and repeated throughout the two cantos to quantify the blood, tears, gore, and slaughter produced by the siege (VII. 50, 68; VIII. 3), culminating in his final picture of Ismail:

> Ismail's no more! The crescent's silver bow
> Sunk, and the crimson cross glared o'er the field,
>   But red with no *redeeming* gore: the glow
> Of burning streets, like moonlight on the water,
> Was imaged back in blood, the sea of slaughter.   (VIII. 122)

Here the blood-besmeared cross, presiding over the scenes of devastations in Ismail, becomes a symbol of the perversion of Christianity, representing not Christ's redemptive sacrifice through crucifixion but the destructiveness of religiously endorsed imperialism. The second of Byron's two major tropes for the siege is Hell (VII. 86; VIII. 6, 20, 42), which he uses for his final attempt to assess the events at Ismail:

> All that the mind would shrink from of excesses;
>   All that the body perpetrates of bad;
> All that we read, hear, dream, of man's distresses;
>   All that the Devil would do if run stark mad;
> All that defies the worst which pen expresses;
>   All by which Hell is peopled, or as sad
> As Hell—mere mortals who their power abuse,—
> Was here (as heretofore and since) let loose.   (VIII. 123)

Byron's representation of the aftermath of Ismail as the result of the devil 'run stark mad' recalls one of his first uses of the siege motif in his poem 'The Devil's Drive' of 1813 in which the devil 'gazed on a town by besiegers taken, | Nor cared he who were winning' (ll. 77–8). It also anticipates the merging of the metaphysical and the historical in *The Deformed Transformed* which dramatizes the conceit by presenting the devilish figure of Caesar observing the bloody sacking of Rome and describing his 'sport' as 'to gaze, since all these labourers | Will reap my harvest gratis' (2. 2. 61–3). In this drama, Byron develops his language of war to render the events of the siege in broader historical terms, merging the literal and symbolic in a way that pushes the play towards the elevated levels and grand schemas of the metaphysical dramas. For example, when Arnold arrives before the walls of Rome he comments 'my path | Has been o'er carcases: mine eyes are full | Of blood' (1. 2. 2–4). His literal meaning is reinforced by Caesar's instructions to him to wipe the blood from his eyes but symbolically his comment represents both his new found role as a conqueror and the atrocities he has seen during it. This merging of the literal and the symbolic is characteristic of the play with its repeated references to the Tiber running with blood (1. 2. 85, 152), the streets of Rome red with gore (1. 2. 152; 2. 2. 10–11), blood contaminating all drinking water (2. 1. 167–8; 2. 2. 48–52) and Arnold 'purple with the blood of Rome' (2. 3. 124) which suggest both the corruption of nature by war, as McGann has argued,[10] and war's devastation of civilization.

While Hemans also emphasizes the devastation of the 'wasting siege' in the 'Songs of the Cid' ('The Cid's Departure into Exile', l. 7) and *The Siege of Valencia* (VI. 7),[11] as this phrase suggests her focus is more often on the suffering caused by famine and pestilence to the civilian population than on the horrors of fighting. In both 'The Wife of Asdrubal' and *The Siege of Valencia*, the central action of the martyring of two brothers in the name of patriotism powerfully enacts the destructiveness of war and patriotic ideology on the family and the home. In her play, Hemans implies that this devastation is felt throughout society during the siege, paralleling the death of the Governor's two sons with those described by an unnamed citizen:

---

[10] Byron, *Poetical Works*, ed. McGann, VI. 746.
[11] References to *The Siege of Valencia* are to *Selected Poems*, ed. Wolfson, and are cited by scene and line within the text.

> This wasting siege,
> Good Father Lopez, hath gone hard with you!
> 'Tis sad to hear no voices through the house,
> Once peopled with fair sons!   (VI. 7–10)

The nation at war is a nation robbed of its sons through death. Through the trope of pestilence, Hemans launches an assault on heroism itself, with martial strength unable to withstand its power: as Ximena comments, in the besieged city 'Death is busy, taming warrior-hearts, | And pouring winter through the fiery blood, | And fettering the strong arm!' (V. 20–2). Rather than providing an arena for the display of physical prowess and the earning of military glory, the siege renders the warrior class both useless and vulnerable, as the knight Garcias himself remarks (II. 75–92).

'Battles, Sieges, and that Kind of Pleasure': The Martial and Erotic in Byron

In revealing 'what a pious pastime war is' in *Don Juan*, Byron maintained the attacks of *Childe Harold's Pilgrimage* on an activity which had gained a central place in British culture and society and developed his criticism of what he saw as the dominant ways in which it was constructed and consumed in the Gazettes and in poetry.[12] These forms of mediation create and feed the illusions of the 'Too gentle reader' (VIII.1), one of the 'panters for newspaper praise' and 'dilettanti in war's art' (VII. 39) who revel in the official accounts of the war without thinking about its costs. Such readers, Byron insists, should 'Think how the joys of reading a Gazette | Are purchased by all agonies and crimes' (VIII. 125). As here, Byron constantly juxtaposes the physical actualities of war with its textual representations, asking 'if a man's name in a *bulletin* | May make up for a *bullet in* his body?' (VII. 21). One of the major fabrications of such idealizing narratives of war is 'glory'—'what story | Sometimes calls "murder," and at others "glory" ' (VII. 26)—and throughout the war cantos Byron seeks to offer 'Glory's dream | Unriddled' (VIII. 1). While Byron exposes glory as illusory—'But Glory's Glory; and if you would find | What that is—ask the pig who sees the wind!' (VII. 84)—he recognizes its abstract yet pervasive power: Suvorov exploits it in his speech to his troops and during the assault Juan battles 'In search of glory' (VII. 64;

---

[12] e.g. VII. 32–4; VIII. 9, 18, 82, 119, 140.

VIII. 31, 52). Byron identifies the ideological force of glory, not only in the role it plays in driving soldiers into battle but in bolstering the established order:

> Yet I love Glory:—glory's a great thing;—
> Think what it is to be in your old age
> Maintained at the expense of your good king:
> A moderate pension shakes full many a sage,
> And heroes are but made for bards to sing,
> Which is still better; thus in verse to wage
> Your wars eternally, besides enjoying
> Half-pay for life, make mankind worth destroying.   (VIII. 14)

Alluding to both Wordsworth, the 'sage' of Grasmere who had taken a governmental 'pension' as Distributor of Stamps for Westmorland, and to Wellington, the subject of numerous poems and whose pensions are alluded to in the opening of canto IX, Byron argues that the concept of 'Glory' has been used not only to justify the destruction of mankind but to maintain the positions of those individuals who have most benefited from the recent wars.

Byron reinforces his unriddling of glory's dream through his highly sceptical treatment of the heroic in his three siege poems. While all three protagonists possess conventionally heroic qualities and play major roles in the actions of the sieges, none of them fights for a justifying 'cause' (*Don Juan*, VII. 40), or even thinks of himself as so doing. Alp in *The Siege of Corinth* is driven by the personal motives of 'revenge and love' (l. 245), while in *Don Juan* Juan and Johnson fight 'thoughtlessly' and 'arm | To burn a town which never did them harm' (VIII. 19; VII. 76). Juan, 'a fine young lad, who fought | He knew not why', is driven on by his desire for glory and by the increasing excitement he feels during the battle (VIII. 29, 32–3, 54–5). Yet Byron's depiction of Juan in battle is also part of the poem's critique of the siege as an act of imperialism. Juan's heroics at Ismail are the product of his education as a member of the gentry class in Spain, trained in the practice of warfare:

> Then for accomplishments of chivalry,
>   In case our lord the king should go to war again,
> He learn'd the arts of riding, fencing, gunnery,
>   And how to scale a fortress—or a nunnery.   (I. 38)

Throughout the siege cantos, Juan is presented as representative of the various aristocrats, including a large number of French émigrés, fighting in what McGann has called a 'classic instance of the imperialism of the monarchist regimes'.[13] For Juan, like many of the other multinational aristocrats in the Russian army, warfare is a gentlemanly pursuit, producing sensations akin to horse-riding and hunting (VIII. 54–5), and he is 'delighted to employ his leisure' 'In such good company as always throng | To battles, sieges, and that kind of pleasure' (VIII. 24). Like Juan, Arnold in *The Deformed Transformed* fights for no explicit cause, chooses the side on which he fights seemingly by chance and becomes frenzied in battle (2. 2. 28–9). Throughout the play, his martial deeds are accompanied by the debunking commentary of his anti-heroic *doppelgänger* Caesar, the 'everlasting Sneerer' (1. 2. 117). Yet if Juan, in his naivety, fights 'without malice' and with ' "the best | Intentions" ' (VIII. 25), Arnold sees his martial 'daring' as the product of his deformity whose 'essence [is] to o'ertake mankind | By heart and soul, and make itself the equal— | Aye, the superior of the rest' (1. 1. 314–16). But such compensations for 'stepdame Nature's avarice' come at a price (1. 1. 320). Arnold's assumption of the heroic form of Achilles is made possible through his Faustian pact with the Stranger which, it transpires, is signed in the blood of all those he kills during the siege of Rome. In this most bloody of all Byron's treatments of war, the achievement of fame through a martial career is represented as nothing less than a compact with the devil.

Byron emphasizes his critique of martial heroism by drawing on the traditional trope of the siege as the assault on the woman's body,[14] seen most obviously in his equation of the taking of the city with the rape of women. In both *The Siege of Corinth* and *Don Juan*, for example, he alludes to Henry V's threats before Harfleur to defile 'your shrill-shrieking daughters' (3. 4. 35) in describing the 'Shriller shrieks' and 'warwhoop and shriller scream' that provide the soundtracks to the sackings of the cities (l. 726; VIII. 127). But this symbolic linking of fortress and woman also operates at the levels of plot and character, as in *The Siege of Corinth*, in which Alp besieges the city not only out of revenge but because it contains Francesca. However, the poem is as critical in its treatment of Alp's attempted sexual conquest of Francesca as it is of the Turk's territorial imperialism: if the assault on Corinth leads only to the city's annihilation, Alp's attempts to gain Francesca lead only to his knowledge of her death and his own destruction. Like the fight between the nameless Venetian aristocrat and the Turk Hassan for possession of

[13] Byron, *Poetical Works*, ed. McGann, V. 719.
[14] See Malcolm Hebron, *The Medieval Siege: Theme and Image in Middle English Romance* (Oxford: Clarendon Press, 1997), 150.

Leila in *The Giaour*, which *The Siege of Corinth* replays on a national scale, the contest for possession of the desired object leads to its destruction along with all those involved, here represented in the staggering apocalyptic explosion of the magazine that annihilates the city and destroys the innocent Greek inhabitants of Corinth as well as the warring Turks and Venetians. Similarly, in *The Deformed Transformed*, the assault on Rome becomes focused on Olimpia, who operates partly as a symbol for Rome itself. In an action that echoes Juan's saving of Leila in *Don Juan*, Arnold saves Olimpia from the rampaging soldiers, but as both Caesar and the soldiers observe, he has as little right to her as they have (2. 3. 73–4, 86–7). Their critique is developed by Olimpia, who is equally suspicious of Arnold's actions, attempts suicide to avoid being taken by him, and even when married to him withholds her love. Through its spirited and independent heroine who refuses to love the 'beautiful and brave' figure of Arnold, *The Deformed Transformed* offers a powerful critique of masculine physical force.

In *Don Juan*, Byron uses the image of the siege to focus one of the poem's major themes, the equation of the martial and the erotic: Juan is trained to 'scale a fortress—or a nunnery', 'cunnus' becomes the best cause of war and reason to 'batter down a wall', the women of society erect 'palisades' to protect their virtue, and Byron ends his account of Ismail with his notorious joke about the middle-aged widows who ask ' "Wherefore the ravishing did not begin!" ' (I. 38; IX. 55–6; XIV. 61; VIII. 132). In the siege cantos, war and love provide not only the subject of the poem—'Oh Love! O Glory!' (VII. 1)—but are deliberately conflated in Byron's invocation: ' "Fierce loves and faithless wars" . . . I sing them both' (VII. 8). Parodying Spenser's *Faerie Queene*, 'Fierce warres and faithfull loues shall moralize my song',[15] Byron not only cynically updates romance values, but suggests a likeness between the martial and the erotic in contemporary society, seen in the sexual and territorial aggressiveness of Catherine the Great, with her excessive appetite for new lands and new lovers, and Potemkin—'a great thing in days | When homicide and harlotry made great' (VII. 37). We might expect Juan, the naïve, feminized hero and saviour of Leila, to be exempted from this linking of the martial with the erotic but his valour is frequently equated with his virility, Johnson commenting to Suvorov, for example, that 'if he hath no greater fault | In war than love, he had better lead the assault.'

<hr />

[15] Edmund Spenser, *The Fairie Queene*, ed. Thomas P. Roche, with the assistance of C. Patrick O'Donnell, Jr. (Harmondsworth: Penguin, 1978), 39.

(VII. 62). While Juan 'wars' as he 'loves' 'with what we call "the best | Intentions" ' according to the narrator (VIII. 25), his complicity in the savagery of Ismail parallels the devastating effect of his romantic adventures on the lives of those involved, such as Donna Julia or Haidee. If the symbolic dimensions of the siege present war as an assertion of masculinity, equating the martial and erotic instincts behind both ' "Fierce loves and faithless wars" ', in *Don Juan* Byron points to the fatal effects that result from the unthinking unleashing of these urges.

'Womanhood . . . Summon'd unto Conflicts': Hemans and the Inspirations of Siege Warfare

In the opening scene of Hemans's *The Siege of Valencia*, Ximena, the daughter of the city's governor, Gonzalez, tells her mother, Elmina, that as a consequence of the Moorish siege 'womanhood | Is summon'd unto conflicts, heretofore | The lot of warrior-souls' (I. 100–2). The siege disrupts the gendered conventions of war, conventions presented in the ballad with which Ximena opens the play in which a warrior returned from the battle of Roncesvalles informs a maiden of her lover's death during it (I. 1–64). In such conventional war narratives, warriors go away to fight while maidens wait for them at home, aligning men with the public sphere and women with the private. But as Ximena's comment emphasizes, by making the home itself the scene of arms, the siege presents a particular challenge to women, compelling them to cross from the private sphere into the public and from a conventionally feminine role into a conventionally masculine one. This structural potential of the siege as a form for examining the relations between war, the home, and gender roles had been recognized by Hannah Cowley in *The Siege of Acre: An Epic Poem, in Six Books* of 1801, the major treatment of the theme prior to Byron's and Hemans's poems on the subject.[16] *The Siege of Acre* celebrates the events of March–May 1799, when a Turkish fortress with the support of Sidney Smith's naval flotilla survived a fierce French siege, and identifies Acre as the place where 'gallic Madness' was stopped by 'sacred Fiat' in what Cowley presents as a holy war.[17] While Cowley

---

[16] Another treatment of a siege from the wars by a woman poet was Laura Sophia Temple's *The Siege of Zaragoza, and Other Poems* (London: William Miller and W. Bulmer and Co., 1812).

[17] Hannah Cowley, *The Siege of Acre: An Epic Poem, in Six Books* (London: J. Debrett, 1801), 4. Further references are to page numbers and are included within text.

emphasizes the 'truth' of her representation of the siege (3, 149), she introduces two fictitious episodes which she justifies as follows: 'It may be almost assumed that there never was a Siege which lasted more than two Months, in which some interesting *family event* did not take place, in consequence of HUSBANDS and FATHERS becoming Military Men' (150). These two episodes not only emphasize the overlap of war and the home as a result of the siege but highlight the potential of this form of warfare to raise questions about wartime gender roles. In the first episode, Ira disguises herself as a man so that she can follow her husband to war, but her adoption of manly dress leads ultimately to her madness, as a result of the horrors that she sees, and her death when she is shot by a French sniper (34–42). In the second episode, two sisters who try to prevent their father from fighting are offered as examples of women who 'endeavour to seduce [the men of their families] from their duty, from an acute sense of their personal danger' (150). As negative examples of women's behaviour in wartime, the two narratives propose by contrast a role for women during conflict which supports the martial endeavours of men without transgressing into the active sphere of fighting. If Ximena's comment in *The Siege of Valencia* raises the issue of women's participation in war that Cowley seeks to proscribe through Ira's narrative, it also points to the different grounds on which conventional gender roles are constructed: women are defined in terms of a natural, essential state—'womanhood'—while the 'warriors' are defined through their 'souls', a spiritual individuality that transcends the bodily. In Hemans's poetry, the state of siege provides an opportunity for women to reconstruct their identity on an entirely different basis, even to transcend what convention presents as their nature and its natural sphere of activities— 'the heart' and the 'domestic affections'—but such reconfigurings of gendered identities away from the naturally feminine threatens women's very existence. The dangers of such reconstructions of women's identities compelled by a state of siege can be illustrated by contrasting two of Hemans's shorter siege poems, before examining her most complex exploration of the issue, *The Siege of Valencia*.

In 'Marguerite of France', the Queen nurses her baby during a Turkish siege 'Deep in the Saracenic gloom | Of the warrior citadel' where 'midst arms the couch was spread, | And with banners curtain'd o'er'.[18] Hemans's description of this 'strange, wild bower' illustrates how

---

[18] As 'Marguerite of France' is not included in Kelly's or Wolfson's editions, I have taken my text from *The Works of Mrs Hemans*, VI. 272 (no line numbers given).

she uses the siege to conflate the sites of the martial and the familial, the national and the domestic. In this poem the Queen inspires her previously reluctant troops to defend the citadel by presenting it as a defence of her child and her sexual purity, linking the gender politics of the home with that of the nation in a Burkean speech which in turn prompts the ideal Burkean response:

> And her babe awoke to flashing swords,
> Unsheath'd in many a hand,
> As they gather'd round the helpless One,
> Again a noble band!

The age of chivalry is not dead and the poem ends with the Queen and the warriors enacting their conventional gender roles, the warriors promising to guard her well so that she can concentrate on the properly feminine activity of mothering—'Rest, with thy fair child on thy breast'. Yet this ending constitutes a restoration of such conventional roles in a poem in which the soldiers' initial 'wavering hearts' had forced the Queen to consider taking on the martial role herself:

> 'Then bring me here a breastplate
> And a helm, before you fly,
> And I will gird my woman's form,
> And on the ramparts die!'

As with Ximena, as a result of the siege the Queen finds herself summoned unto the manly world of conflict, but while Hemans presents her as a potentially heroic figure, she also emphasizes her femininity. Marguerite is a 'fragile thing' with a 'flute-like voice' and 'pale aspect' whose 'soft sad eyes of weeping love' are compared to 'the Virgin Mother's mild'. The Queen remains entirely natural, her 'deep strength' derived from her 'gentle heart' and her embrace extending from her son to her country. If the siege calls upon women to play a role beyond that normally scripted for them, in 'Marguerite of France' Hemans suggests that so long as women remain true to their 'heart' and their nature they have resources of strength that can influence the public sphere.

In 'Marguerite of France' Hemans draws back from presenting the transgressive possibilities of a mother figure dying 'on the ramparts', but it is just such a scene that she represents in another of her siege poems, 'The Wife of Asdrubal'. Like 'Marguerite of France', the action of the poem is generated by the failure of manliness on the part of the citadel protector, in this case the Carthaginian consul Hasdrubal, who surrendered to the Roman general Scipio during the siege of Carthage in 146 BC, deserting his wife and their two sons.[19] The unnamed 'wife' addresses Asdrubal from the roof of a burning temple, the last refuge of those left in the city, before stabbing her two sons and plunging with them into the flames. As for Queen Marguerite, the situation of the siege locates the mother within the arena of war, and like the Queen, the 'wife' is presented in martial terms, though here through simile: 'The dark profusion of her locks unbound, | Waves like a warrior's floating plumage round' (ll. 29–30). But whereas Marguerite's potential adoption of a martial identity was presented as the extension of her maternal role, the 'wife' appears inspired by some higher power, like the priestess of the Delphic Oracle:

> She might be deem'd a Pythia in the hour
> Of dread communion and delirious power;
> A being more than earthly, in whose eye
> There dwells a strange ascendancy. . . .
> Flush'd is her cheek, inspired her haughty mien,
> She seems th'avenging goddess of the scene.   (ll. 19–32)

Hemans emphasizes the unnaturalness of this figure by fusing her feminine qualities with elements more characteristic of the masculine sublime, describing her as 'sternly beauteous in terrific ire' (l. 18). The crisis of the wife's situation raises her beyond the earthly but destabilizes her gendered identity, literally calling into question her role as mother:

> Are those *her* infants . . .
> Is that a mother's glance, where stern disdain,
> And passion awfully vindictive, reign?   (ll. 33–8)

This tension between the wife's inspired but unearthly position and her maternal role as mother is dramatized in her killing of her sons. Though this act is presented as both an act of revenge on their traitorous father—' "thou, their sire, | In bondage safe, shalt yet in them expire" ' (ll. 57–8)—and a culminating act of loving motherhood that has been left with no alternative in a world of masculine violence—' "the arms that cannot save | Have been their cradle, and shall be their grave" ' (ll. 62–5)—in its final lines the poem also suggests it may be a result of madness (ll. 64–9).

These two shorter pieces illustrate how the state of siege brings

---

[19] Felicia Hemans, *Selected Poems, Prose, and Letters*, ed. Gary Kelly (Peterborough, Ontario: Broadview, 2002), 173, n. 1.

women into the arena of war but also reveals the limitations that are placed on their roles as a result of the constructions of gender. In *The Siege of Valencia*, Hemans gives her fullest examination of war's liberating and devastating effect on women through the figure of Ximena, using the dramatic form of the play to voice her ambivalence towards the involvement of women in conflict. If Ximena presents herself as compelled to take on a new role as a result of the siege, Elmina presents her daughter's besieged situation as a removal from the natural world which prefigures her death (I. 73–9, 107–19, 350–68). But Gonzalez figures his daughter's transformation not in relation to nature but through martial imagery (and in language that recalls Roderick's vision of his mother transformed by war in Southey's *Roderick, The Last of the Goths*):

> I see a change
> Far nobler on her brow!—She is as one,
> Who, at the trumpet's sudden call, hath risen
> From the gay banquet, and in scorn cast down
> The wine-cup, and the garland, and the lute
> Of festal hours, for the good spear and helm,
> Beseeming sterner tasks.   (I. 368–74)

Rather than lamenting the severing of Ximena's ties through the heart to nature, Gonzalez celebrates her transformation as inspired by her soul:

> Her eye hath lost
> The beam which laugh'd upon th' awakening heart,
> E'en as morn breaks o'er earth. But far within
> Its full dark orb, a light hath sprung, whose source
> Lies deeper in the soul.   (I. 374–8)

Even though at this stage of the play Ximena is only nursing the sick and wounded, Gonzalez represents her new role within the besieged city in martial terms: 'She hath put on | Courage, and faith, and generous constancy, | Ev'n as a breastplate' (I. 381–3). Like the heroines of Hemans's other siege poems, the crisis of her situation compels her to adopt a martial identity, but such a reconstructed identity is potentially dangerous to a woman if it is not founded on the basis of her 'nature' and her 'heart', as we saw in 'The Wife of Asdrubal'. Elmina sees her daughter in just the same way as the poet of that lyric sees the 'wife', as both transformed and threatened as the result of an inspiring 'unearthly power':

And seest thou not
In that high faith and strong collectedness,
A fearful inspiration?—*They* have cause
To tremble, who behold th'unearthly light
Of high, and, it may be, prophetic thought,
Investing youth with grandeur! (I. 390–5)

Elmina's and Gonzalez's contrasting responses to Ximena's new role as a woman summoned unto conflicts is representative of Hemans's use of them to dramatize the competing demands of the 'heart' and 'soul'. This conflict is produced by the central action of the play in which Gonzalez's and Elmina's two sons, Alphonso and Carlos, are captured by the Moorish Prince, Abdullah, who threatens to execute them unless Gonzalez yields the city to him. Gonzalez refuses to do, despite Elmina's powerful pleadings and criticisms of the values of patriotism and patriarchy, which have provided the focus for some of the excellent recent readings of the play.[20] As Hemans's biographer Henry Chorley commented, this situation, 'a thrilling conflict between maternal love and the inflexible spirit of chivalrous honor—afforded to [Hemans] an admirable opportunity of giving utterance to the two master interests of her mind'.[21] Elmina's response to learning of the threat to her sons is rooted in 'Nature' and the 'heart', as she comments: 'Nature is all-powerful, and her breath | Moves like a quickening spirit o'er the depths | Within a father's heart' (I. 246–8). Gonzalez, however, seeks to subordinate 'Nature's voice' to 'Th'austere and yet divine remonstrances | Whisper'd by faith and honour' and equated throughout the play with the soul (I. 259–63). While Gonzalez acknowledges the power of his own feelings, located within his heart—'Thinkst thou *I* feel no pangs? | He that hath given me sons doth know the heart | Whose treasure she recalls' (I. 302–4)—Elmina presents his refusal to yield up the city as the triumphant separation of his 'soul' from his 'heart':

[20] See Marlon B. Ross, *The Contours of Masculine Desire: Romanticism and the Rise of Women's Poetry* (New York and Oxford: Oxford University Press, 1989), 274–85; Anne K. Mellor, *Romanticism and Gender* (New York and London: Routledge, 1993), 135–40; Susan Wolfson, 'Felicia Hemans and the Revolving Doors of Reception' in Harriet Kramer Linkin and Stephen C. Behrendt (eds.), *Romanticism and Women Poets: Opening the Doors of Reception* (Lexington: University of Kentucky Press, 1999), 214–41; and 'Editing Felicia Hemans for the Twenty-First Century', *Romanticism on the Net*, 19 (August 2000).
[21] Quoted in Mellor, *Romanticism and Gender*, 135.

> Oh, cold and hard of heart!
> Thou shouldst be born for empire, since thy soul
> Thus lightly from all human bonds can free
> Its haughty flight!   (I. 272–5)

Elmina and Gonzalez, then, speak as representatives not only of different sets of values but of the different models of identity underlying Ximena's distinction between 'womanhood' and 'warriors', the first based on the natural affections of the heart, the second on the patriotic and religious values of the soul. They both recognize the power of the values for which the other speaks, Gonzalez acknowledging that God demands a 'terrible sacrifice . . . | From creatures in whose agonizing hearts | Nature is strong as death!' (I. 404–6) and Elmina describing her husband as one who 'bears a soul | Stronger than love or death' (IV. 162–3). The parallel of these two comments indicates the play's overall trajectory, with the 'soul', associated throughout with Gonzalez and his religious and patriotic ideology, presented as stronger than both the 'love' of the 'heart' and death.

The Siege of Valencia offers another version of the wartime transformations of gender, nation, and poetry that have been examined throughout this book. Ximena's reconstruction of her self from an identity based on the natural affections of the heart to one based on the spiritual values of the soul is also registered as a shift in poetic mode, as Elmina announces in the play's opening speech:

> Your songs are not as those of other days,
> Mine own Ximena!—Where is now the young
> And buoyant spirit of the morn, which once
> Breath'd in your spring-like melodies, and woke
> Joy's echo from all hearts?   (I. 64–8)

Against Elmina's figuring of Ximena's songs prior to the siege in natural terms and in relation to the heart, Gonzalez presents the current crisis as requiring a different form that addresses the 'spirit' and cuts it free from nature:

> If there be strains of power
> To rouse a spirit, which in triumphant scorn
> May cast off nature's feebleness, and hold
> Its proud career unshackled, dashing down
> Tears and fond thoughts to earth; give voice to those!
> I have need of such, Ximena! we must hear
> No melting music now!   (I. 148–54)

Ximena, then, becomes representative of a wartime poetics that articulates and inspires a model of identity severed from nature. And her
successful attempts to rouse the citizens of Valencia to attempt to save
her two brothers replays the conflict between 'heart' and 'soul' at a civic
level. In response to a citizen's explanation of the reason for the city's
apathy—'Sickness, and toil, and grief, have breath'd upon us, | Our
hearts beat faint and low' (VI. 77–8)—Ximena sets the bodily heart
against the higher power of the soul:

> Are ye so poor
> Of soul, my countrymen! That ye can draw
> Strength from no deeper source than that which sends
> The red blood mantling through the joyous veins,
> And gives the fleet step wings?—Why, how have age
> And sensitive womanhood ere now endured,
> Through pangs of searching fire, in some proud cause,
> Blessing that agony?—Think ye the Power
> Which bore them nobly up, as if to teach
> The torturer where eternal Heaven had set
> Bounds to his sway, was earthy, of this earth,
> This dull mortality?
>
> (VI. 78–89)

Contrary to Marlon Ross's argument that Ximena 'is always cognizant
that the source of her power is the heart, which binds the hearth and the
state, the past and the present, passivity and activity, suffering and
passion, life and death',[22] her speech to the citizens emphasizes the
necessity of finding in the soul a power and an identity which can transcend those defined in terms of the mortal strength of the heart.

Though Ximena dies during the siege, ostensibly of disease, in many
ways the play endorses her transformation. Gonzalez's elegiac tribute to
her as one who 'for all her life | Breath'd of a hero's soul' (IX. 95–6)
presents her as having achieved the status of the 'warrior-souls' against
which 'womanhood' was initially defined. But the importance of
Ximena's transformation is felt not only by Gonzalez, the embodiment
of faith and honour, or the citizens, themselves transformed by her
patriotic oratory. It is also acknowledged by Elmina, for so long the
spokesperson in the play for the natural and the heart's affections. It is
these values that prompt Elmina to betray the city to Abdullah in return
for the release of her sons, but Abdullah does not keep his word, and the

---

[22] Ross, *Contours*, 284.

two boys are executed below the walls of the city. In her initial response
to the news of their deaths, Elmina collapses in what feels like a potential end to the play, signalled in the stage directions by 'a long pause'
(VIII. 210). But, as if offering an alternative conclusion, Elmina 'rises',
struck by the power of revelation:

> —A light, a light springs up from grief and death,
> Which with its solemn radiance doth reveal
> Why we have thus been tried!
>
> (VIII. 213–15)

This imagery of heavenly light is of course associated with Ximena
throughout the play, and in her valediction to her, Elmina presents
herself as transformed by her influence into a second version of her:

> Be at peace!
> Thou whose bright spirit made itself the soul
> Of all that were around thee!—And thy life
> E'en then was struck, and withering at the core!
> —Farewell!—thy parting look hath on me fall'n,
> E'en as a gleam of heaven, and I am now
> More like what thou hast been!—My soul is hush'd,
> For a still sense of purer worlds hath sunk
> And settled on its depths with that last smile
> Which from thine shone forth.—Thou hast not lived
> In vain—my child, farewell!
>
> (VIII. 285–95)

Transformed by the influence of Ximena, Elmina now constructs herself
in terms of her 'soul' rather than her heart, a shift emphasized by her
previous speech to Gonzalez in which she presents herself through the
imagery of the rising soul she had previously used to criticize her
husband:

> My soul hath risen
> To mate itself with thine; and by thy side
> Amidst the hurtling lances I will stand,
> As one on whom a brave man's love hath been
> Wasted not utterly.   (VIII. 272–6)

By the end of the play, then, Elmina places herself in one of the conventional roles scripted for women in wartime, located in the scene of
conflict but playing a secondary role to her husband and defining herself
in terms of his love for her.

In its three main figures, then, *The Siege of Valencia* appears to celebrate the ability of the 'soul' to rise above the immediate affections of

the 'heart', offering examples of what Hemans in her 'Advertisement' describes as 'the severe and self-devoting heroism, which forms the subject of the . . . poem' (p. 177). All three figures ultimately articulate the connection of 'a religious feeling with the patriotism and high-minded loyalty which had thus been proved "faithful unto death" ' (p. 178). However, Hemans's ambivalence about the triumph of this patriotic discourse of the soul over the affections of the heart is illustrated by the play's dramatic action which presents both Ximena and Gonzalez as unable to free themselves from the body. Stepping beyond the conventional roles of womanhood, Ximena has 'cross'd | The paths of Death' (I. 111–12), as her mother comments, catching disease by entering the public sphere. Yet it is not only disease which kills her, as she tells the citizens:

> But even now,
> I have that within me, kindling through the dust,
> Which from all time hath made high deeds its voice
> And token to the nations;—Look on me!
> Why hath Heaven pour'd forth courage, as a flame
> Wasting the womanish heart, which must be still'd
> Yet sooner for its swift consuming brightness,
> If not to shame your doubt, and your despair,
> And your soul's torpor?
>
> (VI. 94–102)

The martial virtue of 'courage', one of the qualities that Gonzalez had described Ximena as wearing as a breastplate, is absorbed into the imagery of fire that not only inspires but also consumes 'the womanish heart' in a manner figured through Hemans's language of siege— 'Wasting'. Ximena's transformation is achieved at the cost of her heart and her 'hero's soul' is gained through the destruction of her woman's body. While Ximena is able to inspire the city to regain its masculinity, redeeming itself through fighting, this civic regendering results in the death of the feminine. In this association of a martial woman and death, Ximena is linked to the heroine of the ballad sung to her by her friend Theresa which tells of a 'maiden' who 'bound the steel, in battle tried, | Her fearless heart above, | And stood with brave men, side by side' (V. 66 8). Literalizing Ximena's figurative putting on of a breastplate, this heroine is killed by her involvement in war, her grave a symbol of the incongruity of her gender and the place and means of her death:

> Why is the Spanish maiden's grave
> So far from her own bright land? . . .
>
> The lowly Cross, with flowers o'ergrown,
> Marks well that place of rest;
> But who hath gráved, on its mossy stone,
> A sword, a helm, a crest?   (V. 42–3, 54–7)

However, this maiden's motives for crossing into the martial sphere seem at first to differ from Ximena's; like the heroine of Hemans's 'Woman on the Field of Battle', she fights and dies 'In the strength and faith of love', throwing herself in front of a javelin that is aimed at her lover's breast in 'a death which saved what she loved so well' (V. 69, 76). While Ximena appears to fight for a divinely sanctioned national cause, the ballad maiden fights for love, her martial activity made properly feminine because motivated by the heart. Yet Ximena is ultimately contained within just such a conventional narrative. As she dies, she confesses to her mother that she had a lover recently killed in battle and that if she were not already dying of disease she would perish of a broken heart. Ximena dies as a conventional figure of womanhood, akin to the bereaved 'maiden' of the ballad she sings at the play's opening. We might compare her return to such a 'natural role' with Hemans's treatment of the most famous warrior woman of history in her poem 'Joan of Arc, in Rheims', in which Joan's recognition of her father and brother during the coronation of the dauphin is presented as 'Winning her back to nature' (l. 81), prompting her to unbind 'The helm of many battles from her head' and request to return home with her family (l. 82).[23]

If Ximena's reinscription within a conventional feminine role based around the natural heart's affection of womanhood is unsurprising, her inability to free herself from her 'womanish heart' is paralleled by Gonzalez's temporary blindness while watching the execution of his sons. Gonzalez insists on his ability to withstand the ordeal, but immediately finds himself unable to carry out his wish, temporarily blinded by his emotional turmoil:

> —my brain whirls fearfully—
> How thick the shades close round!—my boy! my boy!
> Where art thou in this gloom?
>
>   (VII. 67–9)

---

[23] I was alerted to this moment in the poem by Susan Wolfson's excellent discussion, ' "Domestic Affections" and "the Spear of Minerva": Felicia Hemans and the Dilemma of Gender', in Carol Shiner Wilson and Joel Haefner (eds.) *Re-Visioning Romanticism: British Women Writers, 1776–1837* (Philadelphia: University of Pennsylvania Press, 1994), 156.

Overcome by feeling, Gonzalez finds himself subject to the condition he had earlier criticized in Elmina, whose 'blinding tears' made her unable to see the guilt of her desire to surrender the city (I. 356). Hemans emphasizes the significance of his temporary blindness by stressing his inability to witness Alphonso's heroic death, despite his son's dying wish that he should 'fall | Knowing thine eye looks proudly on thy child' (VII. 56–7). In a poignant moment of recognized failure—'He bade me keep mine eye upon him, | And all is darkness round me!' (VII. 80–1)—Gonzalez's emotions undermine Alphonso's commitment to a heroic death undertaken on behalf of the father. As in Hemans's most famous poem, 'Casabianca', the father's failure to witness his son's martyrdom calls into question the patriotic and filial values for which the sacrifice was made.

Ultimately, then, their affections prevent either Ximena or Gonzalez from entirely severing their ties with the natural and the heart. The demands of the 'heart' and the 'soul' remain in conflict, part of what Wolfson has described as the staging and restaging of a 'restless debate between domestic affections and the spear of Minerva'.[24] Nor is this debate resolved by the ending of the play; to quote Wolfson again, 'the ideological conflicts between patriotism and maternal affection, between aristocratic honor and common misery, are not soluble by historical process'.[25] But what the ending of the play does reveal is that even if these conflicts are not soluble at an ideological level, they can be resolved in formal terms through a double transformation that turns siege into battle and drama into romance. With the the arrival of the Castilian forces the siege, with its conflation of the domestic and the martial and its emphasis on inner tension, is replaced by an open battle in which the Spanish forces can heroically defeat the Moors and the 'noble king' of Castile triumph over 'the man of blood' (IX. 164, 178). Immediately after Gonzalez's tribute to Ximena's heroic soul, there is a 'sound of trumpets and shouting from the plain', as the two armies close and the focus of attention shifts from the walled city to the battlefield, described by the priest Hernandez in the picturesque terms of Scottian narrative romance:

> The first bright sparks of battle have been struck
> From spear to spear, across the gleaming field!
> —There is no sight on which the blue sky looks
> To match with this!   (IX. 103–6)

With Ximena's burial, war again becomes an all-male affair—'the lot of warrior souls'—and its particular value lies in realigning the natural and

²⁴ Wolfson, ' "Domestic Affections" ', 162.
²⁵ Wolfson, 'Revolving Doors', 237.

the spiritual, as Hernandez comments: 'The very nature and high soul of man | Doth now reveal itself' (IX. 108–9). It is through battle against the other that the individual and the city, divided during the siege, regain their unity (and we might recall Hemans's youthful description of herself as an 'enthusiast . . . in the cause of Castile and liberty' whose 'whole heart and soul are interested for the gallant patriots').[26] No longer torn between heart and soul, Gonzalez dies triumphant, claiming the victory for God, his country, and his sons—'For Afric's lance is broken, and my sons | Have won their first good field!' (IX, 198–9). Similarly, in the final speech of the play, Elmina is able to align the heroic and familial, the heart and soul, and the human and divine:

> Aye, 'tis thus
> Thou shouldst be honour'd!—And I follow thee
> With an unfaltering and a lofty step,
> To that last home of glory. She that wears
> In her deep heart the memory of thy love,
> Shall thence draw strength for all things, till the God,
> Whose hand around her hath unpeopled earth,
> Looking upon her still and chasten'd soul,
> Call it once more to thine!
> [to the Castilians]   Awake, I say,
> Tambour and trumpet, wake!—And let the land
> Through all her mountains hear your funeral peal!
> —So should a hero pass to his repose.
>
> (IX. 219–30)

The ease with which the turn to battle and Scottian romance resolves the conflicts of The Siege of Valencia emphasizes the structural value of Hemans's choice of the martial situation of the siege. While the romance of battle works to unite the state and the individual, the drama of siege provides a format in which Hemans can explore the construction of gender in terms of the 'heart' and 'soul' and examine how these roles are both questioned and reconfirmed by the crisis of war.

Sieges and the Lessons of History

Byron and Hemans both drew on the allegorical potential of siege warfare to represent the more general process of history of which it is a part. When Ismail is entered in Don Juan, Byron presents history as a

---

[26] Hemans, Selected Poems, ed. Kelly, 411–12.

sequence of sieges: 'I see cast down | Rome, Babylon, Tyre, Carthage, Nineveh, | All walls men know, and many never known' (VIII. 60). The great sieges of the past here represent a model of history as a series of falls; the siege of Rome, the first example in this list, provides Byron with the subject for his dramatic exploration of the theme in *The Deformed Transformed* in which the city, the 'World's Wonder'(2. 1. 87) and the high point of Western civilization is destroyed. In *The Last Constantine*, Hemans uses the fall of Constantinople to the Turks in 1453, the events which marked the end of the Roman empire—'that last night of empire!' when a 'thousand years of Christian pomp are o'er' (63–4)—for her fullest examination of the historical process, one that she undertakes in the mode and form (Spenserian stanza) of *Childe Harold's Pilgrimage* and one in which she draws on the narrative of wartime national remasculinization that has been traced throughout this book.

Addressing the stars that shine above Constantinople on the night prior to its destruction, Hemans constructs history as a cyclical series of sieges:

> But ye! that beam'd on Fate's tremendous night,
> When the storm burst o'er golden Babylon,
> And ye, that sparkled with your wonted light
> O'er burning Salem, by the Roman won;
> And ye, that calmly view'd the slaughter done
> In Rome's own streets, when Alaric's trumpet-blast
> Rang through the Capitol; bright spheres! roll on!
> *Still* bright, though empires fall; and bid man cast
> His humbled eyes to earth, and commune with the past.　(46)

Hemans's historical model has contemporary relevance, both in the wake of the collapse of the Napoleonic empire and in the context of the resurgence of Greek nationalism which she addresses in the poem's close, prophesying that in Istanbul 'the Tartar sways: | But not for long!' (104). For Hemans the past 'hath mighty lessons' (47) and it speaks from the sites that so often form the subject matter of her shorter pieces, graves and ruins:[27]

> 　　　　　　　　from the tomb,
> And from the ruins of the tomb, and where,
> 'Midst the wreck'd cities in the desert's gloom,
> All tameless creatures make their savage lair,
> *Thence* comes its voice　　　　　　　　(47)

---

[27] e.g., 'The Graves of England', 'The Image in Lava', 'Marius amidst the Ruins of Carthage'.

Yet this historical voice is not one of Byronic lament, for it 'bids us not despair,':

> But make one rock our shelter and our stay,
> Beneath whose shade all else is passing to decay!   (47)

If for Byron, history is a cycle of sieges in the man-made catastrophe of civilization, for Hemans it is a divinely sanctioned process which she presents as a gendered process of history.[28] The Byzantine empire is punished for its enactment of a familiar historical narrative as the feminized city Constantinople, 'great ocean's bride' (1), declines from greatness and glory into decadence and 'luxury' (3), its self-indulgence and over-exquisite sensibility leaving it open to attack:

> The pure high faith of old
> Was changed; and on her silken couch of sleep
> She lay, and murmur'd if a rose-leaf's fold
> Disturb'd her dreams; and call'd her slaves to keep
> Their watch, that no rude sound might reach her o'er the deep.
>
> But there are sounds that from the regal dwelling
> Free hearts and fearless only may exclude;
>
> (2–3)

Like Wordsworth in his sonnet on Venice, and Scott, Byron, and Southey in their writing on Spain, Hemans represents Constantinople's decline as a narrative of gender, the city's feminization contrasted with the manly heroism of the Greece of classical times—'Oh! for a soul to fire thy dust, Thermopylæ!' (6)—and of the 'sainted chivalry' of the Crusades (9). *The Last Constantine* is another siege poem like 'The Wife of Asdrubal' and 'Marguerite of France' which combines historical and gender crises, the failure of masculinity compelling the feminized city to take on the martial role:

> Then gird thou on
> Thine armour, Eastern Queen! And meet the hour
> Which waits thee ere the day's fierce work is done
> With a strong heart; so may thy helmet tower
> Unshiver'd through the storm, for generous hope is power!   (10)

But like the 'wife', the city is doomed as the 'degenerate Greeks' fail to respond to the poet's rallying cry, continuing to indulge themselves in 'every brief delight' of 'luxurious ease' (12, 14).

Hemans presents the Greeks of fifteenth-century Constantinople as

---

[28] See stanzas 38, 40, and 50.

having fallen away from the standards of the heroic and manly past and she looks to the models of classical Greece to inspire 'Freedom's fight' against the Turks in 1820, invoking the 'kindling' 'spirit' of Plataea (101), Marathon (103), and Thermopylae and calling on the Greeks to 'Wash from that soil the stains, with battle-showers' (104). Here Hemans's cyclical model of history becomes incorporated within a divinely ordained teleological scheme which progresses towards a state of 'peace' and 'Freedom' and a triumphing of Christianity over Islam (105). The process of remasculinization necessary to enact this divine historical schema is anticipated in Hemans's treatment of the figure of Constantine and his followers, who fight 'in the strength of a collected heart, | To dare what man may dare—and know 'tis vain' (77). While both Kelly and Sweet have argued that this last Roman ruler is a femi-nized figure, who embodies a revised male subjectivity,[29] Constantine redeems himself through the assumption of a heroic role that parallels the city's need to reman itself. Like Ximena in *The Siege of Valencia* (and Adosinda in *Roderick: The Last of the Goths*), his strength comes from a divine source, though one which Hemans certainly emphasizes may inspire women as well as men:

> Yet then that Power, whose dwelling is on high,
> Its loftiest marvels doth reveal, and speak,
> In the deep human heart more gloriously,
> Than in the bursting thunder!—Thence the weak,
> They that seem'd form'd, as flower-stems, but to break
> With the first wind, have risen to deeds, whose name
> Still calls up thoughts that mantle to the cheek,
> And thrill the pulse!—Ay, strength no pangs could tame
> Hath look'd from woman's eye upon the sword and flame!   (54)

Rather than 'transcend[ing] the forces of masculine history to be the inspired liberal subject of the future' as Kelly has argued,[30] Constantine invokes and appeals to the classical heroism of the past to inspire the masculinity necessary in this crisis, calling on 'the strong names of Rome and Liberty' to 'fire the eye, | And rouse the heart of manhood' (56). In fighting to win 'A soldier's death—the all now left an empire's lord' (90)

[29] Gary Kelly, 'Death and the Matron: Felicia Hemans, Romantic Death, and the Founding of the Modern Liberal State', in Nanora Sweet and Julie Melnyk (eds.), *Felicia Hemans: Reimagining Poetry in the Nineteenth Century* (Basingstoke and New York: 2001), 204–5; Nanora Sweet, 'The Bowl of Liberty: Felicia Hemans and the Romantic Mediterranean', Ph.D. thesis (University of Michigan, 1993), 362–4.

[30] Kelly, 'Death and the Matron', 205.

and in dying 'unfetter'd, arm'd, and free, | And kingly to the last' (99), Constantine embodies redemption through masculine action which provides the model for Greece in its war against the Turks in the 1820s. If it can regain the values of its heroic past, it can bring about a triumph of Christianity that is, in fact, fated.

While Hemans uses the siege of Constantinople to allegorize a divine model of history, Byron uses the dramatic structure of *The Deformed Transformed* to reveal both the ambiguities in historical understanding and the way historical models serve particular ideologies. For Arnold, Rome represents the centre of Christianity and the epitome of historical grandeur and he believes that modern Romans are innocent and undeserving of their impending destruction (1. 2. 90–3). Yet for Caesar, their deaths and the near-total destruction of Rome are part of the cycle of history: Rome was founded in blood with Romulus's murder of Remus and its sacking will only replay the devastation of the Romans themselves who made 'the Ocean and the Earth | . . . their never-ceasing scene of slaughter | For ages' (1. 2. 83–9). On the night before the assault, Bourbon presents his impending sacking of Rome in terms of this vision of history as a repeated refrain of destruction:

> The world's
> Great capital perchance is ours to-morrow.
> Through every change the seven-hilled city hath
> Retained her sway o'er nations, and the Caesars
> But yielded to the Alarics, the Alarics
> Unto the Pontiffs. Roman, Goth, or Priest,
> Still the world's masters! Civilized, Barbarian,
> Or Saintly, still the walls of Romulus
> Have been the Circus of an Empire. Well!
> 'Twas *their* turn—now 'tis ours; and let us hope
> That we will fight as well, and rule much better.
> (1. 2. 274–84)

Bourbon presents the history of Rome as cyclical, but in his hope that he will 'rule much better' he shows how this model of history can be used to serve his own purpose and justify his invasion of Rome. Shortly after, he will describe Rome as his 'treasury' (1. 2. 303). A similar, self-justifying construction of history is given by the dying Lutheran soldier who represents the sacking of Rome not as an exercise in plunder (despite the looting of St Peter's) but as part of a divine teleological scheme (2. 3. 24–7). Byron sets these contrasting historical models against Caesar's version of the cycle of sieges as ants 'tearing down each other's nests' (1. 2. 328).

Caesar's cosmic perspective further questions the human understandings of history and the ideological uses that are made of it.

'Bellona as a Muse': War and Poetic Identity in Byron and Hemans

Byron's and Hemans's siege poems provide a valuable focus for examining the way in which they shaped their poetic identities in relation to war
as a subject and a context of their careers as writers. For Byron, war had
always been part of his epic agenda for Don Juan (I. 200) and in canto
VIII he makes a claim for the special, if ambiguous, role of 'the blaze | Of
conquest and its consequences, which | Make Epic poesy so rare and
rich' (VIII. 90). In choosing a siege, he sets up a parallel with the major
epic model, 'eternal Homer', arguing that if he cannot match Homer
poetically, his modern siege outdoes in its devastation the great siege of
classical history and literature, Troy (VII. 80–1). Byron uses the parallel
with Homer as part of the grand claims he makes for the poem and for
himself as a poet. Homer's skill is registered in terms of the martial forms
of his own epic: he can 'charm | All ears . . . By merely wielding with
poetic arm, | Arms to which men will never more resort' (VII. 79).
Similarly, despite Byron's savage critique of siege warfare, he uses it as a
framing metaphor for his own poetic performance, introducing the
subject with 'I . . . am about to batter | A town which did a famous siege
endure' and concluding it when he is 'Worn out with battering Ismail's
stubborn wall' (VII. 8; VIII. 139). Of course, Byron had a strong sense of
his own poetic militancy, describing himself as one who 'will war, at least
in words (and—should | My chance so happen—deeds)' (IX. 24),[31] but
in Don Juan he uses the siege metaphor to image the power of his own
poetic performance rather than his readiness to take up arms in a particular cause. Similarly, when at the end of canto VI Byron introduces his
martial theme with 'The Muse will take a little touch at warfare' (VI.
120), he not only echoes the Chorus's famous description of Henry V on
the night before Agincourt (' "A little touch of Harry in the night" ' (4.
0. 47)) but also recalls the 'touch' of the linstock on 'the devilish cannon'
at the siege of Harfleur (3. 0. 33). Byron's dazzling display of poetic skills
in Don Juan is often described in terms of pyrotechnics; here he suggests
it is better thought of as a cannonade, as powerful as those of the great
poets of war, Homer and Shakespeare.

---

[31] See also his description of the siege cantos in BLJ, IX. 191.

It is through the figure of Suvorov, the Russian general appointed to lead the siege, that Byron represents the force of history as it enacts itself through war, and it is in response to this figure that he offers his own alternative vision of it and his own statement of his poetics. In his efficiency, ruthlessness, and willingness to expend any number of soldiers to achieve his aim, Suvorov, whose 'trade | Is butchery' (VII. 69), comes to represent both the professionalism and the devastation of modern war. But his position as one of the 'great men' who makes history, possessed of 'the spirit of a single mind [that], | Makes that of multitudes take one direction' (VII. 48), is achieved only as a result of his limited vision of history:

> Suwarrow,—who but saw things in the gross,
>   Being much too gross to see them in detail,
> Who calculated life as so much dross   (VII. 77)

This limited vision is echoed by history's own limitations, described in the next canto:

> History can only take *things in the gross*;
>   But could we know them *in detail*, perchance
> In balancing the profit and the *loss*,
>   War's merit it by no means might enhance,
> To waste *so much* gold for a little *dross*
>   As hath been done, mere conquest to advance.
>   (VIII. 3; italics added)

It is against this 'gross' vision of history that Byron writes in *Don Juan*. Throughout the cantos, as here, he counters history's Suvorovian values by offering his reader an account 'in detail' of the true cost of war, redefining territory rather than human life as 'so much dross', and emphasizing the importance of 'one good action in the midst of crimes' (VIII. 90). Jerome McGann has convincingly argued that Byron's choice of the siege of Ismail at the moment he was reconceiving *Don Juan* was 'extremely important' because it indicates 'its new, self-conscious, and more comprehensive aspirations towards political and ideological commentary and commitment'.[32] This new seriousness and militancy is seen in the way Byron defines his own role as a poet against Suvorov's embodiment of history enacted though war. In his description of Suvorov's victorious message to the Empress Catherine, Byron presents him as 'a poet' who 'Could rhyme, like Nero, o'er a burning city' (VIII.

---

[32] Byron, *Poetical Works*, ed. McGann, V. 718.

134 and p. 1057). Just as Suvorov's embodiment of history's 'gross' vision prompts Byron's alternative detailed vision, so the fatuous and inappropriate 'couplet' of this 'Russ so witty' stimulates Byron's climatic statement of his own poetic role in the siege cantos:

> He wrote this Polar melody, and set it,
>   Duly accompanied by shrieks and groans,
> Which few will sing, I trust, but none forget it—
>   For I will teach, if possible, the stones
> To rise against Earth's tyrants. Never let it
>   Be said that we still truckle unto thrones;—
> But ye—our children's children! think how we
> Showed *what things were* before the world was free!   (VIII. 135)

Defining his own song against Suvorov's 'Polar melody', Byron here gives his most ambitious statement of the function of his poetry and the part it will play in the bringing about of a 'free' world in the future. Adapting the 'things as they are' slogan and aesthetic of the English Jacobin novelists, Byron presents his role as an educative one that will lead to change: he will 'teach' by showing '*what things were*'. While Byron uses the disasters of the sieges of Corinth and Ismail to reveal the pattern of history as shaped by 'thrones, | And those that sate upon them' (VIII. 137), he presents as startlingly different the ultimate outcome of this pattern of history in the two texts. Despite its occasional wishing for 'better days' (l. 341), *The Siege of Corinth* ends on an apocalyptic note of total destruction with no envisioning of a world after the apocalypse. By contrast, the account of the siege of Ismail in *Don Juan* concludes with a millennial vision of an ideal, republican world to come (VIII. 135–7). The factor that will make the difference between these two outcomes, Byron suggests, is his own insistence on singing the 'shrieks and groans' of war and his decision to 'throw away the scabbard' in the 'present clash of philosophy and tyranny', as he described his intention in the siege cantos in a letter to Moore (*BLJ*, IX. 191).

If the siege provided Hemans with a means of bringing together the competing but related themes of her poetry, what her sister and biographer identified as 'the two strains dearest to her nature, the chivalrous and the tender',[33] it also provides a figure for her poetry itself. With its fusion of the domestic and martial spheres, the siege summoned her as a poet, as it did Ximena as an embodiment of 'womanhood', 'unto

---

[33] *The Works of Mrs Hemans*, 1. 56. References to this *Memoir* are hereafter cited by volume and page within the text.

conflicts, heretofore, | The lot of warrior-souls.' As Marlon Ross has reminded us, Hemans's biographer Henry Chorley had pointed out that Ximena's voice represents Hemans's own,[34] and Ximena's transformation from singer of natural lyrics for a family audience within the bower into an inspiring singer of martial ballads in the public sphere offers a figure for the wartime transformation of poetry as well as for Hemans's own poetic ambition; Ximena's rousing of the public with 'The Cid's Battle Song' (VI. 193–224) parallels Hemans's inclusion of 'Songs of the Cid' in *The Siege of Valencia* volume. Yet Ximena's fate illustrates the potential cost of such a public career, her death enacting Hemans's anxiety about the cost of fame for a woman writer. As Susan Wolfson has shown, there is a 'fundamental and unresolvable conflict' in her work which sees 'female fame as a purchase against female happiness'.[35] As she argues of 'Woman and Fame', the poem's 'disparage[ment of] woman's fame against the durable nurture of "home-born love" ' are at war with its 'aesthetic elaborations' which associate 'artistic achievement with the thrill of life itself':[36]

> Thou hast a voice, whose thrilling tone
> Can bid each life-pulse beat,
> As when a trumpet's note hath blown,
> Calling the brave to meet:
> But mine, let mine—a woman's breast,
> By words of home-born love be bless'd.

What is striking here is that the figure which Hemans uses to register the thrill of life is a call to battle. War becomes symbolic of life's excitements, linked in the poem to creativity and artistic achievement, but denied to the poet as a woman dutifully disciplining herself to the demands of the home.

Hemans explores this tension between the life-affirming stimulations of the imagination, war and poetic creativity, on the one hand, and the duties of the home, on the other, in 'An Hour of Romance', another example of the imagining of war facilitated by the writing of Walter Scott.[37] In this poem, published in *Records of Woman* (1828), the poet describes her retreat into a bower where she 'read | Of royal chivalry and

---

[34] Ross, *Contours*, 284.   [35] Wolfson, 'Editing Felicia Hemans', 19.
[36] Ibid.

[37] My attention was first drawn to this poem by E. Douka Kabitoglou's 'The Pen and Sword: Felicia Hemans's Records of Man', in ed. Tony Pinkney, Keith Hanley, and Fred Botting, (eds.), *Romantic Masculinities: News from Nowhere 2, Theory and Politics of Romanticism* (Keele, Staffs: Keele University Press, 1997), 101–20. The poem is also the subject of an excellent discussion by Jacqueline Labbe in *The Romantic Paradox: Love, Violence and the Uses of Romance, 1760–1830* (Basingstoke and London: Macmillan, 2000), 121–2.

old renown, | A tale of Palestine', in the 'magic page' of Scott's novel *The Talisman*.[38] Scott's text acts as a stimulation to the poet's martial imagination, as indeed the man himself would when Hemans met him in 1830, an encounter which it is worth outlining before returning to the poem. Describing her stay at Abbotsford, Hemans explains how, hearing Scott 'pour forth, from the fulness of his rich mind and peopled memory, song, and legend, and tale of old . . . I could almost fancy I heard the gathering-cry of some chieftain of the hills, so completely does his spirit carry me back to the days of the slogan and the fire-cross.'[39] Like his poetry, Scott's tales transport Hemans back through history, and as her fancy begins to take a visual form she sees 'many a cairn and field of old combat, the heroes of which seemed to start up before me, in answer to the "mighty master's" voice, which related their deeds as we went by' (I. 178). And the power of Scott's voice over the imagination is such that Hemans presents herself as taking on the role of Marmion:

like the war-horse at the sound of the trumpet . . . in reciting a verse of old martial song, he will suddenly spring up, and one feels ready to exclaim—

'Charge, Chester, charge!—on, Stanley, on!'

so completely is the electric chain struck by his own high emotion. (I. 179)

Hemans responds to Scott's recitations as readers did to his poetry, his oral and textual performances enabling hearers and readers to picture and become part of the imaginative world that he creates. And it is this process of imagining war that Hemans presents in 'An Hour of Romance', the 'magic page' gradually facilitating the imaginative transformation of the natural bower in which she is reading into the martial environment of his novel, the 'bee' becoming 'A drowsy bugle' and the 'purple dragon-fly' 'a fairy javelin', until 'the spell' of the 'high gorgeous tale' on the poet's 'chain'd soul' transports her to the scene of war:

'twas not the leaves I heard;—
A Syrian wind the lion-banner stirr'd,
Through its proud floating folds;—'twas not the brook
Singing in secret through its glassy glen;—
A wild shrill trumpet of the Saracen
Peal'd from the desert's lonely heart, and shook
The burning air.—Like clouds when winds are high,
O'er glittering sands flew steeds of Araby,

[38] Text from *The Works of Mrs Hemans*, V. 274–5 (no line numbers).
[39] Ibid., I. 178. Further references are included within parentheses in the main text.

> And tents rose up, and sudden lance and spear
> Flash'd where a fountain's diamond wave lay clear,
> Shadow'd by graceful palm-trees. Then the shout
> Of merry England's joy swell'd freely out,
> Sent through an eastern heaven, whose glorious hue
> Made shields dark mirrors to its depth of blue;
> And harps were there—I heard their sounding strings,
> As the waste echoed to the mirth of kings.—

But from these imagined animations of romantic conflict, Hemans is recalled to the domestic sphere:

> The bright mask faded. Unto life's worn track,
> What call'd me from its flood of glory back?
> A voice of happy childhood!—and they pass'd,
> Banner and harp, and Paynim's trumpet's blast;
> Yet might I scarce bewail the splendour gone,
> My heart so leap'd to that sweet laughter's tone.

In a poem primarily inspired by Scott, Hemans here rewrites Wordsworth's 'Immortality Ode' and 'My heart leaps up' lyric to present the joys of motherhood as compensating for the fading of the visionary world of 'splendour' and 'glory'. The poem celebrates only a temporary escape from the demands of the home, an *hour* of romance, and the poet's use of the language of enchantment emphasizes the illusory nature of her imaginings when set against the spell-breaking 'sweet laughter's tone'. However, the poem does emphasize how the imagining of war that provides the poetic subject and the inspiration for poetic creativity cannot be found on 'life's worn track'. This implicit argument in the poem can be glossed with one of Hemans's letters from the late 1820s, in which she compares the world of romance heroes with her own:

I send Herder's beautiful ballads of *The Cid*, and I wish you may take as much pleasure as I have always done in their proud *clarion music*. I often think what a dull, faded thing life—such life as we lead in this later age—would appear to one of those fiery knights of old. Only imagine *my Cid*, spurring the good steed Bavieca through the streets of Liverpool, or coming to pass an evening with me at Wavertree![40]

Though Hemans is ostensibly making a comparison between two ages here, much of the pathos of the passage comes from the juxtaposition of the Cid's romantic adventures with her own constricted domestic life.

In 'An Hour of Romance', then, war provides the subject for

---

[40] *The Works of Mrs Hemans*, I. 159.

Hemans's poetic imagination, and in her 'Advertisement' to *The Siege of Valencia* she emphasizes the extent to which the play is a product of her imagination, again drawing on Theseus's account of the poetic imagination in *A Midsummer Night's Dream* in describing herself as having 'employed the agency of imaginary characters, and fixed upon "*Valencia del Cid*" as the scene to give them "A local habitation and a name" ' (p. 178). 'An Hour of Romance' ends by restoring the poet to the domestic sphere, just as Ximena is restored to the role of broken-hearted maiden lamenting the death of her lover in battle. For the woman writer, war, the imagination, and poetry must be subordinated to the duties of the home and the affections of the heart. Yet if in 'An Hour of Romance' the thrill of the imaginative process and the linked exhilarations of martial conflict seem to overwhelm the supposed joy of the return to 'life's worn track', so in *The Siege of Valencia* Ximena's martial instincts survive not only her recuperation into a more conventional model of wartime but also her death. Ximena's final words are of her 'father's banner' and the 'trumpet of Castile' (VIII. 137–41) and her military spirit lives on not only in the citizens of Valencia but also in Elmina who, as we have seen, bids farewell by saying 'Thou hast not lived | In vain' (VIII. 294–5). Elmina's elegizing of her daughter here draws attention to the fact that Ximena is a poetic figure, for it echoes the opening of Byron's famous self-elegizing in the climax to *Childe Harold's Pilgrimage*, IV (1818):

> But I have lived, and have not lived in vain:
> My mind may lose its force, my blood its fire,
> And my frame perish even in conquering pain,
> But there is that within me which shall tire
> Torture and Time, and breathe when I expire;
> Something unearthly, which they deem not of,
> Like the remembered tone of a mute lyre,
> Shall on their softened spirits sink, and move
> In hearts all rocky now the late remorse of love.   (IV. 137)

Elmina suggests that Ximena's voice will endure and be influential, just as the most famous poet of the period did of himself. Moreover, in granting her daughter poetic status akin to Byron's, Elmina endorses Ximena's own self-conception, for in her address to the citizens Ximena had also presented herself through echoes of Byron's stanza:

> But even now,
> I have that within me, kindling through the dust,
> Which from all time hath made high deeds its voice
> And token to the nations;   (VI. 94–7)

If Ximena (and Hemans) aspire to a Byronic timelessness, they also rewrite poetry away from the autonomous voice of Byronic selfhood and towards the poet as the voice of a divinely inspired patriotism. By the end of the play, these poetics have been inherited by Elmina who, no longer the voice of domestic affections, is now 'More like what [Ximena] hast been!' (VIII. 291). While many critics have rightly emphasized the dark undercurrents of the play's close, with Elmina left on stage as a symbol of both the value and the destruction of the domestic sphere, these readings must be set beside the fact that Elmina presents herself as a reincarnation of the martial spirit of her daughter; what survives at the end of the play is that 'Which from all time doth make high deeds its voice | And token to the nations'. Indeed, so strong is the poem's martial voice that in its review of *The Siege of Valencia* the *British Critic* presented the Roman goddess of war as the presiding deity of Hemans's poetry: '[S]he has a strong predilection for warlike affairs, for bold, fervid, and daring characters. We must, however, remark, that the military spirit that breathes and glows in many of her pages, does not add to their real excellence. We do not like Bellona as a Muse'.[41] While the *British Critic*'s response illustrates once again the ideological pressure which Hemans as a woman had to negotiate in her writing on war, it also registers the extent to which her poetry was shaped by being produced in an age in which Bellona was indeed one of the Muses of British poetry.

[41] Quoted in Wolfson, 'Revolving Doors', 233.

Epilogue: The 'Sir Walter Disease' and the Legacy of Romantic War

ADAM FERGUSON'S READING of *The Lady of the Lake* to 'the rough sons of the Fighting Third Division', with which this book began, and Felicia Hemans's poetic imagining of war in response to the 'magic page' of *The Talisman*, with which it has ended, illustrate the centrality of Walter Scott's writing to the envisioning of conflict during the romantic period. While the popularity of Scott's metrical romances was superseded by the phenomenal sales of Byron's poetry and his own success as a novelist in the years after the war, his reimagining of war remained tremendously influential throughout the nineteenth century, playing a major role in the chivalric revival, in the elevation of the warrior to heroic status, and in the romanticization of war that Michael Paris has seen as defining the 'warrior nation' from 1850 to 2000.[1] For example, Scott's description of the battle of Flodden in *Marmion* continued to be regarded by many as the greatest ever battle poem throughout the nineteenth century. In 1833, W. B. O. Peabody described the 'glorious battle scene' as 'one of the finest passages of narrative poetry in the language',[2] while in the 1880s John Ruskin assessed it as 'the truest and grandest battle-piece that, so far as I know, exists in the whole compass of literature', adding in a note: 'I include the literature of all foreign languages, so far as known to me: there is nothing to approach the finished delineations and flawless majesty of conduct in Scott's Flodden'.[3] Indeed,

---

[1] Michael Paris, *Warrior Nation: Images of War in British Popular Culture, 1850–2000* (London: Reaktion Books, 2000). On Scott and the chivalric revival, see Mark Girouard, *The Return to Camelot: Chivalry and the English Gentleman* (New Haven and London: Yale University Press, 1981), *passim*.

[2] John O. Hayden, *Scott: The Critical Heritage* (London: Routledge and Kegan Paul, 1970), 338.

[3] *Præterita, The Works of John Ruskin*, ed. E. T. Cook and Alexander Wedderburn, 39 vols. (London and New York: George Allen and Longmans, Green, and Co., 1908), XXXV. 546.

Marmion became the benchmark for assessing all poetic accounts of war. Thomas Hardy once responded to criticism of Homer's *Iliad*, 'Oh, but I admire the *Iliad* greatly. Why, it's in the *Marmion* class!'[4]

The continued influence of Scott's poetry on the imagining of conflict can be felt in verses written at the opening of the First World War, such as Julian Grenfell's 'Into Battle' with its emphasis on 'the joy of battle' and Herbert Asquith's 'The Volunteer' with its portrayal of a clerk fearing that 'his days would drift away | With no lance broken in life's tournament'.[5] And the attacks of the poets of that war on the idealization of conflict were in part a response to a verse tradition, as well as a broader cultural movement, that can be traced back to Scott. For example, when Siegfried Sassoon condemns the conception of the war as romance in 'Glory of Women'—'you believe | That chivalry redeems the war's disgrace'[6]—he does so by invoking and undermining a typically chivalric moment in *The Lord of the Isles* when the King sends his cavalry into battle:

> 'Forward, each gentleman and knight!
> Let gentle blood show generous might,
> And chivalry redeem the fight!'   (VI. 24)

And Scott's influential transformation of the imagining of war was not limited to Great Britain. In *Life on the Mississippi* (1883), Mark Twain diagnosed the 'Sir Walter disease' which infected the Southern states of America prior to the American Civil War through Scott's creation of a 'Middle-Age sham civilization' (while Twain's particular target is the novel *Ivanhoe*, his account of Scott refers equally to the poetry).[7] The 'Sir Walter disease' attacked the imaginative self-conception of Scott's readers, turning many of them into warriors (as the *Eclectic Review* argued Scott's poetry had done to his British readers). Twain writes that 'It was Sir Walter that made every gentleman in the South a Major or a Colonel, or a General or a Judge, before the war' (469) and that 'Sir Walter had so large a hand in making Southern character, as it existed before the war,

---

[4] Quoted in John Sutherland, *The Life of Walter Scott: A Critical Biography* (Oxford: Blackwell Publishers, 1997), 125.

[5] Jon Stallworthy (ed.), *The Oxford Book of War Poetry* (Oxford: Oxford University Press, 1988), 164–5, 163.

[6] Ibid. 178.

[7] Mark Twain, *Life on the Mississippi*, The Oxford Mark Twain (New York and Oxford: Oxford University Press, 1996), 468. Page references are hereafter included within the text. As an example of 'Sir Walter's starchier way of phrasing' things, Twain cites 'Southron' (468), a word used in *Marmion* ('Introduction to Canto Third') but not in *Ivanhoe*.

that he is in great measure responsible for the war' (469). While Twain qualifies this argument by describing it as a 'wild proposition', it remains one for which 'something of a plausible argument might, perhaps, be made' (469). And Twain concludes by restating his argument, commenting that 'The change of Character [responsible for the war] can be traced rather more easily to Sir Walter's influence than to that of any other thing or person' (469). Scott's influence was such, Twain argues, that he can be held responsible for the American Civil War. While Twain symbolically enacted the end of Scott's influence in *Huckleberry Finn* when he named the wrecked steamboat the *Walter Scott*,[8] it was the First World War which marked the culmination and the conclusion of the cult of chivalry and of Scott's century of influence. But to borrow the formula of Twain's 'wild proposition', in his poetry Scott transformed the writing of conflict during the Napoleonic wars and it is to the influence of Walter Scott, more than to that of any other thing or person, that we can trace the changed imagining of war in the nineteenth century.

[8] Mark Twain, *Adventures of Huckleberry Finn*, The Oxford Mark Twain (New York and Oxford: Oxford University Press, 1996), 105.

Bibliography

PRIMARY SOURCES

AMPHLETT, J., *Invasion: A Descriptive and Satirical Poem* (London: Longman and Co., 1804).

Anon., *An Accurate and Impartial Narrative of the War, by an Officer of the Guards; . . . Containing the Second Edition of a Poetical Sketch of the Campaign of 1793, revised . . . and . . . enlarged; . . . also a similar sketch of the Campaign of 1794. To which is added a narrative of the Retreat of 1795*, 2 vols. (London: T. Cadell and W. Davies, 1795).

The Anti-Gallican; or, Standard of British Loyalty, Religion, and Liberty, including a Collection of the Principal Papers, Tracts, Speeches, and Songs, that have been Published on the Threatened Invasion; together with many Original Pieces on the Same Subject, nos. 1–12 (London, 1804).

The Anti-Jacobin, ed. Graeme Stones, vol. I of *Parodies of the Romantic Age* ed. Graeme Stones and John Strachan, 5 vols. (London: Pickering and Chatto, 1999).

BARBAULD, ANNA, 'Art. XXXIV. *The Lay of the last Minstrel; a Poem*', *Annual Review and History of Literature for 1804*, 3 (1805), 600–4.

BLAKE, WILLIAM, *Complete Writings, with Variant Readings*, ed. Geoffrey Keynes (Oxford: Oxford University Press, 1966).

BLOOMFIELD, NATHANIEL, *An Essay on War, in Blank Verse* (London: Thomas Hurst and Vernor and Hood, 1803).

BOWLES, WILLIAM LISLE, *The Poetical Works*, ed. Revd George Gilfillan, 2 vols. (Edinburgh: James Nichols, 1845).

BROWN, ROBERT, *The Campaign: A Poetical Essay, in Two Books* (London: John Stockdale, 1797).

BURKE, EDMUND, *A Philosophical Enquiry into the Origins of our Ideas of the Sublime and Beautiful*, ed. Adam Phillip (Oxford: Oxford University Press, 1990).

—— *Reflections on the Revolution in France and on the Proceedings in Certain Societies in London Relative to that Event*, ed. Conor Cruise O'Brien (Harmondsworth, Middlesex: Penguin, 1983).

BURNS, ROBERT, *The Poems and Songs of Robert Burns*, ed. James Kinsley, 3 vols. (Oxford: Clarendon Press, 1968).

BYRON, GEORGE GORDON, LORD, *Byron's Letters and Journals*, ed. Leslie A. Marchand, 12 vols. (London: John Murray, 1973–82).

—— *Byron: The Oxford Authors*, ed. Jerome J. McGann (Oxford: Oxford University Press, 1986).

—— *Complete Poetical Works*, ed. Jerome J. McGann, 6 vols. (Oxford: Clarendon Press, 1980–91).

—— *Poetical Works*, ed. Frederick Page, new edition, corrected by John Jump (Oxford: Oxford University Press, 1970).

—— *The Works of Lord Byron: Letters and Journals*, ed. Rowland E. Prothero, 6 vols. (London and New York: John Murray and Charles Scribner's Sons, 1898–1901).

—— *The Works of Lord Byron: Poetry*, ed. Ernest Hartley Coleridge, 7 vols. (London and New York: John Murray and Charles Scribner's Sons, 1898–1904).

CAMPBELL, THOMAS, *The Complete Poetical Works*, ed. J. Logie Robertson (London, New York, and Toronto: Oxford University Press, 1907).

CLARE, JOHN, *The Early Poems of John Clare, 1804–1822*, ed. Eric Robinson and David Powell, 2 vols. (Oxford: Clarendon Press, 1989).

CLARENDON, EDWARD, EARL OF, *The History of the Rebellion and Civil Wars in England, begun in the Year 1641*, ed. W. Dunn Macray, 6 vols. (Oxford: Clarendon Press, 1888).

COLERIDGE, SAMUEL TAYLOR, *Biographia Literaria, or, Biographical Sketches of my Literary Life and Opinions*, ed. James Engell and W. Jackson Bate, *The Collected Works of Samuel Taylor Coleridge*, Bollingen Series, 75, 2 vols. (London and Princeton: Routledge and Kegan Paul and Princeton University Press, 1983).

—— *Collected Letters of Samuel Taylor Coleridge, 1785–1834* ed. Earl Leslie Griggs, 6 vols. (Oxford: Clarendon Press, 1956–71).

—— *Essays on His Times: In the Morning Post and the Courier*, ed. David V. Erdman, *The Collected Works of Samuel Taylor Coleridge*, Bollingen Series, 75, 3 vols. (London and Princeton: Routledge and Kegan Paul and Princeton University Press, 1978)

—— *The Friend*, ed. Barbara E. Rooke, *The Collected Works of Samuel Taylor Coleridge*, Bollingen Series, 75, 2 vols. (London and Princeton: Routledge and Kegan Paul and Princeton University Press, 1969).

—— *Lay Sermons*, ed. R. J. White, *The Collected Works of Samuel Taylor Coleridge*, Bollingen Series, 75 (London and Princeton: Routledge and Kegan Paul and Princeton University Press, 1972).

—— *Lectures 1795: On Politics and Religion*, ed. Lewis Patton and Peter Mann, *The Collected Works of Samuel Taylor Coleridge*, Bollingen Series, 75 (London and Princeton: Routledge and Kegan Paul and Princeton University Press, 1971).

—— *Lectures 1808–1819 on Literature*, ed. R. A. Foakes, *The Collected Works of Samuel Taylor Coleridge*, Bollingen Series, 75, 2 vols. (London and Princeton: Routledge and Kegan Paul and Princeton University Press, 1987).

—— *The Notebooks of Samuel Taylor Coleridge*, ed. Kathleen Coburn, 6 vols. (Princeton and New York: Pantheon Books, 1957–73).

—— *The Poetical Works of Samuel Taylor Coleridge*, ed. Ernest Hartley Coleridge, 2 vols. (Oxford: Oxford University Press, 1912; repr. 1983).

COLERIDGE, SAMUEL TAYLOR, *The Watchman*, ed. Lewis Patton, *The Collected Works of Samuel Taylor Coleridge*, Bollingen Series, 75 (London and Princeton: Routledge and Kegan Paul and Princeton University Press, 1970).

COWPER, WILLIAM, *The Poetical Works of William Cowper*, ed. H. S. Milford (London, New York, and Toronto: Oxford University Press, 1950).

COLLINS, WILLIAM, *The Poems of Gray, Collins, and Goldsmith*, ed. Roger Lonsdale (London and Harlow: Longmans, Green and Co., 1969).

COWLEY, HANNAH, *The Siege of Acre: An Epic Poem, in Six Books* (London: J. Debrett, 1801).

CROKER, JOHN WILSON, Review of Anna Barbauld 'Eighteen Hundred and Eleven', *Quarterly Review*, 7 (1812), 309–13.

DIBDIN, CHARLES, *The Songs of Charles Dibdin*, 2 vols. (London: Chidley, 1839).

ECLECTIC REVIEW, 'Art. II. *The Vision of Don Roderick. A Poem*. By Walter Scott', 7 (1811), 672–88.

ELIZABETH, PRINCESS, *Cupid Turned Volunteer in a Series of Prints, Designed by Her Royal Highness, The Princess Elizabeth and Engraved by W. N. Gardiner, BA, with Poetical Illustrations by Thomas Park, FSA* (London: E. Harding, 1804.)

FAWCETT, JOSEPH, *The Art of War: A Poem* (London: J. Johnson, 1795).

—— *War Elegies* (London: J. Johnson, 1801).

GILPIN, WILLIAM, *Three Essays: On Picturesque Beauty; On Picturesque Travel; and On Sketching Landscape. To which is added a Poem, On Landscape Painting* (Farnborough: Gregg International, 1972, photographic reprint of edition first published London: R. Blamire, 1794).

GODWIN, WILLIAM, *Enquiry Concerning Political Justice and its Influence on Modern Morals and Happiness*, ed. Isaac Kramnick (Harmondsworth, Middlesex: Penguin Classics, 1985).

GRAY, THOMAS, *The Poems of Thomas Gray, William Collins, and Oliver Goldsmith*, ed. Roger Lonsdale (London and Harlow: Longmans, Green and Co., 1969).

HAZLITT, WILLIAM, *The Complete Works of William Hazlitt*, ed. P. P. Howe, 21 vols. (London and Toronto: J. M. Dent, 1930–4).

HEMANS, FELICIA (née Browne), *The Domestic Affections, and Other Poems* (London: T. Cadell and W. Davies, 1812).

—— *Poems* (London: T. Cadell and W. Davies, 1808).

—— *Selected Poems, Letters, Reception Materials*, ed. Susan J. Wolfson (Princeton and Oxford: Princeton University Press, 2000).

—— *Selected Poems, Prose, and Letters*, ed. Gary Kelly (Peterborough, Ontario: Broadview Press, 2002).

—— *The Works of Mrs Hemans, with a Memoir by her Sister*, 7 vols. (Edinburgh and London: William Blackwood and Sons and Thomas Cadell, 1839).

HUNTER, ANNE, *Poems* (London: T. Payne, 1802).

JONES, WILLIAM, *The Nature, Uses, Dangers, Sufferings, and Preservatives, of the Human Imagination: A Sermon, Preached in the Cathedral Church of St. Paul, London, on Sunday, Jan 31, 1796* (London: F. and C. Rivington, G. G. and J. Robinson, and H. Gardner, 1796).

MATHIAS, T. J., *The Pursuits of Literature: A Satirical Poem in Four Dialogues, With Notes* (London: T. Becket, 1798).

MAURICE, THOMAS, *The Crisis, or, The British Muse to the British Minister and Nation, By the Author of Indian Antiquities* (London: R. Fauldner, 1798).

MILTON, JOHN, *Complete Shorter Poems*, ed. John Carey (London and New York: Longman, 1968; repr. with corrections 1981).

—— *Paradise Lost*, ed. Alastair Fowler. (London: Longman, 1968; repr. with minor corrections 1971).

MOODY, ELIZABETH, *Poetic Trifles* (London: T. Cadell, jun., and W. Davies, 1798).

MORE, HANNAH, *Selected Writings of Hannah More*, ed. Robert Hole (London: William Pickering, 1996).

NAPIER, W. F. P., *History of the War in the Peninsula and in the South of France, from the Year 1807 to the Year 1815* (London: William and Thomas Boone, 1838).

OPIE, AMELIA, *Poems* (London: T. N. Longman and O. Rees, 1802).

PAINE, THOMAS, *Rights of Man*, ed. Eric Foner (Harmondsworth, Middlesex: Penguin, 1984).

PYE, HENRY J., *The War-Elegies of Tyrtæus, Imitated, and Addressed to the People of Great Britain, with some Observations on the Life and Poems of Tyrtæus* (London: T. Cadell jun. and W. Davies, 1795).

—— *Naucratia: or, Naval Dominion, a Poem* (London: 1798).

ROBINSON, MARY, *Selected Poems*, ed. Judith Pascoe (Peterborough, Ontario: Broadview Press, 2000).

RUSKIN, JOHN, *The Works of John Ruskin*, ed. E. T. Cook and Alexander Wedderburn, 39 vols. (London and New York: George Allen and Longmans, Green, and Co., 1908).

SCOTT, SIR WALTER, *The Letters of Sir Walter Scott*, ed. Herbert J. C. Grierson, 12 vols. (London: Constable, 1932–7).

—— *The Miscellaneous Works of Walter Scott, Bart.*, 28 vols. (Edinburgh: Adam and Charles Black, 1880–1).

—— *The Poetical Works of Sir Walter Scott*, ed. J. Logie Robertson, The Oxford Complete Edition (London: Henry Frowde, 1904).

—— *The Poetical Works of Sir Walter Scott, Bart., Author's Edition*, ed. J. G. Lockhart (Edinburgh: Adam and Charles Black, 1869).

—— *Scott on Himself*, ed. David Hewitt (Edinburgh: Scottish Academic Press, 1981).

—— *Waverley; or, 'Tis Sixty Years Since*, ed. Claire Lamont, World's Classics (Oxford and New York: Oxford University Press, 1986).

SHAKESPEARE, WILLIAM, *King Henry V*, ed. by Andrew Gurr (Cambridge: Cambridge University Press, 1992).
—— *A Midsummer Night's Dream*, ed. R. A. Foakes (Cambridge: Cambridge University Press, 1984).
—— *Macbeth*, ed. Kenneth Muir (London and New York: Routledge, 1984).
SMITH, CHARLOTTE, *Elegiac Sonnets* (Oxford and New York: Woodstock Books, 1992).
—— *The Poems of Charlotte Smith*, ed. Stuart Curran (New York and Oxford: Oxford University Press, 1993).
SOUTHEY, ROBERT, *Common-Place Book*, ed. John Wood Warter, 4 vols. (London: Reeves and Turner, 1876).
—— *The Contributions of Robert Southey to the 'Morning Post'*, ed. Kenneth Curry (Tuscaloosa: University of Alabama Press, 1984).
—— *Joan of Arc: An Epic Poem* (Bristol and London: Joseph Cottle, Cadell and Davies, and G. G. and J. Robinson, 1796).
—— *Poems* (Bristol and London: Joseph Cottle and G. G. and J. Robinson, 1797).
—— *Poems: The Second Volume* (London: T. N. Longman and O. Rees, 1799).
—— *Poems of Robert Southey*, ed. Maurice H. Fitzgerald (London: Oxford University Press, 1909).
—— *Selections from the Letters of Robert Southey*, ed. J. W. Warter, 4 vols. (London: 1856).
SPENSER, EDMUND, *The Fairie Queene*, ed. Thomas P. Roche, with the assistance of C. Patrick O'Donnell, Jr. (Harmondsworth, Middlesex: Penguin, 1978).
STOCKDALE, PERCIVAL, *The Invincible Island: A Poem, with Introductory Observations on the Present War* (London: W. Clark, 1797).
TEMPLE, LAURA SOPHIA, *The Siege of Zaragoza, and Other Poems* (London: William Miller and W. Bulmer and Co., 1812).
THELWALL, JOHN, *The Trident of Albion, An Epic Effusion; and an Oration on the Influence of Elocution on Martial Enthusiasms; with an Address to the Shade of Nelson: Delivered at the Lyceum, Liverpool, on Occasion of the Late Glorious Naval Victory* (Liverpool: G. F. Harris, 1805).
Twain, Mark, *Adventures of Huckleberry Finn*, The Oxford Mark Twain (New York and Oxford: Oxford University Press, 1996).
—— *Life on the Mississippi*, The Oxford Mark Twain (New York and Oxford: Oxford University Press, 1996).
WARTON, JOSEPH, *The Three Wartons: A Choice of their Verse*, ed. Eric Partridge (Freeport, NY: Books for Libraries, 1927; repr. 1970).
WILLIAMS, HELEN MARIA, *Poems (1786)* (Oxford and New York: Woodstock Books, 1994).
WORDSWORTH, DOROTHY, *The Journals of Dorothy Wordsworth*, ed. Mary Moorman, 2nd edn. (New York and Oxford: Oxford University Press, 1976).
WORDSWORTH, WILLIAM, *Wordsworth and Coleridge, Lyrical Ballads 1805*, ed. Derek Roper, (Plymouth: MacDonald and Evans, 1968; 2nd edn., 1982).

—— *Letters of William and Dorothy Wordsworth: The Early Years, 1787–1805,* ed. E. de Selincourt, 2nd edn., revised Chester L. Shaver (Oxford: Clarendon Press, 1967).

—— *Letters of William and Dorothy Wordsworth: The Middle Years, Part I, 1806–1811,* ed. E de Selincourt, 2nd edn., revised Mary Moorman (Oxford: Clarendon Press, 1969).

—— *Letters of William and Dorothy Wordsworth: The Middle Years, Part II, 1812–1820,* ed. Ernest de Selincourt, 2nd edn., revised Mary Moorman and Alan G. Hill (Oxford: Clarendon Press, 1967).

—— *Poems, in Two Volumes,* ed. Jared Curtis, The Cornell Wordsworth (Ithaca, NY, and London: Cornell University Press, 1983).

—— *The Poetical Works of William Wordsworth,* ed. E. de Selincourt and Helen Darbyshire, 5 vols. (Oxford: Clarendon Press, 1940–49).

—— *The Prelude: 1799, 1805, 1850,* ed. Jonathan Wordsworth, M. H. Abrams, and Stephen Gill (New York and London: W. W. Norton & Co., 1979).

—— *The Prelude; or, Growth of a Poet's Mind,* ed. E. de Selincourt, revised Helen Darbyshire (Oxford: Clarendon Press, 1959).

—— *The Prose Works of William Wordsworth,* ed. W. J. B. Owen and Jane Worthington Smyser, 3 vols. (Oxford: Clarendon Press, 1974).

—— *The Salisbury Plain Poems of William Wordsworth,* ed. Stephen Gill, The Cornell Wordsworth (Ithaca, NY, and London: Cornell University Press and Harvester Press, 1975).

—— *William Wordsworth: The Oxford Authors,* ed. Stephen Gill (Oxford and New York: Oxford University Press, 1986).

—— *Wordsworth's Poems of 1807,* ed. Alun R. Jones (Basingstoke and London: Macmillan, 1987).

SECONDARY SOURCES

ABRAMS, M. H., *The Mirror and the Lamp: Romantic Theory and the Critical Tradition* (London and New York: Oxford University Press, 1953).

—— *Natural Supernaturalism: Tradition and Revolution in Romantic Literature* (New York and London: W. W. Norton and Co., 1971).

ADAMS, M. RAY, *Studies in the Literary Backgrounds of English Radicalism, with Special Reference to the French Revolution* (New York: Greenwood Press, 1968).

ALEXANDER, J. H., *Two Studies in Romantic Reviewing: Edinburgh Reviewers and the English Tradition, vol. 2: The Reviewing of Walter Scott's Poetry: 1805–1817,* Salzburg Studies in English Literature; Romantic Reassessment, 49, ed. James Hogg (Salzburg: Institut für Englische Sprache und Literatur, Universität Salzburg, 1976).

—— *'Marmion': Studies in Interpretation and Composition,* Salzburg Studies in English Literature; Romantic Reassessment, 30, ed. James Hogg (Salzburg: Insitut für Anglistik und Amerikanistik, Universität Salzburg, 1981).

ALLENTUCK, MARCIA, 'Scott and the Picturesque: Afforestation and History', in Alan Bell (ed.), *Scott Bicentenary Essays: Selected Papers Read at the Sir Walter Scott Bicentenary Conference* (Edinburgh: Scottish Academic Press, 1973), 188–98.

ALTICK, RICHARD D., *The English Common Reader: A Social History of the Mass Reading Public, 1800–1900* (Chicago: University of Chicago Press, 1957).

ANDERSON, BENEDICT, *Imagined Communities: Reflections on the Origin and Spread of Nationalism* (London: Verso, 1983).

ASHFIELD, ANDREW (ed.), *Romantic Women Poets, 1770–1838* (Manchester: Manchester University Press, 1995).

—— *Romantic Women Poets, 1788–1848, vol. II* (Manchester and New York: Manchester University Press, 1998).

ASHTON, JOHN, *English Caricature and Satire on Napoleon I* (London: Chatto and Windus, 1888).

ASPINALL, ARTHUR, *Politics and the Press, 1780–1850* (Brighton: Harvester Press, 1973).

AVERILL, JAMES H., *Wordsworth and the Poetry of Human Suffering* (Ithaca, NY: Cornell University Press, 1980).

BAINBRIDGE, SIMON, *Napoleon and English Romanticism* (Cambridge: Cambridge University Press, 1995).

BAKER, KENNETH (ed.), *The Faber Book of War Poetry* (London: Faber and Faber, 1996).

BANKS, BRENDA, 'Rhetorical Missiles and Double-Talk: Napoleon, Wordsworth, and the Invasion Scare of 1804', in Stephen C. Behrendt (ed.), *Romanticism, Radicalism, and the Press* (Detroit: Wayne State University Press, 1997), 103–19.

BANN, STEPHEN, *The Clothing of Clio: A Study of the Representation of History in Nineteenth-Century Britain and France* (Cambridge: Cambridge University Press, 1984).

BARKER-BENFIELD, G. J., *The Culture of Sensibility: Sex and Society in Eighteenth-Century Britain* (Chicago and London: University of Chicago Press, 1992).

BARRELL, JOHN, *Imagining the King's Death: Figurative Treason, Fantasies of Regicide, 1793–1796* (Oxford: Oxford University Press, 2000).

BATE, JONATHAN, *Shakespeare and the English Romantic Imagination* (Oxford: Clarendon Press, 1986).

—— *Shakespearean Constitutions: Politics, Theatre, Criticism 1730–1830* (Oxford: Clarendon Press, 1989).

—— 'Inventing Region and Nation: Wordsworth's Sonnets', *Swansea Review* (1994), 2–22.

BEATTY, ARTHUR, 'Joseph Fawcett: The Art of War. Its Relation to the Early Development of William Wordsworth', *University of Wisconsin Studies in Language and Literature*, 2 (1918), 224–69.

BEER, JOHN, *Coleridge the Visionary* (London: Chatto and Windus, 1959).

—— 'The "Revolutionary Youth" of Wordsworth and Coleridge: Another View', *Critical Quarterly*, 19 (1977), 79–87.

BEHRENDT, STEPHEN C., 'Placing the Places in Wordsworth's 1802 Sonnets', *SEL* 35 (1995), 641–67.

—— 'British Women Poets and the Reverberations of Radicalism in the 1790s', in Stephen C. Behrendt (ed.), *Romanticism, Radicalism, and the Press* (Detroit: Wayne State University Press, 1997), 83–102.

—— 'The Gap that is not a Gap: British Poetry by Women, 1802–1812', in Harriet Kramer Linkin and Stephen C. Behrendt (eds.), *Romanticism and Women Poets: Opening the Doors of Reception* (Lexington: University of Kentucky Press, 1999), 25–45.

—— ' "A Few Harmless Numbers": British Women Poets and the Climate of War, 1793–1815' in Philip Shaw (ed.), *Romantic Wars: Studies in Culture and Conflict, 1793–1822* (Aldershot: Ashgate, 2000), 13–36.

—— (ed.), *History and Myth: Essays on English Romantic Literature*. (Detroit: Wayne State University Press, 1990).

—— and LINKIN, HARRIET KRAMER (eds.), *Approaches to Teaching British Women Poets of the Romantic Period* (New York: Modern Language Association of America, 1997).

BEIDERWELL, BRUCE, 'Scott's *Redgauntlet* as a Romance of Power', *Studies in Romanticism*, 28 (1989), 273–89.

BENIS, TOBY R., *Romanticism on the Road: The Marginal Gains of Wordsworth's Homeless* (Basingstoke and New York: Macmillan and St Martin's Press, 2000).

BENNETT, BETTY T.(ed.), *British War Poetry in the Age of Romanticism: 1793–1815* (New York and London: Garland, 1976).

BEST, GEOFFREY, *War and Society in Revolutionary Europe, 1770–1870* (Stroud, Gloucestershire: Sutton Publishing, 1998).

BLACK, JEREMY, 'The Military Revolution II: Eighteenth-Century War' in Charles Townshend (ed.), *The Oxford Illustrated History of Modern War* (Oxford and New York: Oxford University Press, 1997), 35–47.

BOLD, ALAN NORMAN (ed.), *The Martial Muse: Seven Centuries of War Poetry* (Exeter: Wheaton, 1976).

BORST, WILLIAM, *Lord Byron's First Pilgrimage* (New Haven: Yale University Press, 1948).

BOWRA, MAURICE, *The Romantic Imagination* (Oxford: Oxford University Press, 1961).

BRAY, MATTHEW, 'Removing the Anglo-Saxon Yoke: The Francocentric Vision of Charlotte Smith's Later Works', *Wordsworth Circle*, 24 (1993), 155–8.

BREEN, JENNIFER (ed.), *Women Romantic Poets, 1785–1832: An Anthology* (London and Rutland, Vt.: J. M. Dent and Charles E. Tuttle, 1992).

BRENNAN, MATTHEW C., 'The "Ghastly Figure Moving at my Side": The Discharged Soldier as Wordsworth's Shadow', *Wordsworth Circle*, 18 (1987), 19–23.

BRIGHT, MICHAEL, ' "Most Capital Enemies of the Muses": War, Art, and "Kubla Khan" ', *Comparative Literature Studies*, 21 (1984), 396–408.

BRONOWSKI, JACOB, *William Blake and the Age of Revolution* (London: Routledge and Kegan Paul, 1972).

BROWN, DAVID, *Walter Scott and the Historical Imagination* (London, Boston, and Henley: Routledge and Kegan Paul, 1979).

BRYANT, ARTHUR, *Years of Endurance, 1793–1802* (London: Collins, 1944; repr. 1975).

—— *Years of Victory, 1802–1812* (London: Collins, 1944; repr. 1975).

—— *Age of Elegance, 1812–1822* (London: Collins, 1944; repr. 1975.)

BUTLER, MARILYN, *Romantics, Rebels and Reactionaries: English Literature and its Background, 1760–1830* (Oxford: Oxford University Press, 1981).

—— (ed.), *Burke, Paine, Godwin and the Revolution Controversy* (Cambridge: Cambridge University Press, 1984).

—— 'Against Tradition: The Case for a Particularized Historical Method', in Jerome J. McGann (ed.), *Historical Studies and Literary Criticism* (Madison: Wisconsin University Press, 1986), 25–47.

—— 'Telling it Like a Story: The French Revolution as Narrative', *Studies in Romanticism*, 28 (1989), 343–64.

—— 'Repossessing the Past: The Case for an Open Literary History', in Marjorie Levinson, Marilyn Butler, Jerome McGann, and Paul Hamilton, *Rethinking Historicism: Critical Readings in Romantic History* (Oxford and New York: Basil Blackwell, 1989), 64–84.

BYGRAVE, STEPHEN, *Coleridge and the Self: Romantic Egotism* (New York: St Martin's Press, 1986).

CANOVAN, MARGARET, ' "Breathes there the Man, with Soul so Dead . . .": Reflections on Patriotic Poetry and Liberal Principles', in John Horton and Andrea T. Baumeister (eds.), *Literature and the Political Imagination* (London and New York: Routledge, 1996), 170–97.

CARLSON, JULIE A., *In the Theatre of Romanticism: Coleridge, Nationalism, Women* (Cambridge: Cambridge University Press, 1994).

CARNALL, GEOFFREY, *Robert Southey and his Age: The Development of a Conservative Mind* (Oxford: Clarendon Press, 1960).

CEADEL, MARTIN, *The Origins of War Prevention: The British Peace Movement and International Relations, 1730–1854* (Oxford: Clarendon Press, 1996).

CHANDLER, ALICE, *A Dream of Order: The Medieval Ideal in Nineteenth-Century English Literature* (London: Routledge and Kegan Paul, 1971).

CHANDLER, DAVID G., *The Campaigns of Napoleon* (London: Weidenfeld and Nicolson, 1966).

—— *Dictionary of the Napoleonic Wars* (London: Greenhill Books, 1993).

—— and BECKETT, IAN (eds.), *The Oxford Illustrated History of the British Army* (Oxford: Oxford University Press, 1994).

CHANDLER, JAMES, *Wordsworth's Second Nature: A Study of Poetry and Politics* (Chicago and London: University of Chicago Press, 1984).

—— *England in 1819: The Politics of Literary Culture and the Case of Romantic Historicism* (Chicago and London: University of Chicago Press, 1998).

CHATTARJI, SUBARNO, *Memoirs of a Lost War: American Poetic Responses to the Vietnam War* (Oxford: Clarendon Press, 2001).

CHRISTENSEN, JEROME, 'Politerotics: Coleridge's Rhetoric of War in *The Friend*', *Clio*, 8 (1979), 339–63.

—— *Lord Byron's Strength: Romantic Writing and Commercial Society* (Baltimore and London: Johns Hopkins University Press, 1993).

—— *Romanticism at the End of History* (Baltimore and London: Johns Hopkins University Press, 2000).

CHRISTIE, IAN R., *Wars and Revolution: Britain 1760–1815* (London: Edward Arnold, 1982).

—— 'Conservatism and Stability in British Society', in Mark Philp (ed.), *The French Revolution and British Popular Politics* (Cambridge: Cambridge University Press, 1991), 169–87.

CLARKE, IGNATIUS FREDERICK, *Voices Prophesying War: Future Wars, 1763–3749* (Oxford and New York: Oxford University Press, 1992).

CLERY, E. J., and MILES, ROBERT (eds.), *Gothic Documents: A Sourcebook, 1700–1820* (Manchester and New York: Manchester University Press, 2000).

COBLEY, EVELYN, *Representing War: Form and Ideology in First World War Narratives* (Toronto, Buffalo, and London: University of Toronto Press, 1993).

COHEN, MICHÈLE, *Fashioning Masculinity: National Identity and Language in the Eighteenth Century* (London and New York: Routledge, 1996).

COLLEY, LINDA, *Britons: Forging the Nation 1707–1837* (London: Vintage, 1996).

COLLINGS, DAVID, *Wordsworthian Errancies: The Poetics of Cultural Dismemberment* (Baltimore and London: Johns Hopkins University Press, 1994).

COLLINS, IRENE, 'Variations on the Theme of Napoleon's Moscow Campaign', *History: The Journal of the Historical Association*, 71/231 (February 1986), 39–53.

COLMER, JOHN, *Coleridge: Critic of Society* (Oxford: Clarendon Press, 1959).

COOK, KAY K., 'The Aesthetics of Loss: Charlotte Smith's *The Emigrants* and *Beachy Head*', in Stephen C. Behrendt and Harriet Kramer Linkin (eds.), *Approaches to Teaching British Women Poets of the Romantic Period* (New York: Modern Language Association of America, 1997), 97–100.

COOKE, MIRIAM, and WOOLLACOTT, ANGELA (eds.), *Gendering War Talk* (Princeton: Princeton University Press, 1993).

COOKSON, J. E., *The Friends of Peace: Anti-War Liberalism in England, 1793–1815* (Cambridge: Cambridge University Press, 1982).

—— *The British Armed Nation, 1793–1815* (Oxford: Clarendon Press, 1997).

—— 'War' in McCalman, Iain *et al.* (eds.), *An Oxford Companion to the Romantic Age: British Culture, 1776–1832* (Oxford: Oxford University Press, 1999), 26–34.

COOPER, HELEN M., MUNICH, ADRIENNE, and SQUIER, SUSAN MERRILL (eds.), *Arms and the Woman: War, Gender, and Literary Representation* (Chapel Hill: University of North Carolina Press, 1989).

COPLEY, STEPHEN, and GARSIDE, PETER (eds.), *Politics of the Picturesque: Literature, Landscape and Aesthetics since 1770* (Cambridge: Cambridge University Press, 1994).

COTTRELL, STELLA, 'The Devil on Two Sticks: Franco-Phobia in 1803', in Raphael Samuel (ed.), *Patriotism: The Making and Unmaking of British National Identity, vol. I: History and Politics*, History Workshop Journal (London and New York: Routledge, 1989), 259–74.

COX, PHILIP, *Gender, Genre and the Romantic Poets* (Manchester and New York: Manchester University Press, 1996).

—— *Reading Adaptations: Novels and Verse Narratives on the Stage, 1790–1840* (Manchester and New York: Manchester University Press, 2000).

CRAWFORD, THOMAS, *Scott* (Edinburgh and London: Oliver and Boyd, 1965).

CREVELD, MARTIN L. VAN, *Men, Women and War* (London: Cassell, 2001).

CRONIN, RICHARD (ed.), *1798: The Year of the Lyrical Ballads* (Basingstoke and New York: Palgrave, 1998).

—— *The Politics of Romantic Poetry: In Search of the Pure Commonwealth* (Basingstoke and New York: Macmillan and St Martin's Press, 2000).

CROZIER, ANNE-JULIE, 'The Influence and Concept of Romance in Scott's Early Narrative Poetry', MA dissertation (University of York, 1989).

CURRAN, STUART, 'The I Altered' in Anne K. Mellor (ed.), *Romanticism and Feminism* (Bloomington and Indianapolis: Indiana University Press, 1988), 185–207.

—— *Poetic Form and British Romanticism* (Oxford and New York: Oxford University Press, 1989).

—— 'Mary Robinson's *Lyrical Tales* in Context', in Carol Shiner Wilson and Joel Haefner (eds.), *Re-Visioning Romanticism: British Women Writers, 1776–1837* (Philadelphia: Pennsylvania University Press, 1994), 17–35.

CURRY, KENNETH, *Southey*, Routledge Author Guides (London, Boston, and Henley: Routledge and Kegan Paul, 1975).

DALLAS, K., *The Cruel Wars: One Hundred Soldiers' Songs* (London: Wolfe Publications, 1972).

DARLINGTON, BETH, 'Two Early Texts: "A Night-Piece" and "The Discharged Soldier" ', in Jonathan Wordsworth and Beth Darlington (eds.), *Bicentenary Wordsworth Studies in Memory of John Alban Finch* (Ithaca, NY: Cornell University Press, 1970), 425–48.

DEANE, SEAMUS, *The French Revolution and the Enlightenment in England, 1789–1832* (Cambridge, Mass.: Harvard University Press, 1988).

DICKINSON, H. T., (ed.), *Britain and the French Revolution* (Basingstoke and London: Macmillan Education, 1989).

DOBRÉE, BONAMY, 'The Theme of Patriotism in the Poetry of the Early Eighteenth

Century: Warton Lecture on English Poetry', *Proceedings of the British Academy*, 35 (1949).

DUFF, DAVID, *Romance and Revolution: Shelley and the Politics of a Genre* (Cambridge: Cambridge University Press, 1994).

DUFFY, CHRISTOPHER, *Fire and Stone: The Science of Fortress Warfare, 1660–1860* (London and Vancouver: David and Charles, 1975).

DUFFY, MICHAEL (ed.), *The Englishman and the Foreigner*, The English Satirical Print, 1600–1832 (Cambridge: Chadwyck-Healey, 1986).

—— 'War, Revolution and the Crisis of the British Empire', in Philp (ed.), *The French Revolution and British Popular Politics* (Cambridge: Cambridge University Press, 1991), 118–45.

DUGAW, DIANNE, *Warrior Women and Popular Balladry, 1650–1850* (Cambridge: Cambridge University Press, 1989).

DUNCAN, JOSEPH E., 'The Anti-Romantic in *Ivanhoe*', reprinted in D. D. Devlin (ed.), *Walter Scott: Modern Judgements* (London: Macmillan, 1968), 142–7.

EBERHART, RICHARD (ed.), *War and the Poet: An Anthology of Poetry Expressing Man's Attitude to War from Ancient Times to the Present* (Westport, Conn.: Greenwood Press, 1974).

ELLISON, JULIE, 'The Politics of Fancy in the Age of Sensibility', in Carol Shiner Wilson and Joel Haefner (eds.), *Re-Visioning Romanticism: British Women Writers, 1776–1837* (Philadelphia: Pennsylvania University Press, 1994), 228–55.

ELSHTAIN, JEAN BETHKE, *Women and War* (Chicago: University of Chicago Press, 1995).

EMSLEY, CLIVE, *British Society and the French Wars, 1793–1815*. (Basingstoke and London: Macmillan, 1979).

—— 'Revolution, War and the Nation State: The British and French Experiences, 1789–1801', in Mark Philp (ed.), *The French Revolution and British Popular Politics* (Cambridge: Cambridge University Press, 1991), 99–117.

ENGELL, JAMES, *The Creative Imagination: Enlightenment to Romanticism* (Cambridge, Mass. and London: Harvard University Press, 1981).

ERDMAN, DAVID V., *Blake, Prophet against Empire: A Poet's Interpretation of the History of his own Times* (Princeton: Princeton University Press, 1984).

ERSKINE-HILL, HOWARD, 'The Prelude and its echoes', *TLS*, 26 September 1975, 1094.

EUBANKS, KEVIN, 'Minerva's Veil: Hemans, Critics, and the Construction of Gender', *European Romantic Review*, 8 (1997), 341–59.

EVEREST, KELVIN, *Coleridge's Secret Ministry: The Context of the Conversation Poems, 1795–1798* (Hassocks, Sussex, and New York: Harvester Press and Barnes and Noble, 1979).

FAIRER, DAVID, and GERRARD, CHRISTINE (eds.), *Eighteenth-Century Poetry: An Annotated Anthology* (Oxford: Blackwell Publishers, 1999).

FARRELL, JOHN P., *Revolution as Tragedy: The Dilemma of the Moderate from Scott to Arnold* (Ithaca, NY: Cornell University Press, 1980).

FAVRET, MARY A., 'Coming Home: The Public Spaces of Romantic War', *Studies in Romanticism*, 33 (1994), 539–48.

—— 'War Correspondence: Reading Romantic War', *Prose Studies*, 19 (1996), 173–85.

FELDMAN, PAULA R., and KELLEY, THERESA M. (eds.), *Romantic Women Writers: Voices and Countervoices* (Hanover, NH, and London: University Press of New England, 1995).

FERGUSON, J. (ed.), *War and the Creative Arts* (London: Macmillan and Open University Press, 1972).

FERRIS, INA, *The Achievement of Literary Authority: Gender, History, and the Waverley Novels* (Ithaca, NY, and London: Cornell University Press, 1991).

FINK, ZERA, 'Wordsworth and the English Republican Tradition', *Journal of English and Germanic Philology*, 1948, 107–26.

FLETCHER, LORAINE, *Charlotte Smith: A Critical Biography* (Basingstoke and New York: Macmillan and St Martin's Press, 1998).

FOOT, MICHAEL, *The Politics of Paradise: A Vindication of Byron* (London: William Collins & Co., 1988).

FORBES, DUNCAN, 'The Rationalism of Sir Walter Scott', *Cambridge Journal*, 7 (1953), 20–35.

FORREST, ALAN, 'The Nation in Arms I: The French Wars' in Charles Townshend (ed.), *The Oxford Illustrated History of Modern War* (Oxford: Oxford University Press, 1997), 48–63.

FOSTER, KEVIN, *Fighting Fictions: War, Narrative and National Identity* (London and Sterling, Va.; Pluto Press, 1999).

FRANKLIN, CAROLINE, 'Cosmopolitan Masculinity and the British Female Reader of *Childe Harold's Pilgrimage*', in Richard A. Cardwell (ed.), *Lord Byron the European: Essays from the International Byron Society* (Lewiston, Queenston, Lampeter: Edwin Mellen Press, 1977), 105–25.

—— *Byron: A Literary Life* (Basingstoke and London: Macmillan, 2000).

FREEMAN, LAWRENCE (ed.), *War*, Oxford Readers (Oxford and New York: Oxford University Press, 1994).

FRIEDMAN, BARTON R., *Fabricating History: English Writers on the French Revolution* (Princeton: Princeton University Press, 1988).

FULFORD, TIM, *Landscape, Liberty and Authority: Poetry, Criticism and Politics from Thomson to Wordsworth* (Cambridge: Cambridge University Press, 1996).

—— *Romanticism and Masculinity: Gender, Politics and Poetics in the Writings of Burke, Coleridge, Cobbett, Wordsworth, de Quincey and Hazlitt* (Basingstoke and London: Macmillan, 1999).

FURLONG, E. J., *Imagination* (London: Allen and Unwin, 1961).

FUSSELL, PAUL, *The Great War and Modern Memory* (Oxford: Oxford University Press, 1975).

—— *Wartime: Understanding and Behaviour in the Second World War* (Oxford: Oxford University Press, 1989).

GAMER, MICHAEL C., 'Marketing a Masculine Romance: Scott, Antiquarianism, and the Gothic', *Studies in Romanticism*, 32 (1993), 523–49.

GARSIDE, PETER. D., '*A Legend of Montrose* and the History of War', *Yearbook of English Studies*, 4 (1974), 159–71.

—— 'Scott and the "Philosophical" Historians', *Journal of the History of Ideas*, 36 (1975), 497–512.

—— 'Picturesque Figure and Landscape: Meg Merrilies and the Gypsies', in Stephen Copley and Peter Garside (eds.), *Politics of the Picturesque: Literature, Landscape and Aesthetics since 1770* (Cambridge: Cambridge University Press, 1994), 145–74.

GATES, DAVID, 'The Transformation of the Army, 1783–1815' in David Chandler and Ian Beckett (eds.), *The Oxford Illustrated History of the British Army* (Oxford: Oxford University Press, 1994), 133–59.

GERRARD, CHRISTINE, 'Political Passions' in John E. Sitter (ed.), *The Cambridge Companion to Eighteenth-Century Poetry* (Cambridge: Cambridge University Press, 2001), 37–63.

GILL, STEPHEN C., 'Wordsworth's Breeches Pocket: Attitudes to the Didactic Poet', *Essays in Criticism*, 19 (1969), 385–401.

—— ' "Adventures on Salisbury Plain" and Wordsworth's Poetry of Protest 1795–97', *Studies in Romanticism*, 11 (1972), 48–65.

—— *William Wordsworth: A Life*, Oxford Lives (Oxford: Oxford University Press, 1989).

GIROUARD, MARK, *The Return to Camelot: Chivalry and the English Gentleman* (New Haven and London: Yale University Press, 1981).

GLECKNER, ROBERT F., *Byron and the Ruins of Paradise* (Westport, Conn.: Greenwood Press, 1967).

GLOVER, MICHAEL, *The Napoleonic Wars, 1792–1815: An Illustrated History* (London: Book Club Associates, 1979).

GOLDSTEIN, WILLIAM S., *War and Gender: How Gender Shapes the War System and Vice Versa* (Cambridge: Cambridge University Press, 2001).

GORDON, CATHERINE, 'The Illustration of Sir Walter Scott: Nineteenth-Century Enthusiasm and Adaptation', *Journal of the Warburg and Courtauld Institute*, 34 (1971), 297–317.

GOSLEE, NANCY MOORE, *Scott the Rhymer* (Lexington: University Press of Kentucky, 1988).

GOSSMAN, LIONEL, *Between History and Literature* (Cambridge, Mass.: Harvard University Press, 1990).

GRIFFIN, DUSTIN H., *Patriotic Poetry in Eighteenth-Century Britain* (Cambridge: Cambridge University Press, 2002).

HAGIN, PETER, *The Epic Hero and the Decline of Heroic Poetry* (Berne: Franke Verlag, 1964).

HALLER, WILLIAM, *The Early Life of Robert Southey, 1774–1803* (New York: Columbia University Press, 1917).

HANLEY, LYNNE, *Writing War: Fiction, Gender, and Memory* (Amherst: University of Massachusetts Press, 1991).

HARDING, ANTHONY JOHN, 'Felicia Hemans and the Effacement of Woman', in Paula R. Feldman and Theresa M. Kelley (eds.), *Romantic Women Writers: Voices and Countervoices* (Hanover, NH, and London: University Press of New England, 1995), 138–49.

HARVEY, A. D., 'The English Epic in the Romantic Period', *Philological Quarterly*, 55 (1976), 241–59.

—— *English Poetry in a Changing Society, 1780–1825* (London: Allison and Busby, 1980).

—— *English Literature and the Great War with France: An Anthology and Commentary* (London: Nold Jonson Books, 1981).

—— *A Muse of Fire: Literature, Art and War* (London and Rio Grande: Hambledon Press, 1998).

HAYDEN, JOHN O. (ed.), *Scott: The Critical Heritage* (London: Routledge and Kegan Paul, 1970).

HAYTHORNWAITE, PHILIP J., *The Napoleonic Source Book* (London: Arms and Armour, 1990).

HEBRON, MALCOLM, *The Medieval Siege: Theme and Image in Middle English Romance* (Oxford: Clarendon Press, 1997).

HESS, JONATHAN M., 'Wordsworth's Aesthetic State: The Poetics of Liberty', *Studies in Romanticism*, 33 (1994), 3–29.

HEWITT, DAVID, 'Scott's Art and Politics', in Alan Bold (ed.), *Sir Walter Scott: The Long Forgotten Melody* (London: Vision Press, 1983).

HILL, DRAPER, *The Satirical Etchings of James Gillray* (New York: Dover Publications, 1976).

HILL, JOHN SPENSER, *Imagination in Coleridge* (Basingstoke and London: Macmillan, 1978).

HINZ, EVELYN J. (ed.), *Troops Versus Tropes: War and Literature* (Winnipeg: University of Manitoba Press, 1990).

HOFKOSH, SONIA, *Sexual Politics and the Romantic Author* (Cambridge: Cambridge University Press, 1998).

HOLE, ROBERT, 'British Counter-Revolutionary Popular Propaganda in the 1790s', in Colin Jones (ed.), *Britain and Revolutionary France: Conflict, Subversion and Propaganda*, Exeter Studies in History, 5 (Exeter: University of Exeter Press, 1983), 53–69.

HOLLANDER, JOHN (ed.), *War Poems* (London: Everyman, 1999).

HOLMES, RICHARD, *Coleridge: Early Visions* (Harmondsworth, Middlesex: Penguin, 1990).

HOPKINS, KENNETH, *The Poets Laureate* (London: Bodley Head, 1954).

HUDSON, CHARLES MELL, JR., 'The Roderick Legend in English Romantic Literature: Scott, Landor and Southey', D.Phil. thesis (Yale, 1943).

HUSTON, NANCY, 'Tales of War and Tears of Women', *Women's Studies International Forum*, 5.3/4 (1982), 271–82.

HYNES, SAMUEL, *A War Imagined: The First World War and English Culture* (London: Bodley Head, 1990).
—— *The Soldiers' Tale: Bearing Witness to Modern War* (London: Pimlico, 1998).
JACKSON, J. R. DE J., *Poetry of the Romantic Period* (London, Boston, and Henley: Routledge and Kegan Paul, 1980.)
JACOBS, SUSIE, JACOBSON, RUTH, and MARCHBANK, JENNIFER (eds.), *States of Conflict: Gender, Violence, and Resistance* (London: Zed Books, 2000).
JACOBUS, MARY, 'Southey's Debt to *Lyrical Ballads* (1798)', *Review of English Studies*, NS, 22 (1971), 20–36.
—— *Tradition and Experiment in Wordsworth's Lyrical Ballads, 1798* (Oxford: Oxford University Press, 1976).
JAMES, LAWRENCE, *Warrior Race: A History of the British at War from Roman Times to the Present* (London: Abacus, 2002).
JEFFORDS, SUSAN, *The Remasculinization of America: Gender and the Vietnam War* (Bloomington and Indianapolis: Indiana University Press, 1989).
JOHNSON, EDGAR, *Sir Walter Scott: The Great Unknown*, 2 vols. (London: Hamish Hamilton, 1970).
JOHNSON, LEE M., *Wordsworth and the Sonnet*, Anglistica, 19 (Copenhagen: Rosenkilde and Bagger, 1973).
JOHNSTON, KENNETH R., *The Hidden Wordsworth* (London: Pimlico, 2000).
JONES, COLIN (ed.), *Britain and Revolutionary France: Conflict, Subversion and Propaganda*, Exeter Studies in History, 5 (Exeter: University of Exeter Press, 1983).
JONES, D. L. (ed.), *War Poetry: An Anthology* (Oxford: Pergamon Press, 1976).
JONES, VIVIEN, 'Femininity, Nationalism and Romanticism: The Politics of Gender in the Revolution Controversy', *History of European Ideas*, 16 (1993), 299–305.
JORDAN, GERALD, and ROGERS, NICHOLAS, 'Admirals as Heroes: Patriotism and Liberty in Hanoverian England', *Journal of British Studies*, 28 (1989), 201–24.
KABITOGLOU, E. DOUKA, 'The Pen and Sword: Felicia Hemans's Records of Man', in Tony Pinkney, Keith Hanley, and Fred Botting (eds.), *Romantic Masculinities: News from Nowhere 2: Theory and Politics of Romanticism* (Keele, Staffs: Keele University Press, 1997), 101–20.
KEACH, WILLIAM, 'A Regency Prophecy and the End of Anna Barbauld's Career', *Studies in Romanticism*, 33 (1994), 569–77.
KEEGAN, JOHN, *The Face of Battle: A Study of Agincourt, Waterloo and the Somme* (Harmondsworth, Middlesex: Penguin, 1978).
—— *A History of Warfare* (London: Pimlico, 1994).
KEEN, PAUL, 'William Wordsworth's Significant Others: Ambivalence and Identification in the 1802–1803 Sonnets', *English Studies in Canada*, 23 (1997), 263–83.
KELLEY, THERESA M., *Wordsworth's Revisionary Aesthetics* (Cambridge: Cambridge University Press, 1989).

KELLY, GARY, 'Revolution and Romantic Feminism: Women, Writing and Cultural Revolution' in Keith Hanley and Raman Selden (eds.), *Revolution and English Romanticism: Politics and Rhetoric* (Hemel Hempstead and New York: Harvester Wheatsheaf and St Martin's Press, 1990), 107–30.

—— 'Death and the Matron: Felicia Hemans, Romantic Death, and the Founding of the Modern Liberal State', in Nanora Sweet and Julie Melnyk (eds.), *Felicia Hemans: Reimagining Poetry in the Nineteenth Century* (Basingstoke and New York: Palgrave, 2001), 196–211.

KELSALL, MALCOLM, *Byron's Politics* (Brighton and New Jersey: Harvester Press and Barnes and Noble, 1987).

KENNEDY, PATRICK JOSEPH, 'War and the Military in British Romantic Poetry', MA thesis (University of South Carolina, 1992).

KHAN, NOSHEEN, *Women's Poetry of the First World War* (New York and Brighton: Harvester Wheatsheaf, 1988).

KITSON, PETER J., 'The Whore of Babylon and the Woman in White: Coleridge's Radical Unitarian Language', in Tim Fulford and Morton D. Paley (eds.), *Coleridge's Visionary Languages: Essays in Honour of J. B. Beer* (Woodbridge, Suffolk: D. S. Brewer, 1993), 1–14.

KLANCHER, JON, *The Making of English Reading Audiences, 1790–1832* (Madison and London: Wisconsin University Press, 1987).

—— 'Romantic Criticism and the Meaning of the French Revolution', *Studies in Romanticism*, 28 (1989) 463–91.

—— 'English Romanticism and Cultural Production', in H. Aram Veeser (ed.), *The New Historicism* (New York and London: Routledge, 1989), 77–88.

KLINGBERG, FRANK J., and HUSTVEDT, SIGURD B. (eds.), *The Warning Drum: The British Home Front Faces Napoleon: Broadsides of 1803*, Publications of the William Andrews Clark Memorial Library (Berkeley and Los Angeles: University of California Press, 1944).

LAMONT, CLAIRE, '*Waverley* and the Battle of Culloden', *Essays and Studies*, 44 (1991), 14–26.

LABBE, JACQUELINE M., 'The Exiled Self: Images of War in Charlotte Smith's *The Emigrants*', in Philip Shaw (ed.), *Romantic Wars: Studies in Culture and Conflict, 1793–1822* (Aldershot: Ashgate, 2000), 37–56.

—— *The Romantic Paradox: Love, Violence and the Uses of Romance, 1760–1830* (Basingstoke and London: Macmillan, 2000).

LEAN, E. TANGYE, *The Napoleonists: A Study in Political Disaffection, 1760–1960* (Oxford: Oxford University Press, 1970).

LEASK, NIGEL, *The Politics of Imagination in Coleridge's Critical Thought* (Basingstoke and London: Macmillan, 1988).

LING, PETER (ed.), *Gentlemen at Arms: Portraits of Soldiers in Fact and Fiction, in Peace and at War: An Anthology of Prose and Poetry* (London: Owen, 1969).

LIU, ALAN, *Wordsworth: The Sense of History* (Stanford, Calif: Stanford University Press, 1989).

LOCKHART, JOHN GIBSON, *The Life of Sir Walter Scott*, 10 vols. (Edinburgh: T. C. and E. C. Jack, 1902).

LONGFORD, ELIZABETH, *Wellington: The Years of the Sword* (London: Panther, 1971).

LONGMATE, NORMAN, *Island Fortress: The Defence of Great Britain 1603–1945* (London: Hutchinson, 1991).

LONSDALE, ROGER (ed.), *Eighteenth-Century Women Poets: An Oxford Anthology* (Oxford and New York: Oxford University Press, 1990).

LOOTENS, TRICIA, 'Hemans and Home: Victorianism, Feminine "Internal Enemies," and the Domestication of National Identity', *PMLA*, 109 (1994), 238–53.

LUKÁCS, GEORG, *The Historical Novel* (Harmondsworth, Middlesex: Penguin, 1969).

McCALMAN, IAIN et al. (eds.), *An Oxford Companion to the Romantic Age: British Culture, 1776–1832* (Oxford: Oxford University Press, 1999).

McCLATCHY, J. D., 'The Ravages of Time: The Function of the *Marmion* Epistles', *Studies in Scottish Literature*, 9 (1972), 256–63.

McCUNN, F. J., *The Contemporary English View of Napoleon* (London: G. Bell and Sons, 1914).

MACDONALD, SHARON, HOLDEN, PAT, and ARDENER, SHIRLEY (eds.), *Images of Women in Peace and War: Cross-Cultural and Historical Perspectives* (Basingstoke and London: Macmillan Education, 1987).

McGANN, JEROME J., *Fiery Dust: Byron's Poetic Development* (Chicago: University of Chicago Press, 1968).

—— *The Romantic Ideology: A Critical Investigation* (Chicago and London: University of Chicago Press, 1983).

—— 'Literary History, Romanticism, and Felicia Hemans', *Modern Language Quarterly*, 54 (1993), 215–35.

McGAVRAN, JAMES HOLT, 'Defusing the Discharged Soldier: Wordsworth, Coleridge, and Homosexual Panic', *Papers on Language and Literature*, 32 (1996), 147–65.

McNEIL, DAVID, *The Grotesque Depiction of War and the Military in Eighteenth-Century English Fiction* (Newark, London, and Toronto: University of Delaware Press and Associated University Presses, 1990).

MADDEN, LIONEL (ed.), *Robert Southey: The Critical Heritage* (London and Boston: Routledge and Kegan Paul, 1972).

MAGNUSON, PAUL, *Coleridge and Wordsworth: A Lyrical Dialogue* (Princeton: Princeton University Press, 1988) .

—— 'The Politics of "Frost at Midnight" ', *Wordsworth Circle*, 22/1 (1991), 3–11.

MAHON, PENNY, 'Towards a Peaceable Kingdom: Women Writers and Anti-Militarism, 1790–1825', Ph.D. thesis (Reading, 1997).

MANNING, PETER J., 'Wordsworth and Gray's Sonnet on the Death of West', *SEL*, 22 (1982), 505–18.

MANNING, PETER J., *Reading Romantics: Texts and Contexts* (Oxford and New York: Oxford University Press, 1990).

MARCHAND, LESLIE A., *Byron: A Biography*, 3 vols. (London: John Murray, 1957).

MARSHALL, MAJOR J. R., TD, 'Walter Scott, Quartermaster', *Blackwood's Magazine*, 227 (1930), 511–32.

MARTIN, PHILIP W., *Mad Women in Romantic Writing* (Brighton and New York: Harvester Press and St Martin's Press, 1987).

MAYO, ROBERT, 'The Contemporaneity of the *Lyrical Ballads*', *PMLA*, 69 (1954), 486–522.

MELLOR, ANNE K., (ed.), *Romanticism and Feminism* (Bloomington and Indianapolis: Indiana University Press, 1988).

—— *Romanticism and Gender* (New York and London: Routledge, 1993).

MITCHELL, JEROME, *Scott, Chaucer and Medieval Romance: A Study in Sir Walter Scott's Indebtedness to the Literature of the Middle Ages* (Lexington: University Press of Kentucky, 1987).

MONK, SAMUEL H., *The Sublime: A Study of Critical Theories in Eighteenth-Century England* (Ann Arbor, Michigan: Ann Arbor Paperbacks, 1960).

MOORMAN, MARY, *William Wordsworth: A Biography; The Early Years; 1770–1803* (Oxford: Clarendon Press, 1957; repr. 1968).

—— *William Wordsworth: A Biography; The Later Years; 1803–1850* (Oxford: Oxford University Press, 1965; repr. 1968).

MURPHY, PETER T., *Poetry as an Occupation and an Art in Britain, 1760–1830* (Cambridge: Cambridge University Press, 1993).

NELSON, J. WALTER, 'War and Peace and the British Poets of Sensibility', *Studies in Eighteenth-Century Culture*, ed. Roseann Runte, 7 (published for American Society for Eighteenth-Century Studies by University of Wisconsin Press, 1978), 345–66.

OMAN, CAROLA, *Britain against Napoleon* (London: Faber and Faber, 1942).

OWEN, W. J. B., 'Imagination, How Impaired . . .', *Wordsworth Circle*, 26 (1995), 51–8.

PAGE, JUDITH W., ' "The Weight of Too Much Liberty": Genre and Gender in Wordsworth's Calais Sonnets', *Criticism*, 30 (1988), 189–203.

—— *Wordsworth and the Cultivation of Women* (Berkeley, Los Angeles, and London: University of California Press, 1994).

PALEY, MORTON D., *Apocalypse and Millennium in English Romantic Poetry* (Oxford: Clarendon Press, 1999).

PALMER, ROY, *The Sound of History: Songs and Social Comments* (London: Pimlico, 1996).

PAOLO, CHARLES DE, 'Kant, Coleridge, and the Ethics of War', *Wordsworth Circle*, 16 (1985), 3–12.

PARET, PETER, *Imagined Battles: Reflections of War in European Art* (Chapel Hill: University of North Carolina Press, 1997).

PARIS, MICHAEL, *Warrior Nation: Images of War in Popular Culture, 1850–2000* (London: Reaktion Books, 2000).

PAULSON, RONALD, *Representations of Revolution (1780–1830)*, (New Haven and London: Yale University Press, 1983).

PECK, JOHN, *War, the Army and Victorian Literature* (Basingstoke and London: Macmillan, 1998).

PEDLEY, COLIN, 'Anticipating Invasion: Some Wordsworthian Contexts', *Wordsworth Circle*, 21 (1990), 64–70.

PHILP, MARK (ed.), *The French Revolution and British Popular Politics* (Cambridge: Cambridge University Press, 1991).

PICK, DANIEL, *War Machine: The Rationalization of Slaughter in the Modern Age* (New Haven: Yale University Press, 1993).

PIETTE, ADAM, *Imagination at War: British Fiction and Poetry, 1939–1945* (London and Basingstoke: Papermac, 1995).

PURKISS, JOHN, *The World of the English Romantic Poets: A Visual Approach* (London: Heinemann, 1982).

PYLE, FOREST, *The Ideology of Imagination: Subject and Society in the Discourse of Romanticism* (Stanford, Calif.: Stanford University Press, 1995).

QUILLEY, GEOFF, 'Duty and Mutiny: The Aesthetics of Loyalty and the Representation of the British Sailor c.1798–1800', in Philip Shaw (ed.), *Romantic Wars: Studies in Culture and Conflict, 1793–1822* (Aldershot: Ashgate, 2000), 80–109.

RAIMOND, JEAN, 'Southey's Early Writing and the Revolution', *Yearbook of English Studies*, 19 (1989), 181–96.

RALSTON, RAMONA MARIE, 'Wordsworth and the Feminized Sonnet: A Suppression of Eighteenth-Century Poetic Influences', Ph.D. thesis (University of Southern California, 1987).

RAWLINSON, MARK, 'Invasion! Coleridge, the Defence of Britain and the Cultivation of the Public's Fear', in Philip Shaw (ed.), *Romantic Wars: Studies in Culture and Conflict, 1793–1822* (Aldershot: Ashgate, 2000), 110–37.

REED, JAMES, *Sir Walter Scott: Landscape and Locality* (London: Athlone Press, 1980).

REIMAN, DONALD H. (ed.), *The Romantics Reviewed: Contemporary Reviews of British Romantic Writers, Part A: The Lake Poets*, 2 vols. (New York and London: Garland Publishing, 1972).

—— (ed.), *The Romantics Reviewed: Contemporary Reviews of British Romantic Writers, Part B: Byron and Regency Society Poets*, 5 vols. (New York and London: Garland Publishing, 1972).

RICHARDSON, ALAN, 'Romanticism and the Colonization of the Feminine', in Anne K. Mellor (ed.), *Romanticism and Feminism* (Bloomington and Indianapolis: Indiana University Press, 1988), 13–25.

RIEDER, JOHN, *Wordsworth's Counterrevolutionary Turn: Community, Virtue, and Vision in the 1790s* (London: Associated University Presses, 1997).

ROBINSON, CHARLES NAPIER, *The British Tar in Fact and Fiction: The Poetry, Pathos, and Humour of the Sailor's Life* (London: Harper, 1909).

ROBINSON, DANIEL, 'Reviving the Sonnet: Women Romantic Poets and the Sonnet Claim', *European Romantic Review*, 6 (1995), 98–127.

ROE, NICHOLAS, 'Coleridge, Wordsworth, and the French Invasion Scare', *Wordsworth Circle*, 17 (1986), 142–8.

—— *Wordsworth and Coleridge: The Radical Years* (Oxford: Clarendon Press, 1988.)

—— 'Wordsworth, Milton, and the Politics of Poetic Influence', *Yearbook of English Studies*, 19 (1989), 112–26.

ROSE, JACQUELINE, 'Why War?', in *Why War?—Psychoanalysis, Politics, and the Return to Melanie Klein* (Oxford: Basil Blackwell, 1993), 15–40.

ROSENBLUM, NANCY L., 'Romantic Militarism', *Journal of the History of Ideas*, 43 (1982), 249–68.

ROSS, ALEXANDER M., *The Imprint of the Picturesque on Nineteenth-Century Fiction* (Waterloo, Ontario: Wilfrid Laurier University Press, 1986).

ROSS, MARLON B., 'Scott's Chivalric Pose: The Function of Metrical Romance in the Romantic Period', *Genre*, 18 (1986), 267–97.

—— 'Romantic Quest and Conquest: Troping Masculine Power in the Crisis of Poetic Identity', in Anne K. Mellor (ed.), *Romanticism and Feminism* (Bloomington and Indianapolis: Indiana University Press, 1988), 26–51.

—— *The Contours of Masculine Desire: Romanticism and the Rise of Women's Poetry* (New York: Oxford University Press, 1989).

—— 'Configurations of Feminine Reform: The Woman Writer and the Tradition of Dissent', in Carol Shiner Wilson and Joel Haefner (eds.), *Re-Visioning Romanticism: British Women Writers, 1776–1837* (Philadelphia: Pennsylvania University Press, 1994), 193–209.

RUDÉ, GEORGES, *Revolutionary Europe 1783–1815* (London: Fontana, 1986).

RUSSELL, GILLIAN, *The Theatres of War: Performance, Politics, and Society, 1793–1815* (Oxford: Clarendon Press, 1995).

RUTHERFORD, ANDREW (ed.), *Byron: The Critical Heritage* (London: Routledge and Kegan Paul; New York: Barnes and Noble, 1970).

SAGLIA, DIEGO, *Byron and Spain: Itinerary in the Writing of Place* (Salzburg: Edwin Mellen Press, 1996).

—— 'Epic or Domestic? Felicia Hemans's Heroic Poetry and the Myth of the Victorian Poetess', *Rivista di Studi Vittoriani*, 2/4 (July 1997), 125–47.

—— ' "O My Mother Spain!" The Peninsular War, Family Matters, and the Practice of Romantic Nation-Writing', *ELH*, 65 (1998), 363–93.

—— 'War Romances, Historical Analogies and Coleridge's *Letters on the Spaniards*', in Philip Shaw (ed.), *Romantic Wars: Studies in Culture and Conflict, 1793–1822* (Aldershot: Ashgate, 2000), 138–60.

SANGER, ERNEST, *Englishmen at War: A Social History in Letters 1450–1900*, with a Foreword by General Sir Anthony Farrar-Hockley (Stroud, Gloucestershire, and Dover, NH: Alan Sutton, 1993).

SCARRY, ELAINE, *The Body in Pain: The Making and Unmaking of the Modern World* (Oxford: Oxford University Press, 1985).

SCHROEDER, PAUL W., *The Transformation of European Politics, 1763–1848* (Oxford: Clarendon Press, 1996).

SCOTT, IAN ROBERTSON, 'From Radicalism to Conservatism: The Politics of Wordsworth and Coleridge, 1787–1818', Ph.D. thesis (Edinburgh, 1987).

—— ' "Things as They Are": The Literary Response to the French Revolution' in H. T. Dickinson, *Britain and the French Revolution, 1789–1815* (Basingstoke and London: Macmillan, 1989), 229–49.

SCRIVENER, MICHAEL (ed.), *Poetry and Reform: Periodical Verse from the English Democratic Press, 1792–1824* (Detroit: Wayne State University Press, 1992).

SHAPIRO, MICHAEL, *Violent Cartographies: Mapping Cultures of War* (Minneapolis and London: University of Minnesota Press, 1997).

SHAW, PHILIP, (ed.), *Romantic Wars: Studies in Culture and Conflict, 1793–1822* (Aldershot: Ashgate, 2000).

—— *Waterloo and the Romantic Imagination* (Basingstoke and New York: Palgrave Macmillan, 2002).

SIMPSON, DAVID, *Wordsworth's Historical Imagination: The Poetry of Displacement* (New York and London: Methuen, 1987).

SKJELSAEK, INGER, and SMITH, D. (eds.), *Gender, Peace and Conflict* (London: Sage, 2001).

SMITH, C. J. P., 'Lamb and the Politics of Literary Fashion in Southey's Female Wanderers', *Charles Lamb Bulletin*, 89 (1995), 2–8.

—— *A Quest for Home: Reading Robert Southey* (Liverpool: Liverpool University Press, 1997).

—— 'Robert Southey and the Emergence of *Lyrical Ballads*', *Romanticism on the Net*, 9 (February 1998).

SMITH, OLIVIA, *The Politics of Language 1791–1819* (Oxford: Clarendon Press, 1984).

SPIEGELMAN, WILLARD, *Wordsworth's Heroes* (Berkeley, Los Angeles, and London: California University Press, 1985).

STABLER, JANE, 'Guardians and Watchful Powers: Literary Satire and *Lyrical Ballads* in 1798', in Richard Cronin (ed.), *1798: The Year of the Lyrical Ballads* (Basingstoke and New York: Palgrave, 1998).

STALLWORTHY, JON (ed.), *The Oxford Book of War Poetry* (Oxford: Oxford University Press, 1988).

STANSFIELD, DOROTHY A., 'A Note on the Genesis of Coleridge's Thinking on War and Peace', *Wordsworth Circle*, 17 (1986), 130–4.

STEPHENSON, WARREN, 'Wordsworth's Satanism', *Wordsworth Circle*, 13 (1982), 176–7.

STONE, LAWRENCE (ed.), *An Imperial State at War: Britain from 1689 to 1815* (London and New York: Routledge, 1994).

STOREY, MARK, *Robert Southey: A Life* (Oxford and New York: Oxford University Press, 1997).

SUTHERLAND, JOHN, *The Life of Walter Scott: A Critical Biography* (Oxford: Blackwell Publishers, 1997).

SWEARINGEN, JAMES E., 'Wordsworth on Gray', *SEL*, 14 (1974), 489–509.

SWEET, NANORA, 'The Bowl of Liberty: Felicia Hemans and the Romantic Mediterranean', Ph.D. thesis (University of Michigan, 1993).

—— 'History, Imperialism, and the Aesthetics of the Beautiful: Hemans and the Post-Napoleonic Moment', in Mary A. Favret and Nicola J. Watson (eds.), *At the Limits of Romanticism* (Bloomington and Indianapolis: Indiana University Press, 1994), 170–84.

—— and MELNYK, JULIE (eds.), *Felicia Hemans: Reimagining Poetry in the Nineteenth Century* (Basingstoke and New York: Palgrave, 2001).

THOMAS, GORDON KENT, *Wordsworth's Dirge and Promise* (Lincoln: Nebraska University Press, 1971).

—— 'Wordsworth's Iberian Sonnets: Turncoats Creed?', *Wordsworth Circle*, 13 (1982), 31–4.

THOMPSON, E. P., 'Disenchantment or Default? A Lay Sermon', in Conor Cruise O'Brien and William Dean Vanech (eds.), *Power and Consciousness* (London and New York: London University Press and New York University Press, 1969), 149–82.

THORSLEV, PETER L., JR., 'Post Waterloo Liberalism: The Second Generation', *Studies in Romanticism*, 28 (1989) 437–61.

TODD, JANET, *Sensibility: An Introduction* (London and New York: Methuen, 1986).

TOWNSHEND, CHARLES (ed.), *The Oxford Illustrated History of Modern War* (Oxford: Oxford University Press, 1997).

UGLOW, JENNY, *Hogarth: A Life and a World* (London: Faber and Faber, 1997).

VAUGHAN, WILLIAM, *Romantic Art* (London: Thames and Hudson, 1978).

VIRILIO, PAUL, *War and Cinema: The Logistics of Perception*, trans. Patrick Camiller (London: Verso, 1989).

WAGNER, JENNIFER ANN, *A Moment's Monument: Revisionary Poetics and the Nineteenth-Century English Sonnet* (Madison, Teaneck, and London: Fairleigh Dickinson University Press and Associated University Presses, 1996).

WALKER, ERIC C., 'Wordsworth, Warriors and Naming', *Studies in Romanticism*, 29 (1990), 223–40.

WARD, WILLIAM S., *Literary Reviews in British Periodicals, 1798–1820: A Bibliography, with a Supplementary List of General, Non-Review, Articles on Literary Subjects*, 2 vols. (New York: Garland, 1972).

WARNER, MARINA, *Monuments and Maidens: The Allegory of the Female Form* (London: Picador, 1987).

WATSON, J. R., *English Poetry of the Romantic Period: 1780–1830* (London and New York: Longman, 1985).

WATTEVILLE, HERMAN GASTON DE, *The British Soldier: His Daily Life from Tudor to Modern Times* (London: Dent, 1954).

WEBB, TIMOTHY, 'Byron and the Heroic Syllables', *Keats–Shelley Review*, 5 (autumn 1990), 41–74.

WEIGHLEY, RUSSELL F., *The Age of Battles: The Quest for Decisive Warfare from Breitenfeld to Waterloo* (London: Pimlico, 1993).

WEST, KENYON, *The Laureates of England: Ben Jonson to William Wordsworth* (London and New York: Frederick H. Stokes, 1895).

WHALE, JOHN, *Imagination under Pressure, 1789–1832: Aesthetics, Politics and Utility* (Cambridge: Cambridge University Press, 2000).

WHEELER, H. F. B., and BROADLEY, A. M., *Napoleon and the Invasion of England: The Story of the Great Terror*, 2 vols. (London and New York: John Lane at the Bodley Head, 1898).

WHITE, DANIEL E., ' "Properer for a Sermon": Particularities of Dissent and Coleridge's Conversational Mode', *Studies in Romanticism*, 40 (2001), 175–98.

WHITE, HAYDEN, *Metahistory: The Historical Imagination in Nineteenth-Century Europe* (Baltimore and London: Johns Hopkins University Press, 1972).

WHITTAKER, JASON, *William Blake and the Myths of Britain* (Basingstoke and London: Macmillan, 1999).

WILKIE, BRIAN, *Romantic Poets and Epic Tradition* (Madison and Milwaukee: Wisconsin University Press, 1965).

WILLIAMS, JOHN, *Wordsworth: Romantic Poetry and Revolutionary Politics* (Manchester and New York: Manchester University Press, 1989).

—— *William Wordsworth: A Literary Life* (Basingstoke and London: Macmillan, 1996).

WILSON, KATHLEEN, *The Sense of the People: Politics, Culture and Imperialism in England, 1715–1785* (Cambridge: Cambridge University Press, 1995).

WINTER, JAY M., 'Imaginings of War: Some Cultural Supports of the Institution of War', in Robert A. Hindle (ed.), *The Institution of War* (Basingstoke and London: Macmillan, 1991), 155–78.

—— *Sites of Memory, Sites of Mourning: The Great War in European Cultural History* (Cambridge: Cambridge University Press, 1996).

WOLFSON, SUSAN J., ' "Domestic Affections" and "the Spear of Minerva": Felicia Hemans and the Dilemma of Gender', in Carol Shiner Wilson and Joel Haefner (eds.), *Re-Visioning Romanticism: British Women Writers, 1776–1837* (Philadelphia: Pennsylvania University Press, 1994), 128–66.

—— 'Felicia Hemans and the Revolving Doors of Reception', in Harriet Kramer Linkin and Stephen C. Behrendt (eds.), *Romanticism and Women Poets: Opening the Doors of Reception* (Lexington: University of Kentucky Press, 1999), 214–41.

—— 'Editing Felicia Hemans for the Twenty-First Century', *Romanticism on the Net*, 19 (August 2000).

WOODRING, CARL R., 'On Liberty in the Poetry of Wordsworth', *PMLA*, 70 (1955), 1033–48.

WOODRING, CARL R., *Politics in the Poetry of Coleridge* (Madison: Wisconsin University Press, 1961).

—— *Politics in English Romantic Poetry* (Cambridge, Mass.: Harvard University Press, 1970).

—— 'Three Poets on Waterloo', *Wordsworth Circle*, 18 (1987), 54–6.

WOOLFORD, JOHN, '*The Prelude* and its echoes', *TLS*, 6 June 1975, 627.

WORDSWORTH, JONATHAN, *The Borders of Vision* (Oxford: Clarendon Press, 1982).

WU, DUNCAN (ed.), *Romantic Women Poets: An Anthology* (Oxford: Blackwell Publishers, 1997).

WYK SMITH, M. VAN, *Drummer Hodge: The Poetry of the Anglo-Boer War* (Oxford: Clarendon Press, 1978).

ZIMMERMAN, SARAH H., 'Charlotte Smith's Lessons', in Stephen C. Behrendt and Harriet Kramer Linkin (eds.), *Approaches to Teaching British Women Poets of the Romantic Period* (New York: Modern Language Association of America, 1997), 121–8.

ZIONKOWSKI, LINDA, 'Gray, the Marketplace, and the Masculine Poet', *Criticism*, 35/4 (fall 1993), 589–608.

Index